PRAISE

"Another successful foray into the complex world of early medieval English manuscripts, Muir's new edition of MS Junius 11 will become as indispensable as his other editions for years to come. He leaves no accent mark out, and no scribal peculiarity unnoted. The book is a welcome contribution to the field."
— Robert E. Bjork, Foundation Professor of English, Arizona State University

"This is an admirably clear and careful edition of a major Old English poetic manuscript. Muir's detailed textual presentation and meticulous attention to the manuscript make this a useful and important addition to the literature on Junius 11."
— R. M. Liuzza, University of Tennessee–Knoxville

"An excellent companion to the Bodleian Library's digitized Junius 11, *The Cædmon Manuscript* provides a foundational review of scholarship on the codex and an edition of its poetry that, with attention to scribal practices and precise notes, is invaluable for understanding the text as it is presented on the page."
—Janet Ericksen, Professor, University of Minnesota Morris

"Bernard Muir's excellent new edition of the four Old English biblical poems preserved in Bodleian Library MS Junius 11 is the first to appear in print in nearly a century. Furnished with an up-to-date Introduction, textual notes and detailed art-historical commentary, this elegant volume will serve as the standard scholarly resource for many years to come."
— Francis Leneghan, Professor of Old English, University of Oxford

The Cædmon Manuscript

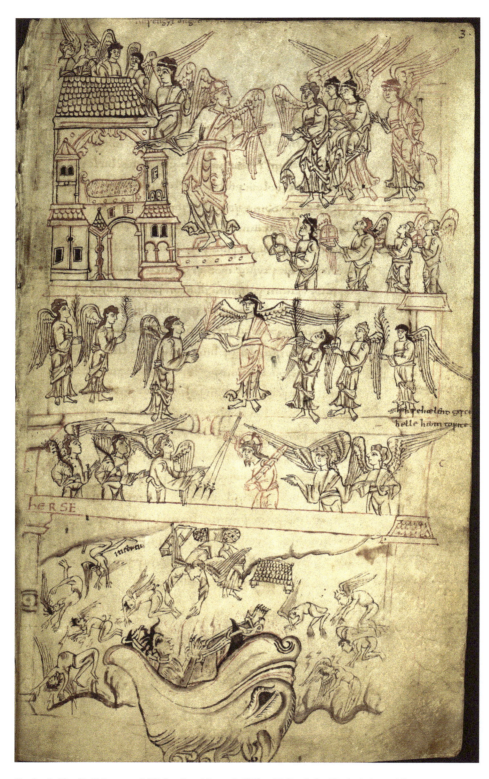

Oxford, Bodl. Library, MS Junius 11, p. 3 ('The Fall of the Rebel Angels')

The Cædmon Manuscript

The Beginnings of English Religious Poetry, I

Bernard J. Muir

ANTHEM PRESS

Anthem Press
An imprint of Wimbledon Publishing Company
www.anthempress.com

This edition first published in UK and USA 2023
by ANTHEM PRESS
75–76 Blackfriars Road, London SE1 8HA, UK
or PO Box 9779, London SW19 7ZG, UK
and
244 Madison Ave #116, New York, NY 10016, USA

© 2023 Bernard J. Muir

The author asserts the moral right to be identified as the author of this work.

All rights reserved. Without limiting the rights under copyright reserved above, no part of this publication may be reproduced, stored or introduced into a retrieval system, or transmitted, in any form or by any means (electronic, mechanical, photocopying, recording or otherwise), without the prior written permission of both the copyright owner and the above publisher of this book.

British Library Cataloguing-in-Publication Data
A catalogue record for this book is available from the British Library.

Library of Congress Cataloging-in-Publication Data: 2023908958
A catalog record for this book has been requested.

ISBN-13: 978-1-83998-974-2 (Hbk)
ISBN-10: 1-83998-974-2 (Hbk)

Cover Credit: Oxford, Bodl. Library, MS Junius 11, p. 1 (detail)

This title is also available as an e-book.

FOREWORD

This edition of Oxford, Bodleian Library, MS Junius 11 supersedes all previous editions, including the present editor's own digital edition of 2004 published as Bodleian Digital Texts 1, in that it is a completely new analysis of the manuscript based on a thorough paleographical and codicological re-examination. Readers today have online access to the complete set of high resolution scans made for the 2004 edition so there is no need to reproduce details of the manuscript itself, including its much admired and commented upon decorated and zoomorphic initials.

The analysis of the manuscript presented here may include a plethora of information not required by individual readers, but it aims to meet the needs of a variety of users for many years to come. For example, the edition reproduces every accent mark in the manuscript because scholars today are still uncertain of their use and relevance, but tomorrow someone may deduce why the scribes and correctors went to the trouble of including them on every page of the manuscript.

So too, a translation of the texts is not included here because Anlezark 2002 presents a new translation of *Genesis A* and *B*, *Exodus* and *Daniel*. *Christ and Satan* is available elsewhere (e.g. Gordon rev. 1954) and since it is not an Old Testament retelling and versification in Old English it is not considered by Anlezark. Other recent translations are included in the online 'Old English Poetry Project' (*q.v.*).

The maxim 'Pride goes before a fall' would be an appropriate subtitle for this anthology of Christian poetry since this is the overriding theme of all four poems, which are about falls resulting from disobedience due to excessive pride and a lack of humility.

Christ and Satan presents a special case since it has been corrected by a later hand, perhaps the scribe of earlier poems in the anthology. Either this corrector or a later reader also added (mostly squeezed in) a plethora of punctuation marks, and those resembling an inverted semicolon (./ – *the punctus elevatus*) can easily be confused for an accent mark by readers not used to this. The practice of the present editor is to privilege that corrector's alterations whenever they make good sense since they present the poem in its latest form and once again this information may be invaluable to readers in the future; those wishing to have access to what was originally recorded in the manuscript have that information readily available to them in the footnotes on each page of this edition.

And lastly, the title chosen here: I have decided to retain the early modern name of the manuscript – *The Cædmon Manuscript* – because of the wealth of history, literature, and allusions that are associated with it, deriving from the fanciful or romantic and folkloric assumption by early readers and scholars that the cowherd mentioned by Bede in the *Ecclesiastical History* (iv. 24) may have been the author of the poems. I think that more people, both scholars and the general public, will be familiar with the early title and not the more technical and correct designation of the work as Oxford, Bodl. MS Junius 11 familiar to the scholarly community.

ACKNOWLEDGEMENTS

This edition follows closely upon my recent edition of *The Peterborough Chronicle* (Anthem Press, 2023) and there I acknowledged the many people who have supported my work in both digital and analogue publication over the past thirty years, and also the Australian Research Council, which has underwritten my publications for the same period of time – moving to Australia forty years ago gave me many opportunities I would not otherwise have had.

My dear friend and programmer, Graeme Smith (†), once again processed the images of MS Junius 11 now available on the Bodleian website; these high-resolution images are essential to my analysis of the manuscript, as they will continue to be for scholars and students in the future.

Slightly further afield, my colleague Dr Andrew Turner with whom I have collaborated for thirty years continues to have essential input into my publications and we continue to work on other projects, mostly on the transmission and reception of Classical texts in the Middle Ages.

Francis Mumme and Daniel Zuzek proofread sections of the text and occasionally found typos and inelegant expressions that had escaped my tired eyes – to them, many thanks.

Robert Turnbull of Melbourne University created the vector diagrams showing the complicated structure of MS Junius 11, for which I am most grateful.

Kerry Greenwood and David Greagg have generously supported my work over many years; without their intellectual and financial support this book would never have come to fruition.

I was fortunate to discover Anthem Press, the publisher of the two-volume *The Peterborough Chronicle* – they have taken on board every suggestion that I have made and produce editions of which I can be proud.

The cover and frontispiece images were provided by the Bodleian Library when the Junius 11 CD was being prepared 25 years ago.

I have not previously dedicated a work to my family: this work is accordingly dedicated to my sons Jeremy and Tristan, and to my grandson Caelan.

CONTENTS

Foreword vii

Acknowledgements ix

Table of Contents xi

Introduction 1
    The Work, its Date, Provenance and Subsequent History 1
    Facsimiles, Transcripts, Catalogue Descriptions, Editions 5
    Codicology 6
        Gathering Analysis 8
    Script and Scribes 14
    Punctuation, Accents, Abbreviations, Word Division 14
    Fitts / Sectional Divisions 15
    Corrections, Glosses, Marginalia 15
    Texts 16
    Artists and Illustrations 24
        Decorated Initials 31
    Captions 32
    Printed Bibliographies and Translations 33
    Editorial Principles 34

Gathering Diagrams 35

Abbreviated References 55

Select Bibliography 57

Poems

    Genesis A & B 69
    Exodus 177
    Daniel 201
    Christ and Satan 231

Art-Historical Commentary 261

INTRODUCTION

1   The Work, its Date, Provenance and Subsequent History

The manuscript presented here is Oxford, Bodleian Library, MS Junius 11. From the beginning it was intended that Junius 11 be an extensively, if not lavishly, illustrated book of Christian poetry; it was perhaps commissioned by a wealthy secular or ecclesiastical patron. It was to be comprised of three poems on the subjects of Creation and the Genesis story down to Abraham and Isaac, the Crossing of the Red Sea recorded in Exodus, and the prophet Daniel; soon after the copying of these poems was completed, however, the final gathering of the manuscript was enlarged and a fourth poem in three sections, dealing with the Fall of the Rebel Angels, the Harrowing of Hell, and the Temptation of Christ was added (whether these were originally three separate poems is discussed later).[1] As was the practice in Anglo-Saxon England, none of the poems was given a title when recorded in the manuscript; they are known today by the names assigned to them by modern editors – *Genesis* (comprised of two poems designated *A* and *B*), *Exodus*, *Daniel* and *Christ and Satan*. The entire manuscript was to be illustrated, but sadly the project was never completed; thus there are blank spaces throughout it where the intended illustrations are lacking (after the final original illustration on p. 88). Two artists were responsible for the Anglo-Saxon illustrations; a third artist of lesser ability added a small number of extra drawings in the twelfth century. One of these, on p. 96, attempts to illustrate an episode in the poem (depicting 'Abraham and the Messenger', it seems), which indicates that the poems were still being read in the late twelfth century. When other manuscripts in the vernacular (i.e. Old English) were no longer being read and were suffering neglect and falling into disrepair, and even being stripped of their bindings so that they could be reused on newly-recorded texts,[2] MS Junius 11 was rebound, indicating that it was still valued; this enduring interest in the manuscript was probably because it was illustrated – a number of its drawings had already been excised by the thirteenth century.[3] Indeed, the first six pages (3 folios) of the manuscript have been removed, with no loss from the text of the first poem, which suggests that there may originally have been a series of up to six full-page illustrations before the drawing which now comes first in the manuscript; such a grand opening would have been consistent with the proposed design of the codex.

Manuscript Junius 11 is one of only four surviving codices of Anglo-Saxon poetry; the others are: i) Exeter, Dean and Chapter MS 3501 (*The Exeter Anthology of Old English Poetry*);[4] ii) London, British Library MS Cotton Vitellius A.xv (the *Beowulf Manuscript*)[5] and iii) Vercelli, Biblioteca Capitolare MS CXVII (*The Vercelli Book* or

---

[1] See Section 8 'Texts'.
[2] This was the fate of another of the surviving manuscripts of Anglo-Saxon poetry, *The Exeter Anthology*; Muir 2000 (I. 2) lists the damage inflicted upon the manuscript in the later Middle Ages after its binding had been stripped from it.
[3] All of the issues raised in this opening parargraph are discussed in detail later in appropriate sections of the Introduction.
[4] The most recent comprehensive edition is Muir 2000.
[5] Cotton MS Vitellius A.xv also contains the fragmentary Anglo-Saxon poem *Judith*, which follows after *Beowulf*. The best recent edition of *Beowulf* is by Bruce Mitchell and Fred C. Robinson (*Beowulf*, Oxford: Blackwell, 1998); the most recent facsimile is the digital one by Kevin S. Kiernan (*The*

Codex Vercellensis).[6] The present manuscript is often referred to as 'The Cædmon Manuscript' in early critical writings and also here, but the attribution of the poems to the cowherd Cædmon is inaccurate and is no longer credited.[7] The manuscript is traditionally dated to the late tenth or early eleventh century (*c*. 975-1010 – Ker 1957 for example, says *s. x/xi*), which would place it after *The Exeter Anthology* and *The Vercelli Book* and probably before the *Beowulf Manuscript*, but in a recent 'integrated' review of the issue, which takes into account the manuscript's illustrations (style and colour), decorated initials, script and other codicological evidence (including punctuation), Lockett 2002 makes the case convincingly for placing it slightly earlier than this, in the period *c*. 960 – *c*. 990 [it should be noted that Lockett is concerned primarily with the work of Artist A and the first scribe of Junius 11].[8] Critical opinion has generally accepted that codicological and art-historical evidence suggest that the manuscript was written at either Christ Church or St Augustine's, Canterbury, but Lucas makes a good case for Malmesbury.[9]

Electronic Beowulf, London and Ann Arbor MI, 1999). The most recent printed facsimile is by Kemp Malone (*The Nowell Codex*, EEMF 12, Copenhagen, 1963).

[6] It contains both poetry (*Andreas*, *The Fates of the Apostles*, *Soul and Body I*, *Homiletic Fragment I*, *Dream of the Rood* and *Elene*) and prose (22 homilies and a *vita* of St Guthlac). Standard editions, facsimiles and codicological analyses of *The Vercelli Book* are by George P. Krapp (*The Vercelli Book*, ASPR II, New York, 1932), Max (Massimiliano) Förster (*Il Codice Vercellese con Omelie e Poesie in Lingua Anglosassone*, Rome, 1913), Celia Sisam (*The Vercelli Book*, EEMF 19, Copenhagen, 1976), Paul E. Szarmach (*Vercelli Homilies IX-XXIII*, Toronto, 1981) and Donald G. Scragg ('The Compilation of the Vercelli Book' in Richards 1994, pp. 317-43), and *The Vercelli Homilies and Related Texts*, ed. D.G. Scragg. EETS 300, London, 1992). The homilies in this manuscript are the earliest surviving collection in Old English. The present editor is preparing a new editon of the *Vercelli Codex* with a complete codicological and paleographical analysis of its poems.

[7] In the *Ecclesiastical History* (iv.24), Bede recounts how the illiterate cowherd miraculously received a divine gift which allowed him to compose religious poetry extemporaneously after a single hearing of the original storyline. The association between Cædmon and the poems in MS Junius 11 was first made by the Dutch scholar Franciscus Junius in his edition of the manuscript's poems. The contents of the manuscript correspond so closely to the description of the poems composed by Cædmon in the seventh century (as detailed by Bede) that it is easy to understand why Junius made this connection – indeed, it must have seemed like a great discovery at the time. Gollancz 1927 gave his facsimile the title *The Caedmon Manuscript of Anglo-Saxon Biblical Poetry*, but reluctantly acknowledged that at best one of the poems might be associated with Cædmon. (In libraries today, facsimiles, editions and translations of the poems are often catalogued with *Caedmon* as the author, which can lead to considerable confusion.) Scholars now believe that the poems were composed in the 'Cædmonian tradition', but that they date from a later period; however, the questions of exactly when they may have been written and by whom still remain unresolved. It is used in the title of the present edition because of its familiarity, historical and folkloric significance.

[8] *The Exeter Anthology* and *The Vercelli Book* are approximately contemporary, and either one could have been written before the other; both are usually associated with the Monastic Revival of the tenth century. Muir 2000 believes that *The Exeter Anthology* was anthologized at one time by one person working *c*. 965-75, and that the scribe responsible for the manuscript may not have been a native Anglo-Saxon (I. 36). Scragg 1994 states that the *The Vercelli Book* is the oldest of the four poetic codices, but does not substantiate his claim (pp. 317-18). Nothing can be said for certain of the origin of either manuscript, and dating must be determined by content and on paleographical evidence, which is notoriously difficult when manuscripts are almost contemporary. A great deal has been written about the date of composition of *Beowulf*, with scholars arguing for a date anywhere between 700 and the early eleventh century (see *The Dating of Beowulf*, ed. Colin Chase, Toronto 1981; rpt. 1997, a collection of scholarly essays specifically discussing the dating of the poem); the manuscript, however, dates from the first quarter of the eleventh century (see Kevin S. Kiernan, *Beowulf and the Beowulf Manuscript*, Ann Arbor MI, 1996, a revision of the 1981 original, for a detailed discussion of the date of the manuscript and the poem; Kiernan associates the manuscript with the reign of Cnut, 1016-35).

[9] Ker 1957 (p. 408), following James 1903 (xxv-xxvi, 51 and 509), observes that the manuscript is 'possibly identical with the *Genesis anglice depicta* in the early fourteenth-century catalogue of Christ

As noted above, MS Junius 11 contains four poems: *Genesis A* and *B*, *Exodus*, *Daniel* and *Christ and Satan*. Poems 1-3 were copied out first, and occupy Gatherings 1-16 and the first folio (or 2 pages – the manuscript is paginated, not foliated) of Gathering 17. The fourth poem, *Christ and Satan*, apparently a conflation or sequence of three independent poems, was added soon afterwards – one of the illustrators of the first part (poems 1-3) added some decorative elements in it (see 'Artists'). The manuscript ends with the words *Finit Liber II. Amen* ('Book 2 ends here. Amen'); consequently, the part of the manuscript containing the first three poems is sometimes referred to as 'Liber I' ('Book 1').[10]

The subject matter of the poems suggests that the compilation was designed to be read at Eastertide (that is, that it may have been designed as a vernacular lectionary for use in a monastery) – the readings for the Easter Vigil service include Biblical passages with strong typological associations describing events from Creation, the Exodus, events in the life of the prophet Daniel, and readings from the prophets foreshadowing Christ's life and mission and his anticipated final triumph over Satan.[11]

Church, Canterbury'. Wormald 1952 (p. 76) also accepts Canterbury as the place of origin. Raw 1994 believes that the manuscript may originally have been bound in limp covers (*in pergameno*, p. 266), a practice associated with St Augustine's, Canterbury. Doane 1978 (pp. 23-4) notes a similarity between some of the Junius illustrations and BL Cotton MS Claudius B.iv, a known Canterbury production. Ohlgren 1975 argues for Newminster, Winchester, but its case seems not as strong as that for Canterbury.

Lucas 1974 (pp. 2-5) details the evidence which he believes supports a Malmesbury attribution:

- the phrase *Genesis anglice depicta* used by James 1903 (xxv-xxvi, 51 and 509) is very general and might refer to some other manuscript (including BL Cotton MS Claudius B.iv, which was known to have once been at Canterbury).
- some of the illustrations in MS Junius 11 bear striking resemblance to some carved medallions of the south porch of Malmesbury Abbey.
- Artist B of MS Junius 11 also drew the Virtues and Vices illustrations in the 'Corpus Prudentius' (Cambridge, CCC MS 23), a known Malmesbury book.
- there was an abbot of Malmesbury from *c.* 1043-6 named Ælfwine, the name in the medallion on p. 2 of MS Junius 11.

He also notes that there is evidence of smoke damage to the folded edge of the gatherings, which occurred before the manuscript was bound; he suggests that this may have been caused by a fire at Malmesbury during the reign of Edward the Confessor (recorded by William of Malmesbury), in which the monastery suffered considerable damage.

[10] A leaf has been lost at the end of Daniel, which, it has been argued, could have contained a corresponding inscription (though this seems unlikely to the present editor); Doane 2013 for example, uses the term 'Liber I' to refer to the part of the manuscript containing the first three poems (p. 34).

[11] The readings focus specifically on the seven days of Creation, the Noah narrative, Abraham and Isaac, the Crossing of the Red Sea, the institution of the Passover, the renewal of the Covenant, the Babylonian Captivity, the Valley of the Dry Bones, Isaiah on the gaping jaws of Hell, the story of Jonah and the whale, the three children in the fiery furnace, and Moses handing down the Law before his death. It will be clear that these themes and incidents are central to the four poems in MS Junius 11, both literally, anagogically and typologically. Garde 1991 (Ch. 2, pp. 25-56) discusses the Junius codex as a vernacular *Heilsgeschichte*, noting that the poems deal with the major events of Salvation History and allude to incidents in each of the six ages of the world throughout (p. 27). Interestingly, there is also a sequence of poems for the Easter season in the *Exeter Anthology of Old English Poetry* though it is on a smaller scale (see Muir 2000, I. 23-4).

The opening words of *Genesis A* – *Us is riht micel* – recall the opening words of the Preface of the Mass – *Vere dignum et iustum est* – which seems intended, given that the overall concern of the

Manuscript Junius 11 is unique among the surviving poetic codices in being illustrated – there are 48 extant illustrations for the *Genesis* poems. The design and layout of the manuscript indicate that the first three poems were meant to be fully illustrated – there are 89 blank spaces throughout them for illustrations which were never completed.[12] It is argued here that *Christ and Satan* was also originally illustrated by several full-page drawings, but these were excised by the early modern period.[13] Scholars often refer to the manuscript's 'Genesis Cycle', and have spent considerable time debating its possible origins, but it is important to remember that it was originally intended that the whole manuscript be illustrated, and thus it is more appropriate to refer to the 'Junius Cycle' of illustration, reflecting this broader scope (this matter is discussed further by Lowden 1992 in his re-evaluation of 'Genesis' cycles of illustration, which either pre-date or are contemporary with Junius 11).

The other well-known, but still remarkable, feature of the manuscript is that the poem known today as *Genesis B* is a translation of an earlier poem composed in Old Saxon, which has been interpolated into the Anglo-Saxon *Genesis A* after the present line 234 (the composite poem is recorded on pages 1-142, with *Genesis B* occupying pages 13-40). Both poems have been edited by Doane – *Genesis A* in 1978 and *Genesis B* in 1991; the latter also contains an edition of the Old Saxon poem and an account of the discovery of the fragments of the original *Genesis* poem in the Vatican Library by Karl Zangemeister in 1894 (pp. 3-8). The hypothesis that lines 235-851 of the Anglo-Saxon *Genesis* poem are a translation of an original Old Saxon poem was fully articulated by Eduard Sievers in 1875, but that a second poem had been interpolated into a pre-existing Anglo-Saxon *Genesis* poem had first been sensed by W.D. Conybeare in 1826 (pp. 186-8);[14] he noted the awkwardness of the connection of its narrative with the preceding Creation story, the repetition of the account of the Fall of the Angels and a distinct change of metre. Sievers' conclusions were:

- that *Genesis B* was not by the poet of *Genesis A*;
- that *A* was later than *B*;
- that the translator may have been an Englishman residing on the continent;
- that *B* underwent further revision after it had been interpolated into *A* and,
- that the *Heliand* poet was the author of the Old Saxon *Genesis*.[15]

The first person associated with the manuscript in modern times is James Ussher (1581-1656), Archbishop of Armagh. Franciscus Junius (1589-1677), received the manuscript from Ussher sometime around 1651, apparently as a gift, and subsequently published a quarto edition of its poems in Amsterdam in 1655. Junius must have met Ussher and become his friend while living in England; he resided there

---

poems in MS Junius 11 is with Salvation History and God's intervention in human affairs, and his plan for making the Heavenly Paradise once again available to them.

[12] There are 22 zoomorphic initials and 33 large plain initials; there are also a number of drypoint etchings, some of which are invisible to the naked eye.

[13] See the detailed analysis of Gathering 17.

[14] He conjectured that it was originally a distinct poem which the Anglo-Saxon paraphrast had 'worked up into the fabric of his poem' (p. 188).

[15] This summary is from Doane 1991 (p. 7).

during the periods 1621-51 and 1674-7.[16] It is not known how Ussher acquired the manuscript, but from 1603 onwards he was buying books for the library at the University of Dublin and he may have discovered it during his travels; from 1640 he lived in England and given their common interests it is easy to imagine how he and Junius were drawn together. William Somner (1598-1669) made a transcript of the manuscript while it was in the library of Sir Simonds D'Ewes (1602-50), according to an inscription at its beginning; the work survives among his books at Canterbury Cathedral. Apparently Somner at first believed that the manuscript belonged to D'Ewes, but discovered subsequently that Ussher was in fact its owner.[17] Junius died in 1677; the codex became part of the collection of the Bodleian Library in 1678, together with Junius's other manuscripts and annotations in manuscript form.[18]

2   Facsimiles, Transcripts, Catalogue Descriptions, and Major Editions

The only complete printed facsimile edition of manuscript Junius 11 is by Gollancz (1927), though the Bodleian Library has now made a full set of digital images available on its website. Ohlgren 1992 reproduces all of the manuscript's illustrations together with succinct captions. Individual pages have been reproduced in numerous publications, most of which are concerned with the manuscript's important illustrations and decorated initials.[19] Ellis 1833 also reproduces the manuscript's illustrations. And as mentioned earlier, William Somner (1598-1669) made a complete transcript of the manuscript while it was in the library of Sir Simonds D'Ewes.

There have been many codicological descriptions of MS Junius 11, the most significant being those in Gollancz 1927, Raw 1994, Doane 1978, Krapp 1931, Timmer 1954, Ker 1957 (no. 334, pp. 406-8) and Lucas 1980; Wanley's description (1705, p. 77) is of historical interest. Temple 1976 (no. 56, pp. 76-8) is the standard catalogue description for art historians, but should be consulted in conjunction with Pächt and Alexander 1973; these are supplemented by Karkov 2001, a more recent monograph study of the manuscript's iconography. Of these analyses, that in Raw 1994 is by far the most detailed and authoritative.

The major editions of the complete manuscript are: Junius 1655, Thorpe 1832 (with an English translation), Bouterwek, 1854 Grein 1857 (the most scholarly of the early editions), Wülker 1894 and Krapp 1931. A new edition of the poems by the present editor, with historical and literary commentary, was published in digital format in 2004.

---

[16] Bremmer 1998 is a collection of essays on the life and work of Junius; it is the most up-to-date source for details of his various scholarly activities.
[17] For a fuller discussion of the Ussher-D'Ewes ownership question, see Gollancz 1927, p. xiv.
[18] Junius began to make annotations on the poetic texts in the manuscript, but never got very far with this project; his reflections are preserved in Bodley MS Junius 73*, reproduced in printed facsimile by Lucas 2000 in 'Appendix 1'):
[19] The 1927 facsimile was published in a limited edition of 250 copies; thus, if scholars and students could not arrange to study the manuscript *in situ*, they have until now had to use images reproduced in photographs, slides or microfilm – the use of digital technology has radically revolutionized the way in which manuscripts are now studied.

3 Codicology

The manuscript has been stitched twice, and the holes from the first stitching can still be seen in many of the gatherings, especially where the binding is now loose. Raw 1994 (p. 254) makes the following observations:

> The present stitching is on three bands, plus head- and tail-bands, at distances of about 70, 165 and 260 mm from the top of each page, with kettle-stitching at about 35 and 290 mm from the top... Holes from earlier stitching are visible at the centre of all gatherings and on stubs of all except five of the singletons at distances of approximately 55, 95, 160, 230 and 265 mm from the top of each page; the marks of this earlier stitching can be seen particularly clearly on the stub of pp. 109/110 in Gathering 9. The centre of the last gathering, which contains *Christ and Satan*, shows the same two sets of stitch-marks as the rest of the manuscript; it can therefore be inferred that *Christ and Satan* had already been added to the rest of the manuscript by the time it was first sewn and that if this text had an earlier, independent existence, as Lucas 1979a has claimed, it was unstitched.

Raw 1994 also notes the positioning of the slots in the front and back covers in her 'Figure 1' (p. 255). On the front boards the slots are at 62, 158 and 258 mm from the top; on the back they are at 63, 163 and 262 mm.

The manuscript is approximately 324 mm tall by 180 mm wide. Today it consists of 116 folios in 17 gatherings and is paginated i-ii, 1-129 (with the last page, which contains two decorative motifs but no original text, being unnumbered); folios are missing throughout, apparently excised by someone interested in their illustrations. Timmer 1954 (p. 1) identifies the hand of the paginator as that of Junius himself. There are normally 26 lines of text on pages 1-212 and 27 on pages 213-29. The arrangement of the surviving folios is:

1^5 (lacks fols 1-3), 2^2 (lacks 1-5, 8), 3^6 (lacks 6-7), 4-6^8, 7^9 (has an extra original singleton), 8^7 (lacks 3), 9^6 (lacks 3, 5), 10^6 lacks 1, 5), 11^7 (lacks 4), 12^6 (lacks 4-5), 13^7 (lacks 6), 14^6 (lacks 4, 8), 15^7 (lacks 2), 16^8 and 17^{10} (lacks 2, 5, 9, 13; originally a normal gathering of 8, but supplemented by the insertion of 3 bifolia (6 folios or 12 pages). See the Gathering Analysis and Diagrams (below).

Thus the original plan for the manuscript was almost uniform, with each of the 17 gatherings intended to have 8 folios (though in the end the seventh represents a minor aberration); a detailed analysis of the original layout and present condition of each gathering follows here. On a number of occasions there is no gap in the poetic text where a folio has been excised, indicating that the excised folio was fully illustrated on both sides.[20] Defective parchment was sometimes used in the manuscript – there are a number of folios where the text is written around original holes. Lockett 2002 (pp. 143-5) notes that the gatherings of Junius 11 are arranged in the pattern H-F F-H, that is, with a hair side on the outside of each gathering and with hair facing hair and

---

[20] Raw 1994 argues for the loss of folios in Gatherings 8, 14, 15 and 17, although there are no gaps in the text (p. 253); Ker 1957 (pp. 407-8) believes that no folios have been lost in these gatherings and that the singletons in them are original – see the detailed analysis of each gathering that follows here.

flesh facing flesh within (allowing, of course, for the presence of singletons which interrupt such an arrangement); with respect to the argument concerning the dating of the manuscript, this arrangement was more common in the eleventh century, but would not have been unusual in the tenth (p. 144).

The gatherings were usually pricked for ruling one at a time after the sheets had been folded; ruling was done with a dry point on the outside of each gathering, so that the outer sheets have the most prominent indentations. There are usually double bounding lines throughout, and the writing area is normally about 120 mm wide.[21] Gatherings 1-7 were generally ruled with the sheets lying flat, and 9-17 on the recto after the sheets had been folded, so that some supplementary ruling was sometimes required. Gathering 8 is anomalous in that it was not ruled in a single operation; it has double vertical bounding lines up to page 94 and then single lines. As noted earlier, Gathering 17 has the most complex structure, since it was originally a normal gathering of 8 folios (or 16 pages), but was enlarged by the addition of three more sheets (12 pages); these modifications are discussed in detail later.

The recto of the first (unnumbered) folio, page i, has a few annotations in various hands on it, including its shelf mark 'MS Junius 11' and the description *Cædmonis Paraphrasis Poetica*;[22] its verso, page ii, contains the first illustration in the manuscript, a picture of 'God enthroned in Majesty' (referred to here as the Frontispiece).

Critics have dated the current binding variously from Anglo-Saxon times to the fifteenth century. Raw 1994 and Lucas 1980 argue for an early date; Raw 1994 (p. 265) places it '1100x1250' (and more precisely, 'the early thirteenth century', p. 266), whereas Lucas 1980 (p. 198) thinks that it dates from the Anglo-Saxon period, *c.* 1040-50. Doane 1978 (p. 6) accepts the fifteenth-century dating of the binding first proposed by Stoddard 1887 (p. 158), as do Gollancz 1927 (p. xxxv) and Timmer 1954 (p. 3). Pächt and Alexander 1973 (p. 5) date the re-sewing of the manuscript to *c.* 1200 and, by implication, the binding. Ker 1957 (p. 408) merely notes that the manuscript has 'medieval binding of white skin over boards'. Raw's analysis (1994), which is based upon a detailed study of the manuscript's stitching patterns, is the most compelling and well argued.[23] Since the manuscript has been re-sewn, it must have been rebound; this is corroborated by the fact that the channels in the oak boards correspond not to the original stitching holes, but to the re-stitching.

---

[21] Raw 1994 notes (p. 265) that the three straps may not be of the same date since they are different widths.

[22] The other annotations are:

> *Seld. cupbd. 42.* That is, the Selden cupboard, the storage place of the manuscript in the Selden End of the Duke Humfrey Library between 1951 (and perhaps earlier) and 1998.
> *G.C. 4.* This stands for 'Glass Case 4'; in the 19th century, the manuscript was permanently on show in a glass case in the Arts End of the Duke Humfrey Library. [There, its illustrations are traditionally said to have been seen by C.L. Dodgson and so to have inspired the phrase 'Anglo-Saxon attitudes' in *Through the Looking Glass*.] *Ego sum bonus puer quem deus amat* ('I am a good boy whom God loves'). This has no known source, and is perhaps just a pen trial.

[23] Instead of the normal pairs of prickings for the vertical bounding lines, Gatherings 9, 10, 14 and 15 have a variety of arrangements of 2, 3 or 4 prickmarks.

The binding boards are made of oak and are covered with whitleather.[24] The gatherings were originally stitched to three leather thongs as well as head- and tailbands made of cord. The cords and thongs were fed through channels in the oak boards and secured to them with wooden pegs (and perhaps short tacks or nails). Raw 1994 (p. 265) notes that 'the arrangement of three bands carried straight across the boards with head- and tailbands threaded at 45° to the corners is typical of twelfth-century bindings'. The head- and tailbands are oversewn in green and beige silk.

The boards of the front and back covers are exposed on the inside because there are now no pastedowns; there is, however, offset text of a now missing bifolium which was once used as a pastedown on the inside of the back board.[25] The three main binding leather straps, which are approximately 10 mm in width, can be clearly seen through breaks in the binding throughout the manuscript (especially in the first gathering) and are reflected in the ridges on the spine; there are two later binding stays as well in Gathering 17. The spine was repaired in modern times (the exact date is unknown) by adding a slip of calf-skin beneath the original leather of the spine. The nail or peg for holding the headband to the inside of the back cover is missing; the slots for the binding cords / thongs are approximately 28 mm from the edge of the board. The manuscript may originally have been held closed by three straps: on the exterior of the front cover part of the central clasp remains; the leather is torn where the top and bottom clasps have been lost. The wooden boards are visible here and there through holes in the leather. Overall, the poor condition of the covers and binding indicates that the manuscript was treated with little care during the early modern period. The back cover is in slightly better condition than the front. The pin to which the middle strap would have been fastened in order to hold the manuscript closed securely remains; small holes indicate where the top and bottom pins have been lost. On the interior of the front board a number of wooden pegs (for securing the binding straps) and nails are visible; a small repair to the leather covering can be seen in the centre of the top edge of the board and the end of the tailband.[26]

3b   Gathering Analysis

There are now 20 singletons in the manuscript (see Raw 1994, 'Appendix I' on p. 274 for details), only one of which, comprising pages 87-8, is apparently original; it is in Gathering 7, which already has four complete bifolia, and there is no loss in the text between the present pages 74 and 75. In addition, this folio is unusual in being unruled. Eleven of the twelve singletons missing in Gatherings 8-17 were lost *before*

---

[24] Whitleather is white or light leather of a soft pliant consistence, prepared by tawing, i.e. dressing with alum and salt so as to retain the natural colour, according to the *Oxford English Dictionary*.
[25] Ker 1957 (p. 408, following Timmer 1954, p. 3) notes, 'The text was apparently a harmony of the Gospels in Latin, written in a clear English Caroline hand, s.xi: parts of Mt. 3:11 and Lk. 3:21-3 are legible'. Gollancz 1927 notes that Henry Bradley tried to read the offset text and thought that it recorded 'an account of the temptation of Christ from a Latin Harmony of the Gospels' (p. xxxv).
[26] Ker 1957 (p. 408) believes that the damaged area in the top centre of the exterior of the front cover 'shows, presumably, that the book was chained at this point'; Raw 1994 (p. 266) notes:

> Books chained at the top of the cover were kept on lecterns, usually with a bar running across the top, whereas books chained in presses like those at Hereford or in the Bodleian Library had the chain fixed to the front edge of the cover.

For further discussion and illustration of chained libraries see Streeter 1931 and Ker 1951.

the medieval re-stitching was done.[27] Four bifolia have also been lost, according to the analysis presented here (which accepts Raw 1994).[28] Before describing each gathering of the manuscript, it is appropriate to summarize Raw's views as stated in her important work of 1984 (rpt. 1994; pp. 252-3):

- that the manuscript has been re-stitched and that the binding dates from the time of the re-stitching;
- that the end of *Daniel* has almost certainly been lost;
- that *Christ and Satan* was not originally a separate manuscript but was copied partly on vellum prepared in connection with the end of *Daniel*;
- that the losses from Gathering 2 are not related to the interpolation of *Genesis B*.

Gathering 1

The first gathering is intriguing in that the text of *Genesis A* begins on what would have been page '9' (it is now numbered '1'), if the gathering were not wanting three folios. These folios, the conjugates of those presently numbered 3-4, 5-6, 7-8, have been excised deep in the gutter near the stitching. A parchment binding stay was wrapped around the outside of the surviving sheets of the second gathering in the thirteenth century in order to reinforce them; one side of it projects out after folio 8 (the recto, which is blank, and the verso, with some thirteenth-century script). Since there is apparently no text missing from the beginning of the poem, it is tempting to speculate that up to six full-page illustrations have been removed.[29] The first extant image, however, is of 'God enthroned in Majesty', apparently above the chaos (*inanis et vacua*, Gen. 1:2) which existed at the moment of Creation; the opening lines of the poem describe exactly this scene, so it is hard to imagine what the subjects of the 'missing' images would have been. If there were six pages of illustrations before the present p. ii, then they were probably not directly related to the story of Genesis[30] The gathering has 3 full-page (3, 5, 7) and 2 half-page (2, 6) drawings. Text: *Genesis A* 1-168.

Gathering 2

If the structure of Gathering 1 is 'intriguing', that of Gathering 2 is 'challenging' for the codicologist, in that only 2 singletons survive of the original 8 folios;[31] critics have interpreted the codicological evidence in different ways and offered a number of possible reconstructions.[32] Raw 1994 (pp. 259-62) demonstrates that the defective

---

[27] The singleton which followed the present p. 180 was lost *after* the re-stitching was done (see Raw 1994, p. 261).
[28] Two in Gathering 2 and one in each of 12 and 17.
[29] The first three missing folios were lost after the manuscript was re-sewn; see Raw 1994 ('Appendix I', p. 274).
[30] Such illustrations might have been typological in nature, since so many of the surviving illustrations have typological significance, as is detailed throughout the Art-Historical Commentary.
[31] The six folios missing in this gathering were lost after the manuscript was re-sewn; see Raw 1994 ('Appendix I', p. 274).
[32] Timmer 1954 (pp. 13-14) argues that the two extant folios were numbers four and six in the original arrangement of the gathering; Gollancz 1927 (pp. l-lii) believes that they were numbers five and seven; Doane 1978 (pp. 7-10) argues that they were numbers two and six, would make a gap of three folios [or 6 pages of text, and perhaps images] at l. 205 of *Genesis A*.

state of this gathering cannot be related directly to the interpolation of *Genesis B* into the pre-existing *Genesis A*, and concludes:

> Evidence that the leaves which survive from Gathering 2 both came from the second half of the gathering and were still bifolia when the manuscript was re-sewn, together with evidence from the contents of these leaves, indicates that the arguments used by Gollancz (1927) and Timmer (1954) to support their view that *Genesis B* was first added to *Genesis A* in the present manuscript cannot be sustained (p. 262).

The Gathering Diagrams include:

- the present state of the gathering,
- ii-iii) two reconstructions proposed by Raw 1994 (p. 260), the first of which seems better supported by the codicological evidence,[33] and,
- iv) Timmer's 1954 reconstruction.

A parchment binding stay was wrapped around the outside of the surviving sheets of this gathering in the thirteenth century in order to reinforce them. There are illustrations in the lower half of pages 9, 10 and 11; the bottom half of p. 12 appears at first to be blank, but Ohlgren 1972a notes that there is an incised drawing here, which he describes as a warrior figure (perhaps meant to be St Michael; see his Fig. 1 and the accompanying discussion). Ruled for 26 lines of text; *Genesis A* 169-234.

Gathering 3

This gathering now consists of two bifolia (pages 13-14, 23-4 and 19-22) and two singletons (15-16 and 17-18); the missing conjugates of the singletons would originally have been positioned between pages 22 and 23 – there is now a gap in the text of *Genesis B* at this point (l. 441), which confirms this.[34] The tabs of the singletons were repositioned after the re-stitching in the thirteenth century so that they are now between pages 18 and 19 (see the diagram). Raw 1994 (p. 258) notes the gathering has two sets of stitching, one between pages 20 and 21 at the normal 5 points and another holding the two singletons to the head- and tailbands and to the second and third main bands. The gathering has 1 full-page (20) and 4 half-page (13, 16-17, 24) drawings. Text: *Genesis B* 235-490.

Gathering 4

This gathering is ruled (unusually) for 28 lines, but only 26 have been used. It is a regular and complete gathering of four bifolia (=16 pages). The gathering has 3 full-

---

[33] Doane 1991 (pp. 32-4) rejects Raw's proposed reconstruction of this gathering and proposes three other possibilities, each of which place pages 9/10 in the first half of the gathering as either the second or the third folio; he does not accept her observation that 9/10 has been re-ruled on the opposite side from its original ruling. He also thinks that a substantial amount of text has been lost between 9/10 and 11/12; his tentative language, however, confirms that fact that there will always be uncertainty about the original structure of this gathering since the poet is freely rendering and rearranging the Biblical source text at this point and the codicological evidence reveals just too little information – it must remain forever a matter of subjective interpretation.

[34] The two folios missing in this gathering were lost after the manuscript was re-sewn; see Raw 1994 ('Appendix I', p. 274).

or near full-page (31, 34, 36) and 2 half-page (28, 39) drawings. Text: *Genesis B* 491-851; *Genesis A* 852-71.

Gathering 5

The gathering has 5 full-page (41, 44, 51, 53-4) and 6 half-page (45-7, 49, 55-6) drawings; the lower half of p. 55 appears to be blank, but it has an unfinished incised etching on it, which seems to depict Jubal and his harp; see Ohlgren 1972a. The lower half of p. 50 is blank. It is a regular and complete gathering of four bifolia (=16 pages). Text: *Genesis A* 872-1142.

Gathering 6

This gathering has 2 full- or near full-page (61, 68) and 8 half-page (57-60, 62-3, 65-6) drawings; p. 70 appears to be blank, but there are some incised etchings on it (see the Art-Historical Commentary). It is a regular and complete gathering of four bifolia (=16 pages). Text: *Genesis A* 1143-1481.

Gathering 7

This gathering has 5 full- or near full-page (77, 81, 84, 87-8) and 5 half-page (73-4, 76, 78, 82) drawings; the lower half of p. 85 is blank. Pages 87-8 make up an *original* singleton containing two full-page illustrations, which augments what was otherwise a normal gathering of four bifolia. The stub of the singleton (87-8) is visible between pages 74 and 75. Text: *Genesis A* 1482-1901.

Gathering 8

This was originally a regular gathering of four bifolia. It now has 5 blank half-pages (99, 101-4) where drawings were never completed; originally the lower half of p. 96 was also blank, but a drawing (of 'Abraham and the Messenger') was added to it in the twelfth century. There is also a folio missing between pages 94 and 95;[35] since there is no gap in the text at this point, it seems likely that the missing folio was intended to record two full-page illustrations. Text: *Genesis A* 1902-2298.

Gathering 9

This was originally a regular gathering of four bifolia (=16 pages). It now has 5 blank half pages (111-14, 116) where drawings were never completed; there are also 4 pages which are almost completely blank (105, 108, 110, 115). Folios have been lost after pages 108 and 110, and there are gaps in the text at these points (i.e. at lines 2381 and 2418).[36] It is possible, of course, that there were also some illustrations planned for the text on the missing folios. Text: *Genesis A* 2299-2512.

---

[35] *Genesis B* is traditionally numbered as lines 235-851 of the composite Anglo-Saxon *Genesis* poem, unless edited as a separate poem.
[36] The folio missing after p. 94 was lost before the manuscript was re-sewn; see Raw 1994 ('Appendix I', p. 274).

Gathering 10

This was originally a regular gathering of four bifolia (=16 pages). It now has 8 blank half pages (117, 121, 123-8) where drawings were never completed; there are also 2 pages which are almost completely blank (118, 122) and one which is completely blank (120). Folios have been lost before page 117 and 123,[37] and there are gaps in the text at these points (i.e. at lines 2381 and 2418). It is possible, of course, that there were also some illustrations planned for the text on the missing folios. Text: *Genesis A* 2513-2707.

Gathering 11

This was originally a regular gathering of four bifolia (=16 pages), but a folio has been lost after p. 134; there is a gap in the text at this point (at l. 2806). Each of its present 14 pages are half blank (129-42) where drawings were never completed, and it is possible, of course, that there were also some illustrations planned for the text on the missing folio. Text: *Genesis A* 2708-2936.

Gathering 12

This was originally a regular gathering of four bifolia (=16 pages), but its middle bifolium has been lost; there is a gap in the text at this point (at l. 141). It is possible, of course, that there were also some illustrations planned for the text on the missing folios. The gathering now has 5 blank half pages (144-5, 147, 149, 153) where drawings were never completed; there are also 2 completely blank pages (150, 152). Two initials, which were to have been decorated, were also never completed (on pages 146 and 148). Text: *Exodus* 1-241.

Gathering 13

This was originally a regular gathering of four bifolia (=16 pages), but a folio has been lost after p. 164; there is a gap in the text at this point (at l. 446). It is possible, of course, that there were also some illustrations planned for the text on the missing folio. The gathering now has 5 blank half pages (155-7, 163, 167) where drawings were never completed; there are also 4 completely blank pages (159, 164-5, 168). Text: *Exodus* 241-510.

Gathering 14

This was originally a regular gathering of four bifolia (=16 pages), but folios have been lost after pages 174 and 180; there is a gap in the text after page 180 (line 177 of *Daniel*), but the text is not interrupted where the first folio has been lost, which indicates that the missing folio probably had two full-page illustrations. It now has 7 blank half pages (171, 175-80; 177 is actually blank at both the top and the bottom, with 9 lines of text in the middle) where drawings were never completed; there is also one completely blank page (172). Text: *Exodus* 511-90; *Daniel* 1-177.

---

[37] The two folios missing in this gathering were lost before the manuscript was re-sewn; see Raw 1994 ('Appendix I', p. 274).

Gathering 15

This was originally a regular gathering of four bifolia (=16 pages). It now has 9 blank half pages (181-7, 189, 193) where drawings were never completed; there is also one completely blank page (194). There is a folio missing between pages 182 and 183; since there is no gap in the text at this point, it appears that two full-page illustrations were planned for the excised folio.[38] Text: *Daniel* 178-429.

Gathering 16

This gathering is a regular and complete gathering of four bifolia (=16 pages). It now has 12 blank half pages (195-201, 203, 205-7, 210) where drawings were never completed; there is also one completely blank page (p. 204). There is a parchment stub visible after p. 210, which must have been added during the rebinding in order to reinforce the last gathering. Text: *Daniel* 430-730.

Gathering 17

Critics cannot agree whether the ending of *Daniel* has been lost or if the poem is complete as it stands. Ker 1957 (p. 407), Hall 1976 (p. 186) and Lucas 1979a (p. 52) believe that the poem is truncated, but Farrell 1974 (pp. 5-6) argues in his edition that it is complete. Raw 1994 (251-2) demonstrates that there is codicological evidence for the loss of a sheet after the current exterior sheet (pages 211-12 and 229-[30]), which probably contained the ending of *Daniel* [the present editor also thinks that there is a folio missing at this point, but that it contained two full-page illustrations (perhaps one for *Daniel* and one for *Christ and Satan*), and that *Daniel* concludes satisfactorily as it stands].

This gathering is irregular in a number of ways. The first folio, pages 211-12, is pricked for 27 lines, but is ruled for only 26; the rest of the folios in the gathering are ruled for 27 lines. The outer bifolium (pages 211-12, 229) has a 120 mm wide writing space, whereas the rest of the gathering has a space 140 mm wide. The first folio has single bounding lines, whereas the rest of the folios have double lines. Pages 213-29 were copied by two scribes.[39] Raw 1994 (267-70) summarizes the codicological evidence which indicates that three sheets were added to the centre of this gathering to provide the 12 pages required to record *Christ and Satan*; this was done before the manuscript was first bound, and not long after the first three poems had been copied out.[40] The two singletons now in this gathering (pages 217-18 and 223-4) were, it seems, originally halves of two bifolia; it is possible that the missing folios were excised because they contained full-page drawings (otherwise, as elsewhere in the manuscript, someone has excised the blank folio for re-use). The stub of the singleton (223-4) is visible between pages 216 and 217 recto and the verso. Finnegan 1977, the most recent editor of the complete poem, does not think that the poem was intended to

---

[38] The folio missing after p. 174 was lost before the manuscript was re-sewn, and that 180 after the re-sewing; see Raw 1994 ('Appendix I', p. 274).
[39] The folio missing after p. 182 was lost before the manuscript was re-sewn; see Raw 1994 ('Appendix I', p. 274).
[40] Ker 1957 thinks that the last page of text (p. 229) was copied out by a different scribe, whose hand resembles the one responsible for the captions on p. 9.

be illustrated, as his collation of the gathering shows. Texts: *Daniel* 731-64; *Christ and Satan* 1-729.

4   Script and Scribes

The texts are written in Anglo-Saxon minuscule script. One scribe (A) was responsible for the copying of the first three poems in the manuscript, the last of which, *Daniel*, concludes on the first folio of Gathering 17. Two scribes were responsible for the final poem, *Christ and Satan*, which is recorded on pages 213-29 or folios 2-10 of the final gathering (the last page, which would have been numbered '230', is blank); the first (B) copied out pages 213-15 and the second (C) 216-29.[41] Scribe A's hand, in Anglo-Saxon Square Minuscule, is larger than that of either B or C, and is more upright and rounded in appearance. Scribe A also spaces the text out more generously than B or C does. Scribe B's hand is more careless than the others, slopes somewhat, and is generally less attractive.

5   Punctuation, Accents, Abbreviations and Word Division

The most interesting aspect of the manuscript's punctuation is the use of a point, sometimes with a small 'check mark' either above (a *punctus elevatus*) or below it, to separate the poetic verses from each other. Lucas 1994 (pp. 17, 20-1) discusses the special function of the point with a small slash above it as a 'continuity marker'; this has been done with remarkable consistency and with minimal error throughout the manuscript (for a detailed analysis of the significance of this pointing, see O'Brien O'Keeffe 1990). Lockett 2002 (pp. 167-72) reviews evidence which suggests that the systematic pointing between verses in Junius 11 may have been done under the influence of a vernacular Germanic poetic manuscript, which is a very plausible hypothesis, given that *Genesis B* was translated in the late ninth or tenth century from an Old Saxon poem. This style of metrical punctuation has classical antecedents. The sequence '.7' is used as an end-of-section marker on occasion (see Lucas 1994, pp. 17, 20). A point is also used occasionally to indicate the deletion of a letter (expunction). Large and small initials may also be considered as 'punctuation', since they indicate the beginning of whole sections of the poems and smaller subsections within them.

Accent marks, added by more than one hand, are used throughout, but just as in the other poetic manuscripts they do not appear to be used systematically.[42] Timmer 1954 notes that pages 1-26 were revised by an eleventh-century corrector (pp. 1-2, 39-41). Ker 1957 (p. 407) notes that 'on p. 23 most of the alterations as well as the added accents are in red ink, which suggests that the corrector added the accents'. Small capitals, which often mark the beginning of long sense units (i.e. modern verse paragraphs), may also be regarded as an aspect of punctuation. The scribes do not mark the end of Fitts or poems with extensive strings of various punctuation signs, as is the habit of the scribe of *The Exeter Anthology* (Exeter, D&C MS 3501).[43] Hyphens

---

[41] Lucas 1979a (pp. 47, 59) argues that the inner part of the last gathering was originally a separate folded booklet, which was subsequently incorporated into the last gathering of the original manuscript.
[42] Timmer 1954 (p. 1), who is followed by Ker 1957 (p. 408) and a number of other critics, believes that yet another (a fourth) hand copied p. 229. Raw 1994 notes that the hand of p. 229 is very similar to that of pp. 216-28, and quotes Francis Wormald as having said he believed the hands to be the same.
[43] Krapp 1931 (p. xxiii) notes that the scribes seem to use accents 'when it struck their fancy', whether to mark long vowels, alliterating or metrically stressed syllables, or 'to make emphatic logically or

are not used to indicate breaks in words at line ends until p. 114. The word spacing in the manuscript is 'better' than in, for example, Exeter MS 3501, *The Exeter Anthology*, in that prepositions are for the most part not joined to the words which they govern. Wrapmarks occur on pages 94, 95 and 139.

The '⁊', *and* or less frequently *ond*, abbreviation symbol is usually joined to the following word when it is a conjunction; sometimes it is used to represent the first syllable of a word, as in *andswarian* or *andsaca*; the scribes used both *and* and *ond* spellings, so their usage is retained here and not normalized. There are only a few other abbreviations used in the manuscript, and these are the ones found most commonly in manuscripts of poetry: *u* and *g* with a macron above for final *-um* and initial *ge-* respectively; *þon* with a macron above for final *-ne* (i.e. *þonne*); *þ* with a crossed ascender for *þæt*. These have been expanded silently in the transcripts.

6   Fitts / Sectional Divisions

Doane 1991 observes that the 'fitts are sporadically but correctly numbered, beginning with vii and running consecutively through the three texts to xli' (p. 29), but this is not so.[44] The Fitts in the first three poems are numbered intermittently *.vii.* (on p. 17) to *.lv.* (on p. 209). It is not clear why the first six divisions are unnumbered (pages 1-16 of the manuscript), but it should be remembered that the interpolated *Genesis B* begins on p. 13, and this may have something to do with the irregularity. The next Fitt number, on p. 19, is also (incorrectly) numbered *.vii.* There are then no more Fitt numbers until *xvi.* on p. 43. Fitt *xviiii* is incorrectly recorded as *.viiii.* on p. 58. Numbers *xxvi* and *xxvii* are missing; they would have fallen between pages 79 and 92; *xxx* and *xxxiii* are missing between pages 94 and 109; *xxxvi* is missing between pages 111 and 121; *xliii*, *xliiii* and *xlv* are missing between pages 143 and 156; *xlviii* is missing between pages 160 and 166 (see the discussion in Lucas 1994, pp. 8-12); *lii* is missing between pages 177 and 191; *liiii* is missing between pages 191 and 209.

7   Corrections, Glosses and Marginalia

The final forms recorded in the manuscript after correcting by either the scribe or a subsequent reader or corrector have generally been adopted throughout, unless they are obvious errors, since they reflect a reading acceptable to a late Anglo-Saxon reader of the poems; the vast majority of such alterations occur in *Christ and Satan*, though pages 1-26 have also been corrected systematically (as noted earlier). When the original reading is preferable to the altered, later reading, this has been noted.

All accents, corrections, glosses and marginalia have been noted and described in the commentary and text; consequently that information is not repeated here in detail. There are very few glosses and marginal annotations, and none has great significance.

The errors in the manuscript are not unusual, and consist mostly of transcription errors, many of which the scribe corrected as he was copying; other errors were corrected later, either by the scribe or a later reader or corrector. Most of the errors

---

rhetorically important words in a passage'. All accents in the manuscript are reproduced in the text – if a black point occurs above a syllable but no tail is visible it is not considered to be an accent (this, of course, is an editorial decision, but the editor is working from extremely high-resolution images).
[44] See Muir 2000 (I. 28-9) for a summary of the punctuation marks in Exeter D&C MS 3501.

arise from one letter being misread as another; the letters read mistakenly here are for the most part the ones which also caused trouble for the scribe of *The Exeter Anthology* (see Muir 2002, I. 34-40): *d-ð, ð-d, r-s, h-n, u-a, wynn-p, wynn-þ, s-f, f-s,* and *r-n*. The evidence here suggests that *h* may not have been pronounced before some letters, just as in Exeter D&C 3051; the combinations affected are *hn, hr, hw* and initial *h* before a vowel. The scribes avoid scratching a letter away completely if it can be corrected by altering it in some way; often when they alter a minim to an ascender they do not bother to erase the original serif of the minim, so that they remain visible. Other forms of correction are expunction (a dot below the letter to be ignored), cancellation and the addition of missing letters interlineally usually with an insertion mark below; none of these occurs with any frequency or regularity. In *forgeaf*, *Exodus* (l. 11), the scribe seems to have written *forgeuf* at first, then underpointed the *u* for deletion; subsequently he realized that he could correct the *u* to *a* by altering it, so he added a second point above the *u / a* to reinstate it in its corrected form. There are a few instances of dittography also (for example in *Exodus* at lines 22 and 146), and on a number of occasions either a word or two or a complete verse or half line has been omitted (all instances are noted). Occasionally the scribe (or the scribe of the exemplar) has substituted a synonym for a word while copying; examples from *Exodus* are *god* for *metod* at l. 414 and *sæs* for *wæges* at l. 467; these went undetected and thus are not corrected. There are a few examples of incorrect word division, but it cannot be known whether they were already in the exemplar or if the Junius scribes introduced them.

The presence of 'nonsense words' in the manuscript, words which would clearly have been unintelligible to an Anglo-Saxon reader, even after a corrector had been through the manuscript (for example, *gewrinc* for *geswinc* at l. 317 of *Genesis B* and *wwa us* l. 1630 of *Genesis A*, which has been altered and remains wrong), raises the question of whether or not the scribes were Anglo-Saxons, that is, native speakers of Old English. This issue was also raised by the present editor with respect to *The Exeter Anthology* (Muir 2000, I. 35-6), in which a larger number of nonsense forms remain even after readings have been 'corrected'. It is noted that some art critics have questioned the nationality of the illustrators of Junius 11, since their work is consistently so out of kilter with the poetic text as to suggest that they could not understand what it said. Since both Junius 11 and Exeter D&C MS 3501 were copied out during the Monastic Reform period in the tenth century, when scholars, abbots, and presumably their support staff of scribes were invited from the Continent to assist in the reforming process, it is possible that these foreign scribes (who probably spoke a related Germanic language) and illustrators became involved in the copying of vernacular texts in order to supplement and expedite the work of native scribes.

8   Texts

Manuscript Junius 11 is an anthology containing four poems on Biblical themes; the first poem, *Genesis*, as noted above, incorporates a translation of an earlier Old Saxon poem into an existing Anglo-Saxon text. The poems in the anthology collectively deal with the major events of Salvation History (*Heilsgeschichte*) as described in the New Testament accounts of Christ's life and mission, and as foreshadowed through major events in the Old Testament; this makes them appropriate reading for all Christians, especially during Eastertide when they are encouraged to reflect upon the Paschal Mystery and how Christ's sacrifice made the attainment of eternal life in the Kingdom of God possible for them. Themes explored in the Biblical readings for the Easter Saturday liturgy and some of its texts, such as the *Exultet*, are central to the poems. Each poem investigates particular moments from the Biblical narrative in the larger context of Salvation History, so that, for example, while *Exodus* recounts the historical Exodus of the Israelites from Egypt, their rescue from slavery and entry into the Promised Land, the poet skilfully explores the typological and allegorical nature of this event both for individuals and for all believers. As such, the poems investigate God's creative act and his plan for humankind from the very beginning until the end of time, the creation of good, the origin of evil in angelic pride and disobedience and, on a cosmic scale (in *Christ and Satan* – see below), the ultimate triumph of good over evil. The Israelites crossing the Red Sea with Moses and journeying towards the Promised Land are described as sailors (*sæmen* l. 105); in the patristic exegetical tradition the Church is the ship in which the Chosen travel towards the heavenly port. The Egyptians, who are described as breakers of faith (*wære fræton*, 'they ate the covenant', l. 147[b]), are referred to as *landmenn* (l. 179), clearly differentiating them from the Israelites, who are faithful and obedient to God and prefigure the followers of Christ. So too, the preservation of the youths in the fiery furnace recounted in *Daniel* prefigures both Christ's Descent into Hell when he freed the Old Testament Just and the promise for all Christians of rescue from the purgatorial fires and rebirth in the heavenly kingdom. Noah, Abraham, Moses, Daniel and the three youths are faithful, righteous, steadfast and obedient; they serve as Old Testament models for all Christians as they relive the life of Christ through the feasts of the Liturgical Year.[45]

Since the appearance of Krapp's edition of the Junius poems in Anglo-Saxon Poetic Records I in 1931, the poems, which are all by different authors, have appeared in a number of separate scholarly editions; these offer detailed analyses of the individual poem's language, metre, punctuation, Fitt numbering, and other linguistic and codicological matters. Readers requiring extensive commentary on these issues are directed to these editions in the various discussions below since this is not the principal remit of the present edition. What follows here is primarily an overview of the integrity, theme and style of each of the poems and a consideration of the overall character of the anthology.[46]

---

[45] By way of comparison, it is interesting to note that the long poems at the beginning of *The Exeter Anthology* seem to have been chosen and arranged so that they present a range of role models for Christians: the first three poems deal with the life of Christ, from his Advent and Incarnation to his Second Coming at the Last Judgement; he is, naturally and inevitably, the epitome of Christian living. Guthlac represents the model for Christian men, and Juliana for women. The three youths in the fiery furnace represent ideal 'pre-Christian' Christians, the Old Testament Just, doomed to wait in bondage until the 'Harrowing' made the heavenly kingdom available to them. And the Phoenix represents a role model for all believers living in the sixth and final age of this world. The word *had,* which denotes a state or way of life (as in modern English '-hood' appended to such words as 'priesthood', 'sisterhood', *etc.*) appears in most of the poems, suggesting the validity of this interpretation of the anthologist's unspoken agenda.

[46] The present editor subscribes to Sisam 1953 where he observes that the surviving Anglo-Saxon poetry is written in a general Old English poetic dialect (or *koiné*), 'artificial, archaic and perhaps mixed in its vocabulary, conservative in inflections that affect the verse structure, and indifferent to non-structural irregularities, which were perhaps tolerated as part of the colouring of the language of verse' (p. 138). [In this context it should be remembered, of course, that certain poems *were* composed in one dialect and then ultimately recorded in a mostly West-Saxon dialect (for example, the 'Advent Lyrics' appear to have been first composed in a Northumbrian dialect — see Muir 2000, I. 385 *et passim*)]

Genesis A & B

The most recent comprehensive edition of *Genesis A* is by Doane 1978; *Genesis B* has been edited as a separate poem by Doane 1991, which should be read in conjunction with the pioneering work of Timmer 1954 (which Ker 1957 draws upon heavily). Vickrey 1960 completed an edition of *Genesis B* in 1960 as a doctoral dissertation.

Genesis is a composite poem, as noted above. Lines 1-234 and 852-2935 are an original Anglo-Saxon poem, probably dating from the eighth century, which is known as *Genesis A*. Lines 235-851 are a translation of an Old Saxon poem which probably dates from the ninth century (see Section 1 above); it is known as *Genesis B*. It is argued below and in the Art-Historical Commentary that the Old Saxon poem was already illustrated when it was brought to England (following Raw 1976).[47]

Genesis A begins with a description of the heavenly bliss in which the angels dwelt with God until Lucifer (the 'Light-bearer', the angel nearest to God himself) began to grow proud and think that he deserved to have a kingdom of his own and need not be subservient to God. The pride of Satan, which caused his fall and ultimately humankind's also, is a theme which is revisited later in two of the 'movements' of *Christ and Satan*, the 'Fall of the Angels' and the 'Harrowing of Hell' (see below); in Daniel, drunken or excessive pride leads to the fall of both the Jews and the Babylonians. God defeats the rebel angels and casts them headlong into the pit of Hell; the battle is described using the conventions and language of Anglo-Saxon epic and heroic poetry. The fallen angels lose their beauty and their wings, and are sexualized as they tumble from Heaven into the dark, fiery abyss of Hell, where they will suffer torment forever. Their fall from grace leaves a multitude of thrones vacant in God's kingdom and moves him to consider how he might best refill them. He determines to create a new world whose inhabitants, a 'better company' (*selran werode*, l. 95), will eventually occupy the thrones (the 'doctrine of replacement'). The narrative then describes the six days of Creation.[48]

One or perhaps two folios are missing at the end of the second gathering, so the text tapers off in the midst of a description of the four rivers which flowed out of the new paradise; *Genesis B* begins on the first page of Gathering 3 with a second account of the bliss in heaven before Lucifer began to grow proud and to plot rebellion against his Creator, and then gives a second, more detailed narrative of the Fall of the Angels. *Genesis B* is a highly-wrought poem, perhaps one of the best of the surviving Anglo-Saxon poems (bearing in mind, of course, that it is a translation from Old Saxon). The poet uses lively dialogue and characterization as he retells the story of the fall of both the angels and of humankind; *Genesis B* ends with Adam and Eve fashioning clothes for themselves from leaves as they await their next, inevitable encounter with God, aware now of their sinful state and of the changed condition of their lives.

---

[47] There are a number of leaves missing in the first and second gatherings of the manuscript; see Gathering Analysis and Diagrams for discussion of the current state of the manuscript and for some proposed reconstructions.
[48] Readers should consult the Art-Historical Commentary on the *Genesis* illustrations for a fuller, step by step discussion of the plot of the poem and the relationship between the manuscript's text and images.

Genesis A is neither a translation nor a synopsis of the Biblical text, and was never intended to be either; it is an original poem woven from materials selected with purpose from the Biblical narrative. The poet brought his work to a conclusion with the story of Abraham and Isaac, which indicates that he had fulfilled his aims at this point. Readers should thus reflect on what he has included in his narrative and try to arrive at an understanding of the rationale of his poem (the assumption of the present editor being that it was not originally a longer poem corresponding to the whole of the Biblical narrative, which was truncated by the anthologist as he designed Junius 11). The major episodes or sections of the poem deal with the following subjects: Adam and Eve and their offspring, with special attention to the family trees of Seth and Cain, which reflects the concern in Genesis with genealogy;[49] the story of Noah and the Flood, and of Noah's descendants; and the many episodes concerning Abraham, culminating in God's testing of his obedience.

Genesis A/B is the story of the relationship between God and humankind, of the latter's repeated lapses into disobedience and of God's willingness to forgive them. It is the story of the Covenant established with Noah and renewed periodically with his descendants, and especially with Abraham. On a more positive note, it is a story with major characters who are steadfast in their faith and obedient to God; these include Abel (p. 49), Seth (p. 56), Enoch (p. 60), Lamech (p. 62), Noah (p. 63) and Abraham and Isaac (pp. 82, 88, 96, 99). A number of these figures are traditionally treated as types of Christ – Adam, in a negative sense, since through the fruit of the tree he earned death and exile for humankind, whereas Christ conquered death through the wood of the Cross. St Augustine says that Abel and Seth prefigured the death of Christ and his resurrection from among the dead – see the commentary for p. 49. Enoch was specially favoured by God and was taken up into heaven by God without having to suffer death. Noah saved humankind through the wood of the ark, just as Christ did through the wood of the Cross; the door in the side of the ark is interpreted figuratively as the wound made by the lance in Christ's side at the Crucifixion. And finally, Abraham, who out of obedience was willing to sacrifice his son, represents God the Father, who let his son be sacrificed in order to redeem humankind.

When considering the poem, readers should recall that the story of Creation is one of the readings in the Holy Saturday liturgy; they should consider also that the anthologist chose *Genesis A/B* as the opening poem for what appears to be a vernacular lectionary for Eastertide, and bear in mind also the themes that are explored in its other poems. The story of the Fall of the Angels, mentioned briefly in Apoc. 12:7-9 but otherwise developed from apocryphal materials, is obviously important to the anthologist since he did not 'edit' either of the Genesis poems by excising one of the two accounts when combining them into a continuous narrative (just as there are two accounts of the Creation of Adam and Eve in the Biblical Genesis – those revising the Old Testament after the return from Exile in Babylon chose not to privilege one over the other). It cannot be known for certain if the original anthologist had planned for the inclusion of *Christ and Satan* from the start – it was added slightly later – but it is important to note that it contains *two* further accounts of the rebellion of the angels in heaven. This strongly suggests that the

---

[49] One would be justified in asking why someone might have excised a *blank* folio: perhaps a piece of blank parchment was needed and there seemed little harm in removing one from Junius 11, if it could be done without damaging the structure of the manuscript. Folios which were blank on only one side and had text recorded on the other were not generally excised.

introduction of evil into the world through pride and disobedience is an essential aspect of the structural principle of the anthology. The surge of evil in this world is countered and quelled by the series of steadfast Old Testament figures from Abel to Abraham who typologically evoke and foreshadow Christ and his ultimate triumph over Satan.

Exodus

The most recent comprehensive editions of *Exodus* are by Irving 1953, Tolkien 1991 (edited from his notes and published posthumously by Joan Turville-Petre) and Lucas 1994. Lucas suggests that the poem was probably composed in the eighth century and although it cannot be known where it was first composed, it may have been transmitted via a West Mercian centre such as Worcester or Lichfield (p. 39).

Exodus, which has no known literary source, is regarded as one of the most highly wrought poems from the Anglo-Saxon period. Like many such poems, it is not well served by its title, since it focuses on the Crossing of the Red Sea by the Israelites (primarily Exod. 13:20-14:31) and pays little attention to the rest of the Exodus narrative. It was chosen for inclusion in Junius 11 (or its exemplar) because the Crossing is a central moment in both Hebrew and Salvation History, and is redolent with typological associations which its readers would have readily identified and appreciated. Its sources are in the poet's knowledge of the Old Testament and the related patristic exegetical tradition and the liturgy. There is no reason not to regard it as an original poem by a learned Anglo-Saxon poet, who was able to invoke the traditional Germanic idiom, rhetoric and ethos in recasting a Biblical narrative in the vernacular, much as Bede relates that Cædmon was able to do after receiving his divine gift (see *EH* iv.24).

In the past, various critics have suggested that three passages in the poem may be interpolations (lines 108-24, 362-446 and 516-48), but this view no longer enjoys favour, since it can be demonstrated that they fit in well and are relevant as they stand (see the summary and argument in Lucas 1994, pp. 30-3). Its intertextual relationship with *Genesis A*, through references to the stories of Noah and Abraham with their typological significance, is in fact particularly relevant, given the nature of the Junius anthology. Lines 516-48, which some scholars believe would be better placed at the end of the poem, are not part of the narrative, but rather describe how readers can understand the hidden meaning of texts with the Holy Spirit's help. Falling as they do just before the concluding section of the poem, these lines seem very appropriately placed to the present editor (as they do also to Lucas 1994 – see his summary of the issue and related bibliographical references, pp. 32-3).

Lucas 1994 (pp. 43-51) offers an excellent appreciation of the style of the *Exodus* poet, focusing on rhetorical strategies, word-play, symbolism and structure. He points out that the poet employs different styles of writing for narrative, description and direct discourse, and that '(h)ints of an allegorical dimension to the poem are to be perceived at the level of style' (p. 46). The poem is rich in compounds, though some critics find other elements of its vocabulary repetitive or limited. The poet uses personification or animation frequently and often with great effect. Lucas also notes the poet's propensity for applying concrete verbs to abstract concepts.

Daniel

The most recent comprehensive edition of *Daniel* is by Farrell 1974; Brennan 1967 edited *Daniel* as a doctoral dissertation.

Daniel occupies all of gatherings 14-16 and p. 212 in the seventeenth (the verso of the first folio, the recto having been left blank for a full-page illustration). As detailed above in Gathering Analysis, the present editor holds different views from Farrell's concerning the structure of these gatherings. It is believed that the conjugate of pages 175-6 has been excised, and that it was intended to record two full-page illustrations (since there is no hiatus in the text after p. 174). In spite of Farrell's arguments to the contrary (1974, pp. 3-4), it would have been extraordinary for a singleton to be bound in the central opening of a gathering, since it could have easily worked itself loose and been lost (as a general practice, medieval scribes avoided positioning singletons in such an exposed manner). Likewise, in Gathering 15 the conjugate of pages 191-2, which was intended to record two full-page illustrations, has been excised (again, there is no loss of text here). Gathering 16 is fully preserved. Gathering 17 has a complex structure and history, as detailed in the Gathering Analysis and Diagrams. The last recorded part of *Daniel* falls on p. 212, where the sentence ends with a full-stop; the previous page (211) was left blank for a full-page illustration. Farrell 1974 argues (pp. 5-6, 32-3) compellingly that the poem is complete as it stands, a view shared by the present editor (who, however, differs from Farrell in thinking that there is a folio missing after the present p. 212 which was intended to record two full-page illustrations). For a summary of critical views on this issue, see Farrell 1974 and Raw 1994 (pp. 252-3).

It has been generally accepted among critics for over a century that *Daniel* contains an interpolated passage after l. 278, which consists of the lines presently numbered 279-361;[50] the original text is sometimes referred to as *Daniel A*, and the interpolated passage as *Daniel B*. Gollancz 1927 (p. lxxxvi) summarizes the evidence which suggests to him that lines 279-361 are an interpolation, but Farrell 1974 (pp. 22-9) counters his arguments and demonstrates compellingly that the Anglo-Saxon poet, who wrote the whole of *Daniel* as it stands in Junius 11, was in fact following the Biblical account (which itself contains some narrative irregularities) and the patristic exegetical tradition.

The poet of *Daniel* essentially constructs his narrative from the first five chapters of the Biblical book of Daniel, thus focusing on its narrative part and not its prophetic section (chapters 7-12).[51] As observed above, *Daniel* was selected for inclusion in the present anthology because it was appropriate reading for Eastertide. In the patristic exegetical tradition, the youths rescued from the fiery furnace represent the Old Testament Just – their release from torment and torture foreshadows the release of all

---

[50] Krapp 1931 (p. xxxii) believes that the intrusive text is longer, comprising lines 279-439.
[51] Part of the story recorded in *Daniel* the song of Azarias and the three youths, is the subject of a poem in *The Exeter Anthology* where it is assigned the title 'The Canticles of the Three Youths' by the present editor, though it is more generally know as 'Azarias'. Farrell 1997 believes that Daniel was written before the Exeter poem and 'served as a source for it' (see his argument on pages 42-5). He also believes that 'Azarias' is the ending of *Guthlac B* (pp. 37-41), a view not held by the present editor (see Muir 2000, II. 461).

the Just from Hell by Christ (the 'Harrowing').[52] Just as the Egyptians were depicted as troth-breakers, evil, and the enemies of God in *Genesis A*, so too here the Babylonians are called *deoflu* ('devils'); the poet says that they are drunken and full of pride (ll. 747-52), which corresponds to the description of the Jews at the beginning of the poem, where the poet describes them as turning to *deofoldædum* ('devilish deeds', l. 18[a]), choosing the *cræft* ('practice, craft', l. 32[b]) of the devil, and losing their city through drunken pride.

Daniel presents further evidence that God continues to honour his Covenant throughout the Old Testament period – even when the Jews fail to honour their obligation to him – and foreshadows the continuation of this relationship with his Chosen People – the followers of Christ – till the end of time (which, of course, is also foreshadowed in the story of the fiery furnace). The Hebrew youths, like Abraham, Noah and Moses before them, are steadfast in their faith and are rewarded for this by God.

Christ and Satan

The most recent comprehensive edition of *Christ and Satan* is Finnegan 1977. The most sustained and comprehensive study of the poem is Sleeth 1982; it offers an extensive analysis of the poem's unity, date, dialect, and also examines issues relating to its sources and the tradition within which it was written. The text was copied out by at least two scribes (see Section 4), and altered or corrected by a person known as 'The Late West-Saxon Corrector', because of his preference for West-Saxon spellings; this same person also altered or updated spellings in the early section of *Genesis A/B*.

Christ and Satan begins on p. 213 of Gathering 17 and ends on p. 229; for a discussion of the complex nature of this gathering, which was enlarged in order to accommodate *Christ and Satan*, see Section 3b. Some early editors and critics (including Ettmüller 1850 and Rieger 1861) considered the poem to be a conflation or sequence of three independent poems, a view which still finds support among many scholars.[53] Other editors considered it to be a single poem, but thought that it had serious textual problems, perhaps related to its transmission (Conybeare 1826 and Thorpe 1832); and still others regarded it simply as a unity (including Bouterwek 1849, Grein 1857, and the most recent editor, Finnegan 1977) – see Sleeth 1982 (pp. 3-8) for a summary of critical opinion.[54] It seems to the present editor that the poem as it stands today was intended to be read as a continuous narrative, but that its three sections or movements were originally composed by three different Anglo-Saxon poets.

---

[52] The songs of Azarias and the three youths are found in the Greek Septuagint, but not in the Hebrew or Aramaic version of Daniel; they are accepted as deuterocanonical by the Catholic Church. The passage, 68 verses in length, is inserted after 3:23, which records the falling of Shadrach, Meshach and Abednego into the fiery furnace; it was included by St Jerome in his fourth-century translation of the Bible into Latin (the 'Vulgate').

[53] Krapp 1931 (pp. xxxiv-xxxv) observes that '(i)t is better described as a set of lyric and dramatic amplifications of a number of Biblical and legendary themes of a familiar character, as a poem therefore more in the manner of Cynewulfian than in that of Cædmonian verse. In a poem of this kind one would not look for as obvious a structural form as would be expected in a narrative poem.

[54] Finnegan 1977 (p. 10) believes that *Christ and Satan* may have been in the projected plan for Junius 11 from the beginning; he suggests that the manuscript may have had 'as its rubric' something like the 'age of man'.

The anthologist or poet responsible for *Christ and Satan* as recorded in the manuscript intended, it seems, to explore the theme of the origin of evil in the universe and of Christ's triumph over it, and the implications of this for humankind, once fallen but now redeemed (Satan is called the *yfles ordfruma* ('the originator / first source of evil', l. 373ª). Its three movements deal with the Fall of the Angels (ll. 1-314), the Harrowing of Hell (ll. 315-662), and the Temptation of Christ by Satan in the desert (ll. 663-729). The poems have no direct literary sources; rather, the poet works within the established Christian patristic and doctrinal tradition, drawing freely upon it and antecedent apocryphal and literary traditions. The Biblical sources for the Fall of the Angels are detailed in the commentary for p. 3. The Letter of Jude (vv. 5-23) is particularly important for a consideration of *Christ and Satan*, and of the Junius anthology as a whole, because it succinctly makes reference to the Exodus, the rebel angels, Judgement Day, Sodom and Gomorrah (which readers are told 'were made an example, suffering the punishment of eternal fire', vs. 7), the archangel Michael, Moses, Cain and Adam. Moreover, the hortatory, homiletic ending of Jude recalls the concluding sections of each of the movements of *Christ and Satan*.[55]

In the 'Fall of the Angels' Satan attributes his fall to pride (*for oferhygdum*, l. 50ª) and acknowledges that he must suffer henceforth for his disobedience. Like Adam and Eve, he realizes the implications of his deeds and the extent of his loss *after* the event; he describes himself as a sinner before God (*ic eom fah wið God*, l. 96ᵇ). He is not the unrepentant Satan of *Genesis B*, but is defeated and suffers reproach from his followers for lying to them and bringing damnation upon them. The poet describes him as an exile in language which clearly evokes the elegiac mood of many Anglo-Saxon poems; the phrase *Hwær com engla ðrym* (l. 36ᵇ) and the ninefold repetition of *Eala* (Alas!, in ll. 163-7) at the beginning of consecutive clauses clearly recalls similar language and anxiety in *The Wanderer*. It is Christ, not God the Father or the Trinity, who opposes and defeats Satan and his followers in the three movements of the poem. The steadfast and faithful will position themselves with Christ at the right hand of the Father after the Last Judgement (ll. 610-11; these are clearly sourced in Matt. 25:31-46). Heaven is referred to as the *eðel* ('native- or homeland') of the righteous throughout. The poem is a cautionary tale, warning that people should not offend Christ, the Son of God: the fate of the fallen angels stands as an example of the harsh rewards for disobedience. The poet notes that '(m)en steadfast in the truth shall shine forth like the sun, fairly clothed, in their Father's kingdom, in his protective city' (ll. 306-8ª).

The 'Harrowing of Hell' opens with another brief account of the Fall of the Angels, which suggests that it had an earlier independent existence. Once again, it is noted that Satan caused his own fall through his pride (*oferhyda*, l. 369ª). Christ is described as crashing through the gates of Hell and rescuing thousands of mortals, whom he leads back up to their homeland. Adam and Eve are among those freed; before ascending, Eve recounts how she was deceived into sinning and asks for Mary to act as intercessor on her behalf. Christ, who is described as *frumbearn Godes* ('Son of God from the beginning', l. 468ᵇ), recounts how he took human mortality upon himself in order to redeem humankind. The remainder of the poem is concerned with

---

[55] See Sleeth 1982 (pp. 50-67) and Finnegan 1977 (pp. 37-42) for detailed discussions of the possible sources for *Christ and Satan*.

activities described at the end of the Gospels and in the Acts of the Apostles: the appearance of Christ after the Resurrection, the establishment of the Church, Christ's Ascension, and the coming of the Holy Spirit at Pentecost. Now, in the sixth and final age of the world,[56] humankind must prepare itself by its words and works for the Second Coming of Christ.

The 'Temptation of Christ' is much shorter than the other two movements of *Christ and Satan* and may be defective in places – for example, it mentions only two of the three ways in which Christ was tempted by Satan. The poet stresses the triumph of Christ over Satan, of good over evil, by repeatedly referring to the demon as 'accursed' (ll. 674^a, 690^a and 698^a); the phrase *Gewit þu, awyrgda* ('Depart, accursed one', l. 674^b) clearly cites the Biblical event (Matt. 4:10), but the poet is more concerned throughout with the cosmic implications of Christ's victory, of its effect on the fate of all mortals.

9   Artists, Illustrations, Initials and Decoration

Artists

Two artists were responsible for most of the decoration in the manuscript; the first is referred to here as Artist A and the second as Artist B.[57] Artist A was responsible for the illustrations down to page 72, the 'portrait of Ælfwine' on p. 2, the ornamental initials to p. 79, and the initial at the beginning of *Exodus* on p. 143. Artist B drew the illustrations on pages 73-88, the binding design on p. 225, (most likely) the initial on p. 226, and the two metalwork designs on the verso of the last unnumbered leaf ('230'). Temple 1976 notes the 'lightness and spontaneity' of Artist B's 'sketchy and impressionistic style, in which the influence from Rheims, perhaps of the *Utrecht Psalter*, is strongly felt' (p. 77). A third artist, working considerably later (probably in the twelfth century), added the unfinished etchings on pages 31 (a lion) and 96 ('Abraham and the Messenger'). The initials on pages 83-136 and 159-209 were made by the scribe; space was left on pages 146, 148 and 149 for large decorated initials which, for reasons unknown, were never drawn. The decorated initial 'h' on p. 226 of *Christ and Satan* seems to be by Artist B, which suggests that this final poem was added to the manuscript not long after the first three poems were copied out. There is one other illustration in the manuscript, which was added after the main illustrations had been drawn – a human head and torso at the top of p. 7. Finnegan 1988 argues that this figure was added later by the Artist B (p. 26), because it is in his style (the face does, in fact, resemble that of God in the lower register on p. 84).

The two main artists work in slightly different ways, and it is generally agreed among critics that B is more skilled than A. Artist A prefers to frame his illustrations, and uses a variety of frame types: a single line frame (e.g. pages 31, 34, 39); double line frame (e.g. pages 2, 44); columns (e.g. pages 3, 9, 16); columns supporting arches (e.g. pages 10, 13, 41, 45); arches with a single line frame (e.g. pages 11, 17, 28, 46); and arches with a double line frame (e.g. p. 24). On a few occasions he does not frame

---

[56] The sixth ages of the world are usually defined as: 1) from the Creation to the Flood; 2) from the Flood to Abraham; 3) from Abraham to David; 4) from David to Daniel; 5) from Daniel to Christ; and 6) the period after Christ's coming.

[57] Artist B also illustrated the Prudentius manuscript in Cambridge, Corpus Christ College, MS 23.

his illustrations (e.g. pages 6, 7). Artist B tends not to use frames and demonstrates a better grasp of perspective in his architectural drawings; he also uses colour tinting more freely than Artist A. Artist B depicts God as youthful and beardless, whereas God is both bearded and beardless in A's illustrations.[58] Each artist depicts God holding a rod / scroll with bands four times (on pages [Artist A] ii, 2, 3, 41; [Artist B] 74, 76, 82 and 84), but Artist B puts dots between the bands, which Raw 1976 (pp. 137-8) suggests is meant to indicate that it is a 'sealed roll'.[59] Artist B's drawing of the naked Noah's torso (p. 78) is much more sophisticated than A's naked Adam and Eve (e.g. on p. 13), and attempts to depict musculature. Both Artists depict God both with and without a nimbus (the nimbus is often crossed) – see, for example, pages 2, 65, 74, and 84. Artist A often depicts God holding the 'Book of Life' (see p. 7 and Commentary), whereas the book is not found in B's illustrations. Artist B does, however, generally attempt to make his illustrations 'match' those of Artist A stylistically, even to the point of associating Eve-Abel with Sarai-Isaac and Mary-Christ typologically (see the Commentary for p. 88).[60] Artist A sometimes 'ignores' his architectural frames by drawing outdoor scenes within them, as on pages 53 and 58, where figures stand on earthen mounds, though apparently indoors.

Artist A interprets the text and sometimes uses his illustrations to comment on it. He occasionally illustrates details found in the Anglo-Saxon poem which are not in the Bible; for example, on p. 49 he depicts the weapon used by Cain to slay Abel (see also the commentaries for pages 46, 54, 58 and 61). And contrariwise, both artists include details in their illustrations which are not mentioned in the poems; these include 'Jacob's Ladder' (p. 3), Enoch listening to an angel (p. 60), and Noah and his son ploughing (p. 77).[61] Artist A freely adapts conventional scenes and iconography, showing a willingness or desire to express himself both artistically and intellectually. For example, during and after the Fall of the Rebel Angels they are depicted naked and sometimes with genitals, whereas the angels in heaven are clothed and not sexualized (nor are Adam and Eve depicted with genitalia before the fall; afterwards, of course, they become aware of their sexuality and cover their nakedness). He simultaneously depicts the tempter as both a serpent and an angelic messenger, merging two traditions (see the Commentary for p. 24). Moreover, he depicts Hell in three ways, as the 'maw or mouth' of Hell personified (p. 3, and see the Commentary

---

[58] It is suggested in the Art-Historical Commentary that through the use of a beard Artist A may have intended to differentiate between God the 'Father' and God the 'Son' and to depict them both as engaged in the act of creating.

[59] The only other English manuscript with a depiction of such a 'sealed scroll' is an 11th-century Boethius at Fleury (Paris, BN fonds lat. 6401, fols.158^v and 159). Raw 1976 associates Junius 11 with the school at Tours, and notes that the *Grandval Bible* (2nd quarter of the 9th century) depicts God as beardless and holding a scroll (which is not sealed, however). She further notes that the Adam and Eve scenes in Junius 11 look like a frieze in that they use trees as frames and to separate scenes, as is also the case in four Bibles from Tours. These four cycles of images are based on the Cotton Genesis cycle (London, BL Cotton MS Otho B.iv) and the mosaics of St. Mark's (Venice). Of these four Bibles the one closest to Junius 11 is the San Callisto Bible (Rome, San Paulo fuori le Mura), especially in its treatment of the creation of Eve, where Adam is positioned identically (but mirrored).

[60] See also the Commentaries for pages 74 and 76 where it is suggested that Artist B may be trying to link later events with earlier ones typologically.

[61] Ohlgren (1972b) thinks that the Junius 11 illustrations elucidate specific portions of the text and 'may also help to clarify and dramatize the underlying thematic purpose of the poem'. Henderson 1975 (p. 168, n. 1), on the other hand, argues the case for a much looser relationship between the text and the illustrations.

there), as a fortress (p. 16) and as a fiery pit (p. 36).[62] On p. 36 the artist shows the devilish messenger returning to Hell to proclaim the success of his mission; on p. 41 he parallels this in the 'serpent' sequence of illustrations by showing the serpent, which has just been cursed by God, slithering off on its belly. As it approaches the vine-entwined column it turns upwards, intending to work its way up the column and back into the animal's mouth at the top, which is surely meant to be or to represent the 'Mouth of Hell' (see the Art-Historical Commentary).

Artist A draws upon the whole of the Bible, not just the book of Genesis, for details in his illustrations (some of this, of course, he inherited as part of the iconographic tradition): Biblical sources for the depiction of the multi-winged seraphim, the 'Book of Life', the 'Mouth of Hell', *inter alia* are given throughout the Commentary. It is suggested in the Art-Historical Commentary for p. 28 that Artist A may sometimes use tinting or colour strategically in his illustrations. The Commentary also demonstrates how the iconography relates to the patristic exegetical tradition, primarily with reference to St Augustine's *City of God*.[63] Artist A occasionally overrides the scribe's original plan for illustrating the *Genesis* poem; consequently, there are blank spaces in the manuscript even in the section where the text has been illustrated (on pages 12, 55 and 70; the scribe probably left the small space at the bottom of p. 50 blank because he knew that a full-page illustration had to be inserted into the narrative on the next page).

Artist B also overrides or ignores the original plan for illustrating the text by leaving the top half of p. 77 blank (see the Art-Historical Commentary);[64] he extends the towers of the building in the lower illustration upwards into the space he has left blank, suggesting that he was trying to compensate for having left out an illustration.[65] Sometimes he does not complete all the details for figures in the background or in groups (see, for example, p. 77, where the hooves and legs of one ox have not been drawn). Though he too has some trouble with the use of perspective, he employs it better than Artist A.

The two artists treat the narrative flow of their illustrations in different ways. If more than one action is depicted in an illustration or sequence of scenes on a single page, Artist B tends to arrange the scenes so that the narrative flow is in what might be called the natural sequence of top to bottom; p. 81 may be an exception to this rule, but critics are not in agreement about the subject matter of the illustrations on that page. Artist A, on the other hand, depicts narrative flow in a number of ways. For example, on p. 20 there is an upper and a lower scene, with the upper scene depicting two separate actions (Adam and Eve gazing upon a tree in Eden and the serpent tempting Eve). The narrative flow is from bottom to top and from right to left at the top. On p. 28 there is only one illustration register, but the picture has a complex

---

[62] For a discussion of the nature of hell and patristic formulations of eternal punishment, see Kelly 1978 (pp. 479-85) and Marthaler 1987 (pp. 167-76). Gardiner 1989 has published a collection of 'visions of hell' in the period up to and including Dante.

[63] The *City of God* has been used here since it contains so much that explains the iconography of the Genesis Cycle in a single volume; it was well known throughout the Middle Ages and continues to be influential today. It is readily available as Bettensen 1972.

[64] Note that the scribe left p. 31 completely blank for a full-page illustration of the 'Fall': it is not clear why Artist A chose to use only the top two-thirds of the page to illustrate this important moment.

[65] Of course, we cannot know exactly why he decided to leave out an illustration at this point.

narrative pattern comprising three stages. The tempter, in angelic form, stands in the centre facing Adam on his right and hands him the fruit. To the left stands Eve; she is involved in two activities though only depicted once: the tempter hands her the fruit, which she takes in her left hand, and she is then shown eating it while holding it with her right hand. In similar fashion, in the single register on p. 44 the artist has depicted two stages of narrative, flowing from left to right; on the left God 'curses' Eve and, on the right, Adam. Whereas on p. 28 one tempter was depicted participating in two different scenes, here the artist has drawn two God the Fathers standing back to back. The narrative sequence on p. 9 is neither vertical nor horizontal; the action begins on the lower right hand side (God removing the rib from Adam's side) and moves to the upper left (the creation of Eve). It is not clear how the 'Jacob's Ladder' and 'Gate of Heaven' scenes relate to the narrative sequence, since they are details added by Artist A which are not found elsewhere in depictions of the Creation of Eve. On p. 61, which depicts the Ascension in two illustrative registers, the narrative flow is from bottom to top, as might be expected logically.

In the illustrations themselves, both artists use gesture to indicate that figures are conversing with each other. On p. 78, in the scene at the top where Cham is shown discovering Noah asleep naked, Artist B uses the placement of Cham's hands to indicate his surprise or shock, a strategy found only here in the manuscript, though in the 'Fall' sequence Adam and Eve hold their hands over their eyes to indicate their remorse (pages 31, 34, 36 and 39).

The 'Genesis Cycle'

The layout of the first three poems in the manuscript indicates that they were all intended to be fully illustrated and, as mentioned earlier, it seems likely that there were once a few full-page illustrations for *Christ and Satan* as well. For whatever reason, the artists only provided illustrations for the *Genesis* poems (and even these poems are not completely illustrated) and consequently art-historical and critical discussions usually focus on the 'Genesis Cycle' and its origins. Several scholars have compiled lists suggesting what illustrations might have been intended for the remaining three poems, from a consideration of treatments of these Biblical books elsewhere and of what would be appropriate for specific blank spaces in their manuscript context; Karkov 2001 summarizes these suggestions ('Appendix', pp. 203-6).[66] Lucas 1994, among others, notes that there were to be more illustrations in Junius 11 than are found in other extant 'parallels' (specifically, the Ashburnham *Pentateuch* (Paris, BnF ms nouv. acq. lat. 2334) and the Old English *Hexateuch* (London, BL Cotton MS Claudius B.iv).[67]

Caution must be used when discussing parallels to and sources for the illustration cycle in Junius 11, however (as Lowden 1992 also warns), because although there are

---

[66] The critics whose work she summarizes are Henderson 1985, Lucas 1979, Lucas 1994, and Gollancz 1927. See also C.R. Dodwell and P. Clemoes, eds., *The Old English Illustrated Hexateuch*. EEMF XVIII. Copenhagen, 1974; pp. 53-8. Lucas (1994, p. 16) rightly notes that any such re-creation must be regarded as very tentative, but they are, in spite of this, informative and helpful.
[67] Interestingly, the illustration programme of Claudius B.iv was also left unfinished. For further discussion of the possible relationship between Junius 11 and the Ælfric manuscript (the Old English prose 'Heptateuch'), see Henderson 1975 (pp. 131-8); he notes that though the sequence of illustrations for Genesis 18-19 tally quite well, 'the proposed cycle in the Junius MS is if anything more substantial'.

a number of similarities between the Junius images and those found in other manuscripts and mosaics, *there is no demonstrable source for the complete cycle*, and many aspects of the illustrations have no parallels anywhere. The integration of the pictures into the text of Junius 11 is complicated by the fact that the *Genesis B* poem has been interpolated into *Genesis A* after being translated from an Old Saxon text, which itself may have been illustrated. Raw 1976 argues that the Old Saxon poem was already illustrated, and that the poem and drawings came to England together; indeed, she argues compellingly that the Junius 11 illustrations have their source in Carolingian models, which in turn are derived from the 'Cotton *Genesis*' (see below). Henderson 1975 cautions that the cycle of illustration in Junius 11 is 'erratic' in nature – being densely illustrated sometimes and at other times sparsely – and this 'should be borne in mind in any estimation of its historical antecedents' (p. 121).

The major studies of the decoration and illustration of Junius 11 are by Gollancz 1927, Henderson 1962, 1963 and 1975), Karkov 2001, Lockett 2002, Lowden 1992, Raw 1976, and Wormald 1945 and 1952). Any critical discussion of the 'sources' of an illustration cycle in a medieval manuscript should be aware of Raw 1992, 'What do we Mean by the Source of a Picture?' Henderson 1975 includes a detailed analysis of the disposition of the illustrations (and of the blank spaces provided for the illustrations that were never completed) with respect to the poetic narrative which demonstrates that there was *not* a close working relationship between the two Anglo-Saxon artists and the scribe; the pictures are often placed a page or two either before or after the narrative they are meant to illustrate. It seems that the scribe of the first three poems had decided upon a set of illustrations when he left the blank spaces throughout his text, but that the artists used their own judgement when adding the illustrations. Indeed, at times, and even at critical points in the narrative (as on p. 70), the illustrators have not even supplied an illustration in the space left blank by the scribe. The lack of synchonization between text and image is so striking that it has led to speculation that the illustrators may not even have been Anglo-Saxon and thus were perhaps unable to fully comprehend the text. Henderson 1975 (pp. 130-1), for example, observes: 'So frequently do the illustrators run counter to the clear intention of the planner of the picture-cycle that they almost make one suspect them of being illiterate in Old English'). Temple 1976 (p. 76) accepts Gollancz's statement that Junius 11 was probably copied from an unillustrated exemplar, and concludes, 'thus it can be assumed that the two Anglo-Saxon artists were responsible for the composition of the cycle'; this oversimplifies a complex situation, as the discussion which follows here shows.

Art historians generally agree in tracing existing early medieval cycles of Genesis illustrations back to Byzantine manuscripts, primarily to the so-called 'Cotton *Genesis*' (London, BL MS Cotton Otho B.vi), which was severely damaged in the Cotton Library fire of 1731, but also to the 'Vienna *Genesis*' (Vienna, Österreichische Nationalbibliothek, cod. theol. gr. 31); the atrium mosaics in the Church of San Marco in Venice, were copied either from the Cotton *Genesis* or from a sister manuscript, and are therefore important to any discussion of the sources for the Junius 11 'Genesis Cycle'. The Cotton manuscript contained only the text of Genesis, which was accompanied by approximately 360 illustrations.[68] The Vienna *Genesis* exists today

---

[68] See Weitzmann and Kressler 1986 for the process of reconstructing the Cotton *Genesis* manuscript; even before the fire of 1731 the manuscript was reduced to 166 folios. There is a succinct summary of

as 24 single leaves, containing passages excerpted from Genesis 3:4-50:4. Lowden 1992, however, reviews the question of the influence of the Cotton and Vienna *Genesis* manuscripts in the West, especially with respect to vernacular 'paraphrases' of the Biblical Genesis, and concludes that they appear to be experimental and unique, and reflect a special interest in Late Antiquity; he observes that 'there was no tradition of illustrated Byzantine Genesis manuscripts, but only two isolated instances'. He notes that even in its own time the Cotton *Genesis* was unusual, and that 'the Cotton and Vienna manuscripts are very different from one another' (p. 41). He says, furthermore, that it is 'inaccurate and tendentious' to refer to the vernacular treatments as 'Genesis manuscripts', since none of them contains solely the text of Genesis (pp. 40-3) [with respect to Junius 11, it is argued in Section 1 that its compiler or anthologist conceived of the collected poems as appropriate reading for Eastertide].

It does not do service to either *Genesis A* or *Genesis B* to refer to them as Biblical paraphrases; the latter in particular is a highly wrought, learned and sophisticated poem, full of lively dialogue and engaging characterizations. That the Anglo-Saxon poems were intended to be original compositions with specific purposes is indicated by the fact that none of them attempts to recount an entire book of the Bible; the poets have selected specific sections or incidents from their Biblical 'source' and fashioned them into poems in their own right.

London, BL Cotton Claudius B.iv, a vernacular *Hexateuch* (in prose) by the Anglo-Saxon monk Ælfric, was illustrated at Canterbury at about the same time that Junius 11 was (most likely) produced there, and so it might be expected that they would be connected in some way, but this is not the case – they are almost totally dissimilar, as Raw 1976 notes (p. 135).[69] She argues that much of Junius 11's illustration cycle must have been derived from a single source, 'because they contain a very unusual iconographic detail, which was misunderstood by both artists'; this is the scroll or rod held by God in eight drawings, four by each artist (A: Frontispiece, 2, 3, 41; B: 74, 76, 82, 84). She believes that these drawings are influenced by or related to a Boethius manuscript held at Fleury in the eleventh century (pp. 138-9). She notes further that the Creator in the Genesis cycle of the Carolingian *Grandval Bible* is beardless and carries a scroll, like the Creator of Artist B (though the scroll there is not sealed).[70] The strongest evidence she presents for associating the Junius *Genesis* illustrations with Carolingian models relates to the treatment of the Adam and Eve sequence. She observes,

> Most of these drawings are framed by pairs of trees and this suggests that they were derived originally from a set of frieze illustrations in which the scenes were divided from one another by trees, as they are in four bibles associated with Tours. ... The Genesis illustrations in these four volumes are based on

---

their findings in Lowden 1992, and also a summary of the proposed reconstruction of the Vienna *Genesis* by Gerstinger, with additional comments by Mazal 1980 (p. 48).

[69] Temple 1976 observes, '(t)his pictorial cycle belongs to a different recension from the one illustrating... Aelfric's Paraphrase of the Pentateuch and Joshua (British Library Cotton, Claudius B. iv)'. Unlike Raw, she believes that the Junius 11 illustrations 'are entirely the invention of the two English illuminators'; she notes, further, that the 'strip narrative' style of the illustration is of 'Late Antique inspiration' (p. 76).

[70] Drawings of God seated and holding a (sealed) scroll are properly associated with illustrations of the Apocalypse (as they are in the Fleury Boethius manuscript).

the Cotton cycle, known from the fragments of the sixth-century Cotton Genesis (London, British Library, Cotton Otho B.vi) and from the mosaics at St Mark's, Venice, which were copied from this manuscript or a sister one (p. 139).

Of the four Carolingian Bibles she associates with Junius 11, its cycle has greatest affinity with the *Grandval* and *San Callisto* Bibles.[71] At the conclusion of her summary of the strong evidence for Carolingian influence on the illustrations of Junius 11, she notes:

> The derivation of both text and illustrations from continental material of a single period suggests that this adaptation was made on the continent and that pictures and text came to England together. A comparison of the Junius drawings of the rebellion and fall of the angels and of the descendants of Adam with the texts of *Genesis A*, *Genesis B* and the Old Saxon *Genesis* confirms this view. The drawings of the rebellion and fall of the angels correspond in detail to *Genesis B*, and hence to its Old Saxon original, even when they ostensibly illustrate *Genesis A* (p. 146).

The evidence Raw presents in this seminal work firmly supports her hypothesis that the main sequence of pictures in Junius 11 came to England with the Old Saxon *Genesis*. She rightly notes that the drawing on p. 2 illustrates *Genesis B*, not *A*, and that the two captions on p. 3 refer to *Genesis B* lines 292-7 and 318-20; there is nothing similar in *Genesis A* (pp. 146-7). She further observes that the illustrations of the descendants of Cain and Enoch do not follow the text of *Genesis A*; she concludes that they are probably following the Old Saxon poem, which is now mostly lost. She conjectures that the manuscript may have been a presentation copy and suggests that it may have been a wedding gift on the occasion of the marriage of Æthelwulf of Wessex to Charles the Bald's daughter Judith in 856.

If Raw is right in what she suggests, then the situation is quite complicated. When Junius 11 was being planned, the scribe (or whoever was overseeing the project, if it was not the scribe) had before him a fully-illustrated Old Saxon *Genesis* poem as well as other manuscripts or individual images, some of which probably derived or evolved from the 'Cotton Genesis' tradition. The overseer and scribe must have determined the disposition of the illustrations, integrating drawings from the Old Saxon manuscript and other sources into the Anglo-Saxon composite poem; as noted earlier, the final cycle is erratic (perhaps 'idiosyncratic' would be a better word) in a number of ways.[72] Despite the effort put into selecting the images for the first *three* poems (not just *Genesis*) and laying out the text to accommodate the selected material

---

[71] See her detailed discussion on pp. 139-43.

[72] Henderson 1975 (p. 135) observes:

> ...the erratic nature of the cycle whose outline we can trace in the blank spaces throughout *Genesis,* its flurry of scenes and its total lack of scenes, does not suggest that the initiative was truly with the scribe, but that he was stimulated by a model or models which gave him an elaborate but only partial programme of scenes. An ancient copy of Genesis, very fully illustrated but impaired and illegible in places, would meet the case.

by the project overseer and / or scribe, the evidence suggests that the illustrators often ignored the original plan and improvised as they went.[73]

9b   Decorated Initials

There are three types of large initials in Junius 11. Quite elaborate decorated and zoomorphic initials are used down to page 79, with a final example occurring at the beginning of *Exodus* on p. 143. From p. 83 down to the end of *Daniel* (p. 212, with the last large initial falling on p. 209) undecorated initials drawn in the same ink as the main text are used. These are of two types: they are either plain and solid or blockish looking, or slightly more elaborate, being drawn with blank spaces left in some of their constituent strokes so that they appear to be two-tone (black and white). Smaller, undecorated initials are generally used in *Christ and Satan*, but those on pages 217-20 are slightly more elaborate and are in red metallic ink. There is one final zoomorphic initial on p. 226, but it was (most likely) drawn by Artist B; the initial at the beginning of the poem (on p. 213) is in the 'second' style as just described ('black and white'), but does not appear to be by the same hand which drew those in the first three poems. Temple 1976 notes that the ornamental initials were drawn before the text was written (p. 77); this concurs with Henderson 1975, who observes:

> On the pages with large zoomorphic initials, the layout of the lines of the text, regularly back from the irregular shape of the initials, shows that the initials were in place, even if only in sketch form, before the adjacent text was written (p. 115).

A good example of this is found on p. 6, where the text moves in and out from the left bounding line in order to accommodate the contours of the large zoomorphic *wynn* (the runic letter for modern *w*). However, there are blank spaces on pages 146, 148 and 149 for three large decorated initials that were never inserted, which complicates the matter, since there is no evidence at these points of any preliminary sketching of the shape of the initials. Beside the blank space on p. 148 there is a small 'h' in the left margin, which serves as a prompt reminding the artist which (decorated) initial needs to be inserted (this is perhaps further evidence that the artist may not have been an Anglo-Saxon, since a native speaker would know that only an *h* can come before the sequence *lud here*).[74]

The evidence just reviewed suggests that the person drawing the decorated initials was working closely with the scribe; it might even be concluded that it *was* the scribe who was drawing the initials, but, if so, why would he have to insert a prompt for himself on p. 148? Henderson 1975, who also thinks that the initials may have been drawn by the scribe, suggests why he might have employed various styles:

> Could not the scribe himself have designed the zoomorphic initials and then, simply tiring of them, have fallen back on his secondary type of letter?

---

[73] Henderson 1975 (p. 138) concurs with this view: 'Untroubled by the chain of anomalies created by lack of respect for the integration of text and illustrations, the artists reorganize the balance and treatment of scenes, and are capable, on occasion, of visual extemporization'. The qualified closing phrases of this statement devalue the creative input of the Junius 11 illustrators, which is unwarranted.
[74] There are prompts for other missing small initials on pages 220 and 224; there is one further missing initial, without a marginal prompt, on page 226.

Alternatively, the change in the form of the initial letters might reflect the written source of the Junius MS text, perhaps supplying visual aids so far and no further, itself having modified its letter form quite independently of the chance of a change of illustrator in the Junius MS at page 73. The matter seems too uncertain in its significance, to be the basis of any firm conception of the level of co-operation between the scribe and the illustrator (p. 115).

Wormald 1945 was the first major study of the ornamental initials in Junius 11 and remains a seminal work; Temple's 1976 catalogue also contains a number of important observations on the style of the decorated initials. Ker 1957 (p. xxxviii) considered them to be tenth-century penwork, and Temple 1976 (p. 77) says that 'they are rather retrospective in style and, composed of full-bodied dragons, interlace, beasts and mask heads, they recall no. 7 (Junius Psalter)'. Wormald 1945, who believed Junius 11 to be firmly planted in the eleventh century because of perceived Scandinavian influences, was consequently forced to speak of the 'artificial antiquity' of the initials (p. 121).[75] Lockett 2002 (pp. 145-8) reviews the scholarship concerning the style of the initials (and the question of Scandinavian influence) and concludes that the initials of Junius 11 'would have been unusual if produced in the eleventh century' (p. 148). Although he cannot 'rule out the possibility that they are a later, very faithful copy of initials in the style of the Junius Psalter', he is inclined to date them *c.* 950-late 970s (when considered in light of the other evidence supporting such a dating, which he also reviews). They exhibit a number of features characteristic of Wormald's 'Type 1' initials (as found in the *Junius Psalter*, *Tollemache Orosius*, *Durham Ritual* and the Tanner *Bede*):

> The animal bodies in the initials are very robust; at their thickest point, they are two or three times as wide as the necks, tongues, tails, and acanthus scrolls which comprise the limbs of the letters and the heavier interlace, which is in turn about twice as wide as the finer interlace. The general aspect of such initials is captured well by Temple's description of 'soft fattish creatures' combined with 'thick worm-like interlace' in the Tanner Bede. In addition, the facial contours and features as well as the execution of the wings follow a relatively predictable pattern in the initials of these five manuscripts (Lockett 2002, p. 147).

10   Captions

There are a number of captions accompanying the illustrations, all but one of which occur early in the manuscript. Ker 1957 (p. 407) notes that the captions on pages 2, 3, 6 and 7 are in the main hand, but thinks that those on p. 9 are by the hand which wrote p. 229. They range from a single word, such as a name identifying a character, to a brief description of a scene; captions are misplaced on pages 3 and 6 (see the Art-Historical Commentary). The Latin words on pages 3 and 7 are perhaps not by the main hand and may have been added later. If some of the captions are in the main hand, as they seem to be, it is odd that two of them are misplaced – this raises further questions about the working relationship between the scribe and the illustrators: for

---

[75] 'The initials in the Caedmon MS. are peculiar, because although the MS. seems to be late, the dragons and even the acanthus ornament have an artificial antiquity about them and look as if they are later copies of initials belonging to a type quite close to the Helmingham Orosius'.

example, if the scribe had originally chosen the illustrations or was at least aware of what was available for copying when he left spaces for them as he laid out the manuscript, why did he not know where to place the captions when he came back later to add them? The captions are:

page 2: *hælendes hehseld* ('The lofty throne of the Healer / Saviour')

page 3.1: *Hu sengyl* (for *se engel*) *ongon ofermod wesan* ('How the angel began to be proud')

page 3.2: *Her se hælend gesco[p] helle heom to wite* ('Here the Healer / Saviour created hell as a torment for them')

page 3.3: *her se* ('Here the...')

page 3.4: *inferni* ('hell')

page 6: *[Her he] gesyndrode wæter and eorðan* ('[Here he] separated water and earth')

page 7.1: *Salvator* ('Saviour')

page 7.2: *her he* (added above) *todælde dæg wið nihte* ('Here he separated day from night')

page 9.1: *Her godes englas astigan of heouenan into paradisum* ('Here the angels of God ascend from Heaven into Paradise')

page 9.2: *michael* ('Michael')

page 9.3: *Her drihten gewearp sclep on adam and genam him an rib of þa sidan and gescop his wif of þam ribbe* ('Here the Lord cast sleep upon Adam and took a rib from his side and created his wife from the rib')

page 9.4: *Her drihten gescop adames wif euam* ('Here the Lord created the wife of Adam, Eve')

page 9.5: *EVA* ('Eve')

page 13: *qoddam* (for *quoddam*) *mare* ('a certain sea')

page 56: *Seth wæs sæli* ('Seth was blest', corresponding to line 1138[a], *Seth wæs gesælig*).

11   Printed Bibliographies and Translations

The following works are either bibliographical or contain an extensive bibliography: Caie 1979, Doane 1978, Doane 1991, Farrell 1974, Finnegan 1977, Irving 1953, Karkov 2001, Krapp 1931, Lucas 1994, and Eriksen 2020. The present edition includes a select bibliography covering codicology, art history and the literary analysis of the poems in the manuscript.

Kennedy 1916 translates the four poems and reprints the manuscript illustrations as published by Ellis 1833, with an art-historical commentary by C.R. Morey. Bradley 1982 translates large portions of the four texts in MS Junius 11 (he translates only the first half of the combined *Genesis* poems – 1542 of 2936 lines – and omits lines 315-64 of *Christ and Satan*.) Mason 1990 is a reprint of his 1915 translation of *Genesis A*, accompanied by Ellis's illustrations (1833). Gordon 1954 translates substantial portions of each of the poems. More recently, Anlezark 2011 translates *Genesis*, *Exodus* and *Daniel*). Other recent translations are included in the online 'Old English Poetry Project' (*q.v.*).

12   Editorial Principles

All the information necessary to facilitate the proper understanding of the text is readily available in the apparatus on each page so that it is not necessary for the user to refer to other sections of the book while reading. These annotations include information relating to the text and how it has been restored where deficient or corrupt, with acknowledgement of the contributions of earlier editors, observations concerning codicology, paleography and decoration, biblical references and allusions, identification of doctrines alluded to, liturgical echoes and influences, and brief descriptions of the illustrations where they occur (full descriptions are included following the texts in the Art-Historical Commentary).

Particular attention has been paid to the scribes' work practices in order to demonstrate how they corrected the text, either while initially copying it, or subsequently when errors were detected either by the scribe or another reader; this information could be of great use to those interested in the reception and transmission of texts in the Anglo-Saxon period. There are sometimes references to the 'Gathering Analysis and Diagrams' included here in order to demonstrate clearly the structure of the manuscript, which has folios missing throughout. Subsection titles have been introduced in the first three poems in order to facilitate reference and to help readers find their way around the texts. In describing the script in the apparatus the word 'bold' is used for the bulkier initials that usually follow the large decorated initials immediately. In the text itself, all accent marks have been indicated, since their use is still not fully understood, and this information may be useful to those interested in prosody. Where they occur, Roman numerals have been replaced with equivalent words in order to show readily how they fit into alliterative patterns. The few common abbreviations have been expanded silently (see Section 5 above).

GATHERING DIAGRAMS

Gathering 1

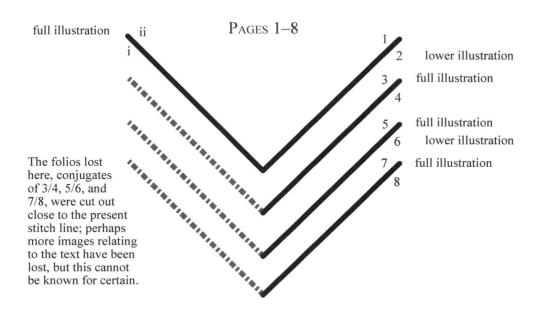

This Gathering Contains Genesis Lines 1–168

Gathering 2 (now)

Pages 9–12

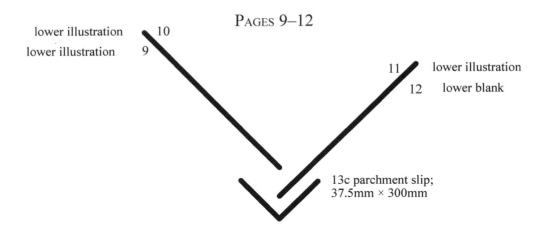

This Gathering Contains Genesis Lines 169–234

Gathering 2 (reconstruction a)

Pages 9–12

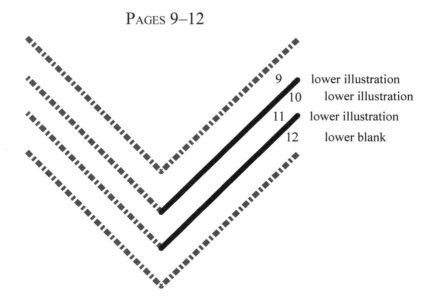

9 lower illustration
10 lower illustration
11 lower illustration
12 lower blank

This Gathering Contains Genesis Lines 169–234

THE CÆDMON MANUSCRIPT

GATHERING 2 (RECONSTRUCTION B)

PAGES 9–12

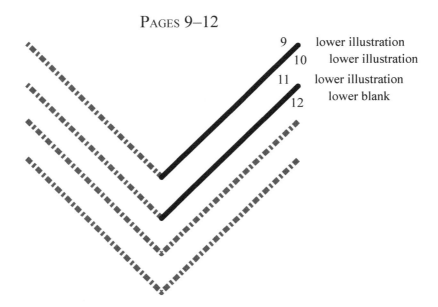

THIS GATHERING CONTAINS GENESIS LINES 169–234

GATHERING 2 (RECONSTRUCTION C)

Timmer's Interpretation

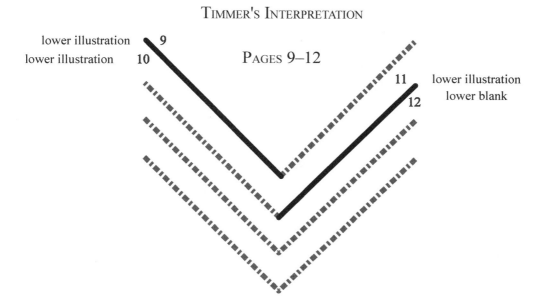

This Gathering Contains Genesis Lines 169–234

Gathering 3

Pages 13–24

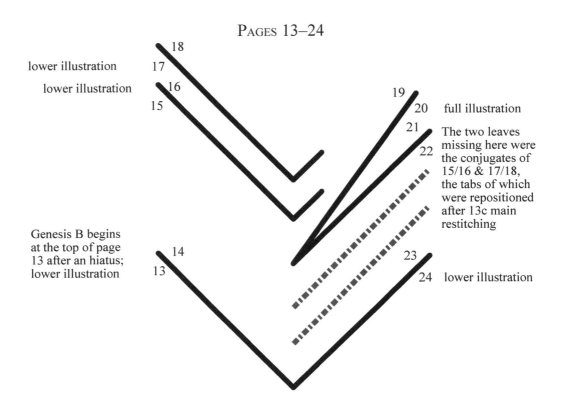

This Gathering Contains Genesis Lines 235–490

Gathering 4

Pages 25–40

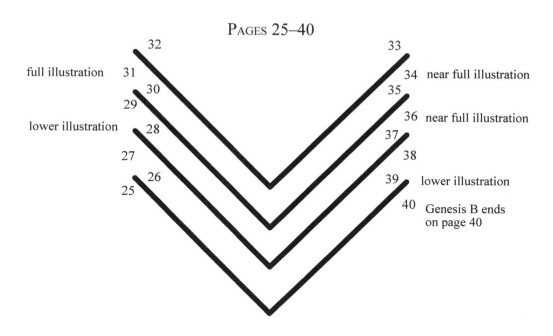

This Gathering Contains Genesis Lines 491–871

Gathering 5

Pages 41–56

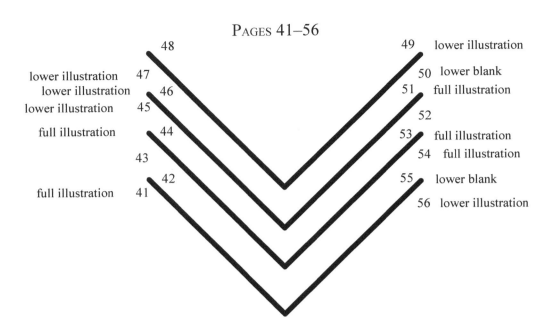

This Gathering Contains Genesis Lines 872–1142

Gathering 6

Pages 57–72

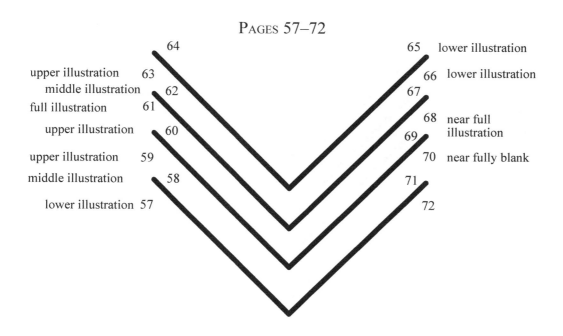

This Gathering Contains Genesis Lines 1143–1481

Gathering 7

Pages 73–90

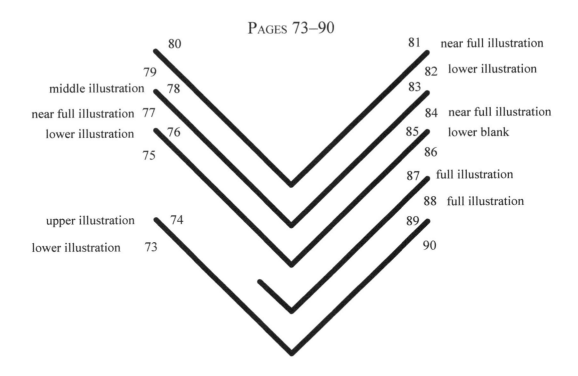

This Gathering Contains Genesis Lines 1482–1901

GATHERING 8

PAGES 91–104

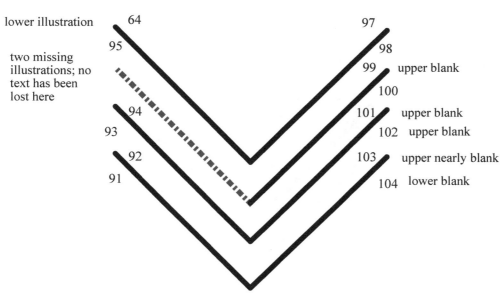

THIS GATHERING CONTAINS GENESIS LINES 1901–2298

Gathering 9

Pages 105–116

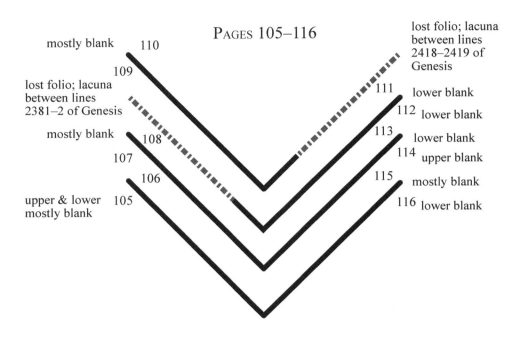

This Gathering Contains Genesis Lines 2299–2512

Gathering 10

Pages 117–128

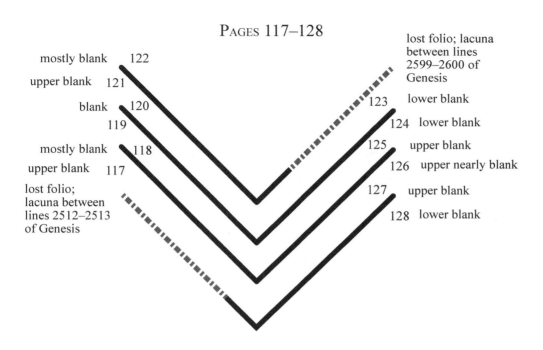

THIS GATHERING CONTAINS GENESIS LINES 2513–2707

Gathering 11

Pages 129–142

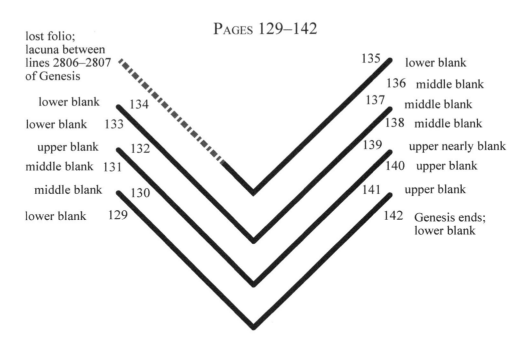

This Gathering Contains Genesis Lines 2708–2936

Gathering 12

Pages 143–154

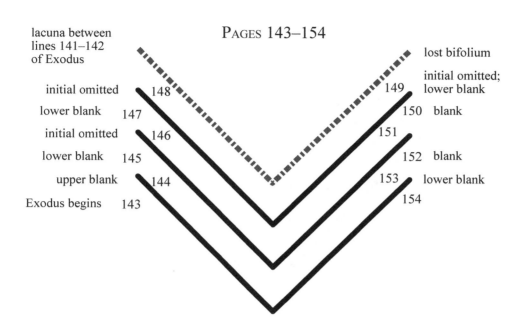

This Gathering Contains Exodus Lines 1–241

Gathering 13

Pages 155–168

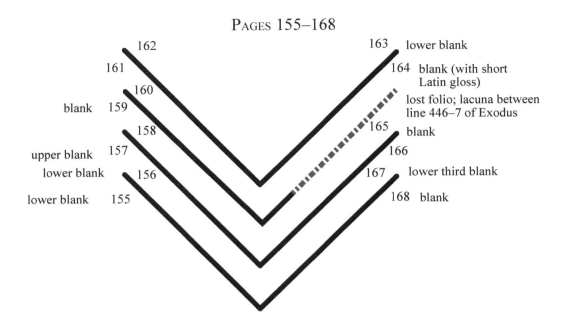

This Gathering Contains Exodus Lines 241–510

Gathering 14

Pages 169–180

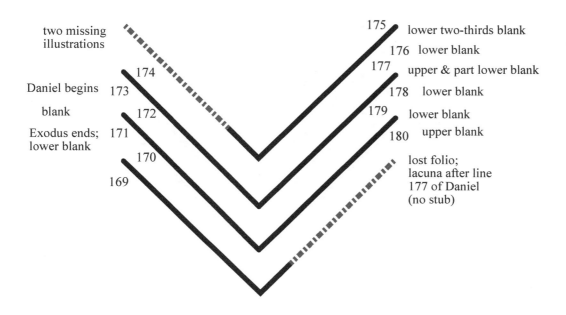

This Gathering Contains Exodus Lines 511–590 and Daniel Lines 1–177

Gathering 15

Pages 181–194

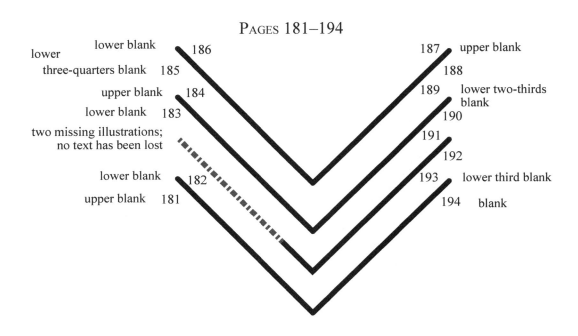

This Gathering Contains Daniel Lines 178–429

Gathering 16

Pages 195–210

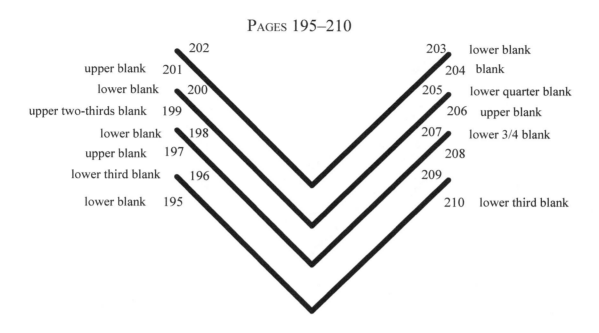

This Gathering Contains Daniel Lines 430–730

Gathering 17

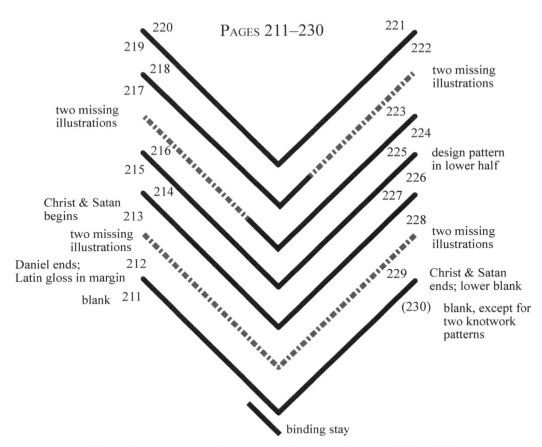

This Gathering Contains Daniel Lines 731–764
and Christ and Satan Lines 1–730

ABBREVIATED REFERENCES

ANQ	*American Notes and Queries*
ASE	*Anglo-Saxon England*
ASPR	Anglo-Saxon Poetic Records
CCSL	*Corpus Christianorum*. Series latina.
CSASE	Cambridge Studies in Anglo-Saxon England
EETS	Early English Text Society
ELN	*English Language Notes*
ES	*English Studies*
JEGP	*Journal of English and Germanic Philology*
LSE	*Leeds Studies in English*
MÆ	*Medium Ævum*
Neophil.	*Neophilologus*
NM	*Neuphilologische Mitteilungen*
PLL	*Papers on Language and Literature*
PMLA	*Publications of the Modern Language Association*
PQ	*Philological Quarterly*
RES	*Review of English Studies*
TPS	*Transactions of the Philological Society*
TSLL	*Texas Studies in Literature and Language*
ZfdA	*Zeitschrift für deutsches Altertum und deutsche Literatur*
ZfdPh	*Zeitschrift für deutsche Philologie*

SELECT BIBLIOGRAPHY

Anderson, Earl R. 'Style and Theme in the Old English *Daniel*'. In Liuzza 2002, pp. 229-60.

Anlezark, Daniel, trans. *Old Testament Narratives*. Dunbarton Oaks Medieval Library, 2002.

– 'Lay Reading, Patronage, and Power in Bodleian Library, Junius 11'. In *Ambition and Anxiety : Courts and Courtly Discourse* c. *700-1600,* ed. Giles, E.M., Gasper and John McKinnell, 76-99. Toronto, 2014.

– 'The Old English *Genesis B* and Irenaeus of Lyon'. *MÆ* 86 (2017) 1 *sqq*.

– 'Aldhelm, Daniel and Azarias'. *MÆ* 89 (2020) 224-43.

Backhouse, Janet *et al*. *The Golden Age of Anglo-Saxon Art*. London, 1984.

Behaghel, Otto. *Heliand und Genesis*. Halle, 1903.

Benskin, Michael and Brian Murdoch. 'The Literary Tradition of Genesis'. *NM* 76 (1975) 389-403.

Bernstein, A.E. *The Formation of Hell*. London, 1993.

Bettenson, Henry, trans. *Concerning The City of God against the Pagans*. Harmondsworth, 1972.

Birkett, Tom. *Reading the Runes in Old English and Old Norse Poetry*. New York, 2017 (esp. essay 1, pp. 13-48).

Blackburn, Francis A. *Exodus and Daniel. Two Old English Poems Preserved in MS Junius 11 in the Bodleian Library of the University of Oxford, England*. Boston and London, 1907.

Bouterwek, Karl W. *Caedmon's des angelsächsen biblische Dichtungen*. Gütersloh and Elberfeld, 1849; 1851; 1854.

Bradley, S.A.J., trans. *Anglo-Saxon Poetry*. London, 1982.

Bremmer, Rolf H. Jr. *Fransiscus Junius F.F. and his Circle*. Amsterdam, 1998.

Brennan, F.C., ed. *The Old English Daniel*. Dissertation, 1967.

Bright, James W. *An Anglo-Saxon Reader*. New York, 1891.

– 'On the Anglo-Saxon Poem *Exodus*'. *MLN* 27 (1912) 13-19.

Brown, Katherine DeVane. 'Antifeminism or Exegesis? Reinterpreting Eve's *wacgeþoht* in *Genesis B*'. *JEGP* 115 (2016) 141-66.

Bugge, John. 'Virginity and Prophecy in the Old English *Daniel*'. *ES* (2006) 127-47.

Burchmore, Susan. 'Traditional Exegesis and the Question of Guilt in the Old English *Genesis B*'. *Traditio* 41 (1985) 117-44.

Caie, Graham D. *Bibliography of Junius XI Manuscript*. Anglica et Americana 6. Copenhagen, 1979.

Carpenter, Stephen H. *An Introduction to the Study of the Anglo-Saxon Language*. Boston, 1875.

Clubb, Merrell D. *Christ and Satan: An Old English Poem*. New Haven, 1925.

Conybeare, John Josias. *Illustrations of Anglo-Saxon Poetry, edited together with additional notes, introductory notices, &c., by his brother William Daniel Conybeare*. London, 1826 [Genesis 356-378, Exodus 447-463a, 489-494a, with translations in Latin].

Cosijn, Peter J. *Anglosaxonica. Beiträge* XIX (1894) 444-61.

– *Anglosaxonica* II *Beiträge* XX (1895) 98-116.

Craigie, W.A. *Specimens of Anglo-Saxon Poetry* I. Biblical and Classical Themes. Edinburgh, 1923.

– *Specimens of Anglo-Saxon Poetry* II. Early Christian Lore and Legend. Edinburgh, 1926.

Cross James E. and S.I. Tucker. 'Allegorical Tradition and the Old English *Exodus*'. *Neophilologus* 44 (1960) 122-7.

Davidson, Cliford, ed. *Gesture in Medieval Drama and Art*. Kalamazoo, 2001.

Dendle, Peter. *Satan Unbound: the Devil in Old English Narrative Literature*. Toronto, 2001.

Doane, Alger N., ed. *Genesis A: a New Edition, Revised*. Madison, Wisconsin, 2013.

– ed. *The Saxon Genesis. An Edition of the West Saxon Genesis B and the Old Saxon Vatican Genesis B*. Madison, Wisconsin, 1991.

Dodwell. C.R. *Anglo-Saxon Gestures and the Roman Stage*. CSASE 28. Cambridge, 2000.

Earl, James W. 'Christian Tradition in the Old English *Exodus*'. In Liuzza 2002, pp. 137-72.

Ellis, Henry. 'Account of Cædmon's Metrical Paraphrase of Scripture History, an illuminated manuscript of the Tenth Century, preserved in the Bodleian Library at Oxford'. London, 1833 [Originally published in *Archaeologia* XXIV (1832) 329-343. Contains reproductions of the MS. illustrations].

Ericksen, Janet Schrunk. 'The Wisdom Poem at the End of Junius 11'. In Liuzza 2002, pp. 302-26.

– 'Legalizing the Fall of Man'. *MÆ* 74 (2005) 205-20.

– *Reading Old English Biblical Poetry: The Book and the Poem in Junius 11*. Toronto, 2020.

Ettmüller, Ludwig, ed. *Engla and Seaxna Scôpas and Bôceras*. Quedlinburg and Leipzig, 1850.

Evans, J.M. *Paradise Lost and the Genesis Tradition*. Oxford, 1968.

Farrell, R.T., ed. *Daniel and Azarias*. London, 1974.

– 'The Structure of the Old English *Daniel*'. In Liuzza 2002, pp. 203-28.

Finnegan, Robert E. 'Eve and 'Vincible Ignorance' in *Genesis B*'. *TSLL* 18 (1976) 329-39.

– ed. *Christ and Satan*. Waterloo, Ont., 1977.

Förster, Max, ed. *Altenglisches Lesebuch für Anfänger*. Heidelberg, 1913 [3d ed., 1928; Genesis 2885-2936].

Fox, Michael. 'Ælfric on the Creation and Fall of the Angels'. *ASE* 31 (2002) 175-200.

Frank, Roberta. 'What Kind of Poetry is *Exodus*?' In *Germania: Comparative Studies in the Old Germanic Languages and Literatures*, ed. Daniel G. Calder and T. Craig Christy, 191-205. Woodbridge, 1998.

– 'Some Uses of Paranomasia in Old English Scriptural Verse'. In Liuzza 2002, pp. 69-98.

Frings, Theodore. '*Christ und Satan*'. *ZfdPh* 45 (1913) 216-36.

Gardiner, E. *Visions of Heaven and Hell before Dante*. New York, 1989.

Gatch, Milton McC. *Preaching and Theology in Anglo-Saxon England: Ælfric and Wulfstan*. Toronto, 1977.

Gestinger, H. *Die Wiener Genesis*. Vienna, 1931.

Gollancz, Sir Israel, ed. *The Caedmon Manuscript of Anglo-Saxon Biblical Poetry, Junius XI in the Bodleian Library*. Oxford, 1927.

Gordon, R.K., trans. *Anglo-Saxon Poetry*. London and New York, 1926; rev. 1954.

Graz, Friedrich. 'Beiträge zur Textcritik der sogenannten Cædmonschen Genesis'. In *Festschrift zum 70. Geburtstage Oskar Schade*, 67-77. Königsberg, 1896.

Grein, Christian W.M., ed. *Bibliothek der angelsächsischen Poesie*. Vol. 1. Göttingen, 1857.

– 'Zur Textcritik der angelsächsischen Dichter'. *Germania* X (1865) 417-20.

Greverus, J.P.E., ed. *Cædmon's Schöpfung und Abfall der bösen Engel aus dem angelsächsischen übersetzt nebst Anmerkungen*. Oldenburg, 1852.

– *Cædmon's Sündenfall aus dem angelsächsischen übersetzt nebst Anmerkungen*. Oldenburg, 1854.

Haines, Dorothy. 'Unlocking *Exodus* ll. 516-32'. *JEGP* 98 (1999) 481-98.

Hall, J.R. '*Geongordom* and *Hyldo* in *Genesis B*'. *PLL* 11 1975) 302-7.

– 'The Old English Epic of Redemption: The Theological Unity of MS Junius 11'. *Traditio* 32 (1976) 185-208.

– 'The Old English Epic of Redemption: Twenty-Five-Year Retrospective'. In Liuzza 2002, pp. 20-52.

– 'Pauline Influence on *Exodus*, 523-48'. *ELN* 15 (1977) 84-8.

– 'Duality and the Dual Pronoun in Genesis B'. *PLL* 17 (1981) 139-45.

– 'Old English *Exodus* and the Sea of Contradiction'. *Mediaevalia* 9 (1986 for 1983) 25-44.

– 'On the Bibliographic Unity of Bodleian MS Junius 11'. *ANQ* 24 (1986) 104-7

– 'Old English *sæborg*: *Exodus* 442a, *Andreas* 308a'. *PLL* 25 (1989) 127-34.

Hall, T.N. 'The Cross as Green Tree in the *Vindicta Salvatoris* and in *Exodus*. *ES* 72 (1971) 297-307.

Harbus, Antonina. 'Nebuchadnezzar's Dreams in the Old English *Daniel*'. In Liuzza 2002, pp. 261-86.

Harsh, Constance D. '*Christ and Satan*: The Measured Power of Christ'. *NM* 90 (1989) 243-53.

Hauer, Stanley R. 'The Patriarchal Digression in the Old English *Exodus*, Lines 362-466'. In Liuzza 2002, pp. 173-87.

Henderson, George. *Studies in English Bible Illustration*. Vol. 1. London, 1985.

Hill, Joyce. 'Confronting *Germania Latina*: Changing Responses to Old English Biblical Verse'. In Liuzza 2002, pp. 1-19.

Hill, Thomas D. 'Apocryphal Cosmography and the *stream uton sæ*': A Note on *Christ and Satan*, Lines 4-12'. *PQ* 48 (1969) 550-4.

– 'The Fall of Satan in the Old English *Christ and Satan*'. *JEGP* 76 (1977) 3-25.

– 'The Fall of the Angels and Man in the Old English *Genesis B*'. In *Anglo-Saxon Poetry: Essays in Appreciation of John C. McGalliard*, ed. Lewis E. Nicholson and Dolores Warewicl Frese, 279-90. Notre Dame, 1975.

– 'The Measure of Hell: *Christ and Satan* 695-722'. *PQ* 60 (1981) 409-14.

– 'Satan's Injured Innocence in *Genesis B*, 360-2, 390-2: A Gregorian Source'. *ES* 65 (1984) 289-90.

– 'Some Remarks on the Site of Lucifer's Throne'. *Anglia* 87 (1969) 303-11.

– 'The *virga* of Moses and the Old English *Exodus*'. *In Old English Literature in Context*, ed. John D. Niles, 57-65. Cambridge, 1980.

Holthausen, Ferdinand. 'Beiträge Erklärung und Textcritik altenglischer Dichter'. *Indogermanische Forschungen* IV (1894) 379-88.

– [Review of Grein -Wülker, Vol. II, Part II.] *Anglia*, Beiblatt V (1895), 193-8, 225-34.

–ed. *Die ältere Genesis*. Heidelberg, 1914 [Addenda and errata in *Anglia* 46 (1922) 60-62].

Hunt, Theodore W. *Cædmon's Exodus and Daniel*. Edited from Grein. Boston, 1883.

Irving, E.B., ed. *The Old English Exodus*. *YSE* 122. New Haven, 1953; rpt. 1970.

Jager, Eric. 'Tempter as Rhetoric Teacher: 'The Fall of Language in the Old English *Genesis B*'. In Liuzza 2002, pp. 99-118.

James, Montague Rhodes. *The Ancient Libraries of Canterbury and Dover*. Cambridge, 1903.

Johnson, David F. 'The Fall of Lucifer in *Genesis A* and Two Anglo-Latin Royal Charters'. *JEGP* 97 (1998) 500-21.

Junius, Franciscus, ed. *Cædmonis Monachi Paraphrasis Poetica Genesios ac præcipuarum Sacræ paginæ Historiarum, abhinc annos M.LXX*. Amsterdam, 1655.

Karkov, Catherine E. *Text and picture in Anglo-Saxon England*. Cambridge, 2001.

Kears, Carl. 'Old English *Mægen:* a Note on the Relationship between *Exodus* and *Daniel* in MS Junius 11'. *ES* 95 (2014) 825-48.

Kelly, J.N.D. *Early Christian Doctrines*. New York, London, 1978.

Kelly, Richard J., ed & trans. *The Blickling Homilies*. London, 2003.

Kendrick, Laura. *Animating the Letter*. Columbus, 1999.

Kennedy, Charles W., trans. *The Cædmon Poems, translated into English prose*. London [includes reproductions of the illustrations as first published by Ellis, with a commentary], 1916.

Ker, Neil R. *Catalogue of Manuscripts containing Anglo-Saxon*. Oxford, 1957.

Klaeber, Fr., ed. *The Later Genesis and Other Old English and Old Saxon Texts Relating to the Fall of Man*. Heidelberg, 1913.

– ed. *The Later Genesis and other Old English and Old Saxon Texts relating to the Fall of Man*. Englische Textbibliothek 15. Heidelberg, 1931.

Klipstein, Louis F., ed. *Analecta Anglo-Saxonica*. Vol. II. New York, 1849.

Kluge, F., ed. *Angelsächishes Lesebuch*. Halle, 1888.

Körner, Karl. *Einleitung in das Studium des Angelsächsischen*. 2. Teil. Heilbronn, 1880.

Krapp, George P. and Arthur G. Kennedy, ed. *An Anglo-Saxon Reader*. New York, 1929.

– ed. *The Junius Manuscript*. Anglo-Saxon Poetic Records I. New York, 1931; rpt. 1964.

Lapidge, Michael. 'Hypallage in the Old English *Exodus*'. *LSE* 37 (2006) 31-9.

Leo, Heinrich. *Altsächsische und angelsächsische Sprachproben*. Halle, 1838.

Liuzza, Roy, ed. *The poems of MS Junius 11 : Basic Readings*. New York, 2002.

Lockett, Leslie. 'An Integrated Re-examination of the Dating of Oxford, Bodleian Library, Junius 11'. *ASE* 31 (2002) 141-73.

Lowden, John. 'Concerning the Cotton Genesis and Other Illustrated Manuscripts of Genesis'. *Gesta* 31 (1992) 40-53.

Lucas, Peter J. 'On the Incomplete Ending of *Daniel* and the addition of *Christ and Satan* in MS Junius 11'. *Anglia* 97 (1979) 46-59.

– 'MS Junius 11 and Malmesbury'. *Scriptorium* 34 (1980) 197-220.

– ed. *Exodus*. Exeter Medieval English Texts and Studies. Exeter, 1977; rpt. 1994.

– ed. *Cædmonis Monachi Paraphrasis Poetica Genesios ac præcipuarum* . Early Studies in Germanic Philology. Amsterdam, 2000 [This is a facsimile reprinting of Junius's 1655 first edition of the manuscript, with Introduction and Bibliography; Junius's annotations for MS Junius 11, found on folios 3-8v of MS Junius 73*, are reproduced in plates at the end of this edition].

Lynch, Clare. 'Enigmatic Diction in the Old English *Exodus*'. Dissertation, Cambridge 2000.

MacLean, G.E. *An Old and Middle English Reader*. New York, 1893.

Major, Tristan. *Undoing Babel: the Tower of Babel in Anglo-Saxon Literature*. Toronto, 2018.

March, Francis A., ed. *Introduction to Anglo-Saxon. An Anglo-Saxon Reader, with Philological Notes, a Brief Grammar, and a Vocabulary*. New York, 1870.

Marthaler, Bernard L. *The Creed*. Mystic, CT, 1987.

Martin, Ellen E. 'Allegory and the African Woman in the Old English *Exodus*'. *JEGP* 81 (1982) 1-15.

Mason, Lawrence, trans. *An Anglo-Saxon Genesis*. Lampeter, 1990.

Mazal, O. *Kommentar zur Wiener Genesis*. Frankfurt, 1980.

Molinari, Alessandra. 'A Crease in Gathering 17 of Bodleian MS. Junius 11'. *Linguae & Revista di lingue e culture moderne* 14 (2015) 55-85.

Muir, Bernard J., ed. *MS Junius 11*. Bodleian Digital Texts 1. Oxford, 2004.

– ed. *The Exeter Anthology of Old English Poetry*. 2 Vols. Exeter Medieval English Texts and Studies. Exeter, 1994; 2nd ed. 2000.

Novacich, Sarah Elliott. ' The Old English *Exodus* and the Read Sea'. *Exemplaria* 23 (2011) 50-66.

Ohlgren, Thomas H. 'The Illustrations of the Caedmonian Genesis: Literary Criticism through Art'. *Medievalia et Humanistica* n.s. 3 (1972) 199-212.

– 'Visual Language in the Old English *Caedmonian Genesis*. *Visible Language* 6 (1972) 253-76.

– 'Some New Light on the Old English *Caedmonian Genesis*. *Studies in Iconography* 1 (1975) 38-73.

– ed. *Insular and Anglo-Saxon Illuminated Manuscripts: An Iconographic Catalogue*. New York and London, 1986.

– ed. *Anglo-Saxon Textual Illustration. Photographs of Sixteen Manuscripts with Descriptions and Index*. Kalamazoo, Michigan, 1992.

O'Brien O'Keeffe, Katherine. *Visible Song. Transitional Literacy in Old English Verse*. CSASE 4. Cambridge, 1990.

Orchard, Andrew. 'Conspicuous Heroism: Abraham, Prudentius, and the Old English Verse *Genesis*'. In Liuzza 2002, pp. 119-36.

O'Sullivan, W. 'Ussher as a Collector of Manuscripts'. *Hermathena*, 88 (1956) 34-58.

Overing, Gillian R. 'On Reading Eve: *Genesis B* and the Readers' Desire'. In *Speaking Two Languages: Traditional Disciplines and Contemporary Theory in Medieval*

Studies, ed. Allen J. Frantzen, 35-63. Albany, 1991.

Pächt, Otto and J.J.G. Alexander, eds. *Illuminated Manuscripts in the Bodleian Library Oxford III*: British, Irish and Icelandic Schools. Oxford, 1973 [Junius 11 is entry no. 34, p. 5].

Pasternack, Carol Braun and Lisa M.C. Weston. *Sex and Sexuality in Anglo-Saxon England.* Binghamton, 2005.

Piper, Paul. *Der altsächsische Bibeldichtung (Heliand und Genesis).* Stuttgart, 1897 [*Genesis B*, pp. 460-86].

– 'Die Heliandhandschriften'. *JVfnS* 21 (1907) 17-59 [Collation of *Genesis B*, pp. 58-9].

Raw, Barbara. 'The Probable Derivation of Most of the Illustrations in Junius 11 from an Illustrated Old Saxon *Genesis*'. *ASE* 5 (1976) 133-48.

– *The Art and Background of Old English Poetry.* London, 1978.

– 'The Construction of Oxford, Bodleian Library, Junius 11'. *ASE* 13 (1984) 187-207. [Reprinted in *Anglo-Saxon Manuscripts: Basic Readings.* Basic Readings in Anglo-Saxon 2, ed. Mary P. Richards, New York, 1994.]

– *Trinity and Incarnation in Anglo-Saxon Art and Thought.* CSASE 21. Cambridge, 1997.

Remley, Paul G. *Old English Biblical Verse.* CSASE 16 (2007).

Rieger, Max. *Alt- und angelsächsisches Lesebuch.* Giesen, 1861 [*Genesis* 246-321, 347-452, *Christ and Satan* 159-88].

Salmon, Paul. 'The Site of Lucifer's Throne'. *Anglia* 81 (1963) 118-23.

Schmidt, Gary D. *The Iconography of the Mouth of Hell.* Selinsgrove PA, 1995.

Schmidt, Wilhelm, ed. 'Die altenglischen Dichtungen Daniel und Azarias, Bearbeiteter Text mit metrischen, sprachlichen und text-kritischen Bemerkungen, sowie einem Wörterbuche'. *BB* 23 (1907) 1-84.

– ed. *Der altenglische Dichtung 'Daniel'* (Bearbeiteter Text). Halle, 1907.

Sedgefield, W.J., ed. *An Anglo-Saxon Verse Book.* Manchester, 1922.

Sharma, Manish. 'The Economy of the Word in the Old English *Exodus*. In *Old English Literature and the Old Testament,* ed. Michael Fox and Manish Sharma, 172-94. Toronto, 2012.

Shepherd, Geoffrey. 'Scriptural Poetry'. In *Continuations and Beginnings*, ed. E.G. Stanley, 1-36. London, 1996.

Sievers, Eduard. 'Collationen angelsächsischer Gedichte'. *ZfdA* 15 (1872) 457-61.

– ed. *Der Heliand und der angelsächsische Genesis*. Halle, 1875.

– 'Zu Codex Junius XI'. *Beiträge* X (1885) 195-9.

Sisam, Kenneth. 'The Cædmonian Exodus 492'. *MLN* 32 (1917) 48.

– '*Genesis B* lines 273-4'. *RES*, n.s. 2 (1951) 371-2.

– 'Dialect Origins of the Earlier Old English Verse'. In *Studies in the History of Old English Literature,* 119-39. Oxford, 1953. [Sisam's Collected Essays, Chapter 8]

Sleeth, Charles R. *Studies in Christ and Satan*. Toronto, 1982.

Solo, Harry J. 'The Twice-Told Tale: A Reconsideration of the Syntax and Style of the Old English *Daniel*, 245-429'. *PLL* (1973) 347-64.

Stévanovitch, Colette, ed. *La Genèse, du manuscrit Junius XI de la Bodleienne*. Publications de l'Association des médiévistes anglicistes de l'enseignment supérieur, hors série 1, 2 vols. Paris, 1992.

Stoddard, Francis. 'The Cædmon Poems in MS. Junius XI'. *Anglia* X (1888) 157-67.

Streeter, B.H. *The Chained Library*. London, 1931

Sweet, Henry. *An Anglo-Saxon Reader*. Oxford, 1876.

Temple, Elzbieta. *Anglo-Saxon Manuscripts 900-1066*. A Survey of Manuscripts Illuminated in the British Isles 2. London, 1976, 76-8 [Junius 11 is no. 56].

Thornley, G.C. 'Accents and Points of MS Junius 11'. *TPS* (1954) 178-205.

Thorpe, Benjamin, ed. & trans. *Cædmon's Metrical Paraphrase of Parts of the Holy Scriptures in Anglo-Saxon*. London, 1832.

Timmer, Benno J., ed. *The Later Genesis*. Oxford, 1948; rev. 1954.

Tolkien, J.R.R. *The Old English Exodus*. Joan Turville-Petre, ed. Oxford, 1991 [Tolkien's papers edited and published posthumously].

Tselos, Dimitri. 'English Manuscript Illumination'. *Art Bulletin* 41 (1959) 137-49.

Turk, Milton H., ed. *An Anglo-Saxon Reader*. New York, 1927.

Utley, Frances Lee. 'The Flood Narrative in the Junius Manuscript and in Baltic Literature'. In *Studies in Old English Literature in Honor of Arthur G. Brodeur,* ed. Stanley Greenfield, 207-26. Eugene, 1963.

Vickrey, John F., ed. *Genesis B: A New Analysis and Edition*. Dissertation. Indiana University, 1960.

– '*Selfsceafte* in *Genesis B*'. *Anglia* 83 (1965) 153-71.

– 'Some Further Remarks on *Selfsceafte*'. *ZfdA* 110 (1981) 1-14.

– 'Adam, Eve, and the *Tacen* in *Genesis B*. *PQ* 72 (1993) 1-14.

Walton, Audrey. '*Gehyre se ðe Wille*: The Old English *Exodus* and the Reader as Exegete'. *ES* 93 (2013) 1-10.

Wanley, H. *Antiquæ literaturæ Septentrionalis Liber Alter*. Seu Humphredi Wanleii Librorum. 1705, 77.

Wehlau, Ruth. 'The Power of Knowledge and the Location of the Reader in *Christ and Satan*'. *JEGP* 97 (1998) 1-14. [Reprinted in Liuzza 2002, pp. 287-301.]

Weitzmann, K. and H.L. Kessler. *The Cotton Genesis, British Library Codex Cotton Otho B.vi.* Princeton, 1986.

Wilcox, Miranda. '*Meotod*, the Meteorologist: Celestial Cosmography in *Christ and Satan*, Lines 9-12a'. *LSE*, n.s. 39 (2008) 17-32.

Williams, O.T., ed. *Short Extracts from Old English Poetry*. Bangor, 1909.

Withers, Benjamin C. and Jonathon Wilcox, eds *Naked before God: uncovering the body in Anglo-Saxon England.* Morgantown, 2003.

Woolf, Rosemary. 'The Devil in Old English Poetry'. *RES*, n.s. 4 (1953) 1-12.

Wormald, Francis. 'Decorated Initials in English MSS, from A.D. 900 to 1100'. *Archaeologia* 91 (1945) 107-35.

– *English Drawings of the Tenth and Eleventh Centuries*. London, 1952.

– *Collected Writings*. Studies in Medieval Art from the Sixth to the Twelfth Centuries. Edited by J.J.G. Alexander, T.J. Brown, Joan Gibbs. Oxford, 1984 (see especially papers III, IV, VII and VIII).

Wright, Charles D. 'The Lion Standard in *Exodus*: Jewish Legend, Germanic Tradition, and Christian Typology'. In Liuzza 2002, pp. 188-202.

Wülker, Richard P., ed. *Bibliothek der angelsächsischen Poesie*. Vol. 2. Leipzig, 1894.

Wyatt, Alfred J. *An Anglo-Saxon Reader*. Cambridge, 1919 [Genesis 304-437].

– ed. *The Threshold of Anglo-Saxon*. New York, 1926.

Zacher, Samantha. *Rewriting the Old Testament in Anglo-Saxon Verse: Becoming the Chosen People*. London and New York, 2013.

Zangemeister, Karl and Wilhelm Braune. *Bruchstücke der altsächsischen Bibeldichtung aus der Bibliotheca Palatina*. Heidelberg, 1894 [Old Saxon Genesis, pp. 42-55].

Zupitza, J. and Schipper, J. *Alt- und Mittelenglisches Übungsbuch*. Wien and Leipzig, 1915 [*Genesis* 2846-2936. This first appeared as J. Zupitza, *Altenglisches Übungsbuch*, Wien, 1874].

POEMS

Genesis A and *B*

    Ús[1] ís riht micel ðæt we rodera Weard,
wereda Wuldorcining wordum herigen,
modum lufien. He is mægna sped,
heafod ealra heahgesceafta,
Frea ælmihtig. Næs him fruma æfre,
ór geworden, ne nu ende cymþ
ecean Drihtnes ac he bið á rice
ofer heofenstolas. Heagum þrymmum
soðfæst and swiðfeorm[2] sweglbosmas heold,
10   þa wæron gesette wide and side
þurh geweald Godes wuldres bearnum,
gasta weardum. Hæfdon gleam[3] and dream,
and heora Ordfruman, engla þreatas,
beorhte[4] blisse. Wæs heora blæd micel.

The Guardian of the Angels rebels against God

    Þegnas þrymfæste Þeoden heredon,
sægdon lustum lof, heora Liffrean
demdon, Drihtenes dugeþum wæron
swiðe gesælige. Synna ne cuþon,
firena fremman ac hie on friðe lifdon,
20   ece mid heora Aldor. Elles ne ongunnon
ræran on roderum nymþe riht and soþ,
ærðon engla weard for oferhygde

---

[1] p. 1. From here to l. 234 is the first part of *Genesis A*. The large initial **U/V** is 6-lines high and zoomorphic and the rest of the first line is in smaller bold capitals. The early modern annotation *Genesis in lingua Saxania* is written in the top margin. *'xb'*, an abbreviation for the word 'Christ' (Lat. *Christus*) and some form of the verb 'to bless' (Lat. *benedicere*). Gollancz 1927 (p. xxv) notes that this stands for a favourite formula used by Irish monks at the beginning of each day's work; he suggests that it is best expanded as *Christe, benedic*.
[2] MS *swið ferom*.
[3] *m* and the following *and* abbreviation written over an erasure.
[4] MS *beorte* with *h* added above and an insertion mark below.

dwæl[5] on gedwilde.   Noldan dreogan leng

heora selfra ræd   ac hie of siblufan

Godes ahwurfon.   Hæfdon gielp micel

þæt hie wið Drihtne   dælan meahton

wuldorfæstan wic   werodes þrymme,

sid and swegltorht.   Him þær sar gelamp,

æfst and oferhygd   and þæs engles mod

30   þe þone unræd ongan   ærest fremman,

wefan and weccean,   þa he worde cwæð,

niþes ofþyrsted   þæt he on norðdæle

ham[6] and heahsetl   heofena rices

agan wolde.   þa wearð yrre God

and þam werode wrað   þe he ær wurðode

wlite and wuldre.   Sceop þam werlogan

wræclicne ham   weorce to leane,

helleheafas,   hearde niðas.

Heht þæt witehus   wræcna bidan,

40   deop, dreama leas,   Drihten ure,

gasta weardas,   þa he hit geare wiste

synnihte beseald   susle geinnod,

geondfolen fyre   and færcyle,

réce and reade lege.   Heht þa geond þæt rædlease hof

weaxan witebrogan;   hæfdon hie wrohtgeteme

grimme wið God gesomnod;   him þæs grim lean becom.

Cwædon þæt heo rice,   reðemode,

agan woldan,   and swa eaðe meahtan.[7]

Him[8] seo wen geleah,   siððan Waldend his,

---

[5] MS *dæl*.

[6] p. 2. The lower part of the page left blank, perhaps for more text. A caption is severely cropped at the top of the page but seems to have read *hu s(e) engyl ongon ofermod wesan*. Beside the illustration here (see the Art-Historical Commentary) is the caption *hælendes hehseld* and above this another *xb*, as on p. 1.

[7] There is no text on p. 3 (see the Art-Historical Commentary). A cropped caption on the right seems to read *Her se hælend gesc<eop> helle heom on wite*. In the space between the third and fourth registers the scribe wrote *her se...* but suddenly stopped before finishing. And in the fourth register the words *in forcu* (?) are written followed by an erasure.

[8] p. 4.

50　　　heofona Heahcining,　honda arærde,
　　　　hehste wið þam herge.　Ne mihton hygelease,
　　　　mæne wið Metode,　mægyn bryttigan[9]
　　　　ac him se Mæra　mod getwæfde,
　　　　bælc forbigde.　Þa he gebolgen wearð,
　　　　besloh synsceaþan　sigore and gewealde,
　　　　dome and dugeðe　and dreame benam
　　　　his feond, friðo　and gefean ealle,
　　　　torhte tire　and his torn gewræc
　　　　on gesacum swiðe　selfes mihtum
60　　　strengum stiepe.　Hæfde styrne mod,
　　　　gegremed grymme,　grap on wraðe
　　　　faum folmum　and him on fæðm gebræc
　　　　yrre[10] on mode;　æðele bescyrede
　　　　his wiðerbrecan　wuldorgestealdum.

　　　　　Sceof[11] þa and scyrede　Scyppend ure
　　　　oferhidig cyn　engla of heofnum,
　　　　wærleas werod.　Waldend sende
　　　　laðwendne here　on langne sið,
　　　　geomre gastas;　wæs him gylp forod,
70　　　beot forborsten　and forbiged þrym,
　　　　wlite gewemmed.　Heo on wrace syððan
　　　　seomodon swearte,　siðe ne þorfton
　　　　hlude hlihhan　ac heo helltregum
　　　　werige wunodon　and wean cuðon,
　　　　sar and sorge,　susl þrowedon
　　　　þystrum beþeahte,　þearl æfterlean
　　　　þæs þe heo ongunnon　wið Gode winnan.
　　　　Þa wæs soð swa ær　sibb on heofnum,
　　　　fægre freoþoþeawas,　Frea eallum leof,
80　　　Þeoden his þegnum;　þrymmas weoxon

---

[9] MS *brittigin.*
[10] MS *yr* at the end of the line.
[11] MS *sceop.*

        duguða mid Drihtne,   dreamhæbbendra.

           Wæron[12] þa gesome   þa þe swegl buað,[13]
wuldres eðel.   Wroht wæs asprungen,
oht mid englum   and órlegnið,
siððan herewosan   heofon ofgæfon,
leohte belorene.   Him on laste setl,
wuldorspedum welig,   wide stodan
gifum growende   on Godes rice,
beorht and geblædfæst,   buendra leas,

90   siððan wræcstowe   werige gastas
under hearmlocan   heane geforan.

       Þa þeahtode   Þeoden ure
modgeþonce   hú he þa mæran gesceaft,
eðelstaðolas   eft gesette,
swegltorhtan seld,   selran werode,
þa hie gielpsceaþan   ofgifen hæfdon,
heah on heofenum.   Forþam halig God
under roderas feng   ricum mihtum
wolde þæt him eorðe   and úproder

100   and síd wæter   geseted[14] wurde
woruldgesceafte   on wraðra gield,
þara þe forhealdene   of hleo sende.

The Six Days of Creation

       Ne wæs her þa giet   nymþe[15] heolstersceado
wiht geworden   ác þes wida grund
stod deop and dim,   Drihtne fremde,
idel and únnyt.   On þone eagum wlat
stiðfrihþ Cining   and þa stowe beheold,
dreama lease   geseah deorc gesweorc

---

[12] p. 5. The large initial **w** (*wynn*) is zoomorphic and the following letters **ÆRON** are in smaller bold capitals.
[13] MS *buan*.
[14] MS *gesetet*, but final *t* may be altered from *d*.
[15] *nymþe heolstersceado*: written over an erased area.

semian sinnihte   sweart under roderum,
110   wonn and weste   oðþæt þeos woruldgesceaft
þurh Word gewearð   Wuldorcyninges.

   Her ærest gesceop   éce Drihten,
Helm eallwihta,   heofon and eorðan,
rodor arærde   and[16] þis rume land
gestaþelode   strangum mihtum,
Frea ælmihtig.   Folde wæs þa gyta[17]
græs ungrene;   garsecg þeahte
sweart synnihte   side and wide
wonne wẹgas.[18]   Þa wæs wuldortorht
120   heofonweardes Gast   ofer hólm boren
miclum spédum.   Metod[19] engla heht,
lifes Brytta,   leoht forð cuman
ofer rumne grund.   Raþe wæs gefylled
Heahcininges hǽs;   him wæs halig leoht
ofer wéstenne   swa se Wyrhta bebead.

   Þa gesundrode   sigora Waldend
ofer laguflode   leoht wið þeostrum,
sceade wið sciman,   sceop þa bam naman,
lifes Brytta;   leoht wæs ærest
130   þurh Drihtnes Word   dæg genemned,
wlitebeorhte gesceaft.[20]   Wel licode
Fréan æt frymðe   forþbæro tid,
dæg æresta;   geseah deorc sceado
sweart swiðrian   geond sidne grund.[21]

   Þa[22] seo tíd gewat   ofer timber[23] sceacan

---

[16] p. 6. There is an illustration in the lower part of this page and a cropped caption *ðan* – see the Art-Historical Commentary

[17] MS *gyt*, followed by an erased *a* (for reasons unclear).

[18] Accented.

[19] Followed by an unusually long space (enough for 2-3 letters), but nothing seems to have been erased.

[20] MS *gescaft*.

[21] There is no text on p. 7; the illustration illustrates stages of Creation – see the Art-Historical Commentary.

[22] p. 8. The large initial **Þ** is zoomorphic and the following letters – *A SEO* – are in smaller bold capitals.

[23] MS *tiber*.

           middangéardes,   Metod æfter sceaf
           scirum sciman,   Scippend ure
           æfen ærest.   Him árn on last,
           þrang þystre genip   þam þe se Þeoden self
140   sceop nihte naman.   Nergend ure
           hie gesúndrode   siððan æfre
           drugon and dydon   Drihtnes willan,
           éce ofer eorðan.   Ða com oðer dæg,
           leoht æfter þeostrum.   Heht þa lifes Weard
           on mereflode   middum weorðan
           hyhtlic heofontimber.   Holmas dælde
           Waldend ure   and geworhte þa
           roderas fæsten   þæt sé Rica áhóf
           úp from eorðan   þurh his agen Word,
150   Frea ælmihtig.   Flod[24] wæs ádæled
           under heahrodore   halgum mihtum,
           wæter óf wætrum,   þam þe wuniað gyt
           under fæstenne   folca hrofes.
           Þá com ofer foldan   fus siðian
           mære mergen þridda.   Næron Metode[25] ða gýta[26]
           wídlond ne wegas nytte   ác stod bewrigen fæste
           folde mid flode.   Frea engla heht
           þurh his Word wesan   wæter gemǽne,
           þa nú under roderum   heora ryne healdað,
160   stowe gestefnde.   Ða stod hraðe
           holm under heofonum   swa se Halga bebead,
           síd ætsomne   ða gesundrod wæs
           lago wið lande.   Geseah þa lifes Weard
           drige stowe,   dugoða Hyrde,
           wíde ætéowde   þa se Wuldorcyning
           éorðan nemde.   Gesette yðum heora

---

[24] MS *fold*.
[25] MS *metod* with *e* added above with an insertion mark below.
[26] MS *gýt* with final *a* erased (for reasons unclear).

onrihtne ryne,   rumum flode,

and gefétero...[27]

GOD CREATES ADAM AND EVE

    Ne[28] þuhte þa gerysne   rodora Wearde,

170   þæt Adam[29] leng   ana wære

neorxnawonges,   niwre gesceafte,

hyrde and healdend.   Forþon him Heahcyning,

Frea ælmihtig   fultum tíode;

wif áweahte   and þa wraðe sealde,

lifes Leohtfruma,   leofum rince.

He þæt andweorc   of Adámes

lice aleoðode   and him listum áteah

ríb of sidan.   He wæs reste fæst,

and softe swǽf,   sár ne wiste,

180   earfóða dæl,   ne þær ænig cóm

blód of bénne   ác him Brego engla

óf lice áteah   liodende bán,

wer únwundod,   óf þam worhte Gód

freolice[30] fæmnan;   feorh in gedyde,[31]

ece saula.[32]   Heo wæron englum gelice,[33]

þá[34] wæs <Eve>,[35]   Adames bryd,

gaste gegearwod.   Hie on geogoðe bú

wlitebeorht wæron   on woruld cenned

Meotodes mihtum.   Mán ne cuðon

---

[27] Several folios have been lost at this point; the missing passage corresponds to Gen. 1:11 – 2:18. See the Gathering Diagrams and Analysis in the Introduction for various proposed reconstructions of Gathering 2.

[28] p. 9. There is an illustration (Creation of Eve) in the lower part of this page – see the Art-Historical Commentary.

[29] Followed by an erased *e*.

[30] MS *freo licu*.

[31] MS *dyde* added above with an insertion mark below.

[32] Final *e* altered to *æ* for reasons unclear.

[33] Final *e* added in a lighter ink.

[34] p. 10. The lower part of this page has an illustration of God addressing Adam and Eve; see the Art-Historical Commentary

[35] Not in the manuscript – reading from Holthausen 1914.

190   dón ne[36] dreogan   ác him Drihtnes wǽs
      bám on breostum   byrnende lufu.
      Þa gebletsode   bliðheort Cyning,
      Metod alwihta,   monna cynnes
      ða forman twá,   fæder and moder,
      wíf and wæpned.   He þa worde cwæð:
      'Temað nú and wexað,   tudre fyllað
      eorðan ælgrene   incre cynne,
      sunum and dohtrum.   Inc sceal sealt wæter
      wunian on gewealde   and eall worulde gesceaft.
200   Brucað blæddaga   and brimhlæste
      and heofonfugla.   Inc ís halig feoh
      and wilde deor   on geweald geseald,
      and lifigende   ða ðe land tredað,
      feorheaceno cynn,   ða ðe flod weccéð
      geond hronrade.   Inc hyrað eall.'
         Þa[37] sceawode   Scyppend ure
      hís weorca wlite   and hís wæstma blæd,
      niwra gesceafta.   Neorxnawong stod
      gód and gastlic   gifena gefylled
210   fremum[38] forðweardum;   fægere leohte
      þæt liðe land   lago yrnende,
      wylleburne.   Nalles wolcnu ða giet
      ofer rumne grund   regnas bæron,
      wann mid winde   hwæðre wæstmum stod
      folde gefrætwod.   Heoldon forðryne
      eastreamas heora   æðele feower
      of þam niwan   neorxnawonge.
      Þá wæron adǽlede[39]   Drihtnes mihtum

---

[36] Abbreviation for *and* (⁊) underpointed for deletion and *ne* added above.

[37] p. 11. The lower part of this page contains an illustration (God blessing Adam and Eve and all creation); see the Art-Historical Commentary. There is an *x* in the upper left margin (elsewhere *xb* stands for *Christe, benedic*).

[38] p. 12. The lower part of this page has been left blank.

[39] MS *adǽlete* with *t* erased and *d* added above with an insertion mark below.

        ealle of anum   þa he þas eorðan gesceop,
220   wætre wlitebeorhtum   and ón woruld sende.
        Þæra[40] <anne>[41] hatað ylde   eorðbúende,
        Físon folcweras;   se[42] foldan dæl
        brade bebugeð[43]   beorhtum stréamum
        Hebeleac útan.   On þære éðyltyrf
        níððas findað   nean and feorran
        gold and gýmcynn,   gumþeoda bearn,
        ða sélestan,   þæs þe ús secgað béc.
        Þonne seo æftre   Ethiopia
        land and leodgeard[44]   belígeð uton,
230   ginne rice   þære ís Géon noma.
        þridda ís Tigris,   seo wið þeodscipe,
        éa inflede,   Assirię belið.
        Swilce ís seo feorðe   þa nu geond folc monig
        weras Éufratén   wide nemnað…[45]

[GENESIS B BEGINS] *ADAM AND EVE IN PARADISE*

'…ác[46] niotað inc þæs oðres ealles,   forlætað þone ænne beam,
        wariað ínc wið þone wæstm.   Ne wyrð inc wilna gǽd.'
    Hnigon þa mid heafdum   Heofoncyninge
        georne togenes[47]   and sædon ealles þanc,
        lísta and þara lára.   He let heo þæt land búan,
240   hwærf him þa to heofenum   halig Drihten,
        stiðferhð Cyning.   Stod his handgeweorc[48]

---

[40] MS *þære*.
[41] Not in the manuscript – reading from Grein 1857.
[42] MS *sǽ*.
[43] MS *bebúgeð* with *u* altered to *i* by scraping (for reasons unclear).
[44] MS *liodgeard* with original *i* altered to *e* (written above)
[45] Two folios are missing in this gathering – see the Gathering Analysis and Diagrams.
[46] p. 13; *Genesis B* begins; it ends at l. 851. The lower part of this page contains an illustration of Adam and Eve in Paradise – see the Art-Historical Commentary.
[47] First *e* altered from *a* by the main hand.
[48] Earlier in the Bible (Gen. 2:7) – the Old English text is missing here due of lost folios – God is described as creating Adam *de limo terrae*, and henceforth in the Old Testament God is sometimes described metaphorically

somod on sande,   nyston sorga wiht

tó begrornianne   butan heo Godes willan

lengest læsten;   heo wæron leof Gode

ðenden[49] heo his halige word   healdan woldon.

   Hæfde[50] se Ealwalda[51]   engelcynna

þurh handmægen,   halig Drihten

tyne[52] getrymede[53]   þæm he getruwode wel

þæt hie his giongorscipe   fyligan wolden,

250 wyrcean hís willan   forþon he heom[54] gewít forgeaf

and mid his handum gesceop,   halig Drihten.

Gesétt hæfde he híe swa gesǽliglice,   ænne hæfde he swa swiðne geworhtne,

swá mihtigne on hís modgeþohte,   he lét hine swa micles wealdan,

hehstne to hím on heofona rice,   hæfde he hine swa hwitne geworhtne,

swa wynlic wæs his wæstm[55] on heofonum   þæt[56] him com from weroda Drihtne,

gelic wæs he þam leohtum steorrum.[57]

LUCIFER GROWS PROUD AND REVOLTS AGAINST HIS MAKER

                                      Lóf sceolde he Drihtnes wyrcean,

dýran sceolde he his dréamas on heofonum   and sceolde hís Drihtne þancian

þæs leanes þe he him on þam leohte gescerede   – þonne lete[58] he his hine

                                                          lange wealdan.

Ác he awende[59] hít hím to wyrsan þinge;   óngán hím winn úp ahebban[60]

260 wið þone hehstan heofnes Wealdend[61]   þe síteð ón þam halgan stole.

---

as a 'Potter' and humans as 'potter's vessels made from clay.' Thus it is appropriate to describe Adam and Eve as his *handgeweorc*. See, for example, Jer. 18:1-11, 2 Cor. 4:7, 2 Tim. 2:21.

[49] MS *ðen den* with a sign above referring to a gloss in the margin – *id est þa hwile*.

[50] p. 14. The large initial **h** is zoomorphic and the following letters **ÆFDE** are in smaller bold capitals

[51] MS *alwalda* with *e* added above.

[52] MS *téne* with *y* added above first *e* underpointed for deletion.

[53] MS *getrimede* with *y* altered from original *i*.

[54] MS *him* with *i* underpointed for deletion and *eo* added above.

[55] MS *wæwtm*.

[56] The abbreviation is accented.

[57] Hence his name – Lucifer.

[58] MS *lǽte* with *ǽ* altered to *e* by scraping.

[59] MS *wénde* with *a* added above and an insertion mark below.

[60] MS *hebban* with *a* added above and an insertion mark below.

[61] MS *waldend* with *e* added above and an insertion mark below.

Deore wæs hé Drihtne urum;[62] ne mihte him bedyrned wyrðan[63]
þæt hís engyl ongan ófermod wesan,
áhóf hine wið hís hearran,[64] sohte hétespræce,
gylpword ongéan, nolde Gode þeowian,
cwæð þæt hís líc wære leoht and scene,
hwit and hiowbeorht. Né meahte hé æt hís hige findan
þæt he[65] Gode wolde géongerdome,
Þeodne þeowian. Þuhte him sylfum
þæt he mægyn and cræft máran hæfde

270 þonne sé halga Gód habban mihte
folcgestælna.[66] Feala worda gespæc
sé engel ofermodes; þohte þurh his anes cræft
hu he him strenglicran stol geworhte,
heahran[67] on heofonum; cwæð[68] þæt hine his hige speonne[69]
þæt he west and norð wyrcean ongunne,
trymede getimbro; cwæð him tweo þuhte
þæt he Gode wolde geongra weorðan.[70]
'Hwæt sceal ic winnan?' cwæð he; nis me wihtæ þearf
hearran to habbanne. Ic mæg mid handum swa fela

280 wundra gewyrcean. Ic hæbbe geweald micel
to gyrwanne godlecran stol,
hearran on heofne. Hwy sceal ic æfter his hyldo ðeowian,
bugan him swilces geongordomes? Ic mæg wesan god swa he.
Bigstandað me strange geneatas þa ne willað me æt þam striðe geswican,
hæleþas heardmode. Hie habbað me to hearran gecorene,
rofe rincas; mid swilcum mæg man ræd geþencean,
fon mid swilcum folcgesteallan. Frynd synd hie mine georne,

---

[62] MS *ure* with *e* underpointed for deletion and *u(m)* added above.
[63] MS *weorðan* with *eo* underpointed for deletion and dotted *y* added above.
[64] MS *herran* with *a* added above and an insertion mark below.
[65] *he* added above with an insertion mark below.
[66] p. 15.
[67] MS *heah_ran* with second *h* altered from original *r* and a letter (*o*?) erased after it.
[68] Followed by a hole in the manuscript.
[69] MS *speonne* with the second *n* underpointed for deletion and then restored.
[70] MS *weorð* with (raised) *an* added after it.

holde on hyra hygesceaftum;   ic mæg hyra hearra wesan,

rædan on þis rice.   Swa me þæt riht ne þinceð,

290   þæt ic oleccan   awiht þurfe

Gode æfter gode ænegum;   ne wille ic leng his geongra wurþan.'

   Þa hit se Allwalda   eall gehyrde

þæt his engyl ongan   ofermede micel

ahebban wið his Hearran   and spræc healic word

dollice wið Drihten sinne   sceolde he þa dæd ongyldan,

worc þæs gewinnes gedælan   and sceolde his wite habban,[71]

ealra[72] morðra mæst.   Swa deð monna gehwilc

þe wið his Waldend   winnan ongynneð

mid mane wið þone mæran Drihten.   Þá wearð se Mihtiga gebolgen,

300   hehsta heofones Waldend,   wearp[73] hine of þan hean stole.

God casts the Rebel Angels into the fiery Pit of Hell

Hete hæfde he æt his Hearran gewunnen,   hyldo hæfde his ferlorene,

grám wearð him se[74] Goda on his mode.   Forþon he sceolde grund gesecean

heardes hellewites   þæs þe he wann wið heofnes Waldend;

ácwæð hine þa fram his hyldo   and hine on helle wearp,

ón þa deopan dala   þær he to deofle wearð,

se feond mid his geferum eallum.   Feollon[75] þá ufon of heofnum

þurhlonge swa   þreo niht and dagas

þa englas of heofnum on helle   and heo ealle forsceop

Drihten to deoflum.   Forþon[76] heo his dæd and word

310   noldon weorðian   forþon he heo on wyrse leoht

under eorðan neoðan,   ællmihtig God

sette sigelease   on þa sweartan helle.

---

[71] This word is written below the main text block on the right-hand side.
[72] p. 16. An illustration in the lower part of the page depicts the Fall of the Rebel Angels – see the Art-Historical Commentary.
[73] MS *wea rp* with a hole after *a*.
[74] *g* scraped away before this word.
[75] *n* abraded.
[76] p. 17. An illustration in the lower part of this page depicts God flanked by angels and Satan chained in the Fortress of Hell – see the Art-Historical Commentary.

Þær hæbbað heo on æfyn   úngemet lange
ealra feonda gehwilc   fýr édneowe
þonne cymð on uhtan   easterne wind,
forst fyrnum cald;   symble fýr oððe gár,
sum heard geswinc[77]   habban sceoldon.
Worhte man hit hím to wite   – hyra woruld wæs gehwyrfed –
forman siðe,[78]   fylde helle
320   mid þam andsacum;   heoldon englas forð
heofonrices hehðe   þé ǽr Godes hýldo gelǽston.

   Lagon þá oðre fynd on þam fyre   þe ǽr swa feala hæfdon
gewinnes wið heora Waldend;   wite þoliað,
hatne heaðowelm   helle tomiddes,
brand[79] and bráde lígas   swilce éac þa biteran récas,
þrosm and þystro   forþon hie þégnscipe
Godes forgymdon.   Hie hyra gál beswác,
engles oferhýgd,   noldon Alwealdan[80]
word weorþian,   hæfdon wite micel,
330   wæron[81] þé befeallene   fýre to bótme
on þa hátan héll   þurh hygeleaste
and þurh ofermetto,   sohton oþer land
þæt wæs leohtes leas   and wæs líges fúll,
fyres fǽr micel.   Fynd ongéaton
þæt hie hæfdon gewrixled   wíta únrím[82]
þurh heora[83] miclan mod   and þurh miht Godes
and þurh ofermetto   ealra swiðost.

   Þa spræc se ofermóda cyning,   þe ǽr wæs engla scynost,
hwittost[84] on heofnon[85]   and his héarran léof,

---

[77] MS *gewrinc*.
[78] *e* squeezed in with an insertion mark below
[79] p. 18. *Brand* has a large zoomorphic initial although a new sentence does not begin here and the following letters **RAND** are in smaller bold capitals. The Fitt number *.vii.* is at the top of the illustration inside the frame.
[80] MS *alwaldan* with *e* added above and an insertion mark below.
[81] *n* added above.
[82] *u* altered from original *i* with an insertion mark under the added stroke.
[83] MS *herra* with the first *r* altered to *o*.
[84] First *t* added above.
[85] MS *heofne* with final *e* altered to *o* and *n* added above.

340	Drihtne dýre, oð hie to dóle wurdon

þæt him for gálscipe   God sylfa wearð

mihtig on móde ýrre;   wearp hine on þæt mórðer ínnan,

niðer on þæt níobedd   and sceop him naman siððan –

cwæð[86] se hehsta   hatan sceolde

Sátan siððan –   hét hine þære swéartan helle

grúndes gyman,   nalles wið God winnan.[87]

Satan maðelode   sorgiende spræc,

se ðe helle forð   healdan sceolde

gyman[88] þæs grundes;   wæs ǽr Godes engel,

350	hwit on heofnon[89] oð hine hís hyge forspéon

and his ofermétto   éalra swiðost

þæt he ne wolde   wereda Drihtnes

word wurðian.   Weoll hím on ínnan

hyge ymb hís héortan,   hát wæs hím utan

wraðlic wite;   he þa worde cwæð:

'Ís þes[90] ænga[91] stede[92]   ungelic swiðe

þam oðrum <ham>[93]   þe we ǽr cuðon,

héan on[94] heofonríce,   þe me mín Hearra[95] onlag

þeah we hine for þam Alwealdan[96]   agan ne moston

360	rómigan ures rices. Næfð he þeah riht gedón

þæt he us hæfð befylled[97]   fýre to botme,

hélle þære hátan   heofonríce benúmen;

háfað hit geméarcod   mid moncynne

to gesettanne.   Þæt me is sorga mæst,

þæt Adam sceal,   þe wæs of eorðan geworht

---

[86] MS *þæt* squeezed in after this word by a corrector, but it seems to be extraneous.
[87] MS *widnan*.
[88] MS *gieman* with *ie* underpointed for deletion and *y* added above.
[89] MS *heofne* with final *e* altered to *o* and *n* added above.
[90] MS *þæs* with *æ* altered to *e* by scraping.
[91] MS *i* added above after *n* and then underpointed for deletion.
[92] MS *styde* with *y* underscored for deletion and *e* added above.
[93] Not in the manuscript – reading from Klaeber 1913.
[94] p. 19. *on* is added in the margin before the first word on this page.
[95] MS *hearra* with *arra* over erased letters.
[96] MS *alwaldan* with *e* added above and an insertion mark below.
[97] MS *befælled* with *y* written over *æ*.

minne stronglican   stol behealdan,

wésan him on wýnne,   and we þis wite þolien,

hearm on þisse helle.   Wá lá. Ahte ic minra hánda gewéald[98]

and moste áne tíd   úte weorðan,

370   wesan ane winterstunde,[99]   þonne ic mid þys werode –[100]

Ác licgað me ymbe   irenbendas,[101]

rideð racentan sal   – íc eom ríces leas –

habbað me swa hearde   helle clommas

fæste befangen.   Hér is fýr micel,

úfan and neoðone;   ic á ne geseah

laðran landscipe –   lig ne aswamað,

hát ofer helle.   Me habbað hringa gespong,

sliðhearda sal   siðes amyrred,

afyrred me mín feðe –   fét synt gebundene,

380   hánda gehæfte;   synt þissa héldora

wegas forwórhte   swa ic mid wíhte ne mǽg

of þissum líoðobendum.   Licgað me ymbutan[102]

héardes irenes   hate geslǽgene

grindlas greate.   Mid þy me God[103] hafað

gehæfted be þam healse   swa íc wat he minne hige cuðe;

and þæt wiste eac   weroda Drihten

þæt sceolde unc Adáme   yfele gewurðan

ymb þæt heofonrice   þær ic ahte minra handa geweald.[104]

Ác[105] ðoliaþ wé nú þrea on helle   – þæt syndon þystro and hæto –

390   grimme, grundlease.   Hafað us God sylfa

forswapen on þas sweartan mistas;   swa he us ne mæg ænige synne gestælan

---

[98] There is no text on p. 20. The Fitt number .vii. is written below the last line of p. 19.
[99] A winter's hour, of course, being shorter than a summer's hour.
[100] An example of aposiopesis, speechlessness caused by extreme emotion.
[101] *i* altered from an earlier letter by scraping and the *tall-s* added by a corrector with an insertion mark below.
[102] MS *ymbe* with *e* scraped away and *után* added above.
[103] *g* altered from an earlier letter.
[104] The Fitt number .vii. is written to the right of this word; earlier on p. 17 the same Fitt number had been recorded, so the one here should be .vii[i]. Page 20 has a full-page illustration in two registers; the bottom part shows the devilish messenger being sent from Hell and the upper part shows him in the shape of the serpent in Paradise tempting Eve – see the Art-Historical Commentary.
[105] p. 21. The large initial *A* is zoomorphic and the rest of the word is in smaller bold capitals.

þæt we him on þam lande lað gefremedon, he hæfð us þeah þæs leohtes[106]
bescyrede,
beworpen on ealra wita[107] mæste. Ne magon we þæs wrace gefremman,
geleanian him mid laðes wihte þæt he us hafað þæs leohtes bescýrede;
he hæfð nu geméarcod anne middangeard þær he hæfð món geworhtne
æfter hís ónlicnesse, mid þam he wile eft gesettan
heofona rice mid hluttrum saulum.[108] Wé þæs sculon hycgan georne
þæt we on Ádáme, gif we æfre mægen,
and on his eafrum swa sóme ándan gebetan,

400   onwendan him þær willan sínes, gif we hit mægen wihte aþencan.
Ne gelyfe ic me nu þæs leohtes furðor þæs þe he heom[109] þenceð lange neotan,[110]
þæs éades mid his engla cræfte; ne magon we þæt on aldre gewinnan
þæt we mihtiges Godes mod onwæcen. Uton oðwendan hit nú monna bearnum,
þæt heofonrice, nu wé hit habban ne moton, gedon þæt hie his hyldo forlæten
þæt hie þæt onwendon þæt he mid his worde bebéad. Þonne weorð he hím wrað
ón mode,
áhwet hie from his hyldo þonne sculon hie þas helle secan
and þas grimman grundas – þonne moton we hie us to giongrum habban,
fira bearn on þissum fæstum clomme. Onginnað nu ymb þa fyrde[111] þencean.

SATAN RECRUITS A FOLLOWER TO ESCAPE AND TO TEMPT ADAM AND EVE

Gif[112] íc ænegum þegne[113] þéodenmadmas
410   géara forgeafe þenden wé on þan gódan rice
gesælige sæton and hæfdon ure setla gewéald,
þonne he me na on leofran tid leanum ne meahte
mine gife gyldan, gif his gien wolde
minra þegna hwilc geþafa wurðan

---

[106] *le* obscured by a stain.
[107] *a* over an erased letter.
[108] This is known as the 'doctrine of replacement.'
[109] MS *him* with *i* underpointed for deletion and *eo* added above with an insertion mark below.
[110] MS *niótan* with *i* altered to *e*.
[111] *-de þencead* is written below the last line of text (to the right).
[112] p. 22.
[113] *é* altered from *ǽ* by scraping.

    þæt he úp heonon   ute mihte
    cuman þurh þas clustro,   and hæfde cræft mid hím
    þæt he mid feðerhóman[114]   fleogan meahte,
    windan on wolcne   þær geworht stondað
    Ádam and Éue   on eorðrice
420   mid welan bewunden,   and we synd aworpene hider
    on þas deopan dalo.   Nu hie Drihtne synt
    wurðran micle   and móton him þone wélan ágan
    þe wé on heofonríce   habban sceoldon
    ríce mid rihte;   ís se ræd gescyred
    monna cynne.   Þæt me ís on minum mode[115] swa sar,
    on minum hyge hreoweð   þæt hie heofonríce
    agan tó aldre;   gif hit eower ænig mæge
    gewendan mid wihte   þæt hie word Godes
    lare forlæten,   sóna híe hím þe laðran beoð.
430   Gif hie brecað hís gebódscipe   þonne he him abolgen wurðeþ;
    siððan bið hím se wela onwended   and wyrð him wite gegearwod,[116]
    súm heard hearmscearu.   Hycgað his ealle,
    hú ge hi beswicen;   siððan ic me sefte mæg
    restan on þyssum racentum,   gif him þæt rice losað.
    Se þe þæt gelæsteð,   him bið lean gearo
    æfter to aldre   þæs we her inne magon
    on þyssum fyre forð   fremena gewinnan.
    Sittan læte íc hine wið me sylfne   swa hwa swa þæt secgan cymeð
    on þas hatan helle   þæt hie Heofoncyninges
440   únwurðlice   wordum and dædum
    lare…'[117]

---

[114] *e* altered from *æ* by scraping and original *d* altered to *ð*.
[115] MS *on mode minum* with marks indicating words to be transposed.
[116] MS *gegarwod* with second *e* added above with an insertion mark below.
[117] Two folios are missing in this gathering – see the Gathering Diagrams and Analysis.

The Tempter prepares for his evil Mission to the earthly Paradise

    Angan[118] hine þa gyrwan   Godes ándsaca,

fús on frǽtwum   – hæfde fǽcne hyge;

hæleðhelm on heafod asette   and þóne fúll héarde gebánd,

speonn[119] mid spángum;   wiste him sprǽca féla,

wora worda.[120]   Wand him up þánon,

hwearf him þurh þa helldora   – hæfde hyge strangne –

léolc on lyfte   laþwendemód,

swáng þæt fýr on twá   féondes cræfte;

450   wolde déarnunga   Drihtnes geongran

mid mándǽdum   ménn[121] beswícan,

forlǽdan and forlǽran   þæt hie wurdon láð Gode.

He þa geferde[122]   þurh feondes cræft

oððæt he Ádám   on eorðrice,

Godes hándgesceaft   géarone fúnde,

wíslice gewórht   and his wíf sómed,

fréo fægroste,   swa hie fela cúðon

Gódes gegéarwigean   þé him to gíngran sélf

Métod[123] mancynnes   mearcode selfa.

460   And him bí twegen[124]   béamas stódon

þa wæron utan   ófætes gehlædene,

gewéred mid wæstme,   swa hie wáldend God,

heah Heofoncyning   handum gesette

þæt þær ýldo béarn   moste ón ceosan

gódes and ýfeles,   gumena æghwilc,

welan and wawan.[125]   Næs se wæstm gelic –

oðer wæs swa wynlic,   wlitig and scene,[126]

---

[118] p. 23. The large initial *A* is 6-lines high and zoomorphic; the rest of the word is in smaller bold capitals.
[119] MS *spenn* with *o* added above and an insertion mark below.
[120] *wora worda*: glossed *uel wraþra worda* in the margin with a mark above *wora* indicating the gloss.
[121] Second *n* added above.
[122] *e* erased after *r*.
[123] MS *métot*.
[124] MS *twegin* with *i* altered to *e*.
[125] *and wawan*: repeated in the margin because defaced in the text.
[126] *and scene*: repeated in the margin because defaced in the text.

    líðe and lofsum   – þæt wæs lifes béam –
    moste on écnisse   æfter lybban,
470 wesan on worulde,   se þæs wæstmes onbát,
    swa him æfter þy   yldo ne derede
    ne súht swáre   ac moste symle wesan
    lungre on lustum   and his lif ágan,[127]
    hyldo Heofoncyninges   her on worulde,
    habban him to wæron   wítode[128] geþingþo[129]
    on þone hean heofon[130]   þonne he[131] heonon wende.
    Þonne wæs se oðer   eallenga sweart,
    dím and þystre   – þæt wæs deaðes beam
    se bær bitres fela.   Scéolde bú witan
480 ylda æghwílc   yfles and godes
    gewanod[132] on þisse worulde;   sceolde on wíte á
    mid swate and mid sorgum   siððan libban,
    swa hwa swa gebyrgde   þæs on þam beame geweox;
    sceolde hine yldo beniman   ellendæda,
    dréamas and drihtscipes   and him beon deað scyred.
    Lytle hwile   sceolde he his lífes niotan,
    secan þonne landa   sweartost on fyre,
    sceolde feondum þeowian   þær is ealra frecna mæste
    leodum to langre hwile.   Þæt wiste se laða georne,
490 dyrne deofles boda   þe wið Drihten wann.

The Tempter changes into a Serpent and approaches Adam

    Wearp[133] hine þa ón wyrmes lic   and wand him þa ymbutan
    þone deaðes beam   þurh deofles cræft,

---

[127] Second *a* altered from *o*.
[128] *e* added above with an insertion mark below.
[129] MS *geþing* with *þ* added over an erased letter and *o* above the punctus.
[130] p. 24. There is an illustration of the devilish messenger, now disguised as an angel, offering the apple to Eve in the lower part of this page – see the Art-Historical Commentary.
[131] MS *heo*.
[132] MS *gewand* with *o* added above and an insertion mark below.
[133] p. 25.

genam þær þæs ofætes   and wende hine eft þanon

þær he wiste handgeweorc   Heofoncyninges.

Ongon hine þa frínan   forman worde

se laða mid ligenum: 'Langað þé awuht,

Ádám, úp tó Gode?   Ic eom on hís ærende hider

feorran geféred;   né þæt nu fyrn ne wæs

þæt ic wið hine sylfne sæt.   Þá het he me on þysne síð faran,

500   het þæt þu þisses ófætes ǽte,   cwæð þæt þin ábal and cræft

and þin módsefa   mara wurde,

and þin lichoma   leohtra micle,

þin gesceapu scenran,   cwæð þæt þe æniges sceattes[134] ðearf

ne wurde on worulde.   Nu þu willan hæfst

hyldo geworhte   Heofoncyninges,

to þance geþénod   þinum Hearran,[135]

hæfst þe wið Drihten dýrne geworhtne;   ic gehyrde hine þine dǽd and word

lofian on his leohte   and ymb þin lif sprecan.

Swa þu læstan scealt   þæt on þis[136] land hider

510   his bodan bringað;   bráde synd on worulde

grene geardas,   and God siteð

on þam hehstan   heofna rice,

úfan Alwalda.   Nele þa earfeðu

sylfa habban   þæt he on þysne sið fare,

gumena Drihten,   ác he his gingran sent

to þinre spræce;   nu he þe mid spellum het

listas læran.   Læste þu georne

hís ambyhto,   nim þe þis ofæt on hand,

bit his and byrige.[137]   Þé weorð on þinum breostum rúm,

520   wæstm þy wlitegra.   Þe sende waldend God,

---

[134] MS *sceates*.
[135] MS *hearan*.
[136] MS *þs* with *i* added above with an insertion mark below.
[137] MS *byrige* with *i* underpointed for deletion (for reasons unclear).

þin Hearra[138] þas[139] helpe[140] of[141] heofonrice.'

 Adam maðelode þær he on eorðan stod,
selfsceafte guma: 'Þonne íc Sigedrihten,
mihtigne God, mæðlan gehyrde
strangre stemne and me her stondan het
his bebodu healdan and me þas bryd forgeaf,
wlitesciene wif, and me warnian het
þæt ic on þone deaðes beam bedroren ne wurde,
beswicen to swiðe; he cwæð þæt þa sweartan helle
530 healdan sceolde sé ðe bi his heortan wuht
laðes gelǽde. Nát þeah þu mid ligenum fare
þurh dyrne geþanc þe þu Drihtnes eart
boda of heofnum. Hwæt. Ic þinra bysna ne mæg,
worda ne wisna wuht oncnawan,
siðes ne sagona. Ic wat hwæt he me self bebead,
Nérgend user þa íc hine nehst geseah;
he het me his word weorðian and wel healdan,
læstan hís lare. Þu gelic ne bist
ænegum his engla þe ic ǽr geseah,
540 ne þu me[142] oðiewdest ænig tacen
þe he me þurh treowe to onsende,
min Hearra þurh hyldo. Þy ic þe hyran ne cann,
ac þu meaht þe forð faran. Ic hæbbe me fæstne geleafan
up to þam ælmihtegan Gode þe me mid his earmum worhte,
hér míd handum sinum. He mæg me of hís héan rice
gyfian[143] mid góda gehwilcum þeah he his gingran ne sende.'

---

[138] The final *-ra* is written below the last line of the text (to the right).
[139] p. 26.
[140] Final *e* altered from *a*.
[141] *f* over a stain – it may have been altered from earlier *n*.
[142] *ne* is inadvertently repeated and then underpointed for deletion.
[143] MS *geofian* with *y* written above original *eo*.

The Tempter subsequently approaches Eve

   Wende[144] hine wráðmód   þær he þæt wif geseah
ón eorðrice   Éuan stondan,
sceone gesceapene,   cwæð þæt sceaðena mæst
550   eallum heora eaforum   æfter siððan
wurde on worulde: 'Íc wat, inc waldend God
abolgen wyrð,   swa[145] íc him þisne bodscipe
selfa secge   þonne íc of þys síðe cume
ofer langne weg   þæt git ne læstan wel
hwilc ærende swa   he easten hider
on þysne sið sendeð.   Nu sceal he sylf faran
to incre andsware;   ne mæg his ærende
his boda beodan;   þy ic wat þæt he inc abolgen wyrð,
mihtig on mode.   Gif þu þeah minum wilt,
560   wif willende,   wordum hyran,
þu meaht his þonne rúme   ræd geþencan.
Gehyge on þinum breostum   þæt þu ínc bam twam meaht
wite bewarigan   swa ic þe wisie.
Æt þisses ofetes –   þonne wurðað þin eagan swa leoht
þæt þu meaht swa wide   ofer woruld ealle
geseon siððan,   and selfes stol
Herran þines,   and habban his hyldo forð.
Meaht þu Adame   eft gestýran,
gif þu his willan hæfst   and he þinum wordum getrywð.
570   Gif þu him to soðe sægst   hwylce þu selfa hæfst
bisne on breostum   þæs þu gebód Godes
lare læstes,   he þone laðan strið,
yfel andwyrde   án forlæteð
on breostcofan,   swa wit him bú tú
an spéd sprecað.   Span þu hine georne

---

[144] The *wynn* is zoomorphic and 10-lines high; the rest of the word is in smaller bold capitals.
[145] p. 27.

  þæt he þine lare læste, þy læs gyt lað Gode,
incrum Waldende, weorðan þyrfen.
Gif þu þæt angin fremest, idesa seo betste,
forhele ic incrum Herran þæt me hearmes swa fela
580 Adam gespræc eargra worda.
Tyhð me untryowða, cwyð þæt ic seo teonum georn,
gramum ambyhtsecg nales Godes engel.
Ac ic cann ealle swa geare engla gebyrdo,
heah heofona gehlidu; wæs seo hwil þæs lang
þæt ic geornlice[146] Gode þegnode
þurh holdne hyge, Herran minum,
Drihtne selfum; ne eom ic deofle gelic.'
  Lædde hie swa mid ligenum and mid listum speon
idese on þæt unriht oðþæt hire on innan ongan
590 weallan wyrmes geþeaht – hæfde hire wacran hige
Metod gemearcod – þæt heo hire mod ongan
lætan æfter þam larum; forþon heo æt þam laðan onfeng
ofer Drihtnes word deaðes beames
weorcsumne wæstm. – ne wearð wyrse dæd
monnum gemearcod. Þæt is micel wundor
þæt hit ece God æfre wolde
Þeoden þolian þæt wurde þegn swa monig
forlædd be þam lygenum þe for þam larum com.

Eve eats the Forbidden Fruit

  Heo[147] þa þæs ofætes æt, Alwaldan bræc
600 word and willan. Þa meahte heo wide geseon
þurh þæs laðan læn þe hie mid ligenum beswac,
dearnenga bedrog þe hire for his dædum com,

---

[146] p. 28. The lower part of this page has a complex illustration of the devilish messenger offering the apple to Adam and then to Eve, and of her eating it – see the Art-Historical Commentary.
[147] p. 29.

þæt hire þuhte[148] hwitre   heofon and eorðe

and eall þeos woruld wlitigre,   and geweorc Godes

micel and mihtig   þeah heo hit þurh monnes geþeaht

ne sceawode;   ác se sceaða georne

swicode ymb þa sawle   þe hire ær þa siene onláh

þæt heo swa wide   wlitan meahte

ofer heofonríce.   Þa se forhatena spræc

610 þurh feondscipe[149] – nalles he hie freme lǽrde:

'Þu meaht nú þe self geseon   swa ic hit þe secgan ne þearf,

Éue seo gode,   þæt þe is ungelíc

wlite and wæstmas   siððan þu mínum wordum getruwodest,

læstes mine lare.   Nu scineð þe leoht fore

glædlic ongean   þæt ic from Gode brohte

hwit of heofonum;   nu þu his hrínan meaht.

Sæge Adame   hwilce þu gesihðe hæfst

þurh minne címe cræfta.   Gif giet þurh cuscne siodo

læst mina lára   þonne gife ic him þæs leohtes genog

620 þæs ic þe swa gódes   gegired hæbbe.

Ne wite ic him þa womcwidas,   þeah he his wyrðe ne sie

to alætanne;   þæs fela he me laðes spræc.'

   Swa hire eaforan sculon   æfter lybban:

þonne hie lað gedoð,   hie sculon lufe wyrcean,

betan heora hearran hearmcwyde   ond habban his hyldo forð.

   Þa gieng[150] to Adame   idesa scenost,

wifa wlitegost   þe on woruld cóme

forþon heo wæs handgeweorc   heofoncyninges,[151]

þeah heo þá dearnenga   fordón wurde,

630 forlǽd mid ligenum   þæt hie lað Gode

þurh þæs wraðan geþanc   weorðan sceoldon,[152]

---

[148] MS *þuht e* with a letter (*r* it seems) erased after *t*; the scribe may have anticipated the *-re* ending on the next word.
[149] MS *feonscipe* with *d* added above and an insertion mark below.
[150] MS *gien*.
[151] MS *heo-/foncyninges*, p. 30.
[152] *o* altered from original *e*.

þurh þæs deofles searo   dóm forlætan,
hierran hyldo,   hefonrices þolian
monige hwile.   Bið þam men full wá
þe hine ne warnað   þonne he his geweald hafað;
sum heo hire on handum bær,   sum hire æt heortan lǽg,
æppel únsælga   þone hire ǽr forbead
drihtna Drihten,   deaðbeames ofet,
and þæt word ácwæð   wuldres Aldor
640   þæt þæt micle morð   menn ne þorfton
þegnas þolian   ac he þeoda gehwam
hefonríce forgeaf,   halig Drihten,
widbradne welan   gif hie þone wæstm án
lætan wolden   þe þæt laðe[153] treow
on his bógum bær   bitre gefylled;
þæt wæs deaðes beam   þe him Drihten forbead.
Forléc hie þa mid ligenum   se wæs lað Gode,
on hete Heofoncyninges,   and hyge Euan,
wifes wac geþoht,   þæt heo ongan hís wordum truwian,
650   læstan his lare,   and geleafan nóm
þæt he þa bysene from Gode   brungen hæfde
þe he hire swa wærlice   wordum sægde,
íewde hire tacen   and treowa gehet,
his holdne hyge.   Þa heo to hire hearran spræc:

EVE OFFERS THE FORBIDDEN FRUIT TO ADAM

  'Adam, frea mín,   þis ofet is swa swete,
bliðe[154] on breostum,   and þes boda sciene
Godes engel gód;   ic on his gearwan geseo
þæt he is ærendsecg   uncres Hearran,
Hefoncyninges.   Hís hyldo is unc betere
660   to gewinnanne   þonne his wiðermedo.

---

[153] MS *lað*.
[154] MS *blið*.

Gif þu him heodæg wuht   hearmes gespręce,[155]
he forgifð hit þeah,   gif wit him geongordóm
læstan willað.[156]   Hwæt scal[157] þe swa laðlic strið
wið þines Hearran bodan?   Unc is his hyldo þearf;
he mæg unc ærendian   to þam Alwaldan,
Heofoncyninge.   Ic mæg heonon geseon
hwær[158] he sylf siteð   – þæt ís suð and east –
welan bewunden   se ðas woruld gesceop;
geseo ic him his englas   ymbe hweorfan
670   mid feðerhaman,   ealra folca mæst,
wereda wynsumast.   Hwá meahte me swelc gewít gifan,
gif hit gegnunga   God ne onsende,
heofones Waldend?   Gehyran mæg íc rume
and swa wide geseon   on woruld ealle
ofer þas sidan gesceaft;   íc mæg swegles gamen
gehyran on heofnum.   Wearð me on hige leohte
utan and innan   siðþan íc þæs ofætes onbat;
nu hæbbe ic his her on handa,   herra se goda,
gife ic hit þe georne.   Ic gelyfe þæt hit from Gode come,
680   broht from his bysene,   þæs me þes boda sægde
wǽrum wordum.   Hit nis wuhte gelic
elles on eorðan   buton swa þes ár sægeð
þæt hit gegnunga   from Gode come.'
   Hio[159] spræc him þicce to   and speon hine ealne dæg
on þa dimman dǽd   þæt hie Drihtnes heora
willan brǽcon.   Stod se wráða boda,
legde him lustas on   and mid listum speon,
fylgde him frecne;   wæs se feond full néah
þe on þa frecnan fyrd   gefaren hæfde

---

[155] MS *gespręce* with *ę* accented.
[156] There is no text on p. 31. The full-page illustration shows Eve offering the apple to Adam (upper) and the devilish messenger casting aspersions on fallen Adam and Eve (lower) – see the Art-Historical Commentary.
[157] p. 32.
[158] MS *hær* with *wynn* added above.
[159] The initial *h* is 12-lines high and zoomorphic; the rest of the word is in smaller bold capitals.

690 ofer langne weg;   leode hogode
     on þæt micle morð   men forweorpan,
     forlæran and forlædan   þæt hie læn Godes,
     Ælmihtiges gife   an forleten,
     heofenrices geweald.[160]   Hwæt. Se hellsceaða
     gearwe wiste   þæt hie Godes yrre
     habban sceoldon   and hellgeþwing,[161]
     þone nearwan nið   niede onfon
     siððan hie gebod Godes   forbrocen hæfdon,
     þa he forlærde   mid ligenwordum
700 to þam unræde   idese sciene,
     wifa wlitegost   þæt heo on his willan spræc;
     wæs him[162] on helpe   handweorc Godes
     to forlæranne.
     Heo spræc ða to Adame   idesa sceonost
     ful þiclice   oð þam þegne ongan
     his hige hweorfan   þæt he þam gehate getruwode
     þe him þæt wif   wordum sægde.
     Heo dyde hit þeah þurh holdne hyge –   nyste þæt þær hearma swa fela,
     fyrenearfeða,   fylgean sceolde
710 monna cynne,   þæs heo on mod genam
     þæt heo þæs laðan bodan   larum hyrde,
     ác wende þæt heo hyldo Heofoncyninges
     worhte mid þam wordum   þe heo þam were swelce
     tacen oðiewde   and treowe gehet
     oðþæt Ádame   innan breostum
     his hyge hwyrfde   and his heorte ongann
     wendan to hire willan.   He æt þam wife onfeng
     helle and hinnsið   þeah hit nære haten swa,
     ác hit ofetes noman   agan sceolde;
720 hit wæs þeah deaðes swefn   and deofles gespon,

---

[160] MS *ge-/weald*, p. 33.
[161] MS *hellgeþwin* with a letter erased after *n* – it may have been *g* but, if so, the erasure would make little sense.
[162] MS *him*.

hell and hinnsið   and hæleða forlor,
menniscra morð   þæt hie tó mete dædon,
ofet únfæle.   Swa hit him on innan cóm,
hrán æt heortan;   hloh þa and plegode
boda bitre gehugod,   sægde begra þanc
hearran sínum:

The Tempter rejoices in his Accomplishments and returns to Hell

              'Nú hæbbe íc þine hyldo me
witode geworhte   and þinne willan gelæst
to ful monegum dæge.   Mén synt forlædde,
Adam and Éue.   Him ís unhyldo

730 Waldendes witod   nú[163] hie wordcwyde hís,
lare forleton.   Forþon[164] hie leng ne magon
healdan heofonrice   ác hie to helle sculon
on þone sweartan sið.   Swa þu hís sorge ne þearft
beran on þinum breostum   þær þu gebunden ligst,
murnan on mode,   þæt her men bún
þone hean heofon   þeah wit hearmas nú,
þreaweorc þoliað   and þystre land,
and þurh þin micle mod   monig forléton
on heofonríce   heahgetimbro,

740 godlice geardas.   Unc wearð God yrre
forþon wit him noldon   on heofonríce
hnígan mid heafdum   halgum Drihtne
þurh geongordom;   ác unc gegenge ne wæs
þæt wit him on þegnscipe   þeowian wolden.
Forþon unc Waldend wearð   wrað on mode,
on hyge hearde   and ús on helle bedraf,

---

[163] p. 34. There is only one line of text at the top of this page. The rest of the page contains an illustration in two registers, the top showing Adam and Eve using a gesture to show their sadness and sorrowing, as they also do in the lower register while covering their genitals with leaves – see the Art-Historical Commentary. For the use of gestures from the Roman stage in Anglo-Saxon illustrations see Dodwell 2000 (esp. Ch. 4).
[164] p. 35.

on þæt fyr fylde   folca mæste,
and mid handum hís   eft on heofonríce
rihte rodorstolas   and þæt ríce forgeaf
750 monna cynne.   Mæg þin mód wesan
blíðe on breostum   forþon her synt bu tu gedón:
ge þæt hæleða bearn   heofonríce[165] sculon
leode forlǽtan   and on þæt líg to þe
hate hweorfan,   eac is hearm Gode,
módsorg gemacod.   Swa hwæt swa wit her morðres þoliað,
hit ís nu Adame   eall forgolden
mid hearran hete   and mid hæleða forlore,
monnum mid morðes cwealme.   Forþon ís min mód gehǽled,
hyge ymb heortan gerúme,   ealle synt uncre hearmas gewrecene
760 laðes þæt wit lange þoledon.   Nú wille íc eft þam lige near,
Satan ic þær sécan[166] wille;   he is on þære sweartan helle
hæft mid hringa gesponne.'   Hwearf him eft niðer
boda bitresta;   sceolde[167] he þa bradan lígas
secan helle gehliðo   þær hís hearra læg
símon[168] gesǽled.

ADAM AND EVE REGRET HAVING DISOBEYED GOD'S COMMAND

Sorgedon bá twá,
Adam and Éue   and him oft betuh
gnornword gengdon;   Godes him ondrédon,
heora Herran hete,   Heofoncyninges nið
swiðe onsæton;   selfe forstodon
770 his word onwended.   Þæt wif gnornode,

---

[165] MS *heofon ríces*.
[166] MS *sé can* with a letter erased after *é*.
[167] p. 36. There are only two lines of text at the top of this page. The rest of the page contains an illustration in two registers, the top showing Adam and Eve using a gesture to show their shame and covering their genitals with leaves; in the lower register (in two merged scenes) the devilish messenger returns to the pit of hell and reports the success of his mission to Satan – see the Art-Historical Commentary. At the top left of the page is another *xb*, as occurs elsewhere in the manuscript (see p. 1, note).
[168] p. 37.

    hof hreowigmod   – hæfde hyldo Godes,
    láre forlæten –   þa heo þæt leoht geseah
    ellor scriðan   þæt hire þurh úntreowa
    tacen iewde   se him þone teonan geræd,
    þæt hie helle nið   habban sceoldon,
    hýnða únrím;   forþam him higesorga
    burnon on breostum.   Hwilum to gebede feollon
    sinhiwan somed   and Sigedrihten
    godne gretton   and God nemdon,
780 heofones Waldend,   and hine bædon
    þæt hie his[169] hearmsceare   habban mosten,
    georne fulgangan   þa hie Godes hæfdon
    bódscipe abrocen.   Bare hie gesawon
    heora líchaman;   næfdon on þam lande þa giet
    sælða gesetena,   ne hie sorge wiht
    weorces wiston   ác hie wel meahton
    libban on þam lande,   gif hie wolden láre Godes
    forweard fremman.   Þa hie fela spræcon
    sorhworda somed   sinhiwan twa.
790   Adam gemælde   and to Éuan spræc:
    'Hwæt. Þu Éue, hæfst   yfele gemearcod
    uncer sylfra sið;   gesyhst þu nu þa sweartan helle
    grædige and gifre.   Nu þu hie grimman meaht
    heonane gehyran;   nis heofonrice
    gelíc þam lige,   ác þis is landa betst
    þæt wit þurh uncres Hearran þanc   habban moston,
    þær þu þam ne hierde   þe unc þisne hearm geræd
    þæt wit Waldendes   word forbræcon,
    Heofoncyninges.   Nu wit hreowige magon
800 sorgian[170] for þis siðe;   forþon he unc self bebead
    þæt wit unc wíte   warian sceolden,

---

[169] Added above with an insertion mark below.
[170] p. 38.

hearma mæstne. Nu slit me hunger and þurst
bitre on breostum, þæs wit begra ǽr[171]
wæron órsorge on ealle tíd.
Hu sculon wit nu libban oððe on þys lande wesan
gif her wind cymð, westan oððe eastan,
suðan oððe norðan? Gesweorc úp færeð,
cymeð hægles scúr hefone getenge,
færeð forst on gemang se byð fyrnum ceald.
810 Hwilum of heofnum háte scineð,
blicð þeos beorhte sunne and wit hér baru standað,
unwered wædo. Nys unc wuht beforan
to scúrsceade, ne sceattes wiht
to mete gemearcod ac unc ís mihtig God,
Waldend wraðmod. To hwón sculon wit weorðan nú?
Nú me mæg hreowan þæt ic bæd heofnes God,
Waldend þone godan þæt he þe hér worhte to me
of liðum minum, nu þu me forlǽred hæfst
on mínes herran hete. Swa me nu hreowan mæg
820 ǽfre to aldre þæt íc þe mínum eagum geseah.'
    Ða[172] spræc Eue eft, idesa scienost,
wifa wlitegost; hie wæs geweorc Godes
þeah heo þa on deofles cræft bedroren wurde:
'Þu meaht hit me wítan, wine mín Adam,
wordum þinum; hit þe þeah wyrs ne mæg
on þinum[173] hyge hreowan þonne hit me æt heortan deð.'
    Hire þa Ádam andswarode:
'Gif ic[174] Waldendes willan cuðe
hwæt ic his to hearmsceare habban sceolde,

---

[171] MS ǽre.
[172] The initial **Ð** is 6-lines high and zoomorphic, and the letters following it, **A SPRÆC**, are in smaller bold capitals.
[173] MS þinu.
[174] Added above.

830 ne gesawe þu[175] nó sniomór   þeah me on sǽ wadan
     hete heofones God   heonone nu þa,
     on flód faran,   nǽre he firnum þæs deop,
     merestream þæs micel   þæt his ó mín mód getweode
     ác ic to þam grunde genge,   gif ic Godes meahte
     willan gewyrcean.   Nis me on worulde niod
     ǽniges þegnscipes   nú íc mines þeodnes hafa
     hyldo forworhte   þæt ic hie habban ne mǽg.
     Ac wit þus baru ne magon   bu tu ætsomne
     wesan to wuhte;   uton gan on þysne weald innan,
840 on þisses holtes hleo.'   Hwurfon hie bá twá,
     togengdon gnorngende   on þone grenan weald,
     sǽton onsundran   bidan selfes gesceapu
     Heofoncyninges,   þa hie þa habban ne moston
     þe him ǽr forgeaf   ælmihtig God.
     Þa hie heora lichoman   leafum beþeahton,
     weredon mid ðy wealde –   wǽda ne hǽfdon;
     ac hie on gebed feollon   bu tu ætsomne
     morgena gehwilce,   bǽdon Mihtigne
     þæt hie ne forgeate   God ælmihtig,
850 and him gewisade   Waldend se góda
     hu hie on þam leohte forð   libban sceolden.[176]

GOD ADDRESSES ADAM AND EVE IN PARADISE

     Þa cóm féran   Frea ælmihtig
     ofer midne dæg,   mǽre Þeoden,
     on neorxnawang   neode sine;
     wolde neosian   Nergend usser,
     bilwit Fæder,   hwæt his bearn dyde;

---

[175] p. 39. The lower part of this page has an illustration with two registers: the upper shows Adam and Eve standing and talking to each other and the lower shows them ashamed and seated in Paradise – see the Art-Historical Commentary.
[176] *Genesis B* ends. *Genesis A* resumes.

wiste forworhte þa he ær wlite sealde.

Gewitan him þam[177] gangan geomermode
under beamsceade blæde bereafod,
860 hyddon hie on heolstre þa hie hálig word
Drihtnes gehyrdon and ondredon him.

Þá sóna ongann swegles Aldor
weard ahsian woruldgesceafta,
het him recene to ríce Þeoden
hís sunu gangan. Him þa sylfa oncwæð,
hean hleoðrade hrægles þearfa:

'Ic wreo me hér wǽda leasne,
Lífffrea mín, leafum þecce;
scyldfull mine sceaðen is me sáre,
870 frecne on ferhðe; ne dear nu forð gan
for ðe andweardne – ic eom eall eall nacod.'[178]

Him[179] ða ædre God andswarede:
'Saga me þæt, sunu mín, for hwon secest ðu
sceade sceomiende? Þu sceonde æt me
furðum <ne>[180] anfenge ác gefean eallum.
For hwon wast þu[181] wéan and wrihst sceome,
gesyhst sorge and þin sylf þecest
lic mid leafum, sagast lifceare
hean hygegeomor þæt þe sie hrægles þearf,
880 nymþe ðu æppel ænne byrgde[182]
of ðam wudubeame þe ic þé wordum forbéad?'

Him þa Ádam eft andswarode:
'Mé ða[183] blæda on hánd bryd gesealde,

---

[177] MS þa.
[178] There is no text on p. 41. The full-page illustration is in two registers: the upper shows God cursing the serpent, who crawls off on his belly and subsequently turns to slither up the border column into a figure representing the mouth of hell; in the lower register God curses / chastises Adam and Eve.
[179] p. 42. The intial h is 7-lines high and zoomorphic; the following letters – **IM** – are in smaller bold capitals.
[180] Not in the manuscript – reading from Krapp 1931 (p. 29).
[181] þ may have been squeezed in later.
[182] MS byrgde with -st squeezed in later and then underpointed for deletion.
[183] MS ðe with e underpointed for deletion and a added above.

freolucu fæmne,   Freadrihten mín,
ðe ic þé on téonan geþah.   Nu ic[184] þæs tacen wege
sweotol on me selfum;   wat ic sorga ðy ma.'
   Ða ðæs Euan frægn   ælmihtig God:
'Hwæt druge þú, dohtor,   dugeþa genohra,
niwra gesceafta   neorxnawanges,
890 growendra gifa   þa þu gitsiende
on beam gripe   blæda name
on treowes telgum   and me on teonan
æte þa únfreme,   Ádame sealdest
wæstme þa inc wæron   wordum minum
fæste forbodene?'   Him þa freolecu mæg,
ídes æwiscmód   andswarode:
'Mé nædre beswac   and me neodlice
to forsceape scyhte   and to scyldfrece,
fah wyrm þurh fægir word   oðþæt ic fracoðlice
900 feondræs gefremede,   fæhðe geworhte
and þa reafode,   swa hit riht ne wæs,
beam on bearwe   and þa blæda ǽt.'
   Þa nædran sceop   Nergend usser,
Frea ælmihtig   fagum wyrme
wide siðas   and þa worde cwæð:
'Þu scealt wideferhð   werig[185] þinum
breostum bearm tredan[186]   bradre[187] eorðan,
faran feðeleas   þenden þe feorh[188] wunað,
gast on innan;   þu scealt greot etan
910 þine lífdagas.   Swa þu laðlice
wrohte onstealdest,   þe þæt wif feoð,
hatað under heofnum   and þín heafod tredeð
fah mid fotum sinum.   Þu scealt fiersna sætan

---

[184] Added above with an insertion mark below.
[185] MS *werg*.
[186] p. 43.
[187] MS *brade*.
[188] MS *feoh* with *r* added above and an insertion mark below.

tohtan niwre;   tuddor bið gemæne
incrum órlegnið   á þenden standeð
woruld under wolcnum.   Nu þu wast and canst,
lað leodsceaða   hu[189] þu lifian scealt.'
 Ða[190] to Euan God   yrringa spræc:
'Wend þe from wynne.   Þu scealt wæpnedmen
920 wesan on gewealde,   mid weres egsan
hearde genearwad,   hean þrowian
þinra dæda gedwild,   deaðes bidan,
and þurh wop and heaf   on woruld cennan
þurh sar micel   sunu and dohtor.'
 Abead eac Adame   éce Drihten,
lífes Leohtfruma,   láð ǽrende:
'Þú scealt oðerne   eðel secean,
wynleasran wic   and on wræc hweorfan
nacod niedwædla,   neorxnawanges
930 dugeðum bedæled;   þe is gedal witod
lices and sawle.   Hwæt.   Þu laðlice
wrohte onstealdest   forþon þu winnan scealt
and on eorðan þe   þine andlifne
selfa geræcan,   wegan swatig hleor,
þinne hlaf etan   þenden þu her leofast,
oðþæt þe to heortan   hearde grípeð
ádl unliðe   þe þu on æple ǽr
selfa forswulge;   forþon þu sweltan scealt.'[191]
 Hwæt.[192] We nu gehyrað   hwær us hearmstafas
940 wraðe onwocan   and woruldyrmðo;
hie þa wuldres Weard   wædum gyrede,
Scyppend usser.   Het heora sceome þeccan
Frea frumhrægle;   het hie from hweorfan

---

[189] MS *nu*.
[190] The *Ð* is 5-lines high and decorated; the following *A* is a smaller bold capital. This Fitt is numbered *xvi*.
[191] There is no text on p. 44. The full-page illustration is divided in half vertically: on the right God (with a crossed nimbus) curses Eve and on the right he curses Adam – see the Art-Historical Commentary.
[192] p. 45.

neorxnawange on nearore lif.
Him on laste beleac liðsa and wynna
hihtfulne ham halig engel
be Frean hæse fyrene sweorde;
ne mæg þær inwitfull ænig geferan
womscyldig mon, ac se Weard hafað
950 miht and strengðo se þæt mære lif
dugeðum deore Drihtne healdeð.
No[193] hwæðre Ælmihtig ealra wolde
Adame and Euan arna ofteon,
Fæder æt frymðe þeah þe hie[194] him from swice,
ác he him to frofre lét hwæðere forð wesan
hyrstedne hróf halgum tunglum
and him grundwelan ginne sealde;
het þam sinhiwum sǽs and eorðan
tuddorteondra teohha gehwilcre[195]
960 to woruldnytte wæstmas fédan.
Gesæton þa æfter synne sorgfulre land,
eard and éðyl unspedigran
fremena gehwilcre þonne se frumstol wæs
þe hie æfter dæde óf ádrifen wurdon.

The Births of Cain and Abel and the Murder of Abel

Ongunnon hie þa be Godes hæse
bearn ástrienan, swa him Metod bebead;
Adames and Euan aforan wæron
freolicu twa frumbearn cenned,
Cain and Abel. Us cyðað bec
970 hu þa dædfruman dugeþa stryndon,
welan and wiste, willgebroðor.

---

[193] p. 46. The lower part of this page has an illustration of the angel armed with a sword expelling Adam and Eve from Paradise – see the Art-Historical Commentary.
[194] MS *he*.
[195] MS *gehilcre*.

Oðer[196] hís to eorðan   elnes tilode,
se wæs ǽrboren;   oðer æhte heold
fæder on fultum   oðþæt forð gewat
dægrimes worn.   Hie þa Drihtne lac
begen brohton;   Brego engla beseah
on Abeles gield   eagum sinum,
Cyning eallwihta,   Caines ne wolde
tiber sceawian.   Þæt wæs torn were

980 hefig æt heortan;   hygewælm asteah[197]
beorne on breostum,   blatende nið,
yrre for æfstum.   He þa únræden
folmum gefremede –   freomæg ofsloh,
broðor sinne   and his blod agéat,
Cain Abeles;   cwealmdreore swealh
þæs middangeard,   monnes swate.

  Æfter wælswenge   wea wæs aréred,[198]
tregena tuddor.   Of ðam twige siððan
ludon laðwende   leng swa swiðor

990 reðe wæstme.   Ræhton wide
geond werþeoda   wrohtes telgan,
hrinon hearmtánas   hearde and sare
drihta bearnum   – doð gieta swa –
of[199] þam brad blado   bealwa gehwilces
sprytan ongunnon.   We þæt spell magon,
wælgrimme wyrd   wópe cwiðan,
nales holunge;   ác us hearde sceod
freolecu fæmne   þurh forman gylt
þe wið Metod æfre   men gefremeden,

1000 eorðbuende,   siððan Adam wearð
of Godes muðe   gaste eacen.

---

[196] p. 47. The lower part of this page has an illustration showing the birth of Seth – see the Art-Historical Commentary.
[197] MS *hyge wælmos teah*.
[198] *r* over an erased letter which had an ascender.
[199] p. 48.

    Ða[200] worde frægn wuldres Aldor
    Cain hwær Abel eorðan wære;
    him ða se cystleasa cwealmes wyrhta
    ǽdre æfter þon andswarode:
    'Ne can íc Abeles ór ne fóre,
    hleomæges sið, ne ic hyrde wæs
    broðer mines.' Him þa Brego engla,
    godspedig Gast géan þingade:
1010 'Hwæt. Befealdest þu folmum þinum
    wraðum on wælbedd wærfæstne[201] rínc,
    broðor þinne and his blod to me
    cleopað and cigeð. Þu þæs cwealmes scealt
    wite winnan and on wræc hweorfan
    awyrged to widan aldre. Ne seleð þe wæstmas eorðe
    wlitige to woruldnytte ác heo wældreore swealh
    halge of handum þinum; forþon heo þe hróðra oftihð,
    glæmes grene folde. Þu scealt geomor hweorfan,
    árleas of earde þinum swa þu Abele wurde
1020 to feorhbanan; forþon þu flema scealt
    widlast wrecan, winemagum lað.'
      Him þa <ædre>[202] Cain andswarode:
    'Ne þearf ic ǽnigre áre wenan
    on woruldríce ac íc forworht hæbbe,
    heofona Heahcyning, hyldo þine,
    lufan and freode; forþon íc lastas[203] sceal
    wéan on wénum wide lecgan,
    hwonne me gemitte mánscyldigne
    se me feor oððe neah fæhðe gemonige,
1030 broðorcwealmes. Ic hís blod ageat,

---

[200] The zoomorphic initial is 7-lines high and the following *A* is 2-lines high and in bold. The Fitt number .*xvii*. is to the right in the line above.

[201] MS *wǽr fæsne*.

[202] Not in the manuscript – reading from Graz 1896.

[203] p. 49. There is an illustration in the lower part of this page showing the narrative of the slaying of Abel by Cain – see the Art-Historical commentary. There is an *x* on the left side of the upper margin.

dreor on eorðan. Þu to dæge þissum
ádemest me fram duguðe and ádrifest from
earde minum. Me to aldorbanan
weorðeð wraðra sum; ic awyrged sceal,
Þeoden, of gesyhðe þinre hweorfan.'

 Him[204] þa selfa oncwæð sigora Drihten:
'Ne þearft ðu þe ondrædan deaðes brógan,
feorhcwealm nu giet þeah þu from scyle
freomágum feor fáh gewitan.

1040 Gif <þe>[205] monna hwelc mundum sínum
aldre beneoteð, hine on cymeð
æfter þære synne seofonfeald wracu,
wite æfter weorce.' Hine Waldend ón,
tírfæst Metod tacen sette,
freoðobeacen Fréa þy læs hine feonda hwilc
mid guðþræce grétan dorste
feorran oððe nean; heht þa from hweorfan
meder and magum mánscyldigne,
cnosle sínum. Him þa Cain gewat

1050 gongan geomormód Gode of gesyhðe,
wineleas wrecca and him þa wíc geceas
eastlandum on, eðelstowe
fædergeardum feor þær him freolecu mæg,
ides æfter æðelum eaforan fedde.

The offspring of Cain

 Se æresta wæs Énos haten,
frumbearn Caines. Siððan <fæsten>[206] ongon
mid þam cneomagum ceastre timbran;
þæt wæs under wolcnum weallfæstenna

---

[204] p. 50.
[205] Not in the manuscript – reading from Grein 1857.
[206] Not in the manuscript – reading from Krapp 1931 (p. 34).

  ærest ealra þara þe æðelingas,
1060 sweordbérende, settan héton.
  Þanon his eaforan ærest wócan,
bearn from bryde on þam burhstede.[207]
Se[208] yldesta wæs Iared haten,
sunu Enoses; siððan wocan,
þa þæs cynnes cneowrim icton,
mægburg Caines. Malalehel wæs
æfter Iarede yrfes hyrde
fæder on laste oðþæt he forð gewát.
  Siððan Mathusal[209] magum dælde,
1070 bearn æfter bearne broðrum sinum
æðelinga gestreon oðþæt aldorgedál
frod[210] fyrndagum fremman sceolde,
lif oflætan. Lameh onfeng
æfter fæder dæge fletgestealdum,
botlgestreonum. Him bryda twa,
idesa on eðle eaforan feddon,
Áda and Sella; þara anum wǽs
Iabal noma, se þurh gleawne geþanc
herbuendra hearpan ærest
1080 handum sinum hlyn awehte,
swinsigende swég, sunu Lamehes.
  Swylce[211] on ðære mægðe maga wæs haten
on þa ilcan tid Tubál-Cain
se þurh snytro sped smiðcræftega wæs
and þurh modes gemynd monna ǽrest,

---

[207] The letters *stede* are written in the last line of this page with a large space between each letter; this is presumably because the scribe knew that a full-page illustration was to follow on p. 51, which shows Cain in the top two registers and Enoch with presumably his wife and Irad/Jared in the bottom register – see the Art-Historical Commentary.

[208] p. 52. The letters *xb* are written to the left side of the top margin as elsewhere in the manuscript (see p. 1, note).

[209] MS *matusal* with *h* added above after *t* and an insertion mark below.

[210] Part of a letter has been erased above this word.

[211] The *S* is zoomorphic and 5-lines; the rest of the word is in large bold letters. The Fitt number *xviii.* is written to the right of the blank line above.

sunu Lamehes, sulhgeweorces
fruma wæs ofer foldan; siððan folca bearn
æres[212] cuðon and isernes,
burhsittende, brucan wíde.

1090 Þa his wifum twæm wordum sægde
Lameh seolfa, leofum gebeddum,
Adan and Sellan unarlic spel:
   'Ic on morðor ofsloh minra sumne[213]
hyldemaga; honda gewemde
on Caines cwealme mine,
fylde mid folmum fæder Enoses,
órdbanan Abeles, eorðan sealde
wældreor weres. Wat <ic>[214] gearwe
þæt þam lichryre on last cymeð
1100 Soðcyninges seofonfeald wracu,
micel[215] æfter mane. Min sceal swiðor
mid grimme gryre golden wurðan
fyll and feorhcwealm, þonne ic forð scio.'

THE BIRTH OF SETH TO ADAM AND EVE, AND HIS OFFSPRING

   Þa wearð Adame on Abeles gyld
eafora on eðle oþer feded,
soðfæst sunu þam wæs Seth noma.
Se wæs eadig and his yldrum ðáh
freolic to frofre, fæder and meder,
Adames and Euan, wæs Abeles gield
1110 on woruldríce. Þa word acwæð
ord moncynnes: 'Me éce sunu

---

[212] MS *ærest*.
[213] MS *sune*.
[214] Not in the manuscript – reading from Graz 1896.
[215] p. 55. The preceding pages (53 and 54) contain full-page illustrations in three registers of the generations of Cain — see the Art-Historical Commentary.

sealde[216] selfa   sigora Waldend,

lífes Aldor   on leofes stæl

þæs þe Cain ofsloh,   and me cearsorge

mid þys magotimbre   of mode ásceaf

Þeoden usser;   him þæs þanc sie.'

    Adam hæfde,   þa he eft ongan

him to eðelstæfe[217]   oðres stríenan

bearnes be bryde,   beorn ellenróf,

1120   þritig and[218] hund[219]   þisses lifes,

wintra on worulde.   Us gewritu secgað

þæt her eahtahund   iecte siððan

mægðum and mæcgum   mægburg sine

Adam on eorðan;   ealra hæfde

nigenhund wintra

and þritig[220] eac,   þa he þas woruld

þurh gastgedal   ofgyfan sceolde.[221]

    Him[222] on laste Seth   leod[223] weardode,

eafora æfter yldrum;   eþelstol heold

1130   and wif begeat.   Wintra hæfde

fif and hundteontig   þa he[224] furðum ongan

his mægburge   men geícean

sunum and dohtrum.   Sethes[225] eafora

se yldesta wæs   Énos haten;

sé nemde God   niðþa bearna

ærest ealra   siððan Adam stop

on gréne græs   gaste geweorðad.

---

[216] MS *sealde sunu.*
[217] MS *edulf stæfe.*
[218] MS has the rune *wynn* for the required *and* abbreviation sign (⁊).
[219] MS *xxx.* and *c.*
[220] MS *xxx.*
[221] MS *sce-/olde*: the scribe had begun to write *eo* at the end of a manuscript line but then erased the *o* and wrote it at the beginning of the next line.
[222] p. 56. The lower part of this page has an illustration depicting Seth and his family – see the Art-Historical Commentary.
[223] MS *leof.*
[224] MS *heo.*
[225] MS *sedes.*

Seth wæs gesælig;[226]   siððan strynde

seofon winter hér   suna and dohtra

1140 ond[227] eahtahund.   Ealra hæfde

twelf[228] and nigonhund,   þa seo tid gewearð

þæt he friðgedál   fremman sceolde.

Hím[229] æfter heold   þa he of worulde gewat,

Enos yrfe,   siððan eorðe swealh

sædberendes   Sethes líce.

Hé wæs leof Gode   and lifde hér

wintra hundnigontig   ǽr he be wife her

þurh[230] gebedscipe   bearn astrynde;

him þa cenned wearð   Cainan ǽrest

1150 eafora on éðle.   Siððan eahtahund

and fiftyno   on friðo Drihtnes

gleawferhð hæleð   geogoðe strynde,

suna and dohtra;   swealt, þa he hafde,

frod fyrnwita,[231]   fif[232] and nigonhund.

Þære cneorisse wæs   Cainan[233] siððan

æfter Énose   aldordema,

weard and wisa;   wintra hæfde

efne hundseofontig   ær him sunu woce.

Þa[234] wearð on eðle   eafora feded,

1160 mago Cainanes,[235]   Malalehel wæs haten;

siððan eahtahund   æðelinga rím

and feowertig[236] eac   feorum geícte

---

[226] The caption in the illustration below is *Seth wæs sæli*.
[227] This is usually written *and*.
[228] MS *.xii.*
[229] p. 57. The lower part of this page has an illustration depicting Cainan, the son of Enos, seated on a faldstool – see the Art-Historical Commentary.
[230] MS *þur*.
[231] MS *-wita*, with *a* altered from *e*.
[232] MS *.v.*
[233] MS *cain* followed by erased *an* (for reasons unclear – here and in l. 1160 the scribe is confused by the similarity between the names *Cain* and *Cainan*).
[234] p. 58. The central part of this page has an illustration depicting Malaleel in an 'orans' pose – see the Art-Historical Commentary.
[235] MS *caines*.
[236] MS *feowertigum*.

Enoses sunu.   Ealra nigonhund
wintra hæfde   þa he woruld ofgeaf
and tyne éac   þa his tíddæge
under rodera rúm   rím wæs gefylled.[237]

   Him[238] on laste heold   land and yrfe
Malalehel siððan   missera worn;
se frumgara   fif and sixtig
1170 wintra hæfde   þa he be wife ongann
bearna strynan.   Him bryd sunu
meowle to monnum brohte;   se maga wæs
on hís mægðe,   mine gefræge,
guma on geogoðe,   Íared haten.
Lifde siððan   and lissa breac
Malalehél lange,   mondreama[239] hér,
woruldgestreona.   Wintra hæfde
fif and hundnigontig   þa he forð gewát,
and eahtahund;   eaforan læfde
1180 land and leodweard.   Longe siððan
Geared gumum   gold brittade;
se eorl wæs æðele,   æfæst hæleð
and se frumgár his   freomagum leof.
Fif and hundteontig   on fyore lifde
wintra gebidenra   on woruldríce
and syxtig eac   þa seo sæl gewearð
þæt his wif sunu   on woruld brohte;
se eafora wæs   Énoc haten,
freolic frumbearn.   Fæder hér þa gýt
1190 his cynnes forð   cneorim icte,
eaforan[240] eahtahund;   ealra hæfde

---

[237] The Fitt number .viiii. is written in the blank space in the middle of this line – it is enclosed in the upper arch of the illustration below.
[238] The *h* is 12-lines high and zoomorphic; the **IM** are 2-lines high and in bold.
[239] p. 59. Two lines of text are followed by an illustration depicting the death of Malaleel – see the Art-Historical Commentary. The illustration is followed by eleven more lines of text.
[240] MS *eafora*.

fif[241] and syxtig, þa he forð gewát,
and nigonhund eac nihtgerímes,
wine frod wintres þa he þas woruld ofgeaf
ond[242] Geared þa gleawum læfde
land and[243] leodweard, leofum rínce.
Enoch siððan ealdordom ahof,
freoðosped folces wisa, nalles feallan let
dóm and drihtscipe

1200 þenden he hyrde wǽs heafodmaga.
bréac blǽddaga, bearna strynde
þreohund wintra. Him wæs Þeoden hold,
rodera Waldend. Se rinc heonon
on lichoman lisse sohte,
Drihtnes duguðe, nales deaðe swealt
middangeardes swa her men dóþ,
geonge and ealde, þonne him god heora
æhta and ǽtwist eorðan gestreona
ón genimeð and heora aldor somed,

1210 ác he cwic gewat mid Cyning engla
of þyssum lænan life feran[244]
on þam gearwum þe his gast onfeng
ǽr hine to monnum modor brohte.
He þam yldestan eaforan læfde
folc,[245] frumbearne; fif[246] and syxtig
wintra hæfde þa he woruld ofgeaf,
and eac ðry[247] hund. Þrage siððan

---

[241] MS .v.
[242] This is usually written *and*.
[243] p. 60. After the first line of text there is an illustration depicting Enoch conversing with an angel – see the Art-Historical Commentary. Below the illustration there are twelve more lines of text.
[244] MS *frean*.
[245] p. 62. Page 61 has no text; its illustration, in two registers, depicts the Assumption of Enoch into heaven – see the Art-Historical Commentary. Page 62 has seven lines of text followed by an illustration depicting the birth of Lamech, Noah's father – see the Art-Historical Commentary. This is followed by eight more lines of text.
[246] MS .v.
[247] MS .iii.

Mathusal heold   maga yrfe,

sé on lichoman   lengest þissa[248]

1220 worulddreama breac.   Worn gestrynde

ær his swyltdæge   suna and dohtra;

hæfde fród hæle   þa he from sceolde

niþþum hweorfan,   nigonhund wintra

and húndseofontig tó.   Sunu æfter heold,

Lamech leodgeard,   lange siððan

woruld bryttade;   wintra hæfde

twa and hundteontig   þa seo tíd gewearð

þæt se eorl ongán   æðele cennan,

sunu and dohtor.   Siððan lifde

1230 fif and hundnigontig,   frea moniges breac

wintra under wolcnum,   werodes aldor,

<and>[249] fif[250] hund eac;   heold þæt folc teala,

bearna strynde,   him býras wócan,

eaforan[251] and idesa.

The Birth of Noah, the Son of Lamech

He þone yldestan

Noę nemde,   se niððum ǽr

land bryttade   siððan Lamech gewat;

hæfde[252] æðelinga   aldorwisa

fif[253] hund wintra   þa he furðum ongan

bearna strynan,   þæs þe bec cweðaþ.

1240 Sém wæs haten   sunu Noes,

se yldesta,   oðer Chám,

þridda Iáfeth.   Þeoda tymdon

---

[248] MS *þisse*.
[249] Not in the manuscript – reading from Graz 1896.
[250] MS *.v.*
[251] MS *eafora*.
[252] p. 63. The upper part of this page has an illustration depicting the birth and life of Noah – see the Art-Historical Commentary.
[253] MS *.v.*

rume under roderum, rím miclade
monna mægðe geond middangeard
sunum and dohtrum. Ða giet wæs Sethes cynn,
leofes leodfruman on lufan swiðe
Drihtne dyre and dómeadig
oðþæt[254] bearn Godes bryda ongunnon
on Cáines cynne sécan,
1250 wergum folce and him þǽr wif curon
ofer Metodes ést monna eaforan,
scyldfulra mægð scyne and fægere.

   Þa reordade rodora Waldend
wrað moncynne and þa worde cwæð:
'Ne syndon me on ferhðe freo from gewitene
cneorisn Caines ác me þæt cynn hafað
sáre[255] ábolgen. Nu me Sethes bearn
torn niwiað and hím tó nimað
mægeð to gemæccum minra feonda;
1260 þǽr wifa wlite onwód grome,
idesa ansien and éce feond
folcdriht wera, þa ǽr on friðe wæron.'

   Siððan hundtwelftig geteled ríme
wintra on worulde wræce bisgodon[256]
fæge þeoda, hwonne Frea wolde
on wærlogan wite settan
and on dead slean dǽdum scyldige
gigantmæcgas, Gode unléofe,
micle mánsceaðan, Metode laðe.
1270 Þa geseah selfa sigoro Waldend
hwæt wæs monna manes on eorðan
and þæt hie wæron womma ðriste,

---

[254] The large initial is 5-lines high and zoomorphic; it does not seem necessary to begin a new sentence here. The Fitt number *xx.* is written to the right in the space above this line.
[255] p. 64.
[256] *e* added above after *s* (for reasons unclear).

inwitfulle.　He þæt únfægere
wera cneorissum　gewrecan þohte,
forgripan gumcynne　grimme and sare,
heardum mihtum.　Hreaw hine swiðe
þæt he folcmægþa　fruman aweahte,
æðelinga ord　þa he Adam sceop,
cwæð þæt he wolde　for wera synnum
1280　eall áæðan　þæt on eorðan wæs,
forleosan lica gehwilc　þara þe lifes gast
fæðmum þeahte.　Eall þæt Frea wolde
on ðære tóweardan[257]　tíde acwellan
þe þa néalæhte　niðða bearnum.
　Nóe wæs gód,　Nergende leof,
swiðe gesælig　sunu Lámeches,
dómfæst and gedéfe.

God rseolves to destroy Humankind but to save Noah

　Drihten wiste
þæt þæs æðelinges　ellen dohte
breostgehygdum;　forðon him Brego sægde,
1290　halig æt hleoðre　Helm allwihta,
hwæt he fah werum　fremman wolde;
geseah únrihte　eorðan fulle,
síde sælwongas　synnum gehladene,
widlum gewemde.　Þa Waldend spræc,
Nergend usser,　and tó Nóe cwæð:
　'Íc wille mid flode　folc acwellan
and cynna gehwilc　cucra[258] wuhta,
þara þe lyft and flod　lædað and fedað,
feoh and fuglas.　Þu scealt frið habban

---

[257] MS *toweardan* with second *a* altered from *e*.
[258] p. 65. After 11 lines of text there is an illustration; it has 2 registers with nothing but the *ground line* dividing them. In the upper register God instructs Noah, and below Noah begins to build the ark – see the Art-Historical Commentary.

1300 mid sunum þinum   ðonne sweart wæter,

wonne wælstreamas   werodum swelgað,

sceaðum scyldfullum.   Ongyn þe scíp wyrcan,

merehús micel;   on þam þú monegum scealt

reste geryman   and rihte setl

ælcum æfter agenum   eorðan tudre.

Gescype²⁵⁹ scylfan   on scipes bósme.

Þu þæt²⁶⁰ fǽr gewyrc   fiftiges wid,

ðrittiges heah   <and>²⁶¹ þreohund lang

elngemeta,   and wið yða gewyrc

1310 gefeg fæste.   Þær sceal fæsl wesan

cwiclifigendra   cynna gehwilces

on þæt wudufæsten   wocor gelæded

eorðan tudres;   earc sceal þy máre.'

Nóe²⁶² fremede²⁶³   swa hine Nergend heht,

hyrde þam halgan   Heofoncyninge;

ongan ofostlice   þæt hof wyrcan,

micle merecieste.   Magum sægde

þæt wæs þrealic þing   þeodum toweard,

reðe wite;   hie ne²⁶⁴ rohton þǽs.

1320   Geseah þa ymb wintra worn   wǽrfæst Metod

geofonhusa mæst   gearo hlifigean,

innan and utan   eorðan líme

gefæstnod wið flode,   fǽr Noes

þy selestan.   Þæt is syndrig cynn;

symle bið þy heardra   þe hit hreoh wæter,

swearte sǽstreamas   swiðor beatað.

---

²⁵⁹ *y* made by altering *i*; the second stroke of *y* is over an erased letter which had a descender (the scribe may have begun to write the next letter, *p*).
²⁶⁰ MS *þær*.
²⁶¹ Not in the manuscript – reading from Holthausen 1922.
²⁶² p. 66. The illustration in the lower part of this page shows cross-nimbed God waiting to close the door of the ark – see the Art-Historical Commentary.
²⁶³ MS *freme*.
²⁶⁴ A *g* has been erased before this word.

Ða[265] to Nóe cwæð   Nergend usser:
'Ic þe þæs míne,   monna leofost,
wǽre gesylle   þæt þu weg nimest
1330 and feora fæsl   þe þu ferian scealt
geond deop wæter   dægrímes worn
on lides bosme.   Lǽd, swa ic þe hate,
under earce bórd   eaforan þine,
frumgáran þry   and eower feower wif.
Ond[266] þu seofone genim   on þæt sundreced
tudra gehwilces   geteled rímes,
þara þe to mete   mannum lifige
and þara oðera[267]   ælces twá.
Swilce þu of eallum   eorðan wæstmum
1340 wiste under wægbórd   werodum gelǽde
þam þe mid sceolon   mereflód nesan.
Féd freolice   feora wócre
oð ic þære láfe   lagosiða eft
reorde under roderum   ryman wille.
Gewit þu nu mid híwum   on þæt hof gangan
gasta werode.   Ic þe godne wát,
fæsthydigne;   þu eart freoðo wyrðe,
ara mid eaforum.   Ic on ándwlitan
nu ofor seofon niht   sigan lǽte
1350 wællregn ufan   widre eorðan.
Feowertig daga   fæhðe ic wille
on weras stælan   and mid wægþreate
æhta and agend   eall acwellan
þa beutan beoð   earce bordum
þonne sweart racu   stigan onginneð.'
    Him þa Nóe gewat,   swa hine Nergend het,

---

[265] p. 67. The large initial *ð* is 7 lines high and zoomorphic; the following *A* is 2-lines high and bold. The Fitt number *xxi.* is written above the first line of text.
[266] Unusually, written out here. The *O* may be over an erased letter.
[267] MS *oðe ra* with an erased letter after *e* – the scribe or a corrector appears to have erased a first *r*.

under earce bórd eaforan lædan,
weras on wægþel²⁶⁸ and heora wif somed;
and eall þæt to fæsle Frea ælmihtig
1360 habban wolde under hróf gefor
to heora ætgifan, swa him ælmihtig
weroda Drihten²⁶⁹ þurh his wórd abead.
Hím²⁷⁰ on hoh beleac heofonríces Weard
merehúses muð mundum sinum,
sigora Waldend and segnade
earce innan ágenum spedum
Nergend usser. Nóe hæfde,
sunu Lameches, syxhund wintra
þa he mid bearnum under bord gestah,
1370 gleaw mid geogoðe be Godes hæse,
dugeðum dyrum. Drihten sende
regn from roderum and eac rume lét
willeburnan on woruld þringan
of ædra gehwære, égorstréamas
swearte swógan.

THE FLOOD

              Sǽs úp stigon
ofer stæðweallas. Strang wæs and reðe
se ðe wætrum weold; wreah and þeahte
manfæhðu bearn middangeardes
wonnan wǽge, wera éðellánd;
1380 hóf hergode, hygeteonan wræc
Metod on monnum. Mere swiðe grap
on fæge folc feowertig daga,
nihta oðer swilc. Nið wæs réðe,

---

²⁶⁸ *e* altered from original *æ* by scraping.
²⁶⁹ p. 68.
²⁷⁰ p. 69. After one line of text, the rest of the page has an illustration in two registers separated by the flood waters. In the lower part God is locking the door to the ark (see lines 1363-4 and 1391ᵇ) and in the upper register the ark floats upon the flood waters – see the Art-Historical Commentary.

wællgrim werum;   Wuldorcyninges
yða wræcon   árleasra feorh
of flæschoman.   Flod ealle wreah,
hreoh under heofonum   héa beorgas
geond sidne²⁷¹ grund   and on sund áhóf
earce from eorðan   and þa æðelo mid,
1390   þa segnade   selfa Drihten,
Scyppend usser   þa he þæt scip beleac.

   Siððan wíde rád   wolcnum under
ofer holmes hrincg   hof seleste,
fór mid fearme;   fære ne moston
wæglidendum   wætres brogan
hæste hrínon   ac hie halig God
ferede and nerede.   Fiftena stod
deop ofer dunum   se²⁷² drenceflod
monnes elna;   þæt is mæro wyrd.

1400   Þam æt niehstan   wæs nan to gedále,
nymþe heof²⁷³ wæs ahafen   on þa hean lyft,
þa se égorhere   eorðan tuddor
eall acwealde   buton þæt²⁷⁴ earce bord
heold heofona Frea,   þa hine halig God
éce upp forlet   édmodne²⁷⁵ <flod>²⁷⁶
streamum stigan,   stiðferhð Cyning.

   Þa²⁷⁷ gemunde God   mereliðende,
sigora Waldend   sunu Lameches
and ealle þa wócre   þe he wið wætre beleac,
1410   lifes Leohtfruma,   on lides bosme.

   Gelædde þa wigend   weroda Drihten

---

²⁷¹ *d* is over an erased *n*.
²⁷² MS *sæ*.
²⁷³ MS *heo*.
²⁷⁴ p. 70. After the first 3 lines of text the rest of the page has been left blank.
²⁷⁵ MS *éd monne*.
²⁷⁶ Not in the manuscript – reading from Wülker 1894.
²⁷⁷ p. 71. The large initial is 10-lines high and zoomorphic; the following *A* is bold and 3-lines high. The Fitt number *xxii.* is in the top margin to the right.

worde ofer wídland;   willflod ongán
lytligan eft.

The Flood Waters Recede

                        Lago ebbade,
sweart under swegle;   hæfde soð Metod[278],
eaforum égstream   eft gecyrred,
torhtne[279] ryne,   regn gestilled.
   Fór famig scip   fiftig and hund[280]
nihta under roderum,   siððan nægledbord,
fær seleste   flod úp ahof

1420   oðþæt rímgetæl   reðre þrage
daga forð gewat.   Ða on dunum gesæt
héah mid hlæste   holmærna mæst,
earc Noes,   þe Armenia
hatene syndon.   Þær se halga bad,
sunu Lameches,   soðra gehata
lange þrage,   hwonne him lifes Weard,
Frea ælmihtig,   frecenra siða
reste ageafe,   þæra[281] he rúme dreah
þa hine on sunde   geond sidne grund

1430   wonne yða   wíde bǽron.
   Holm wæs heononweard;   hæleð langode,
wæglíðende,   swilce wif heora
hwonne hie of nearwe   ofer nægledbord
ofer streamstaðe   stæppan mosten

---

[278] This is a complex word used in Germanic literature largely to describe fate, death, or God. The present editor entertains the idea that the use of this word to describe God as Ordainer or Measurer in Christian writings may be related to Acts 1:7, where the Lord describes the Father as 'controlling the times and seasons' – *Non est vestrum nosse tempora vel momenta quae Pater posuit in sua potestate...* This understanding recognizes the noun's linguistic relationship to the verb *metan*, and in a Christian context such as the poems edited here seems probable. Of course, the epithet has other meanings in non- or pre-Christian literature. The present passage describes God performing in his rôle as Measurer or Controller. Compare the following from *Beowulf* where the passage in Acts also seems to be relevant: *ðonne forstes bend Fæder onlæteð, / onwindeð wælrapas, se weald hafað / sæla ond mæla* (1609-11ª). [Acts 1:7 is also referred to in *Blickling Homily XI* – see Kelly 2003 (pp. 82-3)].
[279] MS *torht*.
[280] That is, 150 (MS *l.* and *c.*); the scribe writes the *l* (*fiftig*) first for alliterative purposes.
[281] MS *þære*.

and of enge út   æhta lædan.

Þá fandode   forðweard scipes,

hwæðer sincende   sæflod þa gyt

wǽre under wolcnum;   lét þa ymb worn daga

þæs þe heah hlioðo   horde onfengon

1440 and æðelum éac   eorðan tudres

sunu Lameches   sweartne fleogan

hrefn ofer heahflod   of húse út.

Nóe tealde   þæt[282] he on neod hine,

gif he on þære láde   land ne funde

ofer síd wæter   secan wolde

on wǽgþele.   Eft him seo wen geleah,

ác se feonde[283] gespearn   fleotende hréaw;

salwigfeðera   secan nolde.

He þa ymb seofon niht   sweartum hrefne

1450 of earce forlet   æfter fleogan

ofer heah[284] wæter   haswe culufran

on fandunga   hwæðer famig sæ

deop þa gyta   dæl ænigne

grenre eorðan   ofgifen hæfde.

Heo wide hire   willan sohte

and rume fleah;   nohweðere reste fand

þæt heo for flode   fotum ne meahte

land gespornan   ne on leaf treowes

steppan for streamum,   ác wæron steap hleoðo

1460 bewrigen mid wætrum.   Gewát se wilda fugel

on æfenne   earce sécan

ofer wonne wǽg,   werig sigan,

hungri to handa   halgum rince.

Ðá[285] wæs culufre éft   of cofan sended

---

[282] p. 72.
[283] MS *feond*.
[284] MS *hea* with second *h* added above with an insertion mark below.
[285] The Ð is larger than usual.

ymb wucan wilde.   Seo wíde fleah
oðþæt heo rumgál   restestowe
fægere funde   and þa fotum stop
on beam hyre;   gefeah bliðemod
þæs þe heo gesittan[286]   swiðe werig
1470 on treowes telgum   torhtum moste.
Heo feðera onsceoc,   gewat fleogan éft
mid lacum hire,   liðend brohte
elebeames twig   án to handa,
grene blædæ.   Þa ongeat hraðe
flotmonna frea   þæt wæs frofor cumen,
earfoðsiða bot.   Þá gyt se eadega wer
ymb wucan þriddan   wilde culufran
áne sende.   Seo eft ne com
to liðe fleogan   ác heo land begeat,
1480 grene bearwas;   nolde gladu æfre
under salwed bord   syððan ætýwan
on[287] þellfæstenne,   þa[288] hire þearf ne wæs.

   Þa[289] to Noe spræc   Nergend usser,
heofonríces Weard   halgan reorde:
   'Þe is eðelstól   éft gerymed,
lisse on lande,   lagosiða rest
fæger on foldan;   gewit on freðo gangan
út of earce   and on eorðan bearm
óf þam héan hofe   hiwan læd þu
1490 and ealle þa wocre   þe ic wægþrea on
liðe[290] nerede   þenden lago hæfde

---

[286] MS *gesette*.
[287] p. 73. The lower part of the page has an illustration depicting God (with a nimbus) holding the ark door open while Noah's family disembarks – see the Art-Historical Commentary. There are two oblong-shaped holes in the upper margin. The Fitt number *xxiii.* is written at the end of the first line of text.
[288] *a* is written over an erasure.
[289] The large initial is 10-lines high and zoomorphic; the following letters *A TO* are bold.
[290] MS *hliðe*.

>   þrymme geþeahtne[291]   þriddan[292] eðyl.'
>
>   He fremede swa   and Frean hyrde,
>   stah ofer streamweall   swa him seo stefn bebead,
>   lustum miclum   and alædde þa
>   of wægþele   wraðra lafe.
>   Þa[293] Noe ongan   Nergende lác
>   rædfæst reðran   and recene genam
>   on eallum dæl   æhtum sinum

1500   ðam ðe him to dugeðum   Drihten sealde,
   gleaw to þam gielde,   and þa Gode selfum
   torhtmod hæle   tiber onsægde,
   Cyninge engla.   Huru cuð dyde
   Nergend usser,   þa he Noe
   gebletsade   and his bearn somed
   þæt he þæt gyld on þanc   agifen hæfde
   and on geogoðhade   gódum dædum
   ær geéarnod   þæt[294] him ealra wæs
   ára este   ælmihtig God,

1510   domfæst dugeþa.   Þa gyt Drihten cwæð,
   wuldris Aldor   word tó Nóe:

>   'Týmað nu and tiedrað,   tíres brucað,
>   mid geféan fryðo;   fyllað eorðan,
>   eall geíceað.   Eow is eðelstol
>   <and>[295] holmes hlæst   and heofonfuglas[296]
>   and wildu deor   on geweald geseald,
>   eorðe ælgrene   and eacen feoh.[297]
>   Næfre ge mid blode   beodgereordu

---

[291] MS *geþeahte.*
[292] MS *þridda.*
[293] p. 74. The upper part of this page has an illustration depicting God (without a nimbus, but holding a ringed scroll) blessing Noah and his sons – see the Art-Historical Commentary.
[294] MS *þa.*
[295] Not in the manuscript – reading from Sievers 1885.
[296] MS *heofon fugla.*
[297] An extraneous *r* is written above *h* (perhaps a later reader is suggesting that instead of fecund 'cattle' the text should read 'life').

        unárlice   eowre þicgeað,
1520 besmiten mid synne   sawldreore.
        Ælc[298] hine selfa   ærest begrindeð
        gastes dugeðum   þæra[299] þe mid gares orde
        oðrum aldor oðþringeð.   Ne ðearf he þy edleane geféon
        modgeþance   ác ic monnes feorh
        to slagan sece[300]   swiðor micle,
        and to broðor banan   þæs þe blodgyte,
        wællfyll weres   wæpnum gespedeð,
        morð mid mundum –   monn wæs to Godes
        anlicnesse   ærest gesceapen.
1530 Ælc hafað magwlite   Metodes and engla
        þara þe healdan wile   halige þeawas.
        Weaxað and wridað,   wilna brucað,
        ára on eorðan;   æðelum fyllað
        eowre fromcynne   foldan sceatas,
        teamum and tudre.   Íc eow treowa þæs
        mine selle   þæt ic on middangeard
        næfre égorhere   eft gelæde,
        wæter ofer wídland.   Ge on wolcnum þæs
        oft <and>[301] gelome   andgiettacen
1540 magon sceawigan   þonne ic scurbogan
        minne iewe,   þæt ic monnum þas
        wære gelæste   þenden woruld standeð.'
            Ða wæs se snotra   sunu Lamehes
        of fere acumen   flode on laste
        mid his eaforum þrim,   yrfes hyrde,
        and heora feower wif;
        nemde wæron   Percoba, Olla,
        Olliua, Olliuani[302] –

---

[298] p. 75.
[299] MS *þære*.
[300] MS *seðe*.
[301] Not in the manuscript – reading from by Krapp 1931 (p. 48).
[302] *nemde...Olliuani*: this line and a half appear to be a marginal gloss incorporated during transmission.

wærfæst[303] Metode,[304] wætra lafe.

1550 Hæleð hygerofe hatene wæron,
suna Nóes Sem and Cham,
Iafeð þridda. From þam gumrincum
folc geludon and gefylled wearð
eall þes middangeard monna bearnum.[305]

Noah and his Family exit the Ark and establish a Homestead

Ða[306] Nóe ongan niwan stefne
mid hleomagum ham staðelian
and to eorðan him ætes tilian;
won and worhte – wingeard sette,
seow sæda fela, sohte[307] georne
1560 þa him wlitebeorhte wæstmas brohte,
géartorhte gife, grene folde.

Ða þæt geeode þæt se eadega wer
on his wicum wearð wíne druncen,
swæf symbelwerig and him selfa sceaf
reaf of líce; swa gerysne ne wæs,
læg þa limnacod. He lyt ongeat
þæt him on his inne[308] swa earme gelamp
þa him on hreðre heafodswima
on þæs halgan hofe heortan clypte.
1570 Swiðe on slæpe sefa nearwode
þæt he ne mihte on gemynd drepen
hine handum self mid hrægle[309] wryon
and sceome þeccan, swa gesceapu wæron

---

[303] The *e* loop of *æ* seems to have been erased but is still visible.
[304] MS *metod*.
[305] The Fitt number *xxiiii.* is written after this word at the end of the manuscript line.
[306] The **Ð** is 3-lines high and bold; it is lightly decorated but is not zoomorphic – it is in the same style as the **Þ** on p. 83.
[307] p. 76. The lower part of this page has an illustration depicting the blessing of Noah by God (no nimbus and holding a ringed scroll) – see the Art-Historical Commentary.
[308] MS *innne*.
[309] *g* over an erased *l*.

werum and wifum   siððan wuldres þegn
ussum fæder and meder   fyrene sweorde
on laste beleac   lifes eðel.

　　Þa cóm ærest   Cám in siðian,
eafora Nóes,   þær his aldor læg
ferhðe[310] forstolen.   Þær he freondlice
1580　on his agenum fæder   áre ne wolde
gesceawian,   ne þa sceonde huru
hleomagum helan,   ác he hlihende
broðrum sægde,   hu se beorn hine
reste on recede.   Hie[311] þa raðe stopon,
heora andwlitan   in bewrigenum
under loðum listum   þæt hie leofum men
géoce gefremede;   góde wæron begen,
Sém and Iafeð.   Ða[312] of slǽpe onbrægd
sunu Lámehes   and þa sóna ongeat
1590　þæt him cynegodum   Chám ne wolde,
þa him wæs áre þearf,   ænige cyðan
hyldo and treowa.   Þæt þam halgan wæs
sár on mode –   ongan þa his selfes bearn
wordum wyrgean;   cwæð, he wesan sceolde
hean under heofnum,   hleomaga þeow,
Chám on eorþan;   him þa cwyde syððan
and his fromcynne   frécne scódon.

　　Þá nyttade   Nóe siððan
mid sunum sinum   sídan rices
1600　ðreohund wintra   þisses lífes,

---

[310] MS *ferðe* with *h* added above.
[311] p. 77. A space has been left in the upper and lower parts of this page for *two* illustrations, but the artist has ignored this and drawn a *single* illustration of Noah plowing, assisted by one of his sons; the drawing runs over the three lines of text in the middle of the page – see the Art-Historical Commentary.
[312] p. 78. The upper part of this page has 10 lines of text, then an illustration in three registers showing Cham looking upon Noah's nakedness and his brothers' reaction to this – see the Art-Historical Commentary. There are a further 4 lines of text below the illustration.

freomen æfter flode, and fiftig eac, þa he forð gewat.[313]

    Siððan his eaforan ead bryttedon,
bearna stryndon;[314] him wæs beorht wela.
Þa wearð Iafeðe geogoð afeded,
hyhtlic heorðwerod heafodmaga,
sunu and dohtra; he wæs selfa til,
heold á rice, eðeldreamas,
blæd mid[315] bearnum, oðþæt breosta hord,
gast ellorfus gangan sceolde
1610 to Gódes dóme. Geomor siððan
fæder flettgesteald freondum dælde,
swæsum and gesibbum, sunu Iafeðes;
þæs teames wæs tuddor gefylled
únlytel dæl eorðan gesceafta.

    Swilce Chames suno cende wurdon,
eoforan on eðle; þa yldestan
Chús and Chánan[316] hátene wǽron,
ful freolice feorh, frumbearn Chámes.
Chús wæs æðelum heafodwisa,
1620 wilna brytta and worulddugeða
broðrum sinum, botlgestreona,
fæder on láste siððan forð gewat
Cham of líce þa him cwealm gesceod.
Se magoræswa mægðe sinre
dómas sægde, oðþæt his dogora wæs
rím aúrnen; þa se rinc ageaf
eorðcunde éad, sohte oðer líf,
fæder Nebroðes.[317] Frumbearn siððan
eafora Chúses yrfestóle weold,

---

[313] See Krapp 1931 (p. 180) for a discussion of the proposals of earlier editors to shorten this unusually long line.
[314] It is possible that what looks like an accent on the *y* here may in fact be part of the illustration.
[315] p. 79.
[316] MS *chám*.
[317] MS *nebreðer*.

1630 wídmǽre wer,　swa[318] us gewritu secgeað,
　　　　þæt he moncynnes　mǽste hæfde
　　　　on þam mǽldagum　mægen and strengo.
　　　　Se wæs Babylones　bregorices fruma,
　　　　ǽrest æðelinga;　eðelðrym onhof,
　　　　rymde and rǽrde;　reord wæs þa gieta
　　　　eorðbuendum　án gemǽne.[319]
　　　　Svilce[320] of Cámes　cneorisse wóc
　　　　wermægða fela;　of þam wídfolce[321]
　　　　cneorim micel　cenned wǽron.
1640　Þa wearð Séme　suna and dohtra
　　　　on woruldrice　worn afeded,
　　　　freora bearna　ǽr ðon frod[322] cure
　　　　wintrum wælreste　werodes aldor.
　　　　On þǽre mægðe　wǽron men tile,
　　　　þara án wæs　Éber haten,
　　　　eafora Sémes;　of þam eorle wóc
　　　　únrím þeoda,　þa nu æðelingas
　　　　ealle eorðbuend,　Ebréi[323] hatað.

　　　　Gewiton him þa eastan　ǽhta lǽdan,
1650　feoh and feorme;　folc wæs ánmod;
　　　　rófe rincas　sohton rumre land,
　　　　oðþæt hie becomon　corðrum miclum,
　　　　folc ferende　þǽr hie fæstlice
　　　　æðelinga bearn,　eard genamon.

　　　　Gesetton þa Sennar　sidne and widne
　　　　leoda rǽswan;　leofum mannum

---

[318] MS *wwa*.
[319] The Fitt number *xxv.* is written in the blank space after this word.
[320] For the usual *Swilce*, but it is an acceptable variant. The **S** is 4-lines high and zoomorphic; the rest of the word is in 2-line high capitals. From this point the style of the large initials changes and becomes more pedestrian, with the exception of one last zoomorphic initial (**h**) on p. 143 – it is hard to account for its appearance there, stranded and so far away from the other intricately decorated initials that have come before it.
[321] MS *wíd folc*.
[322] MS *forð*.
[323] p. 80.

heora geardagum   grene wongas,
fægre foldan,   him forðwearde
on ðære dægtíde   duguðe wæron,
1660 wilna gehwilces   weaxende sped.

The Tower of Babel

Ða þær mon mænig   be his mǽgwine,
æðeling ánmod,   oðerne bæd
þæs hie him to mærðe,   ǽr seo mengeo eft
geond foldan bearm[324]   tofaran sceolde,
leoda mægðe   on landsocne
burh geworhte   and to beacne torr
úp arǽrde   to rodortunglum.
Þæs þe hie gesohton   Sennera feld
swa þa foremeahtige   folces ræswan,
1670 þa yldestan   oft and gelome
liðsum gewunedon;   lárum sohton
weras to weorce   and to wrohtscipe,
oðþæt for wlence   and for wonhygdum
cyðdon cræft heora   ceastre[325] worhton
and to heofnum úp   hlǽdræ rǽrdon,
strengum stepton   stænnene[326] weall
ofer monna gemet,   mærða georne,
hæleð mid honda.   Þa com halig God
wera cneorissa   weorc sceawigan,
1680 beorna burhfæsten,   and þæt beacen somed,
þe to roderum úp   rǽran ongunnon
Adames eaforan,   and þæs únrǽdes
stiðferhð Cyning   steore gefremede,
þa hé réðemód   reorde gesette

---

[324] MS *bearn*.
[325] -*ea*- are written over an original *m*.
[326] MS *stænnene*.

eorðbuendum úngelice,
þæt hie þære spæce sped ne ahton.
   Þa hie gemitton mihtum spedge,
teoche æt torre, getalum myclum,
weorces wisan, ne þær wermægða
1690 ænig wiste hwæt oðer cwæð.
Ne meahte[327] hie gewurðan weall stænenne
úp forð timbran ác hie earmlice
heapum tohlócon,[328] hleoðrum gedælde;
wæs óðerre[329] æghwilc worden
mægburh fremde siððan Metod tobræd
þurh his mihta sped monna spræce.
Toforan[330] þa on feower wegas
æðelinga bearn ungeþeode
on landsocne; him on laste bú
1700 stiðlic stantorr and seo steape burh
samod samworht on Sennar stod.
   Weox þa under wolcnum and wriðade
mægburh Semes oðþæt mon awóc
on þære cneorisse, cynebearna rím,
þancolmod wer, þeawum hydig.
Wurdon þam æðelinge eaforan acende,
in Babilone bearn afeded
freolicu tu and þa frumgaran,
hæleð higerofe hatene wæron
1710 Abraham and Ááron; þam eorlum wæs[331]
Frea engla bám freond[332] and aldor.
   Ða wearð Ááron eafora feded,

---

[327] MS *meah-/te*: p. 81. After 4 lines of text the rest of the page is filled with an illustration in two registers – there is some disgreement about who is being portrayed here; see the Art-Historical Commentary.
[328] MS *tohlódon*.
[329] MS *óðere*.
[330] p. 82. The lower part of this page contains an illustration in three registers to be read from the top to the bottom depicting the construction of the Tower of Babel – see the Art-Historical Commentary.
[331] MS *wees* with the first *e* altered to *a*.
[332] MS *freod*.

leoflic on life,   ðam wæs Loth noma.
Ða magorincas   Metode geþungon,
Abraham and Loth,   unforcuðlice,
swa him from yldrum   æðelu wæron
on woruldrice;   forðon hie wide nú
dugeðum demað   drihtfolca bearn.[333]

  Þá[334] þæs mæles wæs   mearc agongen
1720 þæt him Abraham   idese brohte,
wif to hame   þær he wic ahte,
fæger and freolic;   seo fæmne wæs[335]
Sarra haten,   þæs þe us secgeað bec.
Hie þa wintra fela   woruld bryttedon,
sinc ætsomne,   sibbe heoldon
géara mengeo –   nohwæðre gifeðe wearð
Abrahame þa gýt   þæt him yrfeweard
wlitebeorht ides   on woruld brohte,
Sarra Abrahame,   suna and dohtra.

1730 Gewat him þa mid cnosle   ofer Caldea folc
feran mid feorme   fæder Abrahames;
snotor mid gesibbum   secean wolde
Cananea land;   hine cneowmægas,
Metode gecorene   mid siðedon
of þære eðeltyrf   Abraham and Loth.
Him þa cynegóde   on Carran
æðelinga bearn   eard genamon,
weras mid wifum.   On þam wícum his
fæder Abrahámes   feorh gesealde,
1740 wærfæst hæle;   wintra hæfde
twa hundteontig,   geteled ríme,
and fife eac   þa he forð gewát

---

[333] MS *drihta bearnum*.
[334] p. 83. The Þ is 3-lines high and bold; it is lightly decorated but is not zoomorphic – it is in the same style as the Ð on p. 75 and A on p. 86. This style of large initial appears regularly throughout the rest of the manuscript.
[335] Added above the line.

  misserum fród metodsceaft séon.
   Ða se Halga spræc, heofonrices Weard,
  to Abrahame, éce Drihten:
  'Gewit þu nú feran and þine fare lǽdan,
  ceapas to cnosle; Carran[336] ofgif,
  fæder eðelstol. Far, swa ic þe hate,
  monna leofost, and þu minum wel
1750 larum hyre and þæt land gesec
  þe ic þe ælgrene ýwan wille,
  brade foldan. Þu gebletsad scealt
  on mundbyrde minre lifigan.
  Gif ðe ænig eorðbuendra
  mid wéan gréteð, ic hine wergðo on
  mine sette and módhete,
  longsumne nið; lisse selle,
  wilna[337] wæstme þam[338] þe wurðiað.[339]
  Þurh þe eorðbuende ealle onfoð,
1760 folcbearn freoðo and freondscipe,
  blisse minre and bletsunge
  on woruldríce. Wriðende sceal
  mægðe þinre monrim wesan
  swiðe under swegle[340] sunum and dohtrum
  oðþæt fromcyme folde weorðeð,
  þeodlond monig þine gefylled.'
   Him[341] þa Abraham gewat æhte lædan
  of Egipta eðelmearce,
  gumcystum gód, golde and seolfre
1770 swiðfeorm and gesælig swa him sigora Weard,

---

[336] MS *carram*.

[337] *n* over an erased letter which had an ascender (probably *l*).

[338] p. 84. After 6 lines of text the rest of the page is filled with an illustration in three registers depicting episodes in the life of Abram, to be read from top to bottom – see the Art-Historical Commentary. There is an oblong-shaped hole in the outer margin opposite lines 8-9.

[339] *-iað* is in a darker, heavier script and seems to be a correction.

[340] MS *segle* with *w* (*wynn*) added above.

[341] p. 85. There is enough space for an illustration in the lower part of this page (but there is not one).

Waldend usser þurh his word abead,
ceapas from Carran; sohton Canánea
lond and leodgeard. Þa com leof Gode
on þa eðelturf idesa lædan,
swæse gebeddan and his suhtrian
wif on willan. Wintra hæfde
fif and hundseofontig ða he faran sceolde,
Carran ofgifan and cneowmagas.
   Him þa feran gewat Fæder ælmihtiges
1780 lare gemyndig land sceawian
geond þa folcsceare be Frean hæse
Abraham wíde oðþæt ellenrof
to Sicem[342] com siðe spedig,
cynne Cananeis. Þa hine Cyning engla
Abrahame iewde selfa,
domfæst wereda and Drihten cwæð:

GOD'S PROMISE OF A KINGDOM TO ABRAHAM

   'Þis is seo eorðe þe ic ælgrene
tudre þinum torhte wille
wæstmum gewló on geweald dón,
1790 rúme ríce.' Þa se rinc Gode
wibed worhte and þa Waldende
lifes Leohtfruman lác onsægde
gasta Helme. Him[343] þa gyt gewat
Ábraham eastan eagum wlitan
on landa[344] cyst – lisse gemunde
Heofonweardes gehat, þa him þurh halig word
sigora Selfcyning soð gecyðde –
oðþæt drihtweras duguþum geforan

---

[342] MS *siem*.
[343] p. 86.
[344] MS *lande*.

    þær is botlwela Bethlem haten.
1800 Beorn bliðemod and his broðor sunu
    forð oferforan folcmæro land
    eastan mid æhtum, æfæste men
    weallsteapan hleoðu and him þa wic curon
    þær him wlitebeorhte wongas geþuhton.
     Abraham[345] þa oðere siðe
    wibed worhte; he þær wordum God
    torhtum cigde, tiber onsægde
    his Líffrean – him þæs lean ageaf
    nalles hneawlice[346] þurh his hand Metend –
1810 on þam gledstyde gumcystum til.
     Ðær ræsbora þrage siððan
    wicum wunode and wilna breac,
    beorn mid bryde oðþæt brohþrea
    Cananea wearð cynne getenge,
    hunger se hearda, hamsittendum,
    wælgrim werum. Him þa wishydig
    Abraham gewat on Egypte,
    Drihtne gecoren drohtað secan,
    fleah wærfæst wean; wæs þæt wíte to strang.
1820 Abraham maðelode, geseah Egypta
    hornsele hwite and hea byrig
    beorhte blican; ongan þa his brýd frea,
    wishydig wer, wordum læran:
     'Siððan Egypte eagum moton
    on þinne wlite wlitan wlance monige
    þonne æðelinga eorlas wenað,
    mæg ælfscieno þæt þu min sie
    beorht gebedda þe wile beorna sum

---

[345] The *A* is 4-lines high and bold; it is slightly decorated but is not zoomorphic – it is in the same style as the *Ð* on p. 75 and *Þ* on p. 86.
[346] MS *hnea lice*, with room for the missing *w* (*wynn*).

```
               him geagnian.   Ic me onegan³⁴⁷ mæg
1830    þæt me wraðra sum³⁴⁸   wæpnes ecge
        for freondmynde   feore beneote.
        Saga þu, Sarra,   þæt þu sie sweoster mín,
        lices mæge   þonne þe leodweras
        fremde fricgen   hwæt sie freondlufu
        ellðeodigra   úncer twega,
        feorren³⁴⁹ cumenra.   Þu him fæste hél
        soðan spræce;   swa þu minum scealt
        feore gebeorgan,   gif me freoðo Drihten
        on woruldríce,   Waldend usser,
1840    án Ælmihtig   swa he ǽr dyde,
        lengran lifes.   Se us þas lade sceop
        þæt we on Egiptum   áre sceolde
        fremena friclan   and us fremu secan.'
           Þa com ellenrof   eorl siðian,
        Abraham mid æhtum   on Égypte,
        þær him folcweras   fremde wæron,
        wine úncuðe.   Wordum spræcon
        ymb þæs wifes wlite   wlonce monige,
        dugeðum dealle;   him drihtlicu mǽg
1850    on wlite modgum   mænegum ðuhte,
        cyninges þegnum.   Hie þæt cuð dydon
        heora folcfrean   þæt³⁵⁰ fægerro lýt
        for æðelinge   idesa³⁵¹ sunnon
        ác hie Sarran   swiðor micle
        wynsumne wlite   wordum heredon,
```

---

[347] MS *on agen*.

[348] p. 89. The letters *xb* are written in the top margin to the left; see the note on p. 1 for clarification of this. There are two small, original holes in the parchment, but in both instances the text has been written around them so that there is no loss of text.
Pages 87-8 contain full-page illustrations depicting events in the life of Abram; that on p. 87 has two registers – see the Art-Historical Commentary.

[349] MS *feorren* with *n* altered from *m* by scraping.

[350] MS has the abbreviation sign for *and* (⁊).

[351] MS *idese*.

oðþæt he lædan heht   leoflic wif to
his selfes sele.   Sinces brytta,
æðelinga helm   heht Abrahame
duguðum stepan.   Hwæðere Drihten wearð,
1860 Frea Faraone   fah and yrre
for wifmyne;   þæs wraðe ongeald
hearde mid hiwum   hægstealdra wyn.
Ongæt hwæðere   gumena aldor
hwæt him Waldend wræc   witeswingum;
heht him Abraham tó   egesum[352] geðreadne
brego[353] Egipto,   and his bryd ageaf,
wif to gewealde;   heht him wine ceosan,
ellor æðelingas,   oðre dugeðe.
Abead þa þeodcyning   þegnum sinum,
1870 ombihtscealcum   þæt hie hine árlice
ealles onsundne   eft gebrohten
of þære folcsceare,   þæt he on friðe wære.
   Ðá Abraham   æhte lædde
of Egypta   eðelmearce;
hie ellenrofe   idese feredon,
brýd and begas   þæt hie tó Bethlem
on cuðe wic   ceapas læddon,
eadge eorðwelan   oðre siðe,
wif on[354] willan   and heora woruldgestreon.
1880 Ongunnon him þa bytlian   and heora burh ræran,
and sele settan,   salo niwian.
Weras on wonge   wibed setton
neah þam þe Abraham   æror rærde
his Waldende   þa westan com.
Þær se eadga eft   écan Drihtnes
niwan stefne   noman weorðade;

---

[352] There is an erased minim between this word and the next.
[353] p. 90.
[354] MS has the abbreviation sign for *and* (⁊).

tilmodig eorl   tiber onsægde
Þeodne engla,   þancode swiðe
lifes Leohtfruman   lisse and ára.

Abraham and Lot

1890   Wunedon[355] on þam wicum,   hæfdon wilna geniht
Abraham and Loth.   Ead bryttedon
oðþæt hie on þam lande   ne meahton leng somed
blædes brucan   and heora begra þær
æhte habban,   ác sceoldon árfæste
þa rincas þy   rumor secan
ellor eðelseld.   Oft wæron teonan
wærfæstra wera   weredum gemæne,
heardum hearmplega.   Þa se halga ongan
ara gemyndig   Abraham sprecan
1900   fægre to Lothe: 'Ic eom fædera þin
sibgebyrdum,   þu[356] min suhterga;
né sceolon unc betweonan   teonan weaxan,
wroht wriðian –   ne þæt wille God.
Ac wit synt gemagas;   unc gemæne ne sceal
elles awiht   nymþe eall tela
lufu langsumu.   Nu þu, Loth, geþenc
þæt unc modige   ymb mearce sittað,
þeoda þrymfæste   þegnum and gesiððum,
folc Cananea   and Feretia,
1910   rofum rincum.   Ne willað rumor unc
landriht heora;   forðon wit lædan sculon,
teon of[357] þisse stowe   and unc staðolwangas
rumor secan.   Ic ræd sprece,
bearn Arones,   begra uncer,

---

[355] The large initial **wynn** is 8-lines high and lightly decorated.
[356] p. 91. There are three extraneous letters written in the top margin – *a*, *s*, and the Latin abbreviation for *pro*.
[357] Preceded by extraneous *wit*.

soðne secge.   Ic þe selfes dóm
lífe, leofa.   Leorna þe seolfa
and geþancmeta   þine mode
on hwilce healfe   þu wille hwyrft don,
cyrran mid ceape   nu ic þe cyst abead.'

1920   Him þa Loth gewát   land sceawigan
be Iordane,   grene eorðan;
seo wæs wætrum weaht   and wæstmum þeaht,
lagostreamum leoht,   and gelíc Godes
neorxnawange[358]   oðþæt[359] nergend God
for wera synnum   wylme gesealde
Sodoman and Gomorran,   sweartan líge.
Him þa eard geceas   and eðelsetl
sunu Arones   on Sodoma byrig;
æhte sine   <ealle lædde>[360]

1930   beagas from Bethlem   and botlgestreon,
welan, wunden gold.   Wunode siððan
be Iordane   geara mænego.
Þær folcstede   fægre wæron,
men árlease,   Metode laðe;
wæron Sodomisc cynn   synnum þriste,
dædum gedwolene,   drugon heora selfra
ecne únræd.   Æfre ne wolde
þam leodþeawum   Loth[361] onfón
ác he þære mægðe   monwisan fleah

1940   þeah þe he on þam lande   lifian sceolde,
facen and fyrene   and híne fægre heold,
þeawfæst and geþyldig   on þam þeodscipe,
emne þon gelicost,   lara gemyndig
þe he ne cuðe   hwæt þa cynn dydon.

---

[358] MS *neoxna-*.
[359] MS *on þæt*.
[360] Not in the manuscript – reading from Krapp 1931 (p. 58).
[361] MS *leoht*. p. 92. The letters *xb* are written in the top margin to the left – see p. 1, note.

    Abraham wunode eðeleardum
    Cananéa forð; hine Cyning engla,
    Metod moncynnes mundbyrde heold,
    wilna wæstmum and worulddugeðum,
    lufum and lissum forþon his lof secgað
1950 wide under wolcnum wera cneorisse,
    foldwonga[362] bearn. He Frean hyrde
    estum on eðle ðenden he eardes breac,
    halig and higefrod; næfre hleowlora[363]
    æt edwihtan æfre weorðeð
    feorhbérendra forht and ácol,
    mon for Metode, þe him æfter á
    þurh gemynda sped mode[364] and dædum,
    worde and gewitte, wise þance
    oð his ealdorgedal oleccan wile.[365]
1960 Ða[366] ic aldor gefrægn Elamitarna
    frómne folctogan, fyrd gebeodan,
    Órlahomar; him Ambrafel
    of Sennar side worulde
    fór on fultum. Gewiton hie feower þa
    þeodcyningas þrymme micle
    secan suð ðanon Sodoman and Gomorran.

     Þa wæs guðhergum be Iordane
    wera eðelland wide geondsended,
    folde feondum. Sceolde forht monig
1970 bláchleor ídes bifiende gan
    on fremdes fæðm; feollon wergend
    bryda and beaga, bennum seoce.
    Hím þa togeanes[367] mid guðþræce

---

[362] MS *full wona*.
[363] MS *hleor lora*.
[364] MS *mod*.
[365] The Fitt number *.xxviii.* is written in the blank space at the end of this manuscript line.
[366] The large initial is 5-lines high and lightly decorated; the following *A* is bold and larger than normal.
[367] MS *to-/geanes*. p. 93

fife fóran folccyningas
sweotum suðon, woldon Sodome burh
wraðum werian; þa wintra twelf[368]
norðmonnum ǽr niede sceoldon
gombon gieldan and gafol sellan
oðþæt þa leode leng ne woldon
1980 Elamitarna aldor swiðan
folcgestreonum ác him from swicon.

    Fóron þa tosomne – francan wæron hlude –
wraðe wælherigas; sang se wanna fugel
under deoreðsceaftum, deawigfeðera,
hræs on wénan. Hæleð ónetton
on mægencorðrum, módum þryðge[369]
oðþæt folcgetrume gefaren hæfdon
síd tosomne suðan and norðan,
helmum þeahte. Þær wæs heard plega,
1990 wælgara wrixl, wigcyrm micel,
hlud hildeswég; handum brugdon
hæleð of scæðum hringmæled sweord,
ecgum dihtig. Þær wæs eaðfynde
eorle orlegceap se ðe ǽr ne wæs
niðes genihtsum. Norðmen wæron
suðfolcum swice; wúrdon Sódomware
and Gomorre, goldes bryttan,
æt þæm lindcródan leofum bedrorene,
fyrdgesteallum. Gewiton feorh heora
2000 fram þam folcstyde fléame nergan,
secgum ofslegene; him on swaðe feollon
æðelinga bearn, ecgum ofþegde,
willgesiððas. Hæfde wigsigor
Elamitarna ordes wísa,

---

[368] MS *xii*.
[369] MS *þrydge*.

```
            weold wælstowe.   Gewát seo wæpna laf
            fæsten secan;   fynd gold strudon,
            áhyðdan³⁷⁰ þa mid herge   hordburh wera,
            Sodoman and Gomorran   þa sæl ageald,
            mære ceastra.   Mægð siðedon,³⁷¹
2010        fæmnan and wuduwan,   freondum beslægene
            from hleowstole.   Hettend læddon
            út mid æhtum   Abrahames mæg
            of Sodoma byrig.   We þæt soð magon
            secgan furður   hwélc siððan wearð
            æfter þæm gehnæste   herewulfa sið,
            þara þe læddon Loth   and leoda god,
            suðmonna sinc,   sigore gulpon.

              Him³⁷² þa secg hraðe   gewat siðian,
            án gara laf   se ða guðe genæs,
2020        Abraham secan.   Se þæt órlegweorc
            þam Ebriscan   eorle gecyðde,
            forslegen swiðe   Sodoma folc,
            leoda duguðe   and Lothes sið.
            Þa þæt inwitspell   Abraham sægde
            freondum sinum;   bæd him fultumes
            wærfæst hæleð   willgeðoftan,
            Aner and Manre,   Escol þriddan;
            cwæð þæt him wære   weorce on mode,
            sorga sarost   þæt his suhtriga
2030        þeownyd þolode;   bæd him þræcrofe
            þa rincas þæs   ræd ahicgan,
            þæt his hyldemæg   ahreded³⁷³ wurde,
            beorn mid bryde.   Him þa broðor þrý
```

---

³⁷⁰ MS *áhudan*.
³⁷¹ p. 94.
³⁷² The large initial **H** is 5-lines high and lightly decorated. The Fitt number *xxviiii.* is written in the blank space before this line of text. The last word of the previous sentence, *gulpon*, is written to the right of this, with a wrapmark before it.
³⁷³ MS *ahred*.

æt spræce þære   spedum miclum
hældon hygesorge   heardum wordum,
ellenrofe,   and Abrahame
treowa sealdon   þæt hie his torn mid hím
gewræcon on wraðum   oððe on wæl feollan.[374]
       Þa se halga heht   his heorðwerod
2040 wæpna onfón.[375]   He þær wigena fand,
æscberendra,   eahtatiene[376]
and ðry hundred[377] eac   þeodenholdra,[378]
þara þe he wiste   þæt meahte wel æghwylc
on fyrd wegan   fealwe linde.
Him þa Abraham[379] gewat   and þa eorlas þry
þe him ǽr treowe sealdon   mid heora folcgetrume;[380]
wolde his mæg huru,
Loth alynnan   of laðscipe.
Rincas wæron[381] rofe,[382]   randas wægon[383]
2050 forð frómlice   on foldwege;
hildewulfas   herewicum neh
gefaren hæfdon.   Þa he his frumgaran,
wíshydig wer,   wordum sægde,
Þáres afera,   him wæs þearf micel
þæt hie[384] on twa healfe
grimme guðgemot   gystum eowdon
heardne handplegan;   cwæð þæt him se Halga,
éce Drihten   eaðe[385] mihte
æt þam spereniðe   spede lænan.

---

[374] MS *feallan*.
[375] MS *ofón* with first *n* added above and an insertion mark below.
[376] MS *.xviii.*
[377] MS *ccc*.
[378] MS *þeonden holdra*.
[379] p. 95.
[380] MS *folce getrume*.
[381] MS *waron*.
[382] *f* altered from *r*.
[383] *g* altered from *t*.
[384] MS *he*.
[385] MS *eað*.

2060　　Þa ic neðan gefrægn　under nihtscuwan
　　　　hæleð to hilde.　Hlyn wearð on wicum
　　　　scylda and sceafta,　sceotendra fyll,
　　　　guðflana gegrind;　gripon únfægre
　　　　under sceat werum　scearpe garas,
　　　　and feonda feorh　feollon ðicce,
　　　　þær hlihende　húðe feredon
　　　　secgas and gesiððas.　Sigor eft ahwearf
　　　　of norðmonna　niðgeteone,
　　　　æsctír wera.　Abraham sealde
2070　　wig to wedde,　nalles wunden gold
　　　　for his suhtrigan,　sloh and fylde
　　　　feond on fitte;　him on fultum grap
　　　　heofonrices Weard.　Hergas wurdon
　　　　feower on fleame,　folccyningas,
　　　　leode ræswan;　him on laste stod
　　　　hihtlic heorðwerod　and hæleð lagon,
　　　　on swaðe sæton,　þa þe Sodoma
　　　　and Gomorra　golde berófan,
　　　　bestrudon stígwitum.　Him þæt stiðe geald
2080　　fædera Lothes;　fleonde <wæron>[386]
　　　　Elamitarna　aldorduguðe
　　　　dóme bedrorene　oðþæt hie Domasco[387]
　　　　únfeor[388] wæron.　Gewát him Abraham ða
　　　　on þa wígrode　wiðertrod seon
　　　　laðra monna;　Loth wæs áhreded,
　　　　eorl mid æhtum,　idesa hwurfon,
　　　　wíf ón willan.　Wide gesawon
　　　　freora feorhbanan　fuglas slitan
　　　　on ecgwale.　Abraham ferede

---

[386] Not in the manuscript – reading from Thorpe 1832.
[387] -*masco* is written in the lower margin after a wrapmark.
[388] p. 96. The letters *xb* are in the upper margin to the left; see p. 1, note. The illustration in the lower part of the page is a later addition – see the Art-Historical Commentary.

2090 suðmonna eft sinc and brýda,
æðelinga bearn, oðle nior
mægeð heora magum. Næfre mon ealra
lifigendra hér lytle werede
þon wurðlicor wigsið áteah,
þara þe wið swa miclum mægne geræsde.
Þa[389] wæs suð þanon Sodoma folce[390]
guðspell wegen,[391] hwelc gromra wearð[392]
feonda fromlád. Gewat him frea léoda,
eorlum bedroren, Abraham sécan,
2100 freonda feasceaft; him ferede mid
Solomia sinces hyrde –
þæt wæs se mæra Melchisedec,
leoda bisceop. Se mid lácum com
fyrdrinca fruman fægre grétan,
Abraham árlice and him on sette
Godes bletsunge, and swa gyddode:
'Wæs[393] ðu gewurðod ón wera ríme
for þæs eagum þe ðe æsca tír
æt guðe forgeaf; þæt is God selfa
2110 se ðe hettendra herga þrymmas
on geweald gebræc and þe wæpnum læt
rancstræte forð rúme wyrcan,
huðe áhreddan and hæleð fyllan.
On swaðe sæton; ne meahton siðwerod
guðe spowan ác hie God flymde,
se ðe æt feohtan mid frumgarum
wið ofermægnes egsan sceolde
handum sinum and halegu treow,

---

[389] p. 97. The large initial **Þ** is 6-lines high and composed of thick black stokes – it is the plainest large initial thus far.
[390] MS *folc*.
[391] MS *wegan*.
[392] ð has been altered from earlier *a*.
[393] MS *wær*.

seo þu wið rodora Weard   rihte healdest.'

2120   Him þa se beorn   bletsunga lean

þurh hand ageaf   and þæs hereteames

ealles teoðan sceat   Abraham sealde

Godes bisceope.   Þa spræc guðcyning,

Sodoma aldor   secgum befylled,

to Abrahame   – him wæs ara þearf:

   'Forgif me mennen   minra leoda,

þe þu áhreddest   herges cræftum

wera wælclommum;   hafa þe wunden gold

þæt ǽr ágen wæs   ussum folce,

2130 feoh[394] and frætwa.   Læt me freo lædan

eft on eðel   æðelinga bearn,

on wéste wíc   wif and cnihtas,

earme wydewan.   Eaforan syndon deade,

folcgesiðas   nymðe fea áne,

þe me mid[395] sceoldon   mearce healdan.'

   Him þa Abraham   andswarode

ædre for eorlum,   elne gewurðod,[396]

dóme and sigore,   drihtlice spræc:

   'Ic þe gehate,   hæleða waldend,

2140 for þam Halgan   þe heofona is

<and>[397] þisse eorðan   Agendfrea,

wordum minum,   nís woruldfeoh

þe ic me ágan wille,

sceat ne scilling,   þæs ic on sceotendum,

þeoden mæra,   þines ahredde,

æðelinga helm   þy læs þu eft cweðe

þæt ic wurde,   willgesteallum,

eadig ón eorðan   ǽrgestreonum

---

[394] p. 98.
[395] *mid...Abraham*: added interlinearly above.
[396] *ge-* written over an erasure.
[397] Not in the manuscript – reading from Grein 1857.

Sodoma ríces;[398]   ác þu <selfa>[399] most heonon

2150   huðe lædan   þe ic þe æt hilde geslóh,

ealle buton dǽle   þissa drihtwera,

Aneres and Mamres   and Escoles.

Nelle íc þa rincas   rihte benǽman

ác hie me fulleodon   æt æscþræce,

fuhton þe æfter frofre.   Gewit þu ferian nú

hám hyrsted gold   and healsmægeð,

leoda idesa.   Þu þe laðra ne þearft

hæleða hildþræce   hwile onsittan,

norðmanna wíg;   ac nefuglas[400]

2160   under beorhhleoþum   blodige[401] sittað,

þeodherga wæle[402]   þicce gefylled.'

   Gewát him þa se healdend   hám siðian

mid þy hereteame   þe him se halga forgeaf,

Ebréa leod   árna gemyndig.[403]

Þa gén Abrahame   eowde selfa

heofona Heahcyning[404]   halige spræce,

trymede tilmodigne   and hím tó reordode:

'Meda[405] syndon micla þina;   ne læt þu þe þín mód asealcan,

wærfæst willan mínes.   Ne þearft þu þe wiht ondrædan

2170   þenden þu mine láre læstest   ac ic þe lifigende her

wið weana gehwam[406]   wreo and scylde

folmum minum;   ne þearft þu forht wesan.'

   Abraham[407] þa   andswarode,

dǽdróf Drihtne sinum,   frægn[408] hine dægrime frod:

---

[398] MS *rice*.
[399] Not in the manuscript – reading from Grein 1865.
[400] MS *éacne fuglas*.
[401] MS *blodig*.
[402] MS *wæl*.
[403] MS *gem* at the end of the manuscript line and *myndig* in the next line, with the *m-* partly erased.
[404] *healf trymt* is written in the margin, an instruction to leave half the page blank for a planned illustration.
[405] p. 99. The upper part of this page left blank for an illustration.
[406] *-wa-* over an erasure.
[407] The large initial is 4-lines high and lightly decorated.
[408] *-æg-* written over an erasure.

'Hwæt gifest þu me, gasta Waldend,
freomanna to frofre nú íc þus feasceaft eom?
Ne þearf íc yrfestol eaforan bytlian
ænegum minra ác me æfter sculon
mine woruldmagas welan bryttian.
2180 Ne sealdest þu me sunu; fórðon mec sorg dreceð
on sefan swiðe; ic sylf ne mæg
ræd⁴⁰⁹ ahýcgan. Gæð gerefa mín
fægen freobearnum; fæste mynteð
ingeþancum þæt me æfter sie
eaforan síne yrfeweardas.
Geseoð þæt me of brýde bearn ne wócon.'
    Him þa ædre God andswarode:
'Næfre geréfan rædað þine
eafora yrfe ác þin agen bearn
2190 frætwa healdeð þonne þin flæsc ligeð.
Sceawa heofon, <and>⁴¹⁰ hyrste gerím,
rodores tungel þa nu rume heora
wuldorfæstne wlite wide dælað
ofer brad brymu beorhte scinan.
Swilc bið mægburge⁴¹¹ menigo þinre
folcbearnum frome; ne læt þu þin ferhð wesan
sorgum asæled.⁴¹² Gíen þe sunu weorðeð,
bearn of bryde þurh gebyrd cumen
se ðe æfter bið yrfes hýrde,
2200 gode mǽre. Ne geomra þu;
ic eom se Waldend se þe for wintra fela
of Caldea ceastre alædde,
feowera⁴¹³ sumne, gehét þe folcstede

---

⁴⁰⁹ p. 100.
⁴¹⁰ Not in the manuscript – reading from Krapp 1931 (p. 66).
⁴¹¹ MS *mæg burh*.
⁴¹² MS *æsæled*.
⁴¹³ *o* altered from *w* (*wynn*).

wíde to gewealde. Ic þe wǽre nú,
mago Ebréa, mine selle
þæt sceal fromcynne folde þine,
sidland manig, geseted wurðan,
eorðan sceatas oð Eufraten,
and from Égypta eðelmearce
2210 swa mid niðas swa[414] Nílus sceadeð
and eft Wendelsǽ[415] wide ríce.
Eall þæt sculon agan eaforan þine,
þeodlanda gehwilc swa þa þreo wæter
steape stánbyrig streamum bewindað
famige flodas folcmægða byht.'
     Þa wæs Sarran[416] sár on móde,
þæt hím Abrahame ænig ne wearð
þurh gebedscipe bearn gemǽne,
freolic to frofre.[417] Ongann[418] þa ferhðcearig
2220 to were sinum wordum mæðlan:
     'Me þæs forwyrnde Waldend heofona
þæt ic mægburge moste þínre
rím miclian roderum under
eaforum þinum; nú íc eom órwena
þæt únc se[419] eðylstæf[420] ǽfre weorðe
gifeðe ǽtgædere. Ic eom geomorfrod;
drihten min, do swa ic þe bidde.
Hér ís famne, freolecu mæg,
ides Egyptisc, án ón gewealde.
2230 Hat þe þa recene reste gestigan,
and áfanda hwæðer Frea wille

---

[414] MS *twa*.
[415] MS *wendeð sæ*.
[416] *sara* at the end of the manuscript line, with second *a* erased, and *ran* at the beginning of the next line. *healf tmt* with an abbreviation mark above is written in the margin (see page 99, *healf trymt*).
[417] *-re* written below the end of the last line of text.
[418] p. 101. The upper part of this page has been left blank.
[419] MS *seo*.
[420] Followed by an erased letter with a descender.

   ænigne þe yrfewearda

   on woruld lætan þurh þæt wif cuman.'

    Þa se eadega wer idese larum

   geðafode, heht him þeowmennen

   on bedd gán bryde larum.

   Hire mod astah þa heo wæs magotimbre

   be Abrahame eacen worden.

   Óngan[421] æfþancum agendfrean

2240 halsfæst herian, higeþryðe wæg,

   wæs laðwendo, lustum ne wolde

   þeowdom þolian ác heo þriste ongan

   wið Sarran swiðe winnan.

    Þa ic þæt wif gefrægn wordum cyðan

   hire mandrihtne[422] módes sorge,

   sárferhð sægde and swiðe cwæð:

    'Ne fremest þu gerysnu and riht wið me;

   þafodest þu gena þæt me þeowmennen,

   siððan Ágar ðe, idese laste,

2250 beddreste gestah swa ic béna wǽs,

   drehte[423] dogora geham dædum and wordum

   unárlice. Þæt Agar[424] sceal <ongieldan>,[425]

   gif ic mót for þe míne wealdan,

   Abraham leofa; þæs sie Ælmihtig,

   <drihtna>[426] Drihten, déma mid unc twih.'[427]

    Hire þa ædre andswarode

   wishidig wér wordum sinum:

    'Ne forlæte ic þe, þenden[428] wit lifiað bú,

   árna lease ác þu þín agen most

---

[421] p. 102. The upper part of this page has been left blank.
[422] *-ih-* written over an erased letter.
[423] MS *drehta*.
[424] MS *agan*.
[425] Not in the manuscript – reading from Krapp 1931 (p. 67).
[426] Not in the manuscript – reading from Thorpe 1832.
[427] *h* added above *g* underpointed for deletion.
[428] MS *þen-/den*: p. 103. After 2 lines of text space has been left for an illustration.

2260 mennen áteon   swa þin mód freoð.'

Sarah and Hagar

    Ða[429] wearð únbliðe   Abrahames cwen,
hire worcþeowe   wrað on móde,
heard and hreðe,   higeteonan spræc
fræcne on fæmnan.   Heo þa fleon gewat
þrea and þeowdóm;   þolian né wolde
yfel and ondlean   þæs ðe ǽr dyde
to Sarran   ac heo on sið gewat
westen secan.   Þær hie wuldres þegn,
éngel Drihtnes   án gemitte
2270 geomormóde   se hie georne frægn:
    'Hwider fundast þu,   feasceaft ides,
siðas dreogan?   Þec Sarre ah.'
    Heo him ædre   andswarode:
'Ic fleah wean, wana   wilna gehwilces,
hlæfdigan hete,   hean of wicum
tregan and teonan;   nu sceal tearighleor[430]
on wéstenne   witodes bídan
hwonne of heortan   hunger oððe wulf
sawle and sorge   somed abrégde.'
2280   Hire þa se engel   andswarode:
'Ne ceara þu feor héonon   fléame dǽlan
somwist íncre   ác þu séce eft,
earna þe ára,   eaðmod ongin
dreogan æfter dugeðum,   wes drihtenhold.
Þu scealt, Agar,   Abrahame sunu
on woruld bringan;   ic þe wordum nú
mínum secge,   þæt se magorínc sceal
mid yldum wesan   Ismahel haten.

---

[429] The large initial is 5-lines high and has a heavy outline; the *A* is 2-lines high and written inside the bow of *Ð*.
[430] p. 104. The lower part of this page left blank for an illustration.

Se bið únhyre,   órlæggifre,
2290 <and>[431] wiðerbreca   wera cneorissum,
mágum sínum;   hine monige ón
wraðe winnað   mid wæpenþræce.
Of þam frumgaran[432]   folc awæcniað,[433]
þeod unmǽte;   gewit þu þinne eft
waldend sécan,   wuna þæm þe ágon.'

   Heo þa ædre gewat   engles larum
hire hlafordum,   swa se halga bebead,
Godes ǽrendgast,   gleawan spræce.
   Þa[434] wearð Abrahame   Ismǽl geboren,
2300 efne þa he on worulde   wintra hæfde
siex and eahtatig[435]   Sunu wéox and ðáh,
swa se engel ǽr   þurh his agen word,
fǽle freoðoscealc,   fǽmnan sægde.

   Þa[436] se Ðeoden   ymb ðreotine[437] gear,
éce Drihten   wið Abrahame spræc:
   'Leofa,[438] swa ic þe lære,   læst uncre wel
treowrædenne;   íc þe on tída gehwone
duguðum stepe.   Wes þu dǽdum fróm
willan mínes;   ic þa wǽre forð
2310 soðe gelæste   þe ic þe sealde geo
frofre to wedde   þæs þin ferhð bemearn.
Þu scealt halgian   hired þinne;
sete sigores tacn   soð ón gehwilcne
wæpnedcynnes,   gif þu wille on me
Hlaford habban   oððe holdne freond

---

[431] Not in the manuscript – reading from Sievers 1885.
[432] MS *frum garum*.
[433] MS *apæcniað*.
[434] p. 105. Space has been left for illustrations in the upper and lower parts of this page, with 4 lines of text in the middle separating them.
[435] MS *vi.* and *lxxx*.
[436] p. 106.
[437] MS *.xiii*.
[438] Glossed *lyfa* in the outer margin.

þinum fromcynne.   Ic þæs folces beo
Hyrde and Healdend,   gif ge hyrað me
breostgehygdum   and bebodu willað
mín fullian.   Sceal monna gehwilc
2320 þære cneorisse   cildisc wesan
wæpnedcynnes   þæs þe on woruld cymð,
ymb seofon niht   sigores tácne
geágnod me,   oððe of eorðan
þurh feondscipe   féor ádǽled,
ádrifen from duguðum.   Doð swa ic hate;
ic eow treowige,   gif ge þæt tacen gegaþ
soðgeleafan.   Þu scealt sunu agan,
bearn be bryde þinre   þone sculon burhsittende
ealle Ísáác hatan.   Ne þearf þe þæs eaforan sceomigan
2330 ác ic þám magorince   mine sylle
godcunde gife   Gastes mihtum,
freondsped fremum.   He onfon sceal
blisse mínre   and bletsunge,
lufan and lisse.   Of þam leodfruman
brad folc cumað,   bregowearda fela
rófe arísað,   ríces hyrdas,
woruldcyningas   wíde mære.'
   Abraham[439] ða   ofestum legde
hleor on eorðan,   and mid hucse bewand
2340 þa hleoðorcwydas   on hige sinum,
módgeðance.   He þæs mældæges
self ne wende   þæt him Sarra,
bryd blondenfeax   bringan meahte
on woruld sunu;   wiste gearwe
þæt þæt wif huru   wintra hæfde
efne hund,[440]   geteled rimes.

---

[439] p. 107. *Abraham*: the large initial is 5-lines high and lightly decorated; the following *A* is 2-lines high and bold.
[440] MS *.c.*

He þa Metode oncwæð missarum fród:

'Lifge Ismael larum swilce,

þeoden, þinum and þe þanc wege,

2350 heardrædne hyge, heortan strange,

to dreoganne dæges and nihtes

wordum and dædum willan þinne.'

Him þa fægere Frea ælmihtig,

éce Drihten andswarode:

'Þe sceal wintrum frod on woruld bringan

Sarra sunu, soð forð gán

wyrd æfter þissum wordgemearcum.

Íc Ismael estum wille

bletsian nú swa þu bena eart

2360 þinum frumbearne þæt feorhdaga

on woruldríce worn gebíde,

tanum tudre; þu þæs tiða beo.

Hwæðre íc Isace, eaforan þinum,

geongum bearne þam þe gen nís

on woruld cumen, willa spedum

dugeða gehwilcre on dagum wille

swiðor stépan and him soðe to

modes wǽre mine gelǽstan,[441]

halige higetreowa[442] and him hold wesan.'

2370 Abraham fremede swa him se Eca bebead,

sette friðotacen be Frean hǽse

on his selfes sunu; heht þæt segn wegan[443]

heah gehwilcne, þe his hina wæs

wæpnedcynnes, wære gemyndig,

gleaw on móde ða him God sealde

soðe treowa and þa seolf[444] onfeng

---

[441] MS *gelætan*.
[442] MS *hige treawa*.
[443] MS *wesan*.
[444] p. 108. After 4 lines of text, the rest of the page was left for an illustration.

torhtum tacne. Á his tir Metod,
domfæst Cyning, dugeðum iecte
on woruldrice; he him þæs worhte to
2380 siððan he on fære furðum meahte
his Waldendes willan fremman...[445]

Þa[446] þæt wif ahloh wereda Drihtnes
nalles glædlice ác heo gearum fród
þone hleoðorcwyde husce belegde
ón sefan swiðe. Soð ne gelýfde,
þæt þære spræce spéd folgode;
þa þæt gehyrde heofona Waldend
þæt on bure ahóf bryd Abrahames
hihtleasne hleahtor, þá cwæð halig Gód:
2390 'Ne wile Sarran soð gelyfan
wórdum mínum; sceal seo wyrd swa þeah
fórð steallian swa ic þe æt frymðe gehet.
Soð íc þe secge, on þas sylfan tíd
of idese bið eafora wæcned;
þonne ic þas ilcan oðre siðe
wíc gesece þe beoð wordgehát[447]
mín gelæsted. Þu on magan wlitest,
þin agen bearn, Abraham leofa.'[448]
Gewiton[449] him þa ǽdre ellorfúse
2400 æfter þære spræce spédum feran
of þam hleoðorstede, halige gástas,
lastas legdon – him wæs Lothes[450] mæg
sylfa on gesiðe – oðþæt hie on Sodoman,
weallsteape burg wlitan meahton.

---

[445] A folio has been excised here; it contained text corresponding to Gen. 18:1-11.
[446] p. 109.
[447] MS *worn gehat*.
[448] The Fitt number *xxxiiii.* is written in the blank space after this.
[449] The large initial is 4-lines high and lacks decoration; the following *E* is bold.
[450] MS *leohtes*.

Gesawon ofer since   salo hlifian,

reced ofer readum golde.   Ongan þa rodera Waldend,

árfæst wið Abraham sprecan,   sægde hím únlýtel spell:

   'Íc on þisse byrig   bearhtm gehýre,

synnigra[451] cyrm   swiðe hludne,

2410 ealogalra gylp,   yfele spræce

werod under weallum habban;   forþon wærlogona sint

folces[452] firena hefige.   Íc wille fandigan nú,

mago Ebréa,   hwæt þa men dón

gif hie swa swiðe   synna fremmað

þeawum and geþancum,   swa hie on þweorh sprecað

facen and ínwit;   þæt sceal <fyr>[453] wrecan,

swefyl and[454] sweart líg   sare and grimme,

hat[455] and hæste   hæðnum folce…'[456]

Sodom and Gamorrah

   Weras[457] basnedon   wítelaces,[458]

2420 wean under weallum   and heora wif somed.

Duguðum wlance   Drihtne guldon

gód mid gnyrne   oðþæt gasta Helm,

lifes Leohtfruma   leng ne wolde

torn þrowigean   ác him to sende

stiðmód Cyning   strange twegen

áras síne   þa on æfentíd

siðe gesohton   Sodoma ceastre.

Hie þa æt burhgeate   beorn gemitton

sylfne sittan   sunu Arones,

---

[451] *g* altered from another letter with a descender.
[452] MS *folce*.
[453] Not in the manuscript – reading from Cosijn 1894.
[454] p. 110. After one and a half lines of text the rest of the page is blank.
[455] A letter with a curved descender erased after this, probably *g*.
[456] A folio has been excised here; its text corresponded to Gen. 18:23-33.
[457] p. 111. The Fitt number *.xxx.v.* is written in the top margin. The large initial is 6-lines high and lacks decoration. The lower part of this page is blank.
[458] MS *wíte loccas*.

2430 þæt þam gleawan were geonge þuhton
men for his éagum. Áras þa Metodes þeow
gastum togéanes, grétan eode
cuman[459] cuðlice; cynna gemunde
riht and gerisno and þam rincum bead
nihtfeormunge. Him þa Nergendes
æðele ærendracan[460] andswarodon:

    'Hafa árna þanc þara þe þu únc bude;
wit be þisse stræte stille þencað
sæles bídan siððan sunnan[461] eft
2440 forð tó morgen Metod úp forlæt.'
Þa[462] to fotum Loth
þam giestum hnah and him georne bead
reste and gereorda and his recedes hleow
and þegnunge. Hie ón þanc curon
æðelinges ést, eodon sona
swa him se Ebrisca eorl wisade,
ín undor edoras. Þær him se æðela geaf,
gleawferhð hæle, giestliðnysse
fægre on flette oðþæt forð gewát
2450 ǽfenscíma. Þa com æfter niht
on lást dæge; lagustreamas wreah,
þrym mid þystro þisses lifes,
sǽs and sídland. Comon Sodomware,
geonge and ealde, Gode únleofe
corðrum miclum cuman ácsian
þæt hie behæfdon herges mægne
Lóth mid giestum. Heton lædan út
of þam hean hofe halige áras,
weras to gewealde wordum cwædon

---

[459] MS *cum* with *an* added above and an insertion mark below.
[460] MS *ærendran*.
[461] MS *sunne*.
[462] p. 112. The lower part of this page is blank.

2460 þæt mid þam hæleðum   hæman wolden
     únscomlice,   árna ne gýmden.

         Þa[463] aras hraðe   se ðe oft rǽd ongeat,
     Lóth on recede,   eode lungre út,
     spræc þa ofer ealle   æðelinga gedriht
     sunu Árones,   snytra gemyndig:
         'Hér syndon inne   únwemme twa
     dohtor míne.   Doð, swa ic eow bidde
     — ne can þara idesa   owðer gieta
     þurh gebedscipe   beorna neawest —
2470 and geswicað þære synne.   Íc eow sylle þa,
     ǽr ge sceonde   wið gesceapu fremmen,
     úngifre yfel   ylda bearnum.
     Ónfoð þæm fæmnum;   lætað frið ágon
     gistas míne   þa ic for Gode wille
     gemundbyrdan,   gif íc mót, for eow.'
         Him[464] þa seo mænigeo   þurh gemǽne word,
     árlease cyn,   andswarode:
         'Þis þinceð gerisne   and riht micel
     þæt þu ðe áferige   of þisse folcsceare;
2480 þu þas werðeode   wræccan laste
     freonda feasceaft   feorran gesohtest,
     wineþearfende.[465]   Wilt ðu, gif þu most,
     wesan usser hér   aldordéma,
     leodum lareow?'   Þa ic on Lothe gefrægn
     hæðne heremæcgas   hándum gripan,
     faum folmum.   Him fylston wel
     gystas síne   and hine of gromra þá,
     cuman árfæste,   clommum abrugdon
     ín under edoras   and þa ofstlice
2490 anra gehwilcum   ymbstandendra

---

[463] p. 113. The lower part of this page is blank.
[464] p. 114. The upper part of this page is blank.
[465] MS *þine þearfende*.

folces Sodoma   fæste forsǽton
heafodsiena;   wearð eal here sona
burhwarena blind.[466]   Abrecan ne meahton
reðemóde   reced æfter gistum,
swa hie fundedon   ác þær fróme wǽron
Godes spellbodan.   Hæfde gistmægen
stiðe strengeo,   styrnde swiðe
werode mid wíte.   Spræcon wordum þa
fæle freoðoscealcas   fægre tó Lóthe:

2500   'Gif[467] þu sunu age   oððe swæsne mæg
oððe on þissum folcum   freond ænigne
éac þissum idesum   þe we her on wlitað,
alǽde of þysse leodbyrig   þa ðe leofe sien,
ofestum miclum   and þin ealdor nere,
þy læs þu forweorðe   mid þyssum wǽrlogan.
Unc hit Waldend heht   for wera synnum
Sodoma and Gomorra   sweartan líge,
fýre gesyllan   and þas folc slean,
cynn on ceastrum   mid cwealmþréa

2510 and his torn wrecan;   þære tide ís
neah geþrungen.   Gewit þu nergean þin
feorh foldwege.   Þe is Frea milde…'[468]

Him[469] þa ædre Loth   andswarode:
'Ne mæg íc mid idesum   aldornere mine
swa feor heonon   feðegange
siðe gesécan;   git me sibblufan
and freondscipe   fægre cyðað,
treowe and hyldo   tiðiað me.
Íc wat hea burh   hér ane neah,

---

[466] p. 115. After 5 lines of text, the rest of the page left blank for an illustration.
[467] p. 116. The lower part of this page is blank.
[468] A folio has been excised here; its text corresponded to Gen. 19:14-17.
[469] p. 117. The upper part of this page is blank.

2520 lytle ceastre. Lýfað me þær
áre and reste   þæt we aldornere
on Sigor up   secan moten.
Gif git þæt fæsten   fyre willað
steape forstandan,   on þære stowe we
gesunde magon   sæles bídan,
feorh generigan.' Him þa freondlice
englas árfæste   andswaredon:
  'Þu scealt þære bene,   nu þu ymb þa burh sprycest,[470]
tiða weorðan. Teng recene tó
2530 þam fæstenne;   wit þe friðe healdað
and mundbyrde   ne moton wyt
on wǽrlogum   wrecan tórn Godes,
swebban synnig cynn   ǽr ðon þu on Sǽgor þin
bearn gelǽde   and bryd somed.'
  Þa onette Abrahames mæg
tó þam fæstenne. Feðe ne sparode
eorl mid idesum[471]   ác[472] he ofstum forð
lastas legde   oðþæt he gelædde
bryd mid bearnum   under burhlocan
2540 in Sægor hís. Þa sunne úp,
folca friðcandel,   furðum eode
þa[473] ic sendan gefrægn   swegles Aldor
swefl of heofnum   and sweartne lig
werum to wite,   weallende fyr,
þæs hie on ærdagum   Drihten tyndon
lange þrage. Him þæs lean forgeald
gasta Waldend;   grap heahþrea
on hæðencynn. Hlynn wearð on ceastrum,

---
[470] MS *spryst*.
[471] This word is written in the bottom margin below *eorl mid*.
[472] p. 118. After 3 lines of text the rest of this page has been left blank for an illustration; the letters *xb* are written in its upper left corner – see p. 1, note.
[473] p. 119.

cirm arleasra cwealmes on ore,
2550 laðan cynnes. Lig eall fornam
þæt he grenes fond goldburgum in
swylce þær ymbutan unlytel dæl
sidre foldan geondsended wæs
bryne and brogan. Bearwas wurdon
to axan and to yslan, eorðan wæstma,
efne swa wide swa ða witelac
reðe geræhton rum land wera.
Strudende fyr steapes and geapes,
swogende <leg>,[474] forswealh eall geador[475]
2560 þæt on Sodoma byrig secgas ahton
and on Gomorra; eall þæt God spilde,
Frea mid þy folce. Þa þæt fyrgebræc,
leoda lifgedal, Lothes gehyrde
bryd on burgum under bæc beseah
wið þæs wælfylles. Us gewritu secgað
þæt heo on sealtstanes sona wurde
anlicnesse. Æfre siððan
se monlica – þæt is mære spell –
stille wunode þær hie strang begeat
2570 wite, þæs heo wordum wuldres þegna
hyran ne wolde. Nu sceal heard and steap
on þam wicum wyrde bidan,
Drihtnes domes, hwonne[476] dogora rim,
woruld gewite; þæt is wundra sum,
þara ðe geworhte wuldres Aldor.[477]

  Him[478] þa Abraham gewat ana gangan

---

[474] Not in the manuscript – supplied following Holthausen 1914. For critical discussion of the restoration of this defective manuscript line, see Krapp 1931 (p. 192).
[475] MS *eador*.
[476] MS *hwone* with a second *a* added above.
[477] *-dor* written in the bottom margin below *al-*.
[478] p. 121. Page 120 is entirely blank. The large initial is lightly decorated and the *IM* following it are 2-lines high and bold. The Fitt number *.xxxvii.* is written to the right in the top margin above the first line.

mid ǽrdæge　þæt he eft[479] gestod

þær wordum ǽr　wið his Waldend spræc

fród frumgára;　he geseah from foldan up

2580　wide fleogan　wælgrimne réc.

Hie þæs wlenco onwód　and wíngedrync

þæt hie firendæda　to frece wurdon,

synna þriste,　soð ofergéaton,

Drihtnes dómas　and hwa him dugeða forgeaf,

blæd on burgum.　Forþon him Brego engla

wylmhatne líg　tó wræce sende;

Waldend usser　gemunde wǽrfæst[480] þa

Abraham árlice,　swa he oft dyde

leofne mannan.　Loth generede,

2590　mǽg þæs oðres,　þa seo mænegeo forwearð.

Lot and his Two Daughters

　Ne dorste þa　dǽdróf hæle

for Frean egesan　on þam fæstenne

leng eardigean　ác him Loth gewat

of byrig gangan　and[481] his bearn somed

wælstowe fyrr　wíc sceawian

oðþæt hie be hliðe　heare dune

eorðscræf fúndon.　Þær se eadega Loth

wǽrfæst wunode,　Waldende leof,

dægrímes worn　and hís dohtor twa…[482]

2600　Hie[483] dydon swa;　druncnum eode

seo yldre tó　ǽr on reste

heora bega fæder.　Ne wiste blondenfeax

---

[479] *he eft*: MS *heft*.
[480] MS *wǽr fæst* with *ær* over an erasure.
[481] p. 122. After 4 lines of text the rest of this page has been left blank for an illustration.
[482] A folio has been excised here; its text corresponded to Gen. 19:31-2.
[483] p. 123. The lower part of this page is blank.

hwonne him fæmnan to bryde   him bu wæron,
on ferhðcofan   fæste genearwod[484]
móde and gemynde   þæt he mægða sið
wíne drúncen   gewitan ne meahte.

   Idesa wurdon eacne,   eaforan brohtan
willgesweostor   on woruld sunu
heora ealdan fæder;   þara æðelinga
2610 modor oðerne   Móab nemde,
Lothes dohter,   seo on life wæs
wintrum yldre.   Us gewritu secgeað,
godcunde béc,   þæt seo gingre
hire ágen bearn   Ammon héte;
of[485] þam frumgarum   folces[486] unrim,
þrymfæste twa   þeoda awocon.
Oðre þara mægða   Moabitare
eorðbuende   ealle hatað,
widmære cynn;   oðre weras nemnað,
2620 æðelinga bearn   Ammonitare.[487]

   Gewát[488] him þa mid bryde   broðor Arones
under Abimelech   æhte lædan
mid his hiwum.   Hæleðum sægde
þæt Sarra his[489]   sweostor wære,
Abraham wordum   – bearh his aldre –
þy he wiste gearwe   þæt he winemaga,
on folce lyt   freonda hæfde.
Þa se þeoden his   þegnas sende,
heht <hie>[490] bringan   to him selfum.

---

[484] MS *genearwot*.
[485] p. 124. The lower part of this page is blank.
[486] MS *folc*.
[487] MS *ammontare* with *i* added above *n*. The Fitt number *.xxxviii.* is written in the blank space below this manuscript line.
[488] The large initial is 4-lines high and not decorated; the following *E* is bold.
[489] MS *hi* with *s* added above and an insertion mark below.
[490] Not in the manuscript – reading from Krapp 1931 (p. 78). For critical discussion of this manuscript line, see Krapp 1931 (p. 193).

	Þa wæs ellþeodig oðre siðe
2630	

    2630 Þa wæs ellþeodig   oðre siðe
          wif Abrahames[491]   from were læded
          on fremdes fæðm;   him þær fylste þa
          ece Drihten,   swa he oft dyde,
          Nergend usser.   Com nihtes self,
          þær se waldend læg   wine druncen.
          Ongan[492] þa Soðcyning   þurh swefn sprecan
          to þam æðelinge   and him yrre hweop:
            'Þu Abrahames   idese gename,
          bryde æt beorne;   þe abregdan sceal
    2640 for þære dæde   deað of breostum
          sawle þine.'   Him symbelwerig
          sinces[493] brytta   þurh slǽp óncwæð:
            'Hwæt, þu ǽfre,   engla Þeoden,
          þurh þín ýrre wilt   aldre lætan,
          heah beheowan,[494]   þæne[495] þe her leofað
          rihtum þeawum,   bið on ræde fæst,
          módgeþance   and him miltse
          to þe seceð?   Me sægde ǽr
          þæt wif hire   wordum selfa
    2650 unfricgendum,   þæt heo Abrahames
          sweostor wære;   næbbe íc synne wið hie,
          facna ænig   gefremed géna.'
            Him þa ædre eft   ece Drihten,
          soðfæst Metod,   þurh þæt swefn óncwæð:
            'Agif Abrahame   idese síne,
          wif[496] to gewealde,   gif þu on worulde leng,
          æðelinga helm,   aldres recce.

---

[491] MS *abrames*.
[492] p. 125. The upper part of this page is blank.
[493] MS *synna*.
[494] MS *beheopan*.
[495] MS *þære*.
[496] p. 126. After 2 lines of text there is a large blank space followed by 10 more lines of text.

He is god and gleaw,   mæg self <wið God>⁴⁹⁷ sprecan,
geseon Sweglcyning;   þu sweltan scealt
2660 mid feo and mid feorme,   gif ðu þam frumgáran
bryde wyrnest.   He abiddan mǽg,
gif he ofstum me   ǽrendu⁴⁹⁸ wile
þeawfæst and geþyldig   þin abeodan
þæt íc þe lissa   lifigendum gíet
on dagum lǽte   duguþa brúcan
sinces gesundne.'   Þá slǽpe tobrægd
forht folces weard;   heht⁴⁹⁹ him fetigean tó
gesprecan⁵⁰⁰ síne,   spedum sægde
eorlum Abimeleh,   egesan geðread,
2670 Waldendes word.   Weras hím ondrédon
for þære dǽde   Drihtnes handa
sweng æfter swefne;   heht⁵⁰¹ sylf cyning
him þa Abraham tó   ofstum miclum.
  Þa reordode   rice þeoden:
'Mago Ebréa,   þæs þu me wylle
wordum secgean   hu geworhte⁵⁰² íc þæt,
siððan þu usic under,   Abraham, þine
on þas eðelturf   æhta læddest
þæt þu me þus swiðe   searo renodest?
2680 Þu ellþeodig   usic woldest
on þisse folcsceare   facne besyrwan,
synnum besmitan,   sægdest wordum
þæt Sarra þin   sweostor wǽre,
líces mæge,   woldest laðlice
þurh⁵⁰³ þæt wif on me   wrohte alecgean,

---

⁴⁹⁷ Not in the manuscript – reading from Grein 1857.
⁴⁹⁸ MS *ǽrenda*.
⁴⁹⁹ MS *heht* with *e* altered from *a*.
⁵⁰⁰ MS *sprecan*.
⁵⁰¹ p. 127. The upper part of this page is blank.
⁵⁰² *-orh-* written over an erasure.
⁵⁰³ MS *þur* with *h* added above and an insertion mark below.

órmæte yfel. Wé þe árlice
gefeormedon   and þe freondlice
on þisse werþeode   wíc getæhton,
land to lissum. Þu us leanast nú
2690　únfreondlice   fremena þancast.'[504]
　　　Abraham[505] þa andswarode:
'Ne dyde íc for facne   ne for feondscipe
ne for wihte þæs   íc þe wean uðe.
Ác ic me, gumena baldor,   guðbórdes sweng
leodmagum feor   lare gebearh
siððan me se Halga   of hyrde Frean,
mínes fæder   fyrn alædde.[506]
Ic fela siððan   folca gesohte,
wina uncuðra   and þis wif mid me,
2700　freonda feasceaft. Íc þæs fǽres á
on wénum sæt   hwonne me wraðra sum
ellþeodigne[507]   aldre beheowe
se ðe him þas idese eft   agan wolde.
Forðon íc wígsmiðum   wordum sægde
þæt Sarra[508] mín   sweostor wære
æghwær eorðan   þær wit earda leas
mid wéalandum[509]   winnan sceoldon.
Ic[510] þæt ilce dreah   on þisse eðyltyrf,
siððan ic þina,   þeoden mæra,
2710　mundbyrde geceas. Ne wæs me ón móde cuð
hwæðer on þyssum folce   Frean ælmihtiges
egesa wære   þa íc hér ærest cóm.
Forþón ic þegnum   þinum dyrnde
and sylfum þe   swiðost micle

---

[504] The Fitt number *xxxviiii.* is written in the blank space at the end of this manuscript line.
[505] p. 128. The large initial is lightly decorated; the following ***B*** is bold. The lower part of the page is blank.
[506] MS *alǽded*.
[507] MS *elþeodigne* with the second *l* added above and an insertion mark below.
[508] The first *r* has been altered.
[509] There is an extraneous insertion mark after the first *a*.
[510] p. 129. The lower part of this page is blank.

    soðan spræce   þæt me Sarra[511]
    bryde laste   beddreste gestáh.'
       Þa ongán Abimæleh   Abraham swiðan
    woruldgestreonum   and him his wif ageaf.
    Sealde him to bóte,   þæs þe he hís brýd genám,
2720 gangende feoh   and glæd seolfor
    and weorcþeos;[512] spræc[513] þa wordum eac
    to Abrahame   æðelinga helm:
     'Wuna mid usic   and þe wíc geceos
    on þissum lande   þær þe leofost sie,
    eðelstowe   þe ic ágan sceal.
    Wes us fæle freond,   we ðe feoh syllað.'
       Cwæð þa eft[514] raðe   oðre worde
    to Sarran   sinces brytta:
    'Ne þearf ðe on edwit   Abraham settan,
2730 ðin freadrihten   þæt þu flettpaðas,[515]
    mæg ælfscieno,   míne træde
    ac him[516] hygeteonan   hwitan seolfre
    deope béte;   ne ceara incit duguða
    of ðisse eðyltyrf   ellor secan,
    winas uncuðe   ac wuniað her.'
       Abraham fremede   swa hine his aldor heht,
    onfeng freondscipe   be Frean hæse,
    lufum and lissum;   he wæs leof Gode.
    Forðon he sibbe   gesælig dreah
2740 and his Scippende[517]   under sceade gefor,
    hleowfeðrum þeaht   her þenden lifde.
       Þa gien wæs yrre   God Abimelehe

---

[511] MS *sarran*.
[512] MS *weorc feos* with *s* over erased *h* followed by 2 more erased letters.
[513] p. 130. This word was the last word on the previous page and has been repeated inadvertently. After 10 lines of text there is a large blank space followed by 3 more lines of text.
[514] *þa eft* over an erasure and followed by 3 erased letters, the first of which had a descender.
[515] MS *flett waðas*.
[516] *m* over an erasure.
[517] p. 131. After 7 lines of text there is a large blank space followed by 7 more lines of text.

for þære synne þe he wið Sarrai
and wið Abrahame ǽr gefremede,
þa he gedælde him deore twa,
wif and wæpned. He þæs weorc gehléat,
frecne wíte. Ne meahton freo ne þeowe
heora bregoweardas bearnum ecan[518]
monrím mægeð ác him þæt Metod forstod

2750 oðþæt se halga his Hlaforde
Abraham ongan árna[519] biddan
écne Drihten. Him engla Helm
getigðode, tuddorsped onléac
folccyninge freora and þeowra,
wera and wifa; let weaxan eft
heora rimgetel rodora Waldend,
ead and æhta. Ælmihtig wearð
milde on móde, moncynnes Weard,[520]
Abimeleche, swa hine Abraham bæd.

The Birth of Isaac and the Exile of Hagar and Ishmael

2760 Þa[521] com féran Frea ælmihtig
to Sarrai swa he self gecwæð,
Waldend usser, hæfde wordbeot
leofum gelæsted, lifes Aldor
eaforan and idese. Abrahame woc
bearn of brýde, þone Brego engla
ǽr ðy magotudre modor wære
eacen be eorle, Isáác nemde.
Hine Abraham on <mid>[522] his agene hand
beacen sette swa him bebead Metod,

---

[518] MS *ágan*.
[519] MS *arra*.
[520] MS *wearð*.
[521] p. 132. The upper part of this page is blank.
[522] Not in the manuscript – reading from Cosijn 1894.

2770 wuldortorht ymb wucan, þæs þe hine on woruld
 to moncynne modor brohte.

 Cniht[523] weox and þag, swa him cynde wæron
 æðele from yldrum; Abraham hæfde
 wintra hundteontig[524] þa him wif sunu
 on þanc gebær. He þæs ðrage bád,
 siððan him ærest þurh his agen[525] word
 þone dægwillan Drihten bodode.

 Þa seo wyrd gewearð þæt þæt wif geseah
 for Abrahame Ismael plegan,
2780 ðær hie æt swæsendum sæton bu tu,
 halig on hige and heora hiwan eall,
 druncon and drymdon. Þa cwæð drihtlecu mæg,
 bryd to beorne: 'Forgif me, beaga weard,
 min swæs frea, hat siðian[526]
 Agar ellor and Ismael
 lædan mid hie. Ne beoð we leng somed
 willum minum gif ic wealdan mot.
 Næfre Ismael wið Isace,
 wið min agen bearn yrfe dæleð
2790 on laste þe þonne þu of lice
 aldor asendest.' Þa[527] wæs Abrahame
 weorce on mode þæt he on wræc drife
 his selfes sunu, þa com soð Metod
 freom on fultum, wiste ferhð guman
 cearum on clommum. Cyning engla spræc
 to Abrahame, éce Drihten:

 'Læt þe aslupan sorge of breostum,
 modgewinnan, and mægeð hire,

---

[523] The large initial is 4-lines high and not decorated. The Fitt number .xl. is in the centre of the blank space before this manuscript line.
[524] MS *hunteontig*.
[525] p. 133.
[526] MS *siððan*.
[527] p. 134. The lower part of this page is blank.

bryde þinre. Hát bu tu aweg
2800 Ágár feran and Ismael,
cniht of cyððe íc his cynn gedo
brad and bresne bearna tudre,
wæstmum spedig swa ic þe wordum gehét.'
Þa se wer hyrde his Waldende,
draf of wícum dreorigmód tú,
idese of earde and his ágen bearn…[528]

'Sweotol[529] ís and gesene þæt þe soð Metod
on gesiððe ís, swegles Aldor
se ðe sigor seleð snytru[530] mihtum
2810 and þin mód trymeð,
godcundum gifum. Forðon ðe giena speow,
þæs þu wið freond oððe feond fremman ongunne
wordum oððe dǽdum; Waldend scufeð,
Frea <on>[531] forðwegas folmum sínum
willan þinne. Þæt is wide cuð
burhsittendum. Ic þe bidde nu,
wine Ebrea, wordum mínum
þæt þu tilmodig treowa selle,
wǽra þina, þæt þu wille me
2820 wesan fæle freond fremena to leane,
þara þe ic to duguðum ðe gedón hæbbe
siððan ðu feasceaft feorran cóme
on þas werþeode wræccan laste.
Gyld[532] me mid hyldo þæt ic þe hneaw ne wæs
landes and lissa. Wes þissum leodum nú
and mægbúrge mínre árfæst
gif þe Alwalda, úre Drihten

---

[528] A folio has been excised here; it related to the text of Gen. 21:15-21.
[529] p. 135. The lower part of this page is blank.
[530] MS *snytrum*.
[531] Not in the manuscript – reading from Holthausen 1914.
[532] p. 136. After 7 lines of text there is a large blank space followed by 5 more lines of text.

scirian wille se ðe gesceapu healdeð
þæt þu randwigum rúmor móte
2830 on ðisse folcsceare frætwa dælan,
modigra gestreon, mearce settan.'
Ða Abraham Abimelehe
wǽre sealde þæt he wolde swá.

Siððan[533] wæs se eadega eafora Þáres
in Filistéa folce eardfæst,
leod Ebréa lange þrage,
feasceaft mid fremdum. Him Frea engla
wíc getæhte þæt[534] weras hatað
burhsittende Bersabéa lond.[535]
2840 Ðær sé halga héahsteap[536] reced,
burh timbrede and bearo sette,
weobedd worhte and his Waldende
on þam glædstede gild onsægde,
lác geneahe þam þe líf forgeaf,
gesǽliglic swegle under.

Þa þæs rinces se ríca ongán
Cyning costigan, cunnode georne
hwilc þæs æðelinges ellen wære,
stiðum wordum spræc him stefne tó:

AS A TEST OF OBEDIENCE, GOD ORDERS ABRAHAM TO SACRIFICE ISAAC

2850 'Gewít þu ofestlice, Abraham, féran,
lastas lecgan and þe lǽde míd
þin agen bearn; þu scealt Isáác me
onsecgan, sunu ðinne, sylf to tibre.
Siððan þu gestigest steape dúne,

---

[533] The Fitt number .xli. is written to the right above this manuscript line. There are 2 small holes in the parchment but they do not affect the text.
[534] MS þær.
[535] MS lono.
[536] MS heah-/steap: p. 137. After 4 lines of text there is a large blank space followed by 9 more lines of text.

         hrincg þæs hean lándes þe ic þe heonon getǽce,
         up þinum agnum fotum þær þu scealt ád[537] gegærwan,
         bǽlfýr bearne þinum and blótan sylf
         sunu mid sweordes ecge and [538] þonne sweartan lige
         leofes líc forbærnan and me lác bebeodan.'
2860   Ne forsæt he þy siðe ác sona ongann
         fysan to fóre; him wæs Frean engla
         word ondrysne and hís Waldend[539] leof.
         Þa se eadga Abraham síne
         nihtreste ofgeaf; nalles Nergendes
         hǽse wiðhogode ác hine se halga wer
         gyrde grǽgan sweorde, cyðde þæt him gasta Weardes
         egesa on breostum wunode. Ongan þa his esolas bǽtan
         gamolferhð goldes brytta, heht hine geonge twegen
         men mid siðian; mǽg wæs hís ágen þridda
2870   and he feorða sylf. Þa he fus gewát
         from his ágenum hofe Isáac[540] lædan,
         bearn únweaxen, swa him bebéad Metod.
         Efste þa swiðe and onette
         forð foldwege swá hím Frea tæhte
         wegas ofer westen oðþæt wuldortorht,
         dæges þriddan up ofer deop wæter
         órd arǽmde. Þa se eadega wer
         geseah hlifigan héa dúne
         swa him sægde ǽr swegles Aldor.
2880   Ða Abraham spræc to his ombihtum:
         'Rincas míne, restað incit
         hér on þissum wícum; wit eft cumað,
         siððan wit ǽrende uncer twega
         Gastcyninge agifen habbað.'

---

[537] p. 138. After 3 lines of text there is a large blank space followed by 10 more lines of text.
[538] MS *frea*.
[539] MS *waldende*.
[540] p. 139. After 1 line of text there is a large blank space followed by 12 more lines of text.

Gewat him þa se æðeling   and his ágen sunu
to þæs gemearces   þe him Metod tæhte,
wadan ofer wealdas.   Wudu bær sunu,
fæder fýr and sweord;   ða þæs fricgean ongann
wer wintrum geong   wordum Abraham:[541]
2890 'Wit[542] her fyr and sweord,   frea min, habbað;
hwær is þæt tiber   þæt þu torht Gode
to þam brynegielde   bringan þencest?'
   Abraham maðelode   – hæfde on án gehogod
þæt he gedǽde[543]   swa[544] hine Drihten het:
'Him þæt Soðcyning   sylfa findeð,
moncynnes Weard,   swa him gemet þinceð.'
   Gestah þa stiðhydig   steape dúne
úp mid his eaforan   swa him se Éca bebead
þæt he on hrófe gestod   héan landes
2900 on þære <stowe>[545]   þe him se Stránga to,
wærfæst Metod   wordum tæhte.
Ongan þa ád hladan,   æled weccan
and gefeterode   fét and honda
bearne sínum   and þa on bǽl áhóf
Isáác geongne   and þa ædre gegrap
sweord be gehiltum;   wolde his sunu cwellan
folmum sínum,   fýre scencan[546]
mæges dreore.   Þa[547] Metodes ðegn,
ufan engla súm,   Abraham hlude
2910 stefne cygde.   He stille gebád
áres spræce   and þam engle oncwæð;
him þa ofstum to   ufan of roderum

---

[541] This is written in the bottom margin beneath *wordum* and has a wrapmark before it.
[542] p. 140. The upper part of this page is blank.
[543] The manuscript reads *gedǽd* with *ed* erased after it.
[544] *s* seems to be over an erased *h*.
[545] Not in the manuscript – reading from Bouterwek 1854.
[546] MS *sencan*.
[547] p. 141. The upper part of this page is blank.

wuldorgast Godes   wordum mælde:

GOD'S ANGELIC MESSENGER INSTRUCTS ABRAHAM NOT TO SLAY ISAAC

'Abraham leofa,   ne sleah þin agen bearn
ác þu cwicne abrégd   cniht of áde,
eaforan þinne.   Him án wuldres God.
Mago Ebrea,   þu medum scealt
þurh þæs halgan hánd,   Heofoncyninges,
soðum sigorleanum   selfa onfon,
2920   ginfæstum gifum.   Þe wile gasta Weard
lissum gyldan   þæt þe wæs leofre[548] his
sibb and hyldo   þonne þin sylfes bearn.'
    Ád stod onǽled;   hæfde Abrahame
Metod moncynnes,   mæge Lothes,
breost geblissad   þa he him his bearn forgeaf,
Isáác cwicne.   Ða[549] se eadega bewlat,
rinc ofer exle   and him þær róm geseah
unfeor þanon   ænne standan,
broðor Árones,   brembrum fæstne.
2930   Þone Abraham genam   and hine on ád ahóf
ofestum miclum   for his ágen bearn.
Abrægd þa mid þy bille,   brynegield onhread,
reccendne weg   rommes blode,
onbleot þæt lác Gode,   sægde leana þanc
and ealra þara <sælða>[550]   þe he him sið and ǽr,
gifena Drihten,   forgifen hæfde.

---

[548] MS *leofra*.
[549] p. 142. The poem ends in line 8 of the manuscript and the rest of the page is blank.
[550] Not in the manuscript – reading from Grein 1857.

Exodus

      Hwæt.[1] Wé feor and neah   gefrigen habað
ofer middangeard   Moyses dómas,
wræclico wordriht,   wera cneorissum –
in uprodor   eadigra gehwam
æfter bealusiðe   bote lifes,
lifigendra gehwam   langsumne ræd –
hæleðum secgan.   Gehyre se ðe wille.

      Þone on westenne   weroda[2] Drihten,
soðfæst Cyning,   mid his sylfes miht
10   gewyrðode   and him wundra fela,
éce Alwalda   in æht forgeaf.[3]
He wæs leof Gode,   leoda aldor,
horsc and hreðergleaw,   herges wisa,
freom folctoga.   Faraónes cyn,
Godes andsacan,[4]   gyrdwíte band
þær him gesealde   sigora Waldend,
modgum magoræswan,[5]   his mága feorh,
onwíst eðles,   Abrahames sunum.
Heah wæs þæt handlean   and him hold Frea,
20   gesealde wæpna geweald   wið wraðra gryre,
ofercom mid þý campe   cnéomága fela,
feonda[6] folcriht.

GOD CALLS UPON MOSES TO RESCUE THE HEBREWS

      Ða wæs forma sið
þæt hine weroda God   wordum nægde

---

[1] p. 143. The 8-line high initial ***h*** is zoomorphic and extends into the upper margin; and the rest of the line is in smaller bold capitals. The Fitt number *xlii.* is above the last word in this line (**NEAH**).
[2] MS *werode*.
[3] *a* deleted by underpointing and then restored by placing another point above it.
[4] MS *andsaca*.
[5] MS *mago ræs wum*.
[6] Written twice.

  þær he him gesægde soðwundra fela,
  hu þas woruld worhte witig Drihten,
  eorðan ymbhwyrft and úprodor,
  gesette sigeríce and his sylfes naman,
  ðone yldo bearn ǽr ne cúðon,
  frod fædera cyn, þeah hie fela wiston.
30 Hǽfde[7] he þa geswiðed soðum cræftum
  and gewurðodne werodes aldor,
  Faraónes feond, on forðwegas.
  Þa wæs ingére ealdum witum
  deaðe gedrenced[8] drihtfolca mæst;
  hordwearda hryre heaf wæs geníwad,
  swæfon seledreamas, since berofene.
  Hǽfde mánsceaðan æt middere niht
  frecne gefylled, frumbearna fela,
  abrocene burhweardas. Bana wíde scrað,
40 lað leodhata, land drysmyde[9]
  deadra hræwum, dugoð forð gewát,
  wóp wæs wíde, worulddréama lýt.
  Wæron hleahtorsmiðum handa belocene,
  alyfed laðsið leode grétan;
  folc[10] férende, feond[11] wæs bereafod,
  hergas on helle. Heofung[12] þider becóm,
  druron deofolgyld. Dæg wæs mǽre
  ofer middangeard þa seo mengeo for.
  Swa þæs fæsten dreah fela missera,
50 ealdwerige, Egypta folc
  þæs þe hie wídeferð wyrnan þohton
  Moyses mágum, gif hie Metod lete,

---

[7] p. 144. The upper part of the page has been left blank for an illustration.
[8] *-renced* is written over an erasure in a different, larger hand.
[9] MS *dryr-/myde*.
[10] p. 145. The lower part of the page has been left blank for an illustration.
[11] MS *freond*.
[12] MS *heofon*.

on langne lust   leofes síðes.

    Fyrd wæs gefysed,   fróm se ðe lædde,
modig magoræswa,[13]   mægburh heora.
Oferfor he míd þý folce   fæstena worn,
land and leodweard   laðra manna,
enge anpaðas,   úncuð gelad
oðþæt hie on Guðmyrce   gearwe bæron

60   – wæron land heora   lyfthelme beþeaht –
mearchofu mórheald.   Moyses ofer þa,
fela meoringa,   fyrde gelædde.

    <H>eht[14] þa ymb twa niht   tírfæste[15] hæleð,
siððan hie feondum   oðfaren hæfdon,
ymbwicigean   werodes bearhtme
mid ælfere   Æthanes[16] byrig,
mægnes mæste   mearclandum ón.
Nearwe genyddon   on norðwegas,
wiston him be suðan   Sigelwara land,

70   forbærned burhhleoðu,   brune leode,
hatum heofoncolum.   Þær halig God
wið færbryne   folc gescylde,
bælce oferbrædde   byrnendne heofon,
halgan nette   hatwendne lyft.

Moses leads the Hebrews out of Egypt

    Hæfde wederwolcen   widum fæðmum
eorðan and uprodor   efne gedæled,
lædde leodwerod,   lígfýr adránc,
háte heofontorht.   Hæleð wafedon,

---

[13] MS *mago ræwa*.
[14] p. 146. A 4-line high space has been left for a large decorated initial (**h/H**) in the first line; the rest of the word (**EHT**) is in bold capitals.
[15] MS *tír fæstne*.
[16] MS *ætanes* with *h* added above and an insertion mark below.

```
             drihta gedrymost.   Dægsceades¹⁷ hleo
 80          wand ofer wolcnum;   hæfde wítig God
             sunnan siðfæt   segle¹⁸ ofertolden
             swa þa mæstrapas   men ne cuðon,
             ne ða seglróde   geseon meahton,
             eorðbuende   ealle cræfte,
             hu afæstnod wæs   feldhusa mæst
             siððan he mid wuldre   geweorðode
             þeodenholde.   Þa wæs þridda wíc
             folce to frofre;   fyrd eall geseah
             hu þær hlifedon   halige seglas,
 90          lyftwundor leoht;   leode ongéton,
             dugoð Israhela,   þæt þær Drihten cwom
             weroda Drihten,   wicsteal metan.
             Hím beforan foran   fýr and wolcen
             in beorhtrodor,   beamas twegen,
             þara æghwæðer   efngedælde
             heahþegnunga¹⁹   Haliges Gastes,
             deormodra sið   dágum and nihtum.
                Þa íc on morgen gefrægn   módes rófan
             hebban herebýman   hlúdan stefnum,
100          wuldres wóman.   Werod eall arás,
             modigra mægen   swa him Moyses bebéad,
             mære magoræswa,   Metodes folce,
             fús fýrdgetrum.   Forð gesáwon
             lifes latþeow   lifweg metan;
             swegl siðe weold,   sǽmen æfter
             foron flodwege.   Folc wæs on salum,
             <h>lud²⁰ herges²¹ cyrm.   Heofonbeacen astáh
```

---

[17] MS *dæg scealdes*.

[18] MS *swegle*.

[19] p. 147. The lower part of the page has been left blank for an illustration.

[20] p. 148. A 3-line high space has been left for a large, decorated initial (**h**) in the first line (there is an *h* prompt in the margin).

[21] MS *heriges* with the *i* underpointed for deletion.

æfena gehwam,   oðer wundor,
syllic æfter sunne[22]   setlráde beheold,
110   ofer léodwerum   líge scínan,
byrnende béam.   Bláce stodon
ofer sceotendum   scíre leoman;
scinon scyldhreoðan,   sceado[23] swiðredon,
neowle nihtscuwan   neah ne mihton
heolstor ahýdan;   heofoncandel barn.
Niwe nihtweard   nyde sceolde
wícian ofer weredum   þy læs him westengryre,
hár hæð\<broga\>,[24]   holmegum wederum
on ferclamme[25]   ferhð getwæfde.[26]
120   Hæfde foregenga   fýrene loccas,
bláce beamas;   bellegsan hwéop
in þam hereþréate,[27]   hatan líge
þæt he on westenne   werod forbærnde,
nymðe hie módhwate   Moyses hyrde.

    Scean scír werod,   scýldas lixton,
gesawon randwigan   rihte strǽte,
segn ofer swéoton,   oðþæt sǽfæsten
landes æt énde   leodmægne[28] forstód,
fus on forðweg.   Fýrdwíc arás;
130   wyrpton hie werige,   wíste genægdon
módige meteþegnas,   hyra mægen beton.
Bræddon æfter beorgum   siððan býme sang,
flotan feldhúsum.   Þa wæs feorðe wíc,
randwigena ræst   be þan Réadan Sǽ;
ðǽr on fýrd hyra   færspell becwóm,
oht inlende.   Egsan stódan,

---

[22] MS *sunnan*.
[23] MS *sceaðo*.
[24] -*broga* not in the manuscript – reading from Cosijn 1894.
[25] MS *ofer clamme*.
[26] MS *getwæf*.
[27] *r* altered from earlier *a*.
[28] MS *leo mægne*.

wælgryre weroda;   wræcmon gebád
laðne lástweard,   se ðe him lange ǽr
eðelleasum   onnied gescraf,
140   wean witum fæst.   Wǽre ne gýmdon,
ðeah þe se yldra cyning   ǽr ge...[29]

   <Þ>a[30] wearð yrfeweard   ingefolca,
manna æfter maðmum   þæt he swa miceles geðáh.
Ealles þæs forgeton   siððan grame wurdon
Egypta cyn   ymbe[31] antwig;
ða heo[32] his mægwinum   morðor fremedon,
wroht berenedon,   wære fræton.
Wæron heaðowylmas   heortan getenge,
mihtmod wera;   manum treowum
150   woldon hie þæt feorhlean   facne gyldan,
þætte hie[33] þæt dægweorc   dreore gebohte,
Moyses leode,   þær him mihtig God
on ðam spildsiðe   spede forgefe.
Þa him eorla mod   ortrywe wearð
siððan hie gesawon   of suðwegum
fyrd Faraonis   forð ongangan,
oferholt wegan,   eored lixan –
garas trymedon,   guð hwearfode,
blicon bordhreoðan,   byman sungon –
160   þufas þunian,   þeod mearc tredan,
on hwæl...[34]

   Hwreopon[35] herefugolas,   hilde grædige,

---

[29] A bifolium (4 pages) is lost here (between pages 148 and 149) – see the Gathering Analysis and Diagrams.
[30] p. 149. A 2-line high space has been left for a large decorated initial in the first line; the following *A* is in bold. The lower part of the page has been left blank for an illustration.
[31] MS *ymb*.
[32] Written twice.
[33] MS *he*.
[34] Folios are missing here – see the Gathering Analysis and Diagrams.
[35] MS *hwreopan* with the *a* underpointed for deletion and an *o* written above.

deawigfeðere   ofer drihtneum,[36]
wonn[37] wælceasega.   Wulfas sungon
atol æfenleoð   ætes on wénan,
carleasan deor,   cwyldróf beodan
on laðra last   leodmægnes fyl.[38]
Hreopon mearcweardas   middum[39] nihtum,
fleah fǽge gást,   folc wæs gehǽged.

170   Hwilum of þam werode   wlance[40] þegnas
mǽton mílpaðas   meara bógum.
Him þær segncyning   wið þone segn foran,
manna þengel,   mearcþreate rád;
guðweard gumena   grimhelm gespeon,
cyning cinberge   – cumbol lixton –
wiges on wénum,   wælhlencan[41] sceoc,
het his hereciste   healdan georne
fæst fyrdgetrum.[42]   Freond ónsegon[43]
laðum eagan   landmanna cyme;

180   ymb hine wǽgon   wigend únforhte,
háre heorowulfas[44]   hilde gretton,
þurstige þræcwiges,   þeodenholde.
Hæfde hím alesen   leoda dugeðe
tíreadigra   twá þusendo
þæt wæron cyningas   and cneowmágas,
on þæt eade riht,   æðelum deore.
Forðon ánra gehwilc   út alædde
wæpnedcynnes,   wigan æghwilcne
þara þe he on ðam fyrste   findan mihte.

---

[36] p. 150 has been left blank for an illustration.
[37] p. 151.
[38] MS *ful*.
[39] MS *midum* with a second *d* added above.
[40] An accent above *a* seems to have been scraped (though it is still visible).
[41] MS *hwæl hlencan*.
[42] MS *syrd getrum*.
[43] MS *ónsígon*.
[44] MS *heora wulfas*.

190 Wæron ingemen ealle ætgædere,
     cyningas on corðre. Cuð oft gebád
     horn on heape to hwæs hægstealdmen,
     guðþreat gumena, gearwe bæron.
     Swa þær eorp werod, écan læddon,
     lað æfter laðum, leodmægnes worn,
     þusendmǽlum; þider wæron fúse.[45]
     Hæfdon[46] hie gemynted to þam mægenhéapum
     tó þam ǽrdæge Israhela cynn
     billum abreotan on hyra broðorgyld.
200 Forþon wæs in wicum wóp up ahafen,
     átol æfenleoð, egesan stodon,
     weredon wælnet þa se wóma cwom.
     Flugon frecne spel, feond wæs ánmód,
     werud wæs wígblác oðþæt wlance forsceaf
     mihtig engel se ða menigeo beheold,
     þæt þær gelaðe mid him leng ne mihton
     geseon tosomne; sið wæs gedǽled.
     Hæfde[47] nydfara nihtlangne fyrst,
     þeah ðe him on healfa gehwam hettend seomedon,
210 mægen oððe merestream; nahton maran hwyrft.
     Wæron orwenan eðelrihtes,
     sæton æfter beorgum in blacum reafum,
     wean on wenum; wæccende bád
     eall seo sibgedriht somod ætgædere
     maran mægenes oð Moyses bebead
     eorlas on úhttíd ærnum bemum[48]
     folc somnigean, frecan árísan,
     habban heora hlencan, hycgan on ellen,
     beran beorht searo, beacnum cígean

---

[45] p. 152 has been left blank for an illustration.
[46] p. 153. The lower part of the page has been left blank for an illustration.
[47] p. 154.
[48] MS *benum*.

| 220 | sweot sande néar.   Snelle gemúndon
| | weardas wígleoð,   werod wæs gefysed,
| | brudon ofer burgum   – byman gehyrdon –
| | flotan feldhusum,   fyrd wæs on ofste.
| | Siððan hie getealdon   wið þam téonhete
| | on þam forðherge   feðan twelfe
| | móderófra;[49]   mægen wæs onhréred.
| | Wæs on ánra gehwam   æðelan cynnes
| | alesen under líndum   leoda duguðe
| | on folcgetæl   fiftig cista;
| 230 | hæfde cista gehwilc   cuðes werodes
| | garberendra,   guðfremmendra,
| | tyn[50] hund geteled   tíreadigra.
| | Þæt wæs wiglic werod;   wáce[51] ne gretton
| | in þæt rincgetæl   ræswan herges
| | þa þe for geoguðe   gyt ne mihton
| | under bordhreoðan   breostnet wera
| | wið flane feond   folmum werigean,
| | ne him bealubenne   gebiden hæfdon
| | ofer linde lærig,   lícwunde swor,
| 240 | gylpplegan gáres.   Gamele ne móston,
| | hare heaðoríncas,   hilde onþeon,[52]
| | gif him módheapum   mægen swiðrade
| | ác hie be wæstmum   <on>[53] wíg curon,
| | hú in leodscipe   læstan wolde
| | mód mid áran,   eac þan mægnes cræft,
| | gárbeames feng.
| | Þa wæs handrofra   here ætgædere,
| | fús forðwegas.   Fana up gerád,[54]

---

[49] MS róde rófa.
[50] MS .x.
[51] MS wác.
[52] p. 155. The lower part of the page has been left blank for an illustration.
[53] Not in the manuscript – reading from Bright 1912.
[54] MS rád.

    beama beorhtost;   bidon[55] ealle þa gen
250 hwonne siðboda   sæstreamum neah
    leoht ofer lindum   lyftedoras bræc.

Moses addresses the Hebrews and divides the Red Sea

    Ahleop[56] þa for hæleðum   hildecalla,
    bald beohata,   bord up ahof,[57]
    heht þa folctogan   fyrde gestillan
    þenden modiges meðel   monige gehyrdon.
    Wolde reordigean   ríces hyrde
    ofer hereciste   halgan stefne,
    werodes wisa   wurðmyndum spræc:
    'Ne beoð ge þy forhtran   þeah þe Fáraón brohte
260 sweordwigendra   síde hergas,
    eorla únrím;   him eallum wile
    mihtig Drihten   þurh mine hand
    to dæge þissum   dædlean gyfan
    þæt hie lifigende   leng ne moton
    ægnian mid yrmðum   Israhela cyn.
    Ne willað eow andrædan   deade feðan,
    fæge ferhðlocan,   fyrst ís æt ende
    lænes lifes.   Eow is lár Godes
    abroden of breostum;   ic on beteran ræd
270 þæt ge gewurðien   wuldres Aldor
    and eow Liffrean   lissa bidde,
    sigora gesýnto   þær ge siðien.
    Þis is se écea   Abrahames God,
    frumsceafta Frea   se ðas fyrd wereð,
    modig and mægenróf   mid þære miclan hand.'

---

[55] MS *butan*.
[56] p. 156. The initial *A* is 4-lines high, extending into the top margin. The Fitt number *xlvi.* is written to the right above the first line.
[57] MS *hof* with a prefixed *a* added above; *-hof* is over an erasure.

Hof[58] ða for hergum   hlude stefne
lifigendra leod[59]   þa he to leodum spræc:
    'Hwæt, ge nú eagum to   on lociað,
folca leofost,   færwundra sum,
280 hu ic sylfa sloh   and þeos swiðre hand
grene tacne   gársecges deop.
Yð úp færeð,   ofstum wyrceð[60]
wæter wealfæsten.[61]   Wegas syndon dryge,
haswe herestræta,   holm gerýmed,
ealde staðolas   þa ic ær ne gefrægn
ofer middangeard   men geferan,
fáge feldas   þa[62] forð heonon
in ece <tid>[63]   yðe þeahton,
sælde sægrundas.   Suðwind fornam
290 bæðweges blæst,   brim[64] is areafod,
sand sæcir spaw.[65]   Ic wat soð gere
þæt eow mihtig God   miltse gecyðde,
eorlas ærglade; ofest is selost
þæt ge of feonda   fæðme weorðen,
nu se Agend   up arærde
reade streamas   in randgebeorh.
Syndon þa foreweallas   fægre gestepte,
wrætlicu wægfaru   oð wolcna hrof.'
    Æfter þam wordum   werod eall aras,
300 modigra mægen. Mere stille bad.
Hofon herecyste   hwite linde,
segnas on sande.   Sæweall astah,
uplang gestod   wið Israhelum

---

[58] p. 157. The upper part of the page has been left blank for an illustration.
[59] MS *þeod*.
[60] *-eð* over an erasure.
[61] MS *wæter and wealfæsten*.
[62] p. 158.
[63] Not in the manuscript – reading from Holthausen 1895.
[64] MS *bring*.
[65] MS *span*.

andægne fyrst.   Wæs seo eorla gedriht
anes modes,
fæstum fæðmum   freoðowære heold.
Nalles hige gehyrdon   haliges lare
siððan leofes leoþ   læste near
sweg swiðrode   and sances bland.

310   Þa þæt feorðe cyn   fyrmest eode,
wod on wægstream,   wigan on heape
ofer grenne grund,   Iudisc feða
on órette on úncuð gelad[66]
for his mægwinum.   Swa him mihtig God
þæs dægweorces   deop lean forgeald
siððan him gesælde   sigorworca hreð
þæt he ealdordom   agan sceolde
ofer cynericu,   cneowmaga blæd.[67]

Hæfdon[68] him to segne,   þa hie on sund stigon
320   ofer bordhreoðan   béacen arǽred
in þam gárheape,   gyldenne leon,[69]
drihtfolca mæst,   deora cenost.
Be þam herewisan   hynðo ne woldon
be him lifigendum   lange þolian
þonne hie to guðe   gárwudu rærdon
ðeoda ænigre.   Þracu[70] wæs on óre,
heard handplega,[71]   hægsteald modige
wæpna wælslihtes,   wigend únfórhte,
bilswaðu blodige,   beadumægnes ræs,
330   grimhelma gegrind,   þær Iudas fór.

---

[66] For this whole line the MS reads: *án on órette ún cuð gelád.* The reconstruction was suggested by Krapp 1931 (p. 100); see the detailed discussion of critical literature there on p. 210.
[67] p. 159 has been left blank for an illustration.
[68] p. 160. The initial **h** is 4-lines high, extending into the top margin. The Fitt number *xlvii.* is written to the right above the first line.
[69] MS *leor.*
[70] MS *þraca.*
[71] MS *hand plega*; the scribe seems to have begun to write *heard* a second time and then tried to alter it to *hand*.

Æfter þære fyrde   flota módgade,[72]
Rubenes sunu.   Randas bæron
sǽwicingas   ofer sealtne mersc,
manna[73] menio;   micel ángetrum
eode únforht.   He his ealdordóm
synnum aswefede   þæt he siðor for
on leofes last.   Him on leodsceare
frumbearnes riht   freobroðor oðþáh,
ead and æðelo;   he wæs gearu swa þeah.
340 Þær <forð>[74] æfter him   folca þrýðum
sunu Siméones   sweotum comon;
þridde þeodmægen –   þufas wundon
ofer gárfare –   guðcyste onþrang
deawig sceaftum.   Dægwóma becwóm
ofer gársecge,[75]   Godes beacna[76] sum,
morgen mǽretorht;   mægen forð gewát.

   Þa þær folcmægen   for æfter oðrum,
ísernhergum;   án wísode
mægenþrymmum mǽst,   þy he mære wearð,
350 on forðwegas   folc æfter wolcnum,[77]
cynn æfter cynne.   Cuðe æghwilc
mægburga riht   swa him Moises bead,
eorla æðelo.   Him wæs an fæder,
leof leodfruma,   lándriht geþáh,
frod on ferhðe,   freomagum leof.
Cende cneowsibbe   cenra manna
heahfædera sum,   halige þeode,
Isráela cyn,   onriht Godes,
swa þæt órþancum   ealde reccað

---

[72] There is an elision mark between the two syllables indicating that they form one word.
[73] MS *man*.
[74] Not in the manuscript – reading from Grein 1857.
[75] MS *gár secges*.
[76] The scribe began to write an *n* after the first *a* but realised his error and altered it to a *c*.
[77] p. 161.

360 þa þe mægburge   mæst gefrunon,
    frumcyn feora,   fæderæðelo gehwæs.

        Niwe flodas   Nóe oferlað,
    þrymfæst þeoden   mid his þrim sunum
    þone deopestan   dréncefloda[78]
    þara ðe gewurde   on woruldríce.
    Hæfde him on hreðre   halige treowa;
    forþon he gelædde   ofer lagustreamas
    maðmhorda mæst,   míne gefræge.[79]
    On feorhgebeorh   foldan hæfde
370 eallum eorðcynne   éce[80] lafe,
    frumcneow gehwæs,[81]   fæder and moder
    tuddorteondra,[82]   geteled ríme[83]
    mismicelra   þonne[84] men cunnon,
    snottor sǽleoda.   Eac þon sǽda[85] gehwilc
    on bearm scipes   beornas feredon[86]
    þara þe under heofonum   hæleð bryttigað.

Abraham's Obedience recalled and the Promise of a Homeland

        Swa þæt wise men   wordum secgað
    þæt from Noe   nigoða wære
    fæder Abrahames   on folctale.[87]
380 Þæt ís se Abraham   se him engla God
    naman[88] niwan asceop;   éac þon neah and feor[89]
    halige héapas   in gehýld bebead,

---

[78] MS *drén floda*.
[79] MS *fr fræge*.
[80] A tear in the page from the end of this word to the gutter in the lower margin has been repaired by stitching.
[81] MS *gehæs*.
[82] Second *o* partly lost when the folio was torn and then repaired.
[83] A letter with a descender has been erased at the end of this word.
[84] Second *n* partly lost.
[85] *æ* partly lost.
[86] *o* partly lost.
[87] *e* partly lost.
[88] Second *a* partly lost.
[89] MS *for*, with *e* added above and an insertion mark below.

werþeoda geweald; he on wræce lifde.
Siððan he gelædde[90] leofost[91] feora
haliges hǽsum; heahlónd stigon[92]
sibgemágas[93] on Seone beorh.
Wǽre hie þær fundon, wuldor gesáwon,
halige heahtreowe, swa hæleð gefrunon.
Þær eft se snottra sunu Dauides,

390 wuldorfæst cyning, witgan larum
getimbrede tempel Gode,
alh[94] haligne, eorðcyninga
se wisesta on woruldríce,
heahst and haligost, hæleðum gefrægost,
mæst and mærost, þara þe manna bearn,
fira æfter foldan, folmum geworhte.
To þam meðelstede mágan gelædde
Abrahám Isáác; ádfýr onbran,
fyrst ferhðbana nó þy fægenra[95] wæs.

400 Wolde þone lastweard líge gesyllan,
in bǽlblyse beorna selost,
his swæsne sunu to sigetibre,
angan ofer eorðan yrfeláfe,
feores frofre ða he swa forð gebád,
leodum to láfe langsumne[96] hiht.
He þæt gecyðde þa he þone cniht genám
fæste mid folmum, folccuð getéag
ealde lafe – ecg grymetode –
þæt he him lifdagas leofran ne wisse

---

[90] The scribe initially wrote *gelifde*; he then erased the *if* and wrote an *æ* over the letters and added a second *d* above the line.
[91] *o* partly lost.
[92] The letters *-gon* are written to the right under the last line of the text block.
[93] p. 162.
[94] MS *alhn*.
[95] MS *fæg ra*, with *æ* accented; a letter (tall *e*?) erased after *g*.
[96] *e* partly lost.

410   þonne[97] he hyrde   Heofoncyninge.
      Úp arǽmde   <Abraham þa>[98]
      se eorl wolde slean   eaferan sinne
      únweaxenne,   ecgum[99] reodan
      magan míd[100] méce,   gif hine Metod[101] lete.
      Ne wolde him beorht Fæder   bearn ætniman,
      halig tiber   ác mid handa befeng.
      Þa him stýran cwom   stefn[102] of heofonum,
      wuldres hleoðor,   wórd æfter spræc:
      'Ne[103] sleh þu, Abraham,   þin ágen bearn,
420   sunu mid sweorde.   Soð is gecýðed,
      nu þin cunnode   Cyning alwihta
      þæt þu wið Waldend   wǽre heolde,
      fæste treowe   seo þe freoðo sceal
      in lífdagum   lengest weorðan,
      áwa to aldre   únswiciendo.
      Hu þearf mannes sunu   maran treowe?
      Ne behwylfan mæg   heofon and eorðe
      his wuldres word,   widdra[104] and siddra
      þonne befæðman mæge   fóldan sceattas,
430   eorðan ymbhwyrft   and uprodor,
      gársecges gín   and þeos geomre lyft.
      He[105] að swereð,   engla Þeoden,
      wyrda Waldend   and wereda God,
      soðfæst sigora   þurh his sylfes lif
      þæt þines cynnes   and cneowmága,

---

[97] An accent mark seems to have been erased above the *o*.
[98] Not in the manuscript – reading from Krapp 1931 (p. 102).
[99] MS *eagum*.
[100] *i* partly lost.
[101] MS *god*. A word for God that alliterates is required here — *metod* is suggested by Krapp 1931 (p. 102). This is an example of audible memory lapse.
[102] *n* partly lost.
[103] p. 163. The lower part of the page has been left blank for an illustration. Some text has been lost here – see the Gathering Analysis and Diagrams.
[104] *-id-* over erased letters, the second of which was an *r*.
[105] MS *ne*.

randwiggendra,   rim ne cunnon,
yldo ofer eorðan,   ealle cræfte
to gesecgenne   soðum wordum
nymðe hwylc þæs snottor   in sefan weorðe
440   þæt he ána mæge   ealle geríman
stanas on eorðan,   steorran on heofonum,
sǽbeorga sand,[106]   sealte yða;
ác hie gesittað   be sæm tweonum
oð Egipte   íncaðeode
land Cananea,   leode þine,
freobeárn fæder,   folca sélost…'[107]

Folc[108] wæs afǽred,   flodegsa becwóm
gastas geomre,   geofon deaðe hweop.
Wæron beorhhliðu   blóde bestemed,
450   holm heolfre spáw,   hream wæs on yðum,
wæter wæpna ful,   wælmist astáh.

The Egyptians are destroyed by the returning Flood Waters

Wæron Egypte   eft oncýrde,
flugon forhtigende,   fǽr ongéton,
woldon herebleaðe   hamas findan,
gylp wearð gnornra.   Him ongen genáp
atol yða gewealc,   ne ðær ænig becwóm
herges to háme   ác behindan beleac
wyrd mid wǽge.   Þær ǽr wegas lagon,
mere modgode,   mægen wæs ádrenced;
460   streamas stodon,   storm up gewát

---

[106] MS *sund*.
[107] There is a 20-line space in the lower part of this page for an illustration; pages 164-5, however, have been left blank for illustrations; the words *tribus annis transactis* are written on p. 164. A folio has been excised here; its text corresponded to Exod. 14:23-4.
[108] p. 166. The initial *F* is 4-lines high and lightly decorated; it extends into the top margin. The Fitt number *xlviiii.* is written to the right above the first line.

heah to heofonum, herewópa mæst.
Laðe cyrmdon – lyft up geswearc –
fægum stæfnum, flod blod gewód.
Randbyrig wæron rofene, rodor swipode
meredeaða mæst, modige swulton,
cyningas on corðre, cyre swiðrode
sǽs æt énde. Wigbord scinon
heah ofer hæleðum, holmweall ástah,
merestream modig. Mægen wæs on cwealme
470 fæste gefeterod, forðganges weg[109]
searwum æsæled, sand basnodon,[110]
witodre fyrde hwonne waðema stream,
sincalda sǽ, sealtum yðum
æflastum gewuna ece staðulas,
nacud nýdboda, neosan cóme,
fah feðegast se ðe feondum geneop.
Wæs seo hæwene lyft heolfre geblanden,
brim berstende blodegesan hweop,
sǽmanna sið oðþæt soð Metod
480 þurh Moyses hand[111] modge rymde,
wíde wæðde, wælfæðmum sweop.
Flod famgode, fæge crungon,
lagu land gefeol, lyft wæs onhrered,
wícon weallfæsten, wǽgas burston,
multon meretorras þa se Mihtiga sloh
mid halige hand, heofonríces Weard,
<on>[112] werbeamas. Wlance ðeode
ne mihton forhabban helpendra pað,
merestreames mod ác he manegum gesceod
490 gyllende gryre. Gársecg wedde,

---

[109] MS *nep.*
[110] MS *barenodon.*
[111] p. 167.
[112] Not in the manuscript – reading from Sedgefield 1922.

up ateah, on sleap.   Egesan stodon,
weollon wælbenna.   Witrod[113] gefeol
heah of heofonum   handweorc Godes,
famigbosma   flodwearde sloh,
unhleowan wæg,   alde méce
þæt ðy deaðdrepe   drihte swæfon,
synfullra sweot.   Sawlum lunnon
fæste befarene,   flodblác here,
siððan hie on bugan[114]   brun yppinge,
500   módewæga mæst.   Mægen eall gedréas
ða gedrencte[115] <wæron>[116]   dugoð Egypta,
Faraon mid his folcum.   He onfond[117] hraðe,
siððan <grund>[118] gestáh   Godes andsaca
þæt wæs mihtigra   mereflodes Weard;
wolde heorufæðmum[119]   hilde gesceadan,
yrre and egesfull.   Egyptum wearð
þæs dægweorces   deop léan gesceod
forðam þæs heriges   ham eft ne cóm
ealles úngrundes   ænig to láfe,
510   þætte sið heora[120]   secgan moste,[121]
bodigean[122] æfter burgum   bealospella mæst,
hordwearda hryre,   hæleða cwenum
ác þa mægenþreatas   meredeað geswealh,
spelbodan <eac>.[123]   Se ðe spéd ahte,
agéat gylp wera –   hie wið God wunnon.

---

[113] MS *wit rod*.
[114] MS *bogum*.
[115] MS *þegedrecte*.
[116] Not in the manuscript – reading from Krapp 1931 (p. 105).
[117] MS *on feond*.
[118] Not in the manuscript – reading from Grein 1857.
[119] MS *huru fæðmum*.
[120] MS *heoro*.
[121] p. 168 has been left blank for an illustration.
[122] p. 169.
[123] Not in the manuscript – reading from Blackburn 1907.

Moses Addresses the Hebrews Once Again

        Þanon Israhelum   éce rædas
        on merehwearfe   Moyses[124] sægde,
        heahþungen wer,   halige spræce,
        déop ǽrende. Dægword[125] nemnað
520   swa gýt werðeode,   on gewritum findað
        dóma gehwilcne   þara ðe him Drihten bebead
        on þam siðfáte   soðum wordum,
        gif onlucan wile   lifes wealhstód,
        beorht in breostum,   banhúses weard,
        ginfæsten god   gastes cǽgon.
        Run bið gerecenod,   ræd forð gæð,
        hafað wislicu   word on fæðme,
        wile meagollice   módum tæcan
        þæt we gesne ne sýn   Godes þeodscipes,
530   Metodes miltsa. He us ma onlyhð,
        nu us boceras   beteran secgað
        lengran lifwynna.[126] Þis is læne dream,
        wommum awyrged,   wreccum alyfed,
        earmra ánbid. Eðellease
        þysne gystsele   gihðum healdað,[127]
        murnað on móde,   mánhus witon
        fæst under foldan   þær bið fýr and wyrm,
        open éce scræf. Yfela gehwylces[128]
        swa nu regnþeofas   ríce dælað,
540   yldo oððe ǽrdeað. Eftwýrd cymð,
        mægenþrymma mǽst   ofer middangeard,
        dæg dædum fáh; Drihten sylfa
        on þam meðelstede   manegum démeð,

---

[124] MS *moyse*.
[125] MS *dæg weorc*.
[126] MS *lyft wynna*.
[127] MS *healdeð*.
[128] MS *gehylces*.

  þonne he soðfæstra[129] sawla lædeð,
eadige gastas, on uprodor,
þær <is>[130] leoht and líf, eac þon lissa blæd;
dugoð on dreame Drihten herigað,
weroda Wuldorcyning to wídan feore.

   Swa reordode ræda gemyndig[131]
550 manna mildost, mihtum swiðed,
hludan stefne; here stille bád
witodes willan, wundor ongeton,
modiges muðhǽl hé tó mænegum spræc:

   'Micel is þeos menigeo, mægenwísa trum,
fullesta mæst se ðas fare lædeð;
hafað us on[132] Cananéa cyn gelýfed
burh and beagas, bráde ríce;
wile nu gelæstan þæt he lange gehét
mid áðsware, engla Drihten,
560 in fyrndagum fæderyncynne,
gif ge gehealdað halige láre
þæt ge feonda gehwone forð ofergangað,
gesittað sigerice be sæm tweonum,
beorselas beorna. Bið eower blǽd micel.'

   Æfter þam wordum werod wæs on salum,
sungon sigebyman – segnas stodon –
on fægerne sweg; folc wæs on lande,
hæfde wuldres beam werud gelæded,
halige heapas on hild Godes.
570 Lífe gefegon[133] þa hie oðlæded hæfdon
feorh of feonda dóme þeah ðe hie hit frecne geneðdon,
weras under wætera hrofas. Gesawon hie þær weallas standan,
ealle him brimu blodige þuhton, þurh þa heora beadosearo wægon.

---

[129] MS *soðfæs-/tra*, p. 170. This page was at some stage ripped in half and has been repaired with clear tape.
[130] Not in the manuscript – reading from Grein 1857.
[131] The scribe initially began to write a *u* for the *y*.
[132] MS *ufon*.
[133] MS *gefeon*.

Hreððon hildespelle siððan hie þam <herge>[134] wiðforon.
Hófon hereþreatas hlúde stefne,
for þam dædweorce Drihten heredon,
weras wuldres sáng; wif[135] on oðrum,
folcsweota mæst, fyrdleoð golan[136]
aclum stefnum, eallwundra fela.

580 Þa wæs éðfynde Afrisc neowle[137]
on geofones staðe golde geweorðod.
Handa hofon halswurðunge,
bliðe wæron, bote gesawon,
heddon herereafes, hæft wæs onsǽled.
Ongunnon sǽlafe segnum dælan
on yðlafe, ealde madmas,
reaf and randas. Heo on riht scéodon[138]
gold and godweb, Iosepes gestreon,
wera wuldorgesteald. Werigend lagon
590 on deaðstede, drihtfolca mæ<st>.[139]

---

[134] Not in the manuscript – reading from Grein 1857.
[135] p. 171.
[136] MS *galan*.
[137] MS *meowle*.
[138] MS *scéo*.
[139] Two letters have been scraped away at the end of this word and are supplied here.

Daniel

THE HEBREWS IN CAPTIVITY IN BABYLON

  Gefrægn[1] ic Hebreos eadge lifgean
in Hierusalem, goldhord dælan,
cyningdóm habban, swa him gecynde wæs
siððan þurh Metodes mægen on Moyses hánd
wearð wíg gifen, wigena mænieo,
and hie of Egyptum út afóron,
mægene micle; þæt wæs módig cyn.
  Þenden hie þy rice rædan moston,
burgum wealdan,[2] wæs him beorht wela.
10 Þenden þæt folc mid him hiera fæder wære
healdan woldon, wæs him hyrde God,
heofonríces Weard, halig Drihten,
wuldres Waldend. Se ðam werude geaf
mod and mihte, Metod alwihta
þæt hie oft fela folca feore gesceodon,
heriges helmum, þara þe him hold ne wæs
oðþæt hie wlenco anwód æt winþege
deofoldǽdum, druncne geðohtas.
  Þa hie æcræftas áne forleton,
20 Metodes mægenscipe swa nó man scyle
his gastes lufan wið Gode dǽlan.
  Þa geseah ic þa[3] gedriht in gedwolan hweorfan,[4]
Israhela cyn únriht dón,
wommas wyrcean; þæt wæs weorc Gode.
Oft he þam leodum <to>[5] láre sende,

---

[1] p.173. The initial *G* is 3-lines high. The Fitt number *.l.* is written to the right above the first line.
[2] MS *weoldon*.
[3] MS *þe*.
[4] A letter erased before this word.
[5] Not in the manuscript; reading from Cosijn 1895 (p. 107).

                heofonríces Weard,   halige gastas,
                þa þam werude   wisdom budon.
                Hie þære snytro   soð gelyfdon
                lytle hwile   oðþæt hie[6] langung beswac
30   eorðan dreamas   eces rædes
                þæt hie æt siðestan   sylfe forléton
                Drihtnes domas,   curon deofles cræft.[7]
                Þa wearð réðemód   ríces ðeoden,
                únhold þeodum[8]   þam þe æhte geaf.
                Wisde[9] him æt[10] frymðe   ða ðe on fruman ær ðon
                wæron mancynnes   Metode dyrust,
                dugoða dyrust,   Drihtne leofost;
                herepað[11] <tæhte>[12]   to þære hean byrig,
                eorlum elðeodigum   on eðelland
40   þær Salem stód   searwum afæstnod,
                weallum geweorðod.   To þæs witgan fóron,
                Caldea cyn   to ceastre forð
                þær Israela   æhta wæron
                bewrigene mid weorcum;   to þam þæt werod gefór,
                mægenþreat mære,   manbealwes georn.
                Awehte þone wælnið   wera aldorfrea,
                Babilónes brego   on his burhstede,
                Nabochodonossor   þurh niðhete
                þæt he sécan ongan   sefan gehygdum
50   hu he Israelum   eaðost meahte
                þurh gromra gang   guman oðþringan.
                   Gesamnode þa   suðan and norðan
                wælhreow werod   and west foran[13]

---

[6] MS *me*.
[7] MS *cræst*.
[8] MS *þeoden*.
[9] MS *wisðe*.
[10] p. 174.
[11] MS *herepoð*.
[12] Not in the manuscript – reading from Schmidt 1907.
[13] MS *faran*.

```
         herige hæðencyninga   to þære héan byrig.
         Israela eðelweardas
         <hæfdon>¹⁴ lufan, lifwelan   þenden hie let Metod.
         Þa ic¹⁵ eðan gefrægn   ealdfeonda cyn
         wínburh wera.   Þa wigan ne gelyfdon,
         bereafodon þa receda wuldor   readan golde,
60       since and seolfre,   Salomones templ;
         gestrúdan gestreona   under stanhliðum,
         swilc eall swa þa eorlas   agan sceoldon
         oðþæt hie burga gehwone   abrocen hæfdon
         þara þe þam folce   to friðe stodon.
         Gehlodon him to huðe   hordwearda gestreon,
         feoh¹⁶ and frætwa¹⁷   swilc þær funden wæs
         and þa mid þam æhtum   eft siðedon,
         and gelæddon eac   on langne sið
         Israela cyn   on eastwegas
70       to Babilonia,   beorna únrim¹⁸
         under hand hæleð   hæðenum deman.
         Nabochodonossor   him on nýd dyde
         Israela bearn   ofer¹⁹ ealle lufen,
         wæpna lafe   to weorcþeowum.
         Onsende þá   sínra þegna
         worn þæs werudes   west²⁰ toferan
         þæt him þara leoda²¹   land geheolde,
         eðne eðel,   æfter Ebréum.
             Het²² þa secan   síne gerefan
80       geond Israela   earme lafe,
```

---

¹⁴ Not in the manuscript – reading from Blackburn 1907.
¹⁵ MS *eac*.
¹⁶ MS *féa*.
¹⁷ MS *freos*.
¹⁸ p. 175. A folio is missing between pages 174 and 175; see the Gathering Analysis and Diagrams. The bottom part of this page has been left blank, perhaps for an illustration.
¹⁹ MS *ótor*.
²⁰ MS *wes*.
²¹ MS *leode*.
²² p. 176. The bottom part of this page has been left blank for an illustration.

hwilc þære geogoðe   gleawost wære

boca bebodes   þe þær brungen wæs.

Wolde þæt þa cnihtas   cræft leornedon,

þæt him snytro on sefan   secgan mihte,

nales ðy þe he þæt moste   oððe gemunan wolde

þæt he þara gifena   Gode þancode

þe him þær to duguðe   Drihten scyrede.

Þa hie þær fundon   þry[23] freagleawe

æðele cnihtas   and ǽfæste,

90   ginge and gode   in godsæde:

án wæs Annanías,   oðer Azarías,

þridda Misael,   Metode gecorene.

Þa þry comon   to þeodne foran,

hearde and higeþancle   þær se hæðena sæt,

cyning[24] corðres georn   in Caldea byrig.

Þa hie þam wlancan   wisdom sceoldon,

weras Ebrea,   wordum cyðan,[25]

higecræft heane   þurh halig mod,

þa se beorn bebead,   Babilone weard,

100 swiðmod cyning,   sínum þegnum

þæt þa frumgaras   be feore dæde

þæt þam gengum þrym   gád ne wære

wíste ne wǽde   in woruldlife.

Nabochodonossor's First Dream

Þa[26] wæs breme   Babilone weard,

mǽre and modig   ofer middangeard,

egesful ylda bearnum.   No he ǽ fremede,

---

[23] MS *to*.
[24] It seems that the scribe began to write a *u* for *y*.
[25] MS *cyðdon*.
[26] p. 177. The upper part of this page has been left blank for an illustration. The initial Þ is 4-lines high and the following A is 2-lines high and bold. The Fitt number *.li.* is above the first line to the right.

ác in oferhygde æghwæs[27] lifde.
Þa þam folctogan on frumslæpe
siððan to reste gehwearf rice þeoden,
110 com on sefan hwurfan swefnes woma
hu woruld wǽre wundrum getéod,
úngelic yldum oð edsceafte.
Wearð him on slǽpe soð gecyðed,
þætte ríces gehwæs reðe sceolde gelimpan,
eorðan dreamas, ende wurðan.
Þa[28] onwoc wulfheort se ǽr wíngal swæf,
Babilone weard; næs him bliðe hige,
ác him sorh astah, swefnes wóma.
No he gemunde þæt him meted[29] wæs.
120 Het þa tosomne sinra leoda
þa wiccungdóm widost bæron,
frægn þa ða mænigeo hwæt hine gemætte
þenden reordberend reste wunode.
Wearð he on þam egesan ácol worden,
þa he ne wisse word ne angin
swefnes sínes; het him secgan þeah.
Þa him unbliðe andswaredon
deofolwitgan – næs him dom gearu
to asecganne swefen cyninge:
130 'Hu magon we swa dygle, drihten, ahicgan
on sefan þinne, hu ðe swefnede
oððe wyrda gesceaft wisdom bude,
gif þu his ǽrest ne meaht ór areccan?'
Þa[30] him únbliðe andswarode
wulfheort cyning, witgum sínum:
'Nǽron ge swa eacne ofer ealle men

---
[27] MS æghæs, with wynn added above.
[28] p. 178.
[29] MS metod.
[30] p. 179.

módgeþances   swa ge me sægdon,
and þæt gecwædon   þæt ge cuðon
mine aldorlege,   swa me æfter wearð,
140   oððe ic furðor   findan sceolde.
Nu[31] ge mætinge   míne ne cunnon,
þa þe me for werode   wísdom berað;[32]
ge sweltað deaðe   nymþe íc dóm wite
soðan swefnes   þæs min sefa myndgað.'
   Ne meahte þa seo mænigeo   on þam meðelstede
þurh witigdóm   wihte aþencean
ne ahicgan,   þa hit forhæfed gewearð
þætte hie sædon   swefn cyninge,
wýrda gerýnu   oðþæt witga cwóm,
150   Daniel to dóme,   se wæs Drihtne gecoren,
snotor and soðfæst   in þæt seld gangan.
Se wæs[33] ordfruma   earmre láfe
þære þe þam hæðenan   hyran sceolde.
Him God sealde   gife of heofnum
þurh hleoðorcwyde   Haliges Gastes
þæt him engel Godes   eall ásægde
swa his mandrihten   gemæted wearð.

Daniel Interprets the Dream

Ða[34] eode Daniel,   þa dæg lyhte,
swefen reccan   sínum frean,
160   sægde him wislice   wereda gesceafte,
þætte sona ongeat   swiðmod cyning
órd and ende   þæs þe him ýwed wæs.
Ða hæfde Daniel   dom micelne,

---

[31] MS *Ne*.
[32] MS *bereð*.
[33] MS *þæs*.
[34] p. 180. The upper part of this page has been left blank for an illustration.

blæd in Babilonia   mid bocerum,
siððan he gesæde   swefen cyninge
þæt he ǽr for fyrenum   onfón ne meahte,
Babilonie weard,   in his breostlocan.
No hwæðere þæt Daniel   gedón mihte
þæt he wolde Metodes   mihte gelýfan
170   ác he wyrcan ongan   weoh[35] on felda
þam þe déormóde   Díran héton,
se wæs on ðære ðeode   ðe swa hatte,
bresne Babilonige.   Þære burge weard
anne manlican   ofer Metodes est,
gyld of golde,   gumum arærde
for þam þe gleaw ne wæs,   gumríces weard,
reðe and rædleas,   riht…[36]

  Þa[37] wearð hæleða hlyst   þa hleoðor cwom
byman stefne   ofer burhware;
180   þa hie for þam cumble   on cneowum sæton,
onhnigon to þam herige   hæðne þeode,
wurðedon wihgyld,   – ne wiston wræstran ræd –
efndon unrihtdom,   swa hyra aldor dyde,
mane gemenged,   mode gefrecnod.
Fremde folcmægen,   swa hyra frea ærest,
unræd efnde   – him þæs æfter becwom
yfel endelean –   unriht dyde.
  Þær þry wæron   on þæs þeodnes byrig
eorlas Israela   þæt hie a noldon
190   hyra þeodnes dom   þafigan onginnan,
þæt hie to þam beacne   gebedu rærde
ðeah ðe ðær on herige   byman sungon;

---

[35] MS *woh*.
[36] There is a loss of text at this point; see the Gathering Analysis and Diagrams. The text on the missing folio corresponds to Dan. 3:2-6.
[37] p. 181. The upper part of this page has been left blank for an illustration.

ða wæron æðelum <god>[38] Abrahames bearn,[39]
wæron wærfæste, wiston Drihten
écne uppe, ælmihtigne.[40]
Cnihtas cynegode cuð gedýdon
þæt hie him þæt gold to gode noldon
habban ne healdan ác þone hean Cyning,
gasta Hyrde ðe him gife sealde.
200 Oft hie to bote balde gecwædon
þæt hie þæs wíges wihte ne rohton,
ne hie to þam gebede mihte gebædon
hæðen heriges wisa þæt hie þider hweorfan wolden,
guman to þam gyldnan gylde þe he him to gode getéode.
Þegnas þeodne sægdon þæt hie þære geþeahte wæron,
hæftas heáran in þisse héan byrig,
þa þis hégan ne willað ne þysne wig wurðigean,
þe ðu þe to <wuldre>[41] wundrum teodest…[42]

Ða[43] him bolgenmod Babilone weard
210 yrre andswarode, eorlum onmælde
grimme þam gingum and geocre oncwæð
þæt hie gegnunga gyldan sceolde
oððe þrowigean þreanied micel,
frecne fyres wylm nymðe hie friðes wolde
wilnian to þam wyrrestan, weras Ebrea,
guman to þam golde þe he him to gode teode.
Noldon þeah þa hyssas hyran lárum
in hige hæðnum. Hogedon georne
þæt æ Godes ealle gelæste,
220 and ne awacodon wereda Drihtne,

---

[38] Not in the manuscript – reading from Krapp 1931 (p. 116).
[39] p. 182. The lower part of this page has been left blank for an illustration.
[40] MS *ælmihtne*.
[41] Not in the manuscript – reading from Blackburn 1907.
[42] A folio has been lost here; see the Gathering Analysis and Diagrams.
[43] p. 183.

> ne þan mæ gehwurfe[44] in hæðendóm,
>
> ne hie to facne freoðo wilnedan
>
> þeah þe him se bitera deað geboden wǽre.[45]

The Hebrew Youths cast into the Fiery Funace

> Þa[46] wearð yrre ánmod cyning, het he ófn onhætan
>
> to cwale cnihta feorum forðam þe hie his cræftas onsocon.
>
> Þa he wæs gegleded[47] swa he grimmost mihte,
>
> frécne fyres lige þa he[48] þyder folc samnode
>
> and gebindan het, Babilone weard,
>
> grim and gealhmód, Godes spelbodan.
>
> 230 Het þa his scealcas scufan þa hyssas
>
> in bǽlblyse, beornas geonge.
>
> Gearo wæs se him geóce gefremede; þeah þe hie swa grome nydde
>
> in fæðm fyres lige, hwæðere heora feorh generede
>
> mihtig Metodes weard. Swa þæt mænige gefrunon,
>
> halige him þær help geteode, sende him of heán rodore
>
> God, gumena Weard, gast þone halgan.

Divine intervention

> Engel in þone ófn innan becwóm þær hie þæt áglac drugon,[49]
>
> freobearn fæðmum beþeahte under þam fyrenan hrofe.
>
> Ne mihte þeah heora wlite gewemman <owiht>[50]
>
> 240 wylm þæs wæfran líges, þa hie se Waldend nerede.
>
> Hreohmod[51] wæs se hæðena þeoden, het hie hraðe bærnan.
>
> Æled wæs ungescead micel; þa wæs se ofen onhæted,

---

[44] MS *gen hwyrfe*.
[45] A folio has been lost here; see the Gathering Analysis and Diagrams.
[46] p. 184. The upper part of this page has been left blank for an illustration. The initial Þ is 5-line high and the following *A* is a bold capital.
[47] MS *gelæded*.
[48] MS *þe* with *þ* altered to *h*.
[49] p. 185. The lower part of this page has been left blank for an illustration.
[50] Not in the manuscript – reading proposed by Cosijn 1895.
[51] p. 186. The lower part of this page has been left blank for an illustration.

ísen eall ðurhgleded.   Hine ðær esnas mænige
wurpon wudu on innan,   swa him wæs on wordum gedemed;
bǽron brandas on bryne   blácan fýres
– wolde wulfheort cyning   wall onsteallan,[52]
íserne ymb æfǽste –   oðþæt up gewát
líg ofer leofum   and þurh lust gesloh
micle máre   þonne gemet wære.

250 Ða se líg gewánd   on laðe men,
hæðne of halgum;   hyssas wæron
bliðemode,   burnon scealcas
ymb ofn útan,   álét gehwearf
teonfullum on teso;   ðær[53] to geseah
Babilone brego.   Blíðe[54] wǽron
eorlas Ebrea,   ofestum heredon
Drihten on dreame,   dydon swa hie cuðon
ofne on innan,   aldre generede.
Guman glædmode   God wurðedon,
260 under þæs fæðme   þe geflymed wearð
frecne fyres hæto.   Freobearn wurdon
alæten líges gange,   ne hie hím þær lað gedydon.
Næs him se sweg to sorge   ðon má þe sunnan scíma,
ne se bryne beot mæcgum   þe[55] in þam beote wæron;
ác þæt fyr fyr scyde   to ðam þe[56] ða scylde worhton,
hwearf on[57] þa hæðenan hæftas   fram þam halgan cnihton,
werigra wlite minsode,   þa ðe ðy worce gefǽgon.
    Geseah ða swiþmód[58] cyning,[59]   ða he his sefan ontreowde,
wundor on wite agangen –   him þæt wrǽclic þuhte.
270 Hyssas hale hwurfon   in þam hatan ofne,

---

[52] MS *onstealle*.
[53] p. 187. The upper part of this page has been left blank for an illustration.
[54] MS *biliðe*.
[55] MS *þen*.
[56] MS *we*.
[57] MS *hweorfon on*.
[58] p. 188.
[59] MS *cynig*.

ealle æfæste ðrý;   him eac þær wæs
án on gesyhðe,   engel Ælmihtiges.
Him þær <on ofne>[60]   owiht ne derede,
ác wæs þær inne   ealles gelicost
efne þonne on sumera   sunne scineð,
and deaw dryge[61]   on dæge weorðeð,
winde geondsawen;   þæt wæs wuldres God
þe hie generede   wið þam niðhete.

   Ða Azarias   ingeþancum
280 hleoðrade halig   þurh hatne líg,
<dreag>[62] dæda georn,   Drihten herede,
wer womma leas   and þa word ácwæð:

   'Metod alwihta, hwæt.   Þu eart mihtum swið
niðas to nergenne.   Is þin nama mære,
wlitig and wuldorfæst   ofer werðeode;
siendon þine dómas   in daga gehwam
soðe and geswiðde   and gesigefæste,
swa þu eac sylfa eart.

   Syndon þine willan   on woruldspedum
290 rihte and gerume,   rodora Waldend.
Geoca user[63] georne nu,   gasta Scyppend,
and þurh <hyldo>[64] help,   halig Drihten,
nu we[65] þec for þreaum   and for ðeonydum
and for eaðmedum   arna biddað,
líge belegde.   We ðæs lifgende
worhton on worulde,   eac ðon wóm dyde
user yldran;   for oferhygdum
bræcon bebodo   burhsittende,[66]

---

[60] Not in the manuscript – reading from Krapp 1931 (p. 118).
[61] MS *drias*.
[62] Not in the manuscript – reading from Cosijn 1895.
[63] MS *geo causer*.
[64] Not in the manuscript – reading from Thorpe 1832.
[65] Added above.
[66] MS *burhsittendum*.

had oferhogedon   halgan lifes.

300   Siendon we towrecene[67]   geond widne grund,

heapum tohworfene,   hyldelease;

is user lif   geond landa fela

fracoð and gefræge   folca manegum,

þa usic[68] bewræcon   to þæs wyrrestan

eorðcyninga   æhta gewealde,

on hæft heorugrimra,   and we nu hæðenra

þeowned þoliað.   Þæs þe þanc sie,

wereda Wuldorcyning,   þæt þu us þas wrace teodest.

Ne[69] forlet þu usic ane,[70]   éce Drihten,

310   for ðam miltsum   ðe ðec men hligað,

and for ðam treowum   þe þu tirum fæst,

niða Nergend,   genumen hæfdest

to Abrahame   and to Isááce

and to Iacobe,   gasta Scyppend.

Þu him þæt gehéte   þurh hleoðorcwyde

þæt þu hyra frumcyn   in fyrndagum

ícan wolde,   þætte æfter him

on cneorissum   cenned wurde

and seo mænigeo   mǽre wǽre,

320   had[71] to hebbanne   swa heofonsteorran

bebugað bradne hwyrft,   oððe[72] brimfaroþes,[73]

sæfaroða sand   geond sealtne wǽg

in[74] eáre[75] gryndeð,   þæt his únrim a[76]

in wintra worn   wurðan sceolde.

Fyl nu frumspræce,   ðeah heora feá lifigen.

---

[67] p. 189. The lower part of this page has been left blank for an illustration.
[68] MS *uséc*.
[69] p. 190.
[70] MS *ana*.
[71] MS *hat*.
[72] MS *oð þ(æt)*.
[73] MS *brim faro . þæs*.
[74] MS *me*.
[75] MS *are*.
[76] MS *únrima*.

Wlitiga þinne wordcwyde and þín wuldor on us.
Gecyð cræft and miht þæt þa[77] Caldeas
and folca fela gefrigen habbað
ða þe under heofenum hæðene lifigeað,
330 and þæt þu ána eart éce Drihten,
weroda Waldend, woruldgesceafta,
sigora Settend, soðfæst Metod.'
Swa se halga wer hergende wæs
Metodes miltse and his mihta sped
rehte þurh reorde. Ða of roderum wæs
engel ælbeorht ufan onsended,
wlitescyne wer on his wuldorhaman
se him cwóm to frofre and to feorhnere
mid lufan and mid lisse. Se ðone lig tosceaf,
340 halig and heofonbeorht, hátan fyres,[78]
tosweop hine and toswende þurh þa swiðan miht
ligges leoman[79] þæt hyra[80] líce ne wæs
owiht geegled, ác he on andan sloh
fyr on feondas for fyrendǽdum.
Þa wæs on þam ofne, þær se engel becwóm,
windig and wynsum, wedere gelicost
þonne hit on sumeres tid sended weorðeð
dropena drearung on dæges hwile,
wearmlic wolcna scúr. Swylc bið wedera cyst,
350 swylc wæs on þam fyre Fréan mihtum
halgum to helpe. Wearð se háta líg
todrifen and todwæsced þær þa dædhwatan[81]
geond þone ofen eodon, and se engel míd
feorh nerigende, se ðær feorða wæs,
Annanias and Azarías

---
[77] MS þæt.
[78] p. 191.
[79] MS leoma.
[80] MS hyre.
[81] Second a altered from e.

and Misael. Þær þa módhwatan
þry on geðancum Ðeoden heredon,
bǽdon bletsian bearn Israela
eall lándgesceaft écne Drihten,
360 ðeoda Waldend. Swa hie þry cwædon,
módum horsce þurh gemæne word:

THE 'BENEDICITE', THE SONG OF THE THREE YOUTHS

'Ðe[82] gebletsige, bylywit Fæder,
woruldcræfta wlite and weorca gehwilc.
Heofonas and englas and hluttor wæter,
þa ðe ofer[83] roderum on rihtne gesceaft
wuniað in wuldre ða þec wurðiað.
And þec, Ælmihtig, ealle gesceafte,
rodorbeorhtan tunglu, þa þe ryne healdað,
sunna and mona, sundor ánra gehwilc[84]
370 herige in hade. And heofonsteorran,
deaw and deor scur, ða ðec domige.
And þec, mihtig God, gastas lofige.
Byrnende fýr and beorht sumor
Nergend hergað. Niht somod and dæg,
and þec landa gehwilc, leoht and þeostro,
herige on háde, somod hát and ceald.
And þec, Frea mihtig, forstas and snawas,
winterbiter weder and wolcenfaru,
lofige on lyfte. And þec lígetu,
380 bláce, berhtmhwate, þa þec bletsige.
Eall eorðan grund, éce Drihten,
hyllas and hrusan and heá beorgas,

---

[82] The initial *Ð* is 4-lines high and the following *E* is written within its bowl. The Fitt number *.liii.* is written above the line to the right.
[83] MS *of.*
[84] p. 192.

sealte sæwægas,   soðfæst Metod,
éastream ýða   and upcyme,
wætersprync wylla   ða ðec wurðiað.
Hwalas ðec herigað,   and hefonfugolas,
lyftlacende,   þa ðe lagostreamas,
wæterscipe wecgað.   And wildu deor
and néata gehwilc   naman bletsie.
390 And manna bearn   módum lufiað
and þec Israela,   æhta Scyppend,
herigað ín hade,   Herran sinne.[85]
And þec haligra   heortan cræftas,
soðfæstra gehwæs   sawle and gastas,
lofiað Liffrean,   lean sellende
eallum <eadmodum>,[86]   éce Drihten.
Annanías ðec   and Adzarias
and Misael   Metod domige
breostgeðancum.   We þec bletsiað,
400 Frea folca gehwæs,   Fæder ælmihtig,
soð Sunu Metodes,   sawla Nergend,
hæleða Helpend,   and þec, Halig Gast,
wurðiað[87] in wuldre,   witig Drihten.
We ðec herigað,   halig Drihten,
and gebedum bremað.[88]   Þu gebletsad eart,
gewurðad[89] <wide>ferhð[90]   ofer worulde hrof,
Heahcyning heofones,   halgum mihtum,
lifes Leohtfruma,   ofer landa gehwilc.'
    Ða þæt ehtode   ealdor[91] þeode,
410 Nabochodonossor,   wið þam nehstum[92]

---

[85] MS þinne.
[86] Not in the manuscript – reading from Blackburn 1907.
[87] MS wurðað.
[88] e altered from i by adding a loop atop it.
[89] p. 193. The lower part of this page has been left blank for an illustration.
[90] MS ferhð.
[91] MS ealde.
[92] MS nehstam.

folcgesiþum: 'Þæt eower fela geseah,
þeode[93] mine,   þæt we þrý sendon,[94]
geboden to bǽle   in byrnende
fyres leoman;   nu ic þær feower men
geseo to soðe,   nales me sela[95] leogeð.'
 Ða cwæð se ðe wæs   cyninges ræswa,
wís and wordgleaw: 'Þæt is wundra sum
þæt we ðær eagum   on lociað.
Geðenc, ðeoden mín,   þine gerysna.
420 Ongyt georne   hwa þa gyfe sealde
gingum gædelingum.[96]   Hie God herigað
anne ecne   and ealles him
be naman gehwam   on neod sprecað,
þanciað þrymmes   þristum wordum,
cweðað he sie ána   ælmihtig God,
witig Wuldorcyning,   worlde and heofona.
Ában þu þa beornas,   brego Caldea,
út of ofne.   Nis hit ówihtes gód
þæt hie sien on þam laðe   leng þonne þu þurfe.'[97]
430 Het[98] þa se cyning to him   cnihtas gangan.
Hyssas hearde   hyrdon láre,
cyrdon cynegóde   swa hie gecýðde wǽron,
hwurfon hæleð geonge   tó þam hæðenan foran.
Wǽron þa bende[99] forburnene   þe him on banum lágon,
laðsearo leoda cyninges   and hyra líce geborgen.
Næs hyra wlite gewemmed,   ne nǽnig wroht on hrægle,
ne feax fýre beswæled   ác hie on friðe Drihtnes
of ðam grimman gryre   glade treddedon,
gleawmóde guman,   on gastes hyld.

---

[93] MS *þeoden*.
[94] MS *syndon*.
[95] MS *selfa*.
[96] MS *gædelinge*.
[97] p. 194 has been left blank for an illustration.
[98] p. 195. The lower part of this page has been left blank for an illustration.
[99] MS *benne*.

440   Ða[100] gewát se engel úp   sécan him éce dreamas
       on heanne hróf   heofona ríces,
       heh þegn and hold   halgum Metode.
       Hæfde on þam wundre gewurðod   ðe þa gewyrhto ahton.
       Hyssas heredon[101] Drihten   for þam hæðenan folce,
       septon[102] hie soðcwidum   and him sædon fela
       soðra tácna   oðþæt he sylfa gelyfde
       þæt se wǽre mihta Waldend   se ðe hie of ðam mirce generede.

Divine Intervention

       Gebead þa se bræsna   Babilóne weard
       swiðmód sinum leodum,   þæt se wære his aldre scyldig,
450   se ðæs onsoce   þætte soð wǽre
       mære mihta Waldend   se hie of þam morðre alysde.
       Agæf him þa his leoda lafe   þe þær gelædde wæron
       on[103] æhte[104] ealdfeondum   þæt hie áre hæfdon.
       Wæs heora blæd in Babilone,   siððan hie þone bryne fandedon,
       dom wearð æfter duguðe gecyðed   siððan hie Drihtne gehyrdon.
       Wæron hyra rædas ríce   siððan hie rodera Waldend,
       halig heofonrices Weard,   wið þone hearm gescylde.
       Þa[105] ic sécan gefrægn   soðum wordum,
       siððan he wundor onget,
460   Babilone weard,   þurh fýres bryne,
       hu þa hyssas þrý   hátan ofnes,
       færgryre fýres,   oferfaren hæfdon.
       Wylm þurhwódon,   swa him wiht ne sceod
       grim gleda nið,   Godes[106] spelbodan,
       frecnan fyres,   ác him frið Drihtnes

---

[100] p. 196. The lower part of this page has been left blank for an illustration.
[101] MS *heredo*.
[102] MS *stepton*.
[103] MS *and*.
[104] MS *nahte*.
[105] p. 197. The upper part of this page has been left blank for an illustration.
[106] There is an extraneous *ác* before this word.

     wið þæs egesan gryre   aldor gescylde.

      Ða se ðeoden ongan   geðinges wyrcan;

     het þa tosomne   síne leode

     and þa on þam meðle   ofer menigo bebead

470 wyrd gewordene   and wundor Godes

     þætte on þam cnihtum   gecyðed wæs:

      'Onhicgað nu   halige mihte,

     wise wundor Godes.   We gesawon

     þæt he wið cwealme gebearh   cnihtum on ofne,

     lacende líg,   þam þe his lof[107] báeron;

     forþam he is ána   éce Drihten,

     <Dema>[108] ælmihtig   se ðe him dóm forgeaf,

     spowende spéd,   þam þe his spel berað.

     Forðon witigað   þurh wundor monig

480 halgum gastum   þe his hýld curon.

     Cuð is þæt me Daniel   dyglan swefnes

     soð[109] gesæde,   þæt ær swiðe oðstod[110]

     manegum on móde   minra leoda,

     forþam Ælmihtig   eacenne gast

     in sefan sende,   snyttro cræftas.'

      Swa wordum spræc   werodes ræswa,

     Babilone weard   siððan he beacen onget,

     swutol tacen Godes.   No þy sel dyde

     ac þam æðelinge   oferhygd gesceod,

490 wearð him hyrra hyge   and on heortan geðanc

     mara on[111] modsefan   þonne gemet wǽre

     oðþæt hine mid nyde   nyðor asette

     Metod ælmihtig,   swa he manegum deð

     þara þe þurh oferhyd   úp astigeð.

---

[107] p. 198. The lower part of this page has been left blank for an illustration.
[108] Not in the manuscript – reading from Blackburn 1907.
[109] MS *soðe*.
[110] A letter erased and underpointed at the beginning of this word with *o* added above.
[111] MS *maran*.

Nabochodonossor's Second Dream

    Þa[112] him wearð on slæpe   swefen ætýwed,

    Nabochodonossor;   him þæt neh gewearð.

    Þuhte him þæt on foldan   fægre stóde

    wudubeam wlitig   se wæs[113] wyrtum fæst,

    beorht on blædum.   Næs he bearwe gelic

500   ác he hlifode[114]   to heofontunglum,

    swilce he oferfæðmde   foldan sceatas,

    ealne middangeard   oð merestreamas,

    twígum and telgum.   Ðær he to geseah,

    þuhte him þæt se wudubeam   wilddeor[115] scylde

    áne æte   eallum heolde;

    swylce fuglas eac   heora feorhnere

    on þæs beames   bledum name.

    Ðuhte him þæt engel   ufan of róderum

    stigan cwome   and stefne abead,

510   torhtan reorde.   Het þæt treow ceorfan

    and þa wildan deor[116]   on[117] weg fleon,

    swylce eac þa fugolas   þonne his fyll cóme.

    Het þonne besnædan   seolfes blædum,

    twigum and telgum,   and þeh tácen wesan,

    wunian wyrtruman[118]   þæs wudubeames

    eorðan fæstne   oðþæt eft cyme

    grene bleda   þonne God sylle.

    Het eac gebindan   beam þone miclan

    ærenum clammum   and isernum,

520   and gesæledne   in susl dón,

---

[112] p. 199. The upper part of this page has been left blank for an illustration. The initial Þ is 7-lines high and the following *A* is a bold capital.

[113] The *wynn* has been altered from a *þ*.

[114] MS *hlfode*.

[115] MS *wild-/deor*, p. 200. The lower part of this page has been left blank for an illustration.

[116] MS *wildeor*.

[117] Two letters have been scraped away after this. The scribe initially wrote *oneg*; he realised his mistake and erased the *eg* and and then wrote the required letters (*weg*) at the beginning of the next line.

[118] MS *wyr trumam*. The letters *yr* appear to be written over and erasure.

þæt his mod wite　þæt migtigra

wíte wealdeð　þonne he him wið mæge.

　　Þa[119] of slæpe onwoc　– swefn wæs æt ende –

eorðlic æðeling,　him þæs egesa stód,

gryre fram ðam gáste　ðe þyder God sende.

Het þa tosomne　síne leode,

folctogan <feran>,[120]　frægn ofer ealle

swiðmód cyning　hwæt þæt swefen bude,

nalles þy he wende　þæt hie hit wiston,

530　ác he cunnode　hu hie cweðan woldon.

　　Ða wæs to ðam dóme　Daniel haten,

Godes spelboda.　Him wæs gæst geseald,

halig of heofonum　se his hyge trymede.

On þam Drihtenweard　deopne wisse

sefan sidne geþanc　and snytro[121] cræft,

wisne[122] wordcwide.　Oft[123] he wundor manig,

Metodes mihta,　for men ætbǽr.

Þa he secgan ongán　swefnes woman,

heahheort and hæðen　heriges wisa,

540　ealne þone egesan　þe him eowed wæs.

Bæd hine areccan　hwæt seo rún bude,

hófe haligu word　and in hige funde

to gesecganne　soðum wordum

hwæt se beam bude　þe he blícan geseah,

and him witgode　wýrda[124] geþingu.

　　He ða swigode,　hwæðere soð ongeat,

Daniel æt þam dóme　þæt his drihten wæs,

gumena aldor,　wið God scyldig.

Wándode se wísa,　hwæðre he worde cwæð,

---

[119] p. 201. The upper part of this page has been left blank for an illustration. The **Þ** is bold.
[120] Not in the manuscript – reading from Schmidt 1907.
[121] The *n* has been altered from another letter.
[122] p. 202.
[123] MS *eft*.
[124] The *ý* seems to be over an erasure.

550 æcræftig[125] ár   to þam æðelinge:

DANIEL INTERPRETS THE SECOND DREAM

'Þæt is, weredes weard,   wundor unlytel,
þæt þu gesawe   þurh swefen cuman,
heofonheane beam   and þa halgan word,
yrre and egeslicu   þa se engel cwæð,
þæt þæt treow sceolde,   telgum besnæded,
foran áfeallan   þæt ǽr fæste stod
and þonne mid deorum   dreamleas beon,
westen wunian   and his wyrtruman
foldan befolen,   fyrstmearc wesan
560 stille on staðole,   swa seo stefn gecwæð,
ymb seofon tida   sæde eft onfón.
Swa þin blǽd lið —   swa se béam geweox,
heah to heofonum,   swa þu hæleðum eart
ána eallum   eorðbuendum
weard and wisa.   Nís þe wiðerbreca,
man on moldan   nymðe Metod ána.
Se ðec áceorfeð   of cyningdóme
and ðec wineleasne[126]   on wræc sendeð,
and þonne onhweorfeð   heortan þine
570 þæt þu ne gemyndgast[127]   æfter mandreame,
ne gewittes wast   butan wildeora þeaw,
ac þu lifgende   lange þrage
heorta hlypum   geond holt wunast.
Ne bið þec mǽlmete   nymþe mores græs,
ne rést witod   ác þec regna scur
weceð and wreceð   swa wildu deor
oðþæt þu ymb seofon winter   soð gelyfest,

---

[125] MS *ár cræftig*.
[126] p. 203. The lower part of this page has been left blank for an illustration.
[127] MS *gemydgast*.

　　　　　þæt sie án Metod　eallum mannum,
　　　　　reccend and rice,　sé on roderum is.
580　　Is me swa þeah willa　þæt se wyrtruma
　　　　　stille wæs on staðole,　swa seo stefn gecwæð,
　　　　　and ymbe seofan tíde　sǽde onfenge.
　　　　　Swa þín ríce　restende bið,
　　　　　ánwalh[128] for eorlum　oðþæt þu eft cymst.
　　　　　Gehyge þu, frea min,　fæstlicne rǽd.
　　　　　Syle ælmyssan,　wes earmra hleo,
　　　　　þinga for Ðeodne,　ǽr ðam seo þrah cyme
　　　　　þæt he þec aworpe　of woruldríce.[129]
　　　　　Oft[130] Metod alǽt　monige ðeode
590　　wyrcan <bote>[131]　þonne hie woldon sylfe,
　　　　　fyrene fæstan,　ǽr him fǽr Godes
　　　　　þurh egesan gryre　aldre gesceode.'
　　　　　　No þæs fela Daniel　to his drihtne gespræc
　　　　　soðra worda　þurh snytro cræft,
　　　　　þæt þæs á se rica　reccan wolde,
　　　　　middangeardes weard　ác his mód astah,
　　　　　heah fram heortan;　he þæs hearde ongeald.
　　　　　Ongan ða gyddigan　þurh gylp micel
　　　　　Caldea cyning　þa he ceastergeweorc[132]
600　　Babilone burh,　on his blǽde geseah,
　　　　　Sennera feld　sidne bewindan,
　　　　　heah hlifigan;　þæt se heretyma
　　　　　werede geworhte　þurh wundor micel,
　　　　　wearð ða ánhydig　ofer ealle men,
　　　　　swiðmod in sefan,　for ðære sundorgife
　　　　　þe him God sealde,　gumena ríce,
　　　　　world to gewealde　in wera life:

---

[128] MS *ánwloh*.
[129] Page 204 has been left blank for an illustration.
[130] p. 205.
[131] Not in the manuscript – reading from Blackburn 1907.
[132] MS *ceastre weold* – reading from Krapp 1931 (p. 128).

Nabochodonossor's Punishment – to live for Seven Years as a Wild Beast

'Ðu eart seo micle and min seo mære burh
þe ic geworhte to wurðmyndum,
610 rúme ríce; ic reste on þe,
eard and eðel agan wille.'
    Ða for ðam gylpe gumena drihten
forfangen wearð and on fleam gewát,
ana on oferhyd ofer ealle men.
Swa wod[133] wera on gewindagum
geocrostne sið in Godes wíte,
ðara þe eft lifigende leode begete,
Nabochodonossor[134] siððan him nið Godes,
hreð of heofonum, hete gesceode.
620 Seofon winter samod susl þrowode,
wildeora westen, winburge cyning.
Ða se earfoðmæcg up locode,
wilddeora gewita, þurh wolcna gang;
gemunde þa on móde þæt Metod wære,
heofona Heahcyning, hæleða bearnum
ána éce Gast. Þa he eft onhwearf
wodan gewittes, þær þe he ǽr wide bær
herewosan hige, heortan getenge.
Þa his gast ahwearf in Godes gemynd,
630 mod to mannum siððan he Metod onget.
    Gewát þa earmsceapen eft siðian,
nacod nýdgenga, nið[135] geðafian,
wundorlic wrǽcca and wǽda leas,
mǽtra on modgeðanc to mancynne
ðonne gumena weard in gylpe wæs.

---

[133] MS *woð*.
[134] p. 206. The upper part of this page has been left blank for an illustration.
[135] p. 207. The lower part of this page has been left blank for an illustration.

   Stod middangeard æfter mandrihtne,
eard and eðel æfter þam æðelinge,
seofon winter samod, swa no swiðrode
ríce under roderum oðþæt se ræswa cóm.
640 Þa[136] wæs eft geseted in aldordom
Babilone weard, hæfde beteran ðeaw,
leohtran geleafan in Liffruman,
þætte God sealde gumena gehwilcum[137]
welan swa wíte swa he wolde sylf.
Ne lengde þa leoda aldor
witegena wordcwyde ac he wide bead
Metodes mihte þær he meld ahte,
siðfæt sægde sinum leodum,
wide waðe þe he mid wilddeorum ateah
650 oðþæt him Frean Godes in gast becwóm
rædfæst sefa ða he to roderum beseah.
Wyrd wæs geworden, wundor gecyðed,
swefn geseðed, susl awunnen,
dóm gedemed swa ær Daniél[138] cwæð,
þæt se folctoga findan sceolde
earfoðsiðas for his ofermedlan.
Swa he ofstlice godspellode
Metodes mihtum for mancynne,
siððan in Babilone burhsittendum
lange hwile lare sægde,
660 Daniel domas. Siððan deora gesið,
wildra wærgenga, of waðe cwóm,
Nabochodonossor of niðwracum,
siððan weardode wíde rice,
heold hæleða gestreon and þa hean burh,
frod, foremihtig folca ræswa,

---

[136] p. 208.
[137] MS *gehlilcum*, with a *wynn* written, as a correction, over the first *l*.
[138] The accent on *e* is obscured by the *l*.

```
         Caldea cyning    oðþæt him cwelm gesceod,
         swa him ofer eorðan   andsaca ne wæs
         gumena ænig    oðþæt him God wolde
670      þurh hryre hreddan   hea ríce.
         Siððan þær his aferan   ead bryttedon,
         welan, wunden gold,   in þære widan byrig,
         ealhstede eorla,   unwaclice,¹³⁹
         heah hordmægen,   þa hyra hlaford læg.
```

Belshazzar's Rise to Power and his Feast

```
         Ða¹⁴⁰ in ðære ðeode¹⁴¹ awóc   his þæt þridde cneow.
         Wæs Baldazar   burga aldor,
         weold wera ríces   oðþæt him wlenco gesceod,
         oferhyd egle.   Ða wæs endedæg
         ðæs ðe Caldéas   cyningdom ahton.
680      Ða Metod onlah   Médum and Persum
         aldordomes ymb¹⁴² lytel fæc,
         let Babilone   blǽd swiðrian,
         þone þa hæleð   healdan sceoldon.
         Wiste he ealdormen   in únrihtum,
         ða ðe ðy ríce   rǽdan sceoldon.
         Ða þæt gehogode   hámsittende,
         Meda aldor   þæt ǽr man ne ongan,
         þæt he Babilone   abrecan wolde,
         alhstede eorla,   þær æðelingas
690      under wealla hleo   welan brytnedon.
         Þæt wæs þara fæstna   folcum cuðost,¹⁴³
         mǽst and mǽrost   þara þe men bun,
         Babilon burga   oðþæt Baldazar
```

---

¹³⁹ p. 209.
¹⁴⁰ The initial **Ð** is 3-lines high and the following *A* is bold. The Fitt number *.lv.* is written above this line.
¹⁴¹ A letter has been scraped away before this word.
¹⁴² MS *ym*.
¹⁴³ *s* is over an earlier *c or t*.

       þurh gylp grome   Godes frasade.[144]
          Sæton him æt wine   wealle belocene,
       ne onegdon na[145]   orlegra nið
       þeah ðe feonda folc   feran cwome
       herega gerædum   to þære heahbyrig
       þæt hie Babilone   ábrecan mihton.
700   Gesæt þa to symble[146]   siðestan dæge
       Caldea cyning   mid cneomagum,
       þær medugal wearð   mægenes wisa.
       Hét þam <æðelum>[147] beran   Israela gestreon,
       huslfatu halegu,   on hand werum,
       þa ǽr Caldeas   mid cyneðrymme,
       cempan[148] in ceastre,   clǽne genámon,
       gold in Gerusalem   ða hie Iudea
       blǽd forbrǽcon   billa ecgum
       and þurh hleoðorcyme   herige genamon
710   beorhte frætwe.   Ða hie tempel strudon,
       Salomanes seld,   swiðe gulpon.[149]
          Ða[150] wearð bliðemod   burga aldor,
       gealp gramlice   Gode on andan,
       cwæð þæt his hergas   hyrran wæron
       and mihtigran   mannum to friðe
       þonne Israela   ece Drihten.

The Writing on the Wall

          Him þæt tacen wearð   þær he to starude,
       egeslic for eorlum   innan healle,
       þæt he for leodum   ligeword gecwæð

---

[144] MS *frea sæde*.
[145] A letter scraped before this word.
[146] *y* altered from *u*.
[147] Not in the manuscript – reading from Blackburn 1907.
[148] p. 210. The lower part of this page has been left blank for an illustration.
[149] *a* altered from *u*.
[150] *a* added above with an insertion mark below.

| 720 | þa þær in egesan   engel Drihtnes |

let his hand cuman   in þæt hea seld,
wrat þa in wáge   worda gerynu,
baswe bócstafas,   burhsittendum.
Ða wearð folctoga   forht on mode,
acul for þam egesan.   Geseah he engles hand
in sele writan   Sennera wíte.
Þæt gyddedon   gumena mænigeo,
hæleð in healle   hwæt seo hand write
to þam beacne   burhsittendum;

| 730 | werede comon   on þæt wundor seon.[151] |

Sohton[152] þa swiðe   in sefan gehydum
hwæt seo hand write   haliges gastes.
Ne mihton arǽdan   runcræftige men
engles ærendbec,   æðelinga cyn
oðþæt Daniel cóm,   Drihtne gecoren,
snotor and soðfæst,   in þæt seld gangan.
Ðam wæs on gaste   Godes cræft micel,
to þam ic georne gefrægn   gyfum ceapian
burhge weardas[153]   þæt he him bocstafas

| 740 | arædde and arehte   hwæt seo run bude. |

Him ǽcræftig   andswarode,
Godes spelboda,   gleaw geðances:

Daniel interprets the Writing on the Wall

'No ic wið feohsceattum   ofer folc bere
Drihtnes domas,   ne ðe dugeðe can
ac þe unceapunga   órlæg secge,
worda gerynu,   þa þu wendan ne miht.

---

[151] Page 211 has been left blank for an illustration.
[152] p. 212. A bifolium, containing two illustrations, has been lost here; its conjugate, also with two illustrations, fell between pages 228-9. See the Gathering Analysis and Diagrams.
[153] MS *burh geweardas*.

   Þu for anmedlan in æht bere
   huslfatu halegu,[154] on hand werum.
   On þam ge deoflu drincan ongunnon,
750 ða ǽr Israela in æ hæfdon
   æt Godes earce oðþæt hie gylp beswac,
   windruncen gewit swa þe wurðan sceal.
   No þæt þin aldor æfre wolde
   Godes goldfatu in gylp beran,
   ne ðy hraðor hremde ðeah ðe here brohte
   Israela gestreon in his æhte geweald
   ac þæt oftor gecwæð aldor ðeoda
   soðum wordum ofer sín mægen,
   siððan him wuldres Weard wundor gecyðde,
760 þæt he wǽre ána ealra gesceafta
   Drihten and Waldend, se him dóm forgeaf,
   unscyndne[155] blæd eorðan ríces,
   and þu lignest nu þæt sie lifgende,
   se ofer deoflum dugeþum wealdeð.'

---

[154] e added above after *l*.
[155] *s* is over an earlier letter (*c*?).

Christ and Satan

Þæt[1] wearð[2] underne   eorðbúendum[3]
þæt Meotod[4] hæfde   miht and stréngðo
ðá he gefestnade   fóldan sceatas.
Seolfa he gesétte   sunnan and mónan,
stanas and eorðan,   stream út on sǽ,
wæter and wolcen,[5]   ðurh his wundra miht.
Deopne ýmblyt   clene ymbhaldeð
Meotod on mihtum   and alne middangeard.
He selfa mæg   sǽ[6] géondwlítan,
10   grundas in geofene,[7]   Godes ágen Bearn,
and he aríman mæg   rǽgnas scúran,
dropena gehwelcne.   Daga énderím
seolua he gesette   þurh his sóðan míht.
Swá se Wyrhta   þurh his wuldres gást
serede and sette   on síx dagum
eorðan dæles,   up on heofonum,
<and>[8] heanne[9] holm.[10]   Hwá ís þæt ðe cunne
orðonc clæne[11]   nymðe[12] éce God?
Dréamas he gedælde,[13]   dúguðe and geþeode,
20   Adam ærest   and þæt æðele cýn,
engla órdfruman   þæt þe eft forwearð.[14]

---

[1] p. 213. The initial is 7-lines high and projects into the upper margin. [*The final readings adopted here generally reflect the changes made by a corrector; they often improve the text and are indeed the final readings in the manuscript. No spaces have been left for illustrations on the surviving folios in this poem, but four folios, assumed here to have contained eight full-page illustrations, have been excised from it.*]
[2] ð is over an erased þ.
[3] MS *eorð buendum* with an e erased at the end of *eorð*.
[4] *him* is added above after this word.
[5] MS *wolcn* with e added above.
[6] æ has been altered from original e.
[7] MS *heofene* with third e altered to o and n added above.
[8] Not in the manuscript – reading from Holthausen 1895.
[9] MS *henne* with a added above.
[10] MS *holme*.
[11] æ altered from original e.
[12] Glossed *buton* above.
[13] æ written above the second e.
[14] e added above before a.

Ðuhte heom[15] on móde   þæt hit mihte[16] swá,
þæt hie wæron[17] sylfe[18]   swegles brytan,
wuldres[19] waldend.   Him ðær wirse[20] gelomp[21]
ða héo in hélle   hám staðeledon,
án æfter oðrum   in þæt[22] átole scref,[23]
þær héo brynewelme   bídan sceoldon[24]
sáran[25] sorge,   náles swegles[26] leoht
habban[27] in heofnum   heahgetimbrad

30   ác gedufan sceolun   in ðone deopan wælm
niðær under néssas   in ðone neowlan grund,
grædige[28] and gifre.   God ana wat
hu he þæt scyldige[29] werud   forscrifen hæfde.[30]

   Cleopað[31] ðonne se ealda[32]   út of hélle,
wriceð wordcwedas[33]   weregan reorde,
eisegan stefne: 'Hwær com engla ðrym,
þe[34] we on heofnum   habban sceoldan?
Þis is ðeostræ[35] ham   ðearle gebunden
fæstum fýrclommum;   flor is on welme
40   attre onæled.   Nis nu ende feor
þæt we sceolun ætsomne   susel þrowian,

---

[15] *eo* written above original *i*.
[16] There is an accent above the *m*.
[17] *æ* written above original *e*.
[18] *y* written above original *eo*.
[19] *d* altered from *r*.
[20] MS *wise* with *ors* above the last three letters.
[21] *o* written above original *a*.
[22] A letter erased after this abbreviated form.
[23] There is an extraneous accent above the *r*.
[24] MS *sceoden* with *l* added above and an insertion mark below and *o* above original *e*.
[25] **S** added in bold in the margin.
[26] MS *swe gles* (a letter erased before *g*).
[27] Second *b* added above.
[28] The *æ* is written above the first *e*.
[29] MS *scyldi* with *ge* added above.
[30] The *æ* is written above original *e*.
[31] MS *cleopad*.
[32] *e* added above with an insertion mark below.
[33] *-word* added above.
[34] MS has an extraneous *ða* before this word.
[35] *þe* erased before this.

wéan and wergu,³⁶ nalles³⁷ wuldres³⁸ blæd

habban in heofnum, hehselda wyn.

Hwæt. We for Dryhtene íu dreamas³⁹ hefdon,⁴⁰

song on swegle selrum tidum

þær nu ymb ðone Ecan⁴¹ æðele stondað,

hæleð⁴² ymb⁴³ héhseld, herigað Drihten

wordum⁴⁴ and wiorcum⁴⁵ and ic in wíte sceal

bídan in béndum and me bættran⁴⁶ ham⁴⁷

50   for oferhygdum æfre ne wene.'

    Ða him andsweradan átole gastas,

swearte⁴⁸ and synfulle, susle begnornende:⁴⁹

    'Þu us gelærdæst ðurh lyge ðinne

þæt we Hælende⁵⁰ heran ne sceoldon;⁵¹

ðuhte þe anum þæt ðu ahtest alles gewald,

héofnes and eorþan, wære halig God,

Scypend seolfa. Nu earttu sceaðana⁵² sum

in fyrlocan feste gebunden.

Wéndes ðú ðurh wuldor ðæt þu woruld ahtest,

60   alra onwald and we englas mid ðec.

Átol is þin onseon – habbað we alle swá

for ðinum leasungum lyðre gefered.

---

³⁶ MS *wergum*.
³⁷ *a* written above a deleted *e*.
³⁸ MS *wulres*.
³⁹ p. 214.
⁴⁰ *n* altered from original *m*.
⁴¹ *e* altered from original *æ*.
⁴² *æ* altered from original *e*.
⁴³ MS *ym* with *b* added above and an insertion mark below.
⁴⁴ MS *wordun*.
⁴⁵ MS *weṛcum*, with *io* added above original *ẹ* (underpointed for deletion).
⁴⁶ *b* erased (for reasons unclear).
⁴⁷ There is an extraneous *for* before this word; it has been struck through for deletion. The scribe seems to have anticipated *for* in the next line.
⁴⁸ *e* added above with an insertion mark below.
⁴⁹ MS *begrorenne*.
⁵⁰ *æ* added above original *e*.
⁵¹ *o* added above original *a*.
⁵² MS *earm sceaða* with an erased letter after *m*, and *a* over an erased letter after *ð*, with *na sum* mostly erased at the beginning of the next line.

Sægdest[53] us to soðe   þæt ðín sunu wære
Meotod moncynnes;   hafustu nu máre susel.'
   Swa firenfulle   facnum wordum
heora aldorðægn   on[54] reordadon,
on cearum cwidum.   Crist heo afirde,
dreamum bedælde.[55]   Hæfdan Dryhtnes leoht[56]
for oferhygdum   ufan[57] forlæten,[58]
70 hæfdon hym to hyhte   helle floras,
beornende bealo.   Bláce hweorfon[59]
scinnan forscepene,   sceaðan hwearfedon,[60]
earme æglecan   geond þæt atole scref,
for ðam ánmedlan[61]   þe hie ær drugon.
   Eft[62] reordade   oðre siðe
feonda aldor.   Wæs þa forht[63] agen,
seoððan he ðæs[64] wítes   wórn gefélde.
He spearcade[65]   ðonne he spreocan ongan
fýre and attre;[66]   ne[67] bið swelc fæger dréam
80 ðonne he in witum   wordum[68] índraf:
   'Ic wæs íu in heofnum   hálig ængel,
Dryhtene[69] deore;   hefde me dréam mid Gode,
micelne for Meotode,   and ðeos menego swa some.
   Þa ic in mode   minum hógade

---

[53] æ is over the e.
[54] MS un.
[55] æ is over an erased e with an insertion mark below.
[56] eo written over erased e.
[57] f over two erased letters.
[58] Original é altered to æ and e altered from original o.
[59] MS hworfon with e added above with an insertion mark below.
[60] MS hwearfdon.
[61] MS medlan with án added above and an insertion mark below.
[62] The Fitt number .li. is written above this manuscript line.
[63] MS for worht.
[64] MS ðes with e erased and æ written above.
[65] MS swearcade with t altered from original c.
[66] MS atre with second t added above.
[67] Original h altered to n by scraping.
[68] MS word.
[69] MS drihtene with first e underpointed for deletion and final e squeezed in.

þæt ic wolde[70] towiorpan[71]   wuldres[72] Leoman,
Bearn Hælendes,[73]   ágan[74] me burga geweald[75]
éall to æhte   and ðeos[76] earme heap
þe ic hebbe to helle   ham gelædde.[77]
Wéne[78] þæt tacen sutol   þa[79] ic aseald wes on wærgðu,
90 niðer under næssas[80]   in ðóne[81] neowlan grund;
nu ic eow hebbe to hæftum   hám geferede[82]
ealle[83] of earde.   Nis her eadiges tír,
wloncra wynsela,[84]   ne worulde dream,
ne engla[85] ðreat,[86]   ne we[87] úppheofon[88]
ágan móten.[89]   Is ðes[90] átóla hám
fyre[91] onæled –   ic eom fah wið God.
Éce[92] æt helle duru   dracan eardigað
hate on reðre;   hy[93] us helpan ne magon.
Is ðes[94] wálica hám   wítes afylled;
100 nágan[95] we ðæs heolstres   þæt we ús gehydan magon[96]

---

[70] Three minims erased before this.
[71] *io* written above original *e*.
[72] MS *wulres*.
[73] *æ* added above original *e*.
[74] p. 215.
[75] *a* added above with an insertion mark below.
[76] *o* written over an erased *s*.
[77] *æ* altered from original *e*.
[78] *ge* added above *ne* (for reasons unclear).
[79] *þa...wærgðu*: MS *and wærgðu þa ic of aseald wes* – reading from Krapp 1931 (p. 138).
[80] MS *nessas* with *e* underpointed for deletion and *æ* added above.
[81] MS *ðónne* with the first *n* deleted.
[82] MS *gef erede* with second *e* altered from original *æ* by scraping (hence the space) and the third *e* added above.
[83] First *e* added above with an insertion mark below.
[84] *y* written over original *i* and original final *e* altered to *a*.
[85] *e* altered from original *æ* by scraping.
[86] Original *d* altered to *ð* by adding a (misaligned) crossbar.
[87] *we* added above.
[88] Second *p* added above.
[89] *ne* added above before this word (for reasons unclear).
[90] *s* written over erased *os*.
[91] *e* crowded in after this word with an insertion mark below.
[92] First *e* altered from *ǽ* by scraping.
[93] *y* written above original *eo*, both of which are underpointed for deletion.
[94] *e* altered from *æ* by scraping.
[95] *n* written over an erased large initial.
[96] *a* altered from *æ* by scraping.

in ðissum neowlan genípe. Hér[97] is nedran sweg,[98]
wyrmas gewúnade;   is ðis wítes clom
fæste[99] gebunden.   Feond seondon réðe,
dimme and[100] deorce;   ne her dæg lyhteð[101]
for scedes sciman,   Sceppendes leoht.
Iu[102] ahte ic[103] gewald   ealles wuldres
ær[104] ic moste in ðeossum átolan   éðele[105] gebidan
hwæt me Drihten God   déman wylle,[106]
fágum on flora.   Nu ic féran com

110   deofla menego   to ðissum dimman ham.
Ác[107] ic sceal on flyge   and on flyhte ðragum
earda neosan,   and eower ma,
þe ðes oferhydes   ord onstealdon.[108]
Ne ðurfon we ðæs[109] wénan   þæt us Wuldorcyning
ǽfre wílle   eard alyfan,[110]
eðel[111] to æhte,   swa he ær dyde,
écne[112] onweald;[113]   ah him ealles[114] geweald,[115]
wuldres[116] and wíta,   Wealdéndes[117] Sunu.

---

[97] *e* altered from *ǽ* by scraping.
[98] *e* altered from *ǽ* by scraping.
[99] *æ* may have been altered from original *e*.
[100] The abbreviation is written over erased *on*.
[101] MS *lyh–* with *teð* added above.
[102] MS *nu*.
[103] Added above after *ahte* with an insertion mark below.
[104] MS *þær*.
[105] First *e* altered from *æ* by scraping.
[106] *y* written over original *i*.
[107] *c* written over erased *h*.
[108] *e* added above with an insertion mark below.
[109] *æ* altered from original *e*.
[110] *y* written over original *e*.
[111] *e* altered from *æ* by scraping.
[112] *n* added above with an insertion mark below.
[113] *e* added above with an insertion mark below.
[114] First *e* added above with an insertion mark below.
[115] *e* added above.
[116] MS *wulres* with *d* added above.
[117] First *e* added above with an insertion mark below.

Forðon ic sceal[118] héan and earm[119] hwyrfan[120] ðy widdor,[121]
120 wadan wræclastas, wúldre benémed,
  duguðum bedeled, nænigne dréam ágan
  úppe mid englum[122] þæs[123] ðe ic ær gecwæð
  þæt ic wære seolfa swegles[124] Brytta,
  wihta[125] Wealdend. Ac[126] hit him wyrse gelamp.'[127]
   Swa[128] se werega gast wordum sæde
  his éarfoðo ealle ætsomne,
  fah in fyrnum – fýrleoma stód
  géond þæt atole scræf attre geblonden:
   'Ic eom limwæstmum þæt ic gelutian ne mæg
130 on þyssum sidan sele synnum forwundod.
  Hwæt. Her hát and ceald hwilum mencgað;
  hwilum ic gehere hellescealcas,
  gnorniende[129] cynn, grundas mænan,
  niðer under næssum; hwilum nacode men
  winnað ymbe[130] wyrmas. Is þés windiga sele
  eall inneweard atole gefylled.
  Ne mot ic hihtlicran hames brucan,
  burga ne bolda, ne on þa beorhtan gescæft
  ne mót ic æfre má eagum starian.
140 Is me nu wyrsǽ[131] þæt ic wuldres leoht
  úppe mid englum æfre cuðe,

---

[118] Added above after *ic*, with an insertion mark below.
[119] Final *m* is lighter and at the end of the manuscript line – it may have been added by the corrector. The letters *ma* are at the beginning of the next line, but have been marked for deletion.
[120] *y* written over original *eo* which are underpointed for deletion.
[121] Second *d* added above.
[122] *e* altered from *æ* by scraping.
[123] *æ* altered from *e* by adding a loop to it.
[124] *e* altered from *æ* by scraping.
[125] MS *wi hta wealdend* over an erased area.
[126] *c* over erased *h*.
[127] *a* added above an *o* underpointed for deletion. The Fitt number *.lii.* has been partly erased when the correction above it was made.
[128] p. 216. The script changes on this folio to a smaller, neater hand, and the intense level of alteration of vowels thus far stops for the most part, and fewer words have accents. The initial **S** is 2-lines high and bold.
[129] *i* added above with an insertion mark below.
[130] *e* added above.
[131] *ǽ* altered from *é*.

song on swegle,   þær Sunu Meotodes
habbað eadige[132] bearn   ealle ymbfangen
seolfa mid sange.   Ne ic þam sawlum ne mót
ænigum sceððan
butan þam anum[133]   þe he agan[134] nyle;
þá ic mot to hæftum   ham geferian,
bringan to bolde   in þone biteran grund.
Ealle we syndon   úngelíce
150 þonne þe we íu in heofonum   hæfdon ærror
wlite and weorðmynt.   Ful oft wuldres <sweg>[135]
brohton to bearme   Bearn Hælendes
þær we ymb hine utan   ealle hofan,
leomu ymb leofne,   lofsonga word,
Drihtne sædon.   Nu ic eom dædum fáh,
gewundod mid wommum;   sceal nu þysne wítes clom
beoran beornende   in bæce minum,
hat on helle   hyhtwillan leas.'
    Þa gyt feola cwiðde[136]   fírna herede,[137]
160 atol æglæca,   út of helle
witum wérig.   Word spearcum fleah
attre gelícost   þonne he út þurhdráf:[138]
    'Eala Drihtenes þrym.   Eala duguða Helm.
Eala Meotodes miht.   Eala middaneard.
Eala dæg leohta.[139]   Eala dréam Godes.
Eala engla þreat.   Eala upheofen.
Eala þæt ic éam ealles leas   ecan dreames
þæt ic mid handum ne mæg   heofon geræcan,

---

[132] MS *eadigne*.
[133] This is in fainter ink and seems to have been added later.
[134] There is an extraneous *to* before this word.
[135] Not in the manuscript – reading from Grein 1857.
[136] MS *cwide* with the interlinear gloss *uel dum*.
[137] MS *herede* with a scrape above the first *e*.
[138] *u* is written above an *o* underpointed for deletion.
[139] *o* may have been altered from earlier *d*.

　　　　　　　　ne mid eagum ne mot　up[140] locian,
170　　　　　　ne huru mid éarum ne scéal　æfre geheran

　　　　　　　　þære byrhtestan[141]　beman[142] stefne.

　　　　　　　　Ðæs ic wolde of selde　Sunu Meotodes,

　　　　　　　　Drihten adrifan　and ágan me þæs dreames gewald,

　　　　　　　　wuldres and wynne;　me þær wyrse gelamp

　　　　　　　　þonne ic to hihte　ágan moste.

　　　　　　　　Nu ic eom ascéaden　fram þære scíran driht,

　　　　　　　　aláeded fram leohte　in þone laðan hám;

　　　　　　　　ne mæg ic þæt gehicgan　hu ic in ðæm becóm,[143]

　　　　　　　　in þis neowle genip,　niðsynnum[144] fáh,

180　　　　　　aworpen of worulde.　Wat ic nu þa

　　　　　　　　þæt[145] bið alles leas　ęcan[146] dreamæs

　　　　　　　　se ðe Heofencyninge　heran[147] ne þenceð,

　　　　　　　　Meotode cweman.　Ic þæt morðer[148] sceal,

　　　　　　　　wéan and wítu　and wrace dreogan,

　　　　　　　　góda bedæled,　íudædum fah

　　　　　　　　þæs ðe ic geþohte adrifan　Drihten of selde,

　　　　　　　　weoroda Waldend;　sceal nu wreclastas

　　　　　　　　settan sorhgcearig,[149]　siðas[150] wíde.'

　　　　　　　　　　Hwearf þa to helle　þa he gehéned wæs,

190　　　　　　Godes andsaca;　dydon his gingran swa,[151]

　　　　　　　　gífre and grædige　þa hig[152] God bedraf

　　　　　　　　in þæt hate hof　þam is hel nama.

　　　　　　　　Forþan sceal gehycgan　hæleða æghwylc

---

[140] There is a faint *g(e)* added after this in the margin (for reasons unclear).
[141] p. 217. A folio containing two illustrations has been lost between pages 216 and 217; see the Gathering Analysis and Diagrams.
[142] *y* written over original *e*.
[143] MS *becwóm* with *w* underpointed for deletion.
[144] MS *mid synnum*.
[145] Added (as an abbreviation) at the end of the previous manuscript line.
[146] Accented.
[147] *he* abraded.
[148] MS *morðre*.
[149] Final *g* added by the corrector.
[150] MS *sidas*.
[151] Glossed *uel some*.
[152] *-ig* written above original *e*.

þæt he ne abelige[153]   Bearn Waldendes.

Læte him to bysne   hu þa blácan feond

for oferhygdum   ealle forwurdon.

Niman[154] us to wynne[155]   weoroda Drihten,

uppe[156] écne geféan,   engla Waldend;

he þæt gecydde   þæt he mægencræft hæfde,

200   mihta miccle   þa he þa mænego adraf,

hæftas of ðæm hean selde.   Gemunan we þone halgan Drihten,

écne in wuldre   mid alra gescefta <ealdre>;[157]

ceosan us eard in wuldre   mid ealra cyninga Cyninge

se is Crist genemned.

Beoran on breostum   bliðe geþohtas,

sibbe and snytero;   gemunan soð and riht,

þonne we to hehselde   hnígan[158] þencað

and þone[159] Ealwaldan[160]   áræ[161] biddan.

Þonne behofað[162]   se ðe her wunað

210   weorulde wynnum   þæt him wlite scine

þonne he oðer lif   eft geséceð,

fægre[163] land   þonne þéos folde seo;

is[164] þær wlitig and wynsum,   wæstmas scinað,

beorhte ofer burgum.   Þær is brade lond,

hyhtlicra[165] hám   in heofonrice,

Criste gecwémra.   Uta[166] cerran þider

þær he sylfa sit,   sigora Waldend,

---

[153] First *e* altered from *æ* by scraping.
[154] MS *neoman* with *i* written above the *eo*.
[155] The accent on this word is very faint.
[156] MS *upne*.
[157] Not in the manuscript – reading from Krapp 1931 (p. 142).
[158] *h* added in the margin before *nígan* by the corrector.
[159] MS *þonne* with the first *n* deleted by scraping.
[160] MS *anwaldan* with *uel eal* written above.
[161] *æ* altered from original *a*.
[162] p. 218.
[163] Glossed *scilicet mycele* above.
[164] *is þær wlitig*: MS *is wlitig* with the gloss *scilicet þær* added above.
[165] MS *hyhtlicran*, with final *n* erased by scraping.
[166] The corrector has inserted *on-* above after *t* with an insertion mark below (for reasons unclear, but suggesting that the final reading should be *uton acerran*).

Drihten hælend, in ðæm deoran ham,
and ymbe[167] þǽt hehsetl hwite standað
220 engla feðan and eadigra,[168]
halige[169] heofenþreatas herigað Drihten
wordum and weorcum. Heora wlite scineð
geond ealra worulda woruld mid Wuldorcyninge.

  Ða get ic furðor gefregen feond[170] ondetan;
wæs him eall ful strang wom and witu; hæfdon Wuldorcyning
for oferhigdum ánforlæten;
cwædon eft hraðe oðrum wordum:[171]
  'Nu is gesene þæt wé gesyngodon[172]
uppe on earde; sceolon nu æfre þæs
230 dreogan domlease gewinn Drihtnes mihtum.
Hwæt. We in[173] wuldres wlite wunian moston
þær we halgan Gode heran woldon
and him sang ymb seld secgan sceoldon
þusendmælum. Þa we þær wæron,[174]
wunodon on wynnum, geherdon wuldres sweg,
beman stefne. Byrhtword arás
engla Ordfruma and to þæm æþelan
hnigan him sanctas; sigetorht aras
éce Drihten, ofer ús gestód
240 and gebletsode bilewitne heap
dogra gehwilcne and his se deora Sunu,
gasta Scyppend. God seolfa wæs
eallum andfeng þe ðær up becom,
and hine on eorðan ær gelyfde.[175]

---

[167] *e* squeezed in later by the corrector, with an insertion mark below.
[168] MS *eadigre*.
[169] MS *halig e* with a letter erased after *g*.
[170] MS *feonda*.
[171] MS *oðre worde* with each of the final letters glossed *uel um*.
[172] *ge-* added above.
[173] Added above with an insertion mark below.
[174] Added above.
[175] *y* written over original *e*.

Þa ðæs ofþuhte   þæt se Þeoden wæs
strang and stiðmod.   Ongan ic þa steppan forð
ána wið englum   and to him eallum spræc:
'Ic can eow[176] læran   langsumne ræd,
gif[177] ge willað mínre[178]   mihte[179] gelefan.
250 Uta[180] oferhycgan   Helm þone micclan,
weroda Waldend,   agan us þis wuldres leoht
eall to æhte;   þis is idel gylp
þæt we ær drugon   ealle hwile.'
    Ða[181] gewearð usic   þæt we woldon swá
Drihten adrifan[182]   of þam deoran ham,
Cyning of cestre;   cuð is wide
þæt wreclastas   wunian moton,
grimme grundas.   God seolfa him
rice haldeð;   he is ana Cyning
260 þe us eorre gewearð,   éce Drihten,
Meotod mihtum swið.[183]   Sceal nu þeos menego her
licgan on leahtrum,   sume on lyft sceacan,[184]
fleogan ofer foldan;   fýr bið ymbutan
on æghwylcum   þæh he uppe seo.
Ne mót he þam sawlum   þe ðær sécað up,
eadige of eorþan   æfre gehrinan[185]
ah ic be hondum mot   hæþenre sceale[186]
gripan to grunde,   Godes andsacan.
Sume sceolon hweorfan   geond hæleða land
270 and únsibbe   oft onstyrian

---

[176] p. 219. *Omnis homo primum bonum* is written in the top margin to the right.
[177] A second *f* erased after this word.
[178] *n* added above with an insertion mark below.
[179] MS *mihta* with *e* written above *a* underpointed for deletion.
[180] MS *uta* with *n* added above (for reasons unclear).
[181] The initial *Ð* is 3-lines high and lightly coloured. The Fitt number *.vi.* is written above this line to the right. The prompt in the margin is *þ*.
[182] *d* appears to be written over an erased letter with a descender.
[183] MS *swilc*.
[184] MS *scacan* with *e* added above after the first *c* and an insertion mark below.
[185] *h* added above with an insertion mark below.
[186] MS *sceal*.

monna mægðum　geond middaneard.
Ic her geþolian sceal　þinga æghwylces,
bitres niðæs[187]　beala gnornian,
seoc[188] and sorhful,　þæs ic seolfa weold
þonne ic on heofonum　ham staðelode,
hwæðer us se Éca　æfre wille
on heofona rice　hám aléfan,
eðel[189] to æhte,　swa he ǽr dyde.'
　Swa gnornedon　Godes andsacan,
280　hate on helle;　him wæs Hælend God
wrað geworden　for womcwidum.
Forþon mæg gehycgan　se ðe his heorte deah
þæt he him afirre　frecne geþohtas,
laðe leahtras,　lifigendra gehwylc.
Gemunan symle on mode　Meotodes strengðo;
gearwian us togénes　grene stræte
up to englum　þær is se ælmihtiga God.
And us befæðman wile　Freobearn Godes,
gif we þæt on eorðan　ǽr geþencað,
290　and us to þam halgan　helpe gelefeð.[190]
Þonne he us no forlæteð　ah lif syleð
uppe mid englum,　eadigne dream.
Tæceð us se Torhta[191]　trumlicne ham,
beorhte burhweallas;　beorhte scinað
gesælige sawle,　sorgum bedælde
þær heo æfre forð　wunian moten
cestre and cynestol.　Uton cyþan þæt.
Deman we on eorðan,　ǽrror lifigend,
onlucan mid listum　locen Waldendes,
300　ongeotan gastlice.　Us ongean cumað

---

[187] MS *in ðæs*.
[188] MS *sic*, with *i* altered (faintly) to *e* and *o* added above with an insertion mark below.
[189] MS *eðle*.
[190] MS *gelefað* with *a* underpointed for deletion and *e* added above.
[191] p. 220.

   þusend engla, gif þider moton
   and þæt on eorðan ǽr gewyrcað.
    Forþon se bið eadig se ðe æfre wile
   man oferhycgen, Meotode cweman,
   synne adwæscan. Swa he sylfa cwæð:
   'Soðfæste men, sunnan gelíce,
   fægre gefrætewod in heora Fæder rice
   scinað in sceldbyrig.' Þær[192] heo Sceppend seolf[193]
   <friðe>[194] befæðmeð, Fæder mancynnes,[195]
310 ahefeð holdlice in heofones leoht
   þær heo mid Wuldorcyninge wunian moton
   áwa to aldre,
   ágan dréama dréam mid Drihtne Gode,
   á to worulde á buton ende.[196]
    <É>ála[197] hwæt. Se awyrgda wraðe geþohte
   þæt he Heofencyninge heran ne wolde,
   Fæder frefergendum. Flor attre weol
   hat under hæftum; hreopan[198] deofla,
   wíde geond windsele[199] wéan[200] cwanedon,
320 mán and morður. Wæs seo[201] menego þær
   swylce onæled; wæs þæt eall full strong,
   þonne wæs heora aldor þe ðær ærest cóm
   forð on feþan, fæste gebunden
   fýre and lige. Þæt wæs fæstlic þreat;
   ec sceoldon his þegnas þær gewunian
   atolan eðles, nalles up þanon
   geheran in heofonum haligne dream,

---

[192] There is an erased *þ* before this word.
[193] At the end of the line followed by 2-3 erased letters, the second of which had a descender.
[194] Not in the manuscript – reading from Grein 1857.
[195] MS *mancyn* with *nes* added above and an insertion mark below.
[196] The *n* is an elongated *N*, perhaps used here to signal the end of a Fitt.
[197] There is a prompt for the initial *e* in the outer margin.
[198] MS *hreowan*.
[199] MS *winsele* with *d* added above and an insertion mark below.
[200] MS *wéa*.
[201] MS *ðær*.

	þær heo oft fægerne folgað hæfdon
	uppe mid englum. Wæron þa alles þæs
330	góda lease²⁰² ah nymþe gryndes <ad>²⁰³
	wunian <ne>²⁰⁴ moten and þone werigan sele
	þær is wom and wóp wide gehered,
	and gristbitungc²⁰⁵ and gnornungc²⁰⁶ mecga.
	Nabbað he²⁰⁷ to hyhte nymþe cyle and fýr,
	wéan and wítu and wyrma þreat,²⁰⁸
	dracan and næddran and þone dimman ham.
	Forðon mihte geheran, se ðe æt hylle wæs
	twelf milum neh þæt ðær wæs tóða geheaw,
	hlude²⁰⁹ and geomre. Godes andsacan
340	hweorfan geond helle hate onæled
	ufan and utan – him wæs æghwær wá –
	witum werige, wuldres bescyrede,
	dreamum bedælde. Heofon deop gehygd,
	þa heo on heofonum ham staðelodon,
	þæt hie woldon benæman nérgendne Crist
	rodera rices ah he on riht geheold
	hired heofona and þæt halige seld.
	Nis nænig swa snotor né swa cræftig,
	ne þæs swa gleaw, nymþe God seolfa
350	þæt asecgan mæge swegles léoman,
	hu scima²¹⁰ þǽr scineð ymbutan
	Meotodes mihte, geond þæt mære cynn
	þær habbað englas eadigne dream,

---

²⁰² MS *leas* with *e* added by a corrector and an insertion mark below.
²⁰³ Not in the manuscript – reading from Clubb 1925.
²⁰⁴ Not in the manuscript – reading from Thorpe 1832.
²⁰⁵ MS *gristbitunge*.
²⁰⁶ MS *gnornunge*.
²⁰⁷ MS *we*.
²⁰⁸ p. 221.
²⁰⁹ *h* added above with an insertion mark below.
²¹⁰ MS *sunnu*.

sanctas singað – þæt[211] is se[212] seolfa – for God.

Þonne beoð þa eadigan þe of eorðan cumað,

bringað to bearme blostman stences,

wyrta[213] wynsume – þæt synd word Godes –

þonne hie befæðmeð Fæder mancynnes,

and hie gesegnað mid his swiðran hond,

360   lædæð to lihte, þær hi lif ágon

a to aldre, uplicne ham,

beorhtne[214] burhstede.[215] Blæd bið æghwæm

þæm ðe Hælende hyran[216] þenceð

and wel is þam ðe þæt <wyrcan>[217] mot.

  Wæs[218] þæt encgelcyn ǽr genemned,

Lucifer haten, 'Leohtberende',

on geardagum in Godes rice.

Þa he in wuldre wrohte[219] onstealde[220]

þæt he oferhyda agan wolde.

370   <Þa>[221] Satanus swearte geþohte

þæt he wolde on heofonum hehseld wyrcan

uppe mid þam Écan. Þæt wæs ealdor heora,

yfeles ordfruma.[222] Him þæt eft gehreaw,

þa he to helle hnigan sceolde,

and his hired mid hine, ín hynðo[223] geglidan,

Nergendes nið and no seoððan

þæt hi mosten in þone Ecan andwlítan <seon>[224]

buton ende. Þa him egsa becom,

---

[211] The scribe first wrote a w (wynn) and then added a crossed ascender to make the þ.
[212] Partly erased (for reasons unclear).
[213] a altered from original e.
[214] eo written above cancelled y.
[215] First e written above cancelled y.
[216] y written above e underpointed for deletion.
[217] Not in the manuscript – reading from Clubb 1925.
[218] The initial is 3-lines high and bold.
[219] MS wroht with e squeezed in later and an insertion mark below.
[220] First e added above with an insertion mark below.
[221] Not in the manuscript – reading from Krapp 1931 (p. 147).
[222] MS ordfruman.
[223] MS to.
[224] Not in the manuscript – reading from Holthausen 1895.

                dyne for Deman,   þa he duru in helle
380   bræc and begde.   Blis wearð monnum
                þa hi Hælendes   heafod gesawon.[225]
                Þonne wæs þam atolán   þe we ær nemdon…[226]

                Þa wæron mid egsan   ealle afyrhte,
                wide geond windsele[227]   wordum mændon:
                  'Þis is stronglic,   nu þes storm becom,
                þegen mid þreate,   Þeoden engla.
                Him beforan féreð   fægere[228] leoht
                þonne we æfre ǽr   eagum gesawon
                buton þa we mid englum   uppe wæron.
390   Wile nu ure witu   þurh his wuldres cræft
                eall toweorpan.   Nu ðes Egsa com,
                dyne for Drihtne,   sceal þes dreorga heap
                ungeara nú   atol þrowian.
                Hit is se seolfa   Sunu Waldendes,
                engla Drihten.   Wile uppe heonan
                sawla lædan   and we seoððan á
                þæs yrreweorces   henðo geþoliað.'
                  Hwearf þa to[229] helle   hæleða bearnum,
                Meotod þurh mihte;   wolde manna rim,
400   fela þusenda   forð gelædan
                up to eðle.   Þa com engla sweg,
                dyne on dægred;   hæfde Drihten seolf
                feond oferfohten.   Wæs seo fæhðe[230] þa gyt
                open on uhtan   þa se egsa becom.
                Let þa up faran   eadige sawle,[231]

---

[225] p. 222.
[226] Some text has been lost here, perhaps just one line; see Krapp 1931 (p. 240) for discussion and proposed restorations.
[227] MS *winsele* with *d* added above and an insertion mark below.
[228] Final *e* added by the corrector and an insertion mark below.
[229] Added above with an insertion mark below.
[230] *e* underpointed for deletion and then restored by placing a dot above it.
[231] *e* altered to *a* (for reasons unclear).

Adámes cyn, and ne moste Éfe[232] þa gyt
wlitan in wuldre ær heo[233] wordum cwæð:
  'Ic þe æne abealh, éce Drihten,
þa wit Adam twa eaples þigdon
410 þurh næddran nið, swa wit na ne sceoldon.
Gelærde unc se atola se ðe æfre nú
beorneð on bendum, þæt wit blæd ahton,
haligne ham, heofon to gewalde.
Þa wit ðæs awærgdan wordum gelyfdon,
namon mid handum on þam halgan treo
beorhte blæda; unc þæs bitere forgeald
þa wit in þis hate scræf hweorfan sceoldon,
and wintra rim wunian seoððan,
þusenda feolo, þearle onæled.
420   Nu ic þe halsige, heofenrices Weard,
for þan hirede þe ðu hider[234] læddest,
engla þreatas þæt ic up heonon
mæge and mote mid minre mægðe.
And ymb þreo niht com þegen Hælendes
ham to helle; is nu hæftum strong,
witum werig, swylce him Wuldorcyning
for onmædlan eorre geworden.
Segdest us to soðe þætte seolfa God
wolde helwarum ham gelihtan.
430 Arás þa anra gehwylc and wið earm gesæt,[235]
hleonade wið handa; þeah hylle gryre
egeslic þuhte, wæron ealle þæs
fægen in firnum þæt Freodrihten[236]
wolde him to helpe helle gesecan.'

---

[232] é altered from *æ* by scraping and second *e* over erased *re* (the scribe originally wrote *æfre*).
[233] MS *he* with *o* squeezed in with an insertion mark below.
[234] *-der* over erased letters.
[235] p. 223. A folio containing two illustrations has been lost between pages 222 and 223; see the Gathering Analysis and Diagrams.
[236] MS *heora drihten*.

Ræhte[237] þa mid handum   to Heofencyninge,
bæd Meotod miltse   þurh Marian hád:
'Hwæt. Þu fram minre[238] dohtor,   Drihten, onwoce
in middangeard   mannum to helpe;
nu is geséne   þæt ðu eart sylfa God[239]
440   and[240] ece Ordfruma   ealra gesceafta.'
   Let þa up faran   éce Drihten;
wuldre hæfde   wites clomma
feondum oðfæsted   and heo furðor sceaf
in þæt neowle genip,   nearwe gebéged
þær nu Satanus   swearte þingað,
earm aglæca   and þa atolan mid him,
witum werige.   Nalles wuldres leoht
habban moton   ah in helle grund,
ne hi edcerres   æfre moton
450   wenan seoððan.   Him wæs Drihten God
wrað geworden,   sealde him wites clom,
atole to æhte   and egsan gryre,
dimne[241] and deorcne   deaðes scuwan,
hatne helle grund,   hinsiðgryre.[242]
   Þæt, la, wæs fæger,   þæt se féða cóm
úp to earde   and se Éca mid him,
Meotod mancynnes   in þa mæran burh;
hofon hine mid him   handum halige
witigan up to eðle,   Abrahames cynn.
460   Hæfde þa Drihten seolf   deað oferwunnen,
feond[243] geflemed;[244]   þæt in fyrndagum

---

[237] æ added above original i underpointed for deletion.
[238] MS *mire*.
[239] Written twice, with the second instance underpointed for deletion.
[240] The abbreviation seems to be partly erased.
[241] MS *dimme*.
[242] MS *in sið gryre*.
[243] 4-5 letters have been erased after this.
[244] ge- added in the outer margin by the main scribe.

witegan sædon þæt he swa[245] wolde.
Þis wæs on uhtan eall geworden,
ær dægrede þæt se dyne becom,
hlud of heofonum þa he helle duru
forbræc and forbegde; ban weornodon
þa hie swa leohtne léoman gesawon.

  Gesæt þa mid þære fyrde Frumbearn Godes,
sæde soðcwidum: 'Snotre gastas,
470 ic eow þurh mine mihte geworhte,
Ádam ærest and þæt æðele wif.
Þa hie begeton on Godes willan
feowertig bearna, þæt forð þonon
<on>[246] middangeard[247] menio onwocon[248]
and wintra feola wunian moston,
eorlas on eðle oððæt eft gelamp
þæt hie[249] afyrde[250] eft feond in firenum;
fáh[251] is æghwær.

  Ic on neorxnawonge niwe asette
480 treow mid telgum þæt ða tanas up
æpla[252] bæron[253] and git æton þa
beorhtan blæda swa inc se balewa het,
handþegen[254] helle. Hæfdon forþon hatne grund,
þæs git ofergymdon Hælendes word,
æten þa egsan; wæs se atola beforan,
se inc[255] bam forgeaf balewe geþohtas.

  Þa me gereaw þæt min handgeweorc[256]

---

[245] MS *swa*.
[246] Not in the manuscript – reading from Ettmüller 1850.
[247] MS final *e* erased by scraping.
[248] MS *on wocon* with *e* underpointed for deletion after *w*.
[249] MS *he*.
[250] MS *afyrhte*.
[251] There is an extraneous insertion mark after this word.
[252] p. 224.
[253] Abraded.
[254] *hand-* abraded.
[255] *c* abraded.
[256] MS *handgeweorc* with *g* partly erased.

<þæs>[257] carcernes clom ðrowade.

Næs ða monna gemet, ne mægen engla,
490 ne witegena weorc, ne wera snytero
þæt eow mihte helpan nimðe Hælend God,
se þæt wite ær to wrece gesette.
Ferde to foldan þurh fæmnan had
ufan from eðle and on eorþan gebad
tintregan fela[258] and teonan micelne.
Me seredon ymb secgas monige
dæges and nihtes hu heo me deaðes cwealm,
rices rædboran,[259] hrefnan mihten.
Þa wæs þæs mæles mearc agangen
500 þæt on worulde wæs wintra gerimes
þreo and þritig geara ǽr ic þrowode.
Gemunde ic ðæs mænego on[260] þa minnan[261] ham
lange þæs ðe ic of hæftum ham gelædde
up to earde þæt heo ágan <sceolon>[262]
Drihtnes domas and duguðe þrym;
wuniað in wynnum, habbað wuldres blæd
þusendmælum. Íc eow þingade
þa me on beame beornas sticedon,
garum on gealgum;[263] heow se giunga þær,
510 and ic eft up becom éce dreamas
to haligum Drihtne.'

Swá[264] wuldres Weard wordum sæde,
Meotod moncynnes ær on morgen
þæs þe[265] Drihten God of deaðe aras.

---

[257] Not in the manuscript – reading from Ettmüller 1850.
[258] MS *and fela*.
[259] MS *boran*.
[260] MS *and* (⁊).
[261] MS *minan* with the second *n* added above and an insertion mark below.
[262] Not in the manuscript – reading from Holthausen 1894.
[263] *e* added above and an insertion mark below.
[264] MS *wa* with space left for *s*; there is a prompt for the *s* in the margin suggesting that it was to be a larger initial.
[265] Added above with an insertion mark below.

Næs nan þæs stronglic stan[266] gefæstnod,
þeah he wære mid irne eall ymbfangen
þæt mihte þam miclan mægne wiðhabban
ac[267] he ut eode, engla Drihten,
on þæm fæstenne and gefætian[268] het
520 englas eallbeorhte andleofan gingran
and[269] huru secgan het Simon Petre
þæt he moste in Galileam God sceawian,
ecne and trumne, swa he ær dyde.

   Þa ic gongan gefregn gingran ætsomne
ealle to Galileam; hæfdon Gastes bled,
<ongeton>[270] haligne Godes Sunu
swá heo gesegon hwær Sunu Meotodes
þa on[271] upp gestod,[272] ece Drihten,
God in Galileam. To ðæs gingran þider
530 ealle urnon, þær se Éca wæs;
feollon on foldan and to fotum[273] hnigon,
þanceden Þeodne þæt hit[274] þus gelomp
þæt hi sceawodon Scyppend engla.

   Þa sona spræc Simon Petrus:
'Eart þu þis, Drihten, dome gewurðad?
We ðe gesawon æt sumum cyrre,
þé[275] gelegdon on laðne bend
hæþene[276] mid hondum; him þæt gehreowan mæg
þonne heo endestæf eft gesceawiað.'
540   Sume hie ne mihton mode[277] oncnawan

---

[266] MS *satan*.
[267] *c* added above *h* underpointed for deletion.
[268] *æ* altered from *a* (the added loop of *e* is faint).
[269] There is an extraneous *winum* before this word.
[270] Not in the manuscript – reading from Grein 1857.
[271] There is an extraneous *gingran* before this word, the first on p. 225.
[272] MS *stod*.
[273] *on to fotum* abraded.
[274] *þæt hit*: these words occur twice in the manuscript.
[275] MS *þéc* with final *c* underpointed for deletion.
[276] MS *hæþenne*.
[277] MS *mod*.

þæt wæs se déora – Didimus[278] wæs haten –
ær he mid hondum Hælend genom
sylfne be sidan þær he his swat forlet;
feollon to foldan fulwihtes bæðe.

Fæger wæs þæt ongin þæt Freodrihten
geþrowode, Þeoden ure.
He on beame astah and his blod ageat,
God on gealgan[279] þurh his gastes mægen.
Forþon men sceolon mæla gehwylce
550 secgan Drihtne þanc dædum and weorcum
þæs ðe he us of hæftum ham gelædde
up to eðle þær we agan <sceolon>[280]
Drihtnes domas
and we in wynnum wunian moton.
Us is wuldres leoht
torht ontyned, þam ðe teala þenceð.[281]

Þa[282] wæs on eorðan ece Drihten
feowertig daga folgad folcum,
gecyðed mancynne,[283] ær he in þa mæran gesceaft,
560 burhleoda Fruma, bringan wolde
haligne gast to heofonrice.
Astáh up on heofonum engla Scyppend,
weoroda Waldend; þa com wolcna sweg,
halig of heofonum. Mid wæs hond Godes,
onfeng Freodrihten and hine forð lædde
to þam halgan ham heofna Ealdor –
him ýmbflugon engla þreatas
þusendmælum. Þa hit þus gelomp,
þa gyt Nergende Crist <gecwæþ>[284] þæt he þæs

---
[278] Another name for (doubting) Thomas; it is only found St John's Gospel (11:26, 20:24).
[279] e added above with an insertion mark below.
[280] Not in the manuscript – reading from Holthausen 1894.
[281] p. 226. There lower half of this page is filled with a square of geometric patterning and interlace.
[282] MS *a* with space left before it for a 2-line high initial.
[283] MS *man cynnes*.
[284] Not in the manuscript – reading proposed by Krapp 1931 (p. 154).

570	ymb tene²⁸⁵ niht twelf apostolas
	mid his gastes gife, gingran geswiðde.
	Hæfde þa gesette²⁸⁶ sawla unrim
	God lifigende; þa wæs Iúdas of,
	se ðe ær on tifre torhtne gesalde,
	Drihten Hælend; him seo dæd ne geþeah,
	þæs he bebohte Bearn Wealdendes
	on seolfres sinc – him þæt swearte forgeald
	earm æglæca innon helle.
	Siteð nu on þa swiðran hond Sunu his Fæderes;
580	dæleð dogra gehwæm Drihten weoroda
	help and hælo hæleþa bearnum
	geond middangeard. Þæt is monegum cuð
	þæt he ana is ealra gescefta
	Wyrhta and Waldend þurh his wuldres cræft.
	Siteð him on heofnum halig encgel,
	Waldend mid witegum. Hafað wuldres Bearn
	his seolfes seld swegl behealden.²⁸⁷
	Laðað²⁸⁸ us þider to leohte þurh his læcedom
	þær we moton seolfe sittan mid Drihtne,
590	uppe mid englum, habban þæt ilce leoht
	þær his²⁸⁹ hired nu halig eardað,
	wunað in wynnum; þær is wuldres bléd
	torht ontyned. Uton <teala>²⁹⁰ hycgan
	þæt we Hælende heran georne,
	Criste cweman;²⁹¹ þær is cuðre lif
	þonne we on eorðan mægen æfre gestreonan.
	Hafað²⁹² nu geþingod to us Þeoden mæra,

---

[285] MS *ane*.
[286] MS *ge sette* with a letter erased after *ge*.
[287] MS *betalden* with *t* scratched away and underpointed for deletion and *he* added above.
[288] *e* erased before the first *a*.
[289] *h* added above with an insertion mark below.
[290] Not in the manuscript – reading from Krapp 1931 (p. 154).
[291] *a* altered from *æ* by scraping.
[292] The **h** is 5-lines high and zoomorphic, extending well below the last line into the bottom margin.

       ælmihtig God,
       on[293] domdæge Drihten seolfa.
600   Hateð heahenglas[294] hluddre stefne
       byman[295] blawan ofer burga geseotu
       geond foldan sceatas.
       Þonne of þisse moldan men onwecniað;[296]
       deade of duste arisað þurh Drihtnes miht.
       Þæt bið daga lengust and dinna[297] mæst
       hlud gehyred þonne Hælend cymeð,
       Waldend mid wolcnum in þas woruld færeð.
       Wile þonne gesceadan[298] wlitige and unclæne
       on twa healfe, tile and yfle.
610   Him þa soðfæstan on þa swiðran hond
       mid rodera Weard reste gestigað.
       Þonne beoð bliðe þa[299] in burh móton
       gangan[300] in Godes rice
       and héo gesenað mid his swiðran hond
       Cynincg alwihta, cleopað ofer ealle:
        'Ge sind wilcuman – gað in wuldres leoht
       to heofona rice þær ge habbað
       á to aldre éce ræste.'[301]
        Þonne stondað þa forworhtan, þa ðe firnedon;
620   beoð beofigende hwonne[302] him Bearn Godes
       deman wille þurh his dæda sped.
       Wénað þæt heo moten tó þære mæran byrig
       up to englum swa oðre dydon,

---

[293] This word is the last on p. 226 and is inadvertently repeated as the first on p. 227.
[294] MS *heh* with *a* added above and an insertion mark below.
[295] MS *beman* with *y* written over the *e*.
[296] MS *onwecnað* with *i* added above and an insertion mark below.
[297] MS *dimma* – reading from Thorpe 1832.
[298] MS *gesceawian*.
[299] *þe* added above with an insertion mark below (for reasons unclear).
[300] *o* altered to *a*.
[301] *æ* altered from original *e* by adding a loop to it.
[302] MS *þonne* with *þ* altered to *wynn* by scraping and *h* added above with an insertion mark below.

ac[303] him bið reordende[304]
éce Drihten, ofer ealle gecwyð:[305]
   'Astigað nu, awyrgde, in þæt witehus
ófostum miclum; nu ic éow ne con.'
   Sona æfter þæm wordum werige gastas,
helle hæftas, hwyrftum scriþað
630 þusendmælum and þider[306] lædað[307]
in þæt sceaðena scræf, scufað to grunde
in þæt nearwe nið and no seoððan
þæt hie up þonan æfre moton
ah þær geþolian sceolon earmlic wíte,
clom and carcern, and þone caldan grund
deopne adreogan and deofles spellunge
hu hie him on edwit oft asettað
swarte suslbonan, stæleð <feondas>[308]
fæhðe and[309] firne, þær ðe hie Freodrihten,[310]
640 écne Anwaldan, oft forgeaton
þone[311] þe[312] hie him to hihte habban sceoldon.
Uton, la, geþencan geond þas worulde
þæt we Hælende hyran[313] onginnen.
Georne þurh Godes gife gemunan gastes bled,
hu eadige þær uppe sittað
sylfe[314] mid swegle, Sunu[315] Hælendes.
Þær is geat gylden[316] gimmum gefrætewod,

---

[303] *c* altered from original *h* by scraping.
[304] MS *reodiende* with *r* added above and an insertion mark below, *en* written above an erasure, and two letters erased after *de*.
[305] *y* written over an *æ* underpointed for deletion.
[306] *he* erased before this by scraping.
[307] MS *lædað* with original *e* altered to *æ* and *a* erased after *e* by scraping, and the first *ð* altered to *d* by scraping away its crossbar.
[308] Not in the manuscript – reading from Krapp 1931 (p. 155 – see the discussion there).
[309] Followed by an extraneous *in*.
[310] MS *drihten* – reading from Krapp 1931 (p. 156).
[311] MS *þonne* with first *n* erased.
[312] Added above with an insertion mark below.
[313] *y* written over original *e*.
[314] *y* written over original first *e*.
[315] An extraneous *torht* before this word.
[316] MS *gyldenne* with final *ne* erased by scraping.

```
              wynnum bewunden   þæm þe in wuldres leoht
              gongan moten   to Godes rice
650           and ymb þa weallas   wlitige scinað
              engla gastas   and eadige sawla,³¹⁷
              þa ðe heonon ferað.
                 Þær martiras   Meotode cwemað
              and herigað Hehfæder   halgum stefnum,
              Cyning in cestre.   Cweþað ealle þus:
                 'Þu eart hæleða Helm   and Heofendéma,³¹⁸
              engla Ordfruma³¹⁹   and eorðan tudor
              <up gelæddest>³²⁰   to þissum eadigan ham.'
                 Swa wuldres Weard   wordum herigað
660           þegnas ymb Þeoden,   þær is þrym micel,
              sang æt selde,   is sylf Cyning,
              ealra Ealdor,³²¹   in ðære écan gesceft.
              Þæt is se Drihten,   seðe deað for ús
              geþrowode,   Þeoden engla.
                 Swylce he fæste   feowertig daga,
              Metod mancynnes,   þurh his mildsa sped.
              Þa gewearð þone weregan,   þe ǽr aworpen wæs
              of heofonum   þæt he³²² in helle gedéaf,
              þa costode   Cyning alwihta;
670           brohte him to bearme   brade stanas,
              bæd him for hungre   hlafas wyrcan –
              'gif þu swa micle   mihte hæbbe.'
                 Þa him andswarode   éce Drihten:
              'Wendest þu, awyrgda,   þæt awriten nære,
```

---

³¹⁷ p. 228.
³¹⁸ MS *heofen deman*.
³¹⁹ MS *ordfruman* with *n* erased by scraping.
³²⁰ Not in the manuscript – reading from Grein 1857.
³²¹ MS *aðor* with *ð* altered to *d* by adding a crossbar, and *e* added above before *a* and *l* after it with an insertion mark below.
³²² Added above with an insertion mark below.

nymþe me ænne…[323]

      ac geseted hafast,   sigores Agend,

      lifigendum liht,   lean butan ende

      on heofenrice,   halige dreamas.'

                Þa he mid hondum genom

680   atol þurh edwit   and on esle[324] ahof,

      herm[325] bealowes[326] gast   and on beorh astah,

      asette on dune   Drihten Hælend:

      'Loca nu ful wide   ofer londbúende.[327]

      Ic þe geselle   <on>[328] þines seolfes dom[329]

      folc and foldan;   foh hider to me

      burh and breotone   bold to[330] gewealde,

      rodora rices,   gif þu seo riht Cyning

      engla and monna   swa ðu ær myntest.'

                Þa him andswarode   ece Drihten:

690   'Gewit þu, awyrgda,   in þæt witescræf,

      Satanus seolf;   þé is susl weotod

      géaro[331] togegnes,   nalles Godes rice.

      Ah ic þe hate   þurh þa hehstan miht

      þæt ðu hellwarum   hyht ne abeode

      ah þu him secgan miht   sorga mæste

      þæt ðu gemettes   Meotod alwihta,

      Cyning moncynnes.   Cyr[332] ðe on bæcling.

      Wite þu éac, awyrgda,   hu wíd and síd

      helheoðo dreorig   and mid hondum amet.

---

[323] The sense is defective here indicating a loss of some text – see Krapp 1931 (p. 246) for a summary of critical proposals for amending of the text.
[324] *h* added above with an insertion mark below after first *e* (for reasons unclear).
[325] MS *her* with *m* added above and an insertion mark below.
[326] Tall *s* added by the scribe – he generally does not use the tall *s*, but does so again six lines later in *hehstan*.
[327] MS *lond b wende* with *ú* written above an original *e* erased by scraping and *wynn* marked for deletion by underlining.
[328] Not in the manuscript – reading from Thorpe 1832.
[329] MS *seoferdum*.
[330] Added above with an insertion mark below.
[331] *o* written above original final *a*.
[332] *y* written over original *e*.

700	Grip wið þæs grundes; gang þonne swa
	oððæt þu þone ymbhwyrft alne cunne,
	and ærest amet ufan to grunde,
	and hu sid seo[333] se swarta eðm.
	Wast þu þonne þe geornor þæt þu wið God wunne,
	seoððan þu þonne hafast handum ametene
	hu heh and deop hell inneweard seo,
	grim græfhus. Gong ricene to,
	ǽr twa seondon[334] tida agongene
	þæt ðu merced hus ameten hæbbe.'
710	Þa[335] þam[336] werigan[337] wearð wracu[338] getenge.
	Satan seolua ran[339] and on susle gefeol,
	earm æglæce.[340] Hwilum mid folmum mæt
	wéan[341] and witu; hwilum se wonna leg[342]
	læhte wið þes laþan; hwilum he licgan geseah
	hæftas in hylle; hwilum hréam[343] astah[344]
	ðonne he on þone atolan eagum gesawun.
	Hæfdon gewunnon Godes ándsacan...[345]
	blac bealowes[346] gast, þæt he on botme stód.
	Þa him þuhte þæt þanon wære
720	to helleduru hund þusenda
	mila gemearcodes, swa hine se Mihtiga het

---

[333] This follows extraneous *eðm* in the manuscript.

[334] MS *seond* with *on* added above and an insertion mark below.

[335] p. 229. A folio containing two illustrations (the conjugate of that lost between pages 212 sand 213) has been lost here; see the Gathering Analysis and Diagrams.

[336] *Þa þam* seem to have been corrected – the *a* of *þam* appears to be altered from original *e* and the *þ* from *s*.

[337] MS *werga* with *i* added above and an insertion mark below, and final *n* also added above.

[338] MS *wrece* with first *e* altered to *a* and *u* written above final *e* underpointed for deletion.

[339] *n* added above.

[340] MS *æglece* with *æ* accented and first *e* altered to *æ* by adding a bow to it.

[341] *wynn* is over an erasure and the top stroke of preceding *t* is extended over another erased letter.

[342] MS *lǽg* with the bow of *æ* scraped away.

[343] *h* added above.

[344] *h* added above original *g* underlined for deletion.

[345] The sense is defective here indicating a loss of some text – see Krapp 1931 (p. 247) for a summary of critical proposals for amending of the text.

[346] MS *bealowe* with final *s* added above.

þæt þurh sinne[347] cræft susle amæte.

Ða he gemunde þæt[348] he on grunde stod.

Locade leas wiht geond þæt laðe scræf,

atol mid egum oððæt egsan gryre

deofla mænego þonne up astag.

Wordum in witum ongunnon þa werigan[349] gastas

reordian and cweðan:

'Lá, þus beo nú on yfele; noldæs ær teala.'

730   *FINIT LIBER .II. AMEN.*[350]

---

[347] MS *synne*.
[348] MS *þa*.
[349] The extraneous words *on þa* are written before this word.
[350] There is no equivalent phrase earlier marking the end of a 'Liber .I.'

ART-HISTORICAL COMMENTARY

ii [Frontispiece; lines 1-16; Artist A] God is seated on a cushioned throne above chaos before Creation. There is a double arch above him which perhaps depicts the vault of heaven; the inner arch is painted yellow. Two multi-winged angels, with eyes on one pair of their wings, flank the Deity and two winged beings support his throne; these are personifications of the winds, inspired by the opening verses of Psalm 103, a celebration of God as Creator:

> …who coverest the higher rooms thereof with water. Who makest the clouds thy chariot: who walkest upon the wings of the winds (Ps. 103:3)

Raw 1976 (p. 143) links these figures to the illustration of this Psalm in the *Utrecht Psalter*, part of the evidence for Continental influence on the illustrations of Junius 11. God is bearded and cross-nimbed; he holds a ringed scroll in his left hand and extends his right hand in a blessing gesture. Raw (p. 137, n. 2) shows the connection between this scroll (with rings) and similar ones depicted in two Carolingian manuscripts with illustrations of the Apocalypse (BnF ms nouv. acq. lat. 1132, f. 1 and Valenciennes, Bibl. mun. ms 99, f. 3). The folds of his robe are naturalistic and the artist attempts to use perspective. In her catalogue, Temple 1976 (p. 77) describes the robed figures throughout Junius 11 thus:

> …the large-headed, somewhat wooden figures with awkward gestures are invigorated by the richly varied patterns of the garments flaring out stiffly at the bottom in wildly agitated but strangely frozen and formalized hemlines…

Surging and swirling lines depict the waters of chaos leaping towards the heavens. An inscription in Latin at the top of the folio reads *Genesis in anglico*, ('Genesis in English'). The related Biblical passage is Gen. 1:1-2.

The Biblical sources for the iconography here are:

> Exod. 25:22, 'Thence will I give orders, and will speak to thee over the propitiatory [the lid of the Ark of the Covenant], and from the midst of the two Cherubim'. Ezech. 10:12 says that the wings of the Cherubims were full of eyes, and 10:21 states that they each had four wings and four faces, and that the likeness of a man's hand was under their wings. Isaiah 6:2, 'Upon it stood the Seraphims: the one had six wings, and the other had six wings: with two they covered his face, and with two they covered his feet, and with two they flew.' Apoc. 4:8, 'And the four living creatures had each of them six wings: and round about and within they are full of eyes.' Ps. 98:1 reads, 'The Lord hath reigned, let the people be angry: he that sitteth on the Cherubims, let the earth be moved'.[1]

2   [lines 20-46; Artist A] God, cross-nimbed and bearded, is seated on the same cushioned throne as in the previous illustration, again holding a ringed scroll and flanked by multi-winged angels (see the commentary for the Frontispiece (p. ii) for a description of these). This time he looks down to his right and addresses Lucifer, who has two wings and is nimbed; while looking up towards God, he is gesturing with his hands, as if reinforcing a

---

[1] Biblical references and citations are to the Latin *Vulgate* and the Douay-Rheims translation of it (Reims 1582, for the New Testament, and Douai 1609-10, for the Old Testament in two volumes).

point in his argument. It is most likely the archangel Michael who is positioned above him, though he is not identified here (see below); he has two wings and a flowing sash or cloak. His hands are raised as if in adoration. A caption in the outer margin reads *hælendes hehseld*, ('the lofty throne of the Saviour/Healer').

Interestingly, St Michael the archangel is not mentioned by name anywhere in the poem; in the illustration of the 'Creation of Eve' on p. 9, however, a caption above the head of the angel standing in the doorway at the top of the ladder identifies him as 'Michael'. Gollancz 1927 (p. xxxix) identifies the upper angel here on p. 2 as St Michael, which since that time has generally been accepted by scholars. Ohlgren 1972a (pp. 28-30) is inclined to identify the unfinished (12th century?) drypoint etching of an advancing warrior with sword and shield in the 'blank' area at the bottom of p. 12 with St Michael. The text immediately before this, however, describes the garden of Paradise, so the identification of the incised image as Michael is less than positive – the image is most likely extraneous doodling by a later reader (it is certainly not well executed, and was not drawn by either Artist A or Artist B). There is a break in the text after p. 12 – *Genesis B* begins at this point) – but there is no reason to expect that the lost portion of the Creation narrative would make reference to Michael. The beginning of *Genesis B* has also been lost.

Below this main scene at the bottom of the folio there is a profile portrait of a beardless man in a double-rimmed medallion; the name *Ælfwine* is written within the medallion. Gollancz 1927, following C.R. Morey (in Kennedy 1916, p. 190), is inclined to identify this Ælfwine with the person who became abbot of the New Minster in Winchester in 1035 but, as he points out the name was quite common in Anglo-Saxon England, so the grounds for making this assumption are at best shaky. He notes that, '[i]t is not likely that the artist is portraying himself, or his fellow-worker the scribe' (p. xxxv). Wormald 1952 (p. 76) notes that artistically Junius 11 bears no resemblance to the two surviving manuscripts associated with Abbot Ælfwine (BL Cotton MSS Titus D.xxvi and xxvii). Ælfwine may well have been a patron – Raw 1976 (p. 148) notes that because Junius 11 is so richly decorated it is 'likely to have been a presentation copy'. She suggests that, 'it may have been a gift on the marriage of Æthelwulf of Wessex to Charles's [Charles the Bald] daughter Judith in 856.' Lucas 1994 (pp. 2-5), who argues that the manuscript was made at Malmesbury, suggests that the Ælfwine portrayed here may be the person who was its abbot from *c.*1043-6.[2]

---

[2] Ker 1957 (p. 408), following James 1903 (pp. xxv-xxvi, 51 and 509), observes that the manuscript is 'possibly identical with the *Genesis anglice depicta* in the early fourteenth-century catalogue of Christ Church, Canterbury'. Wormald 1952 (p. 76) also accepts Canterbury as the place of origin. Raw 1984 believes that the manuscript may originally have been bound in limp covers (*in pergameno,* p. 266), a practice associated with St Augustine's, Canterbury. Doane 1978 (pp. 23-4) notes a similarity between some of the Junius illustrations and BL Cotton MS Claudius B.iv, a known Canterbury production. Ohlgren 1975 argues for Newminster, Winchester, but its case seems not to be as strong as that for Canterbury.

Lucas 1994 (pp. 2-5) details the evidence which he believes supports a Malmesbury attribution:

- the phrase *Genesis anglice depicta* used by James 1903 (xxv-xxvi, 51 and 509) is very general and might refer to some other manuscript (including BL Cotton MS Claudius B.iv, which was known to have been at Canterbury at some time).

- some of the illustrations in M Junius 11 bear striking resemblance to some carved medallions of the south porch of Malmesbury Abbey.

For the Biblical sources for the iconography here, see the Frontispiece (p. ii). It should be noted that the illustrations on this folio go with *Genesis B*, the Old English rendition of the original Old Saxon Genesis poem (which survives in fragmentary form), and not with *Genesis A* – Satan's rebellion and the Fall of the rebel angels into the depths of Hell are recounted in the former. Moreover, the two complete captions on p. 3 are derived from lines 292-7 and 318-20 of the poem. Raw 1976 (p. 146) argues convincingly that,

> [t]he derivation of both text and illustrations from continental material of a single period suggests that this adaptation [of the Genesis cycle pictures] was made on the continent and that pictures and text came to England together. A comparison of the Junius drawings of the rebellion and Fall of the angels and of the descendants of Adam with the texts of *Genesis A*, *Genesis B* and the Old Saxon *Genesis* confirms this view.

She connects the Junius illustrations of Adam and Eve with 'four ninth-century Bibles associated with Tours and with the court school of Charles the Bald (reigned 840-77)'; she continues:

> The pictures of Cain and Able show similarities of detail to a painting in a manuscript known to have been at Tours by the ninth century. The picture of God enthroned and holding a scroll resemble a painting which has connections with the Court School at Aachen, and the Frontispiece includes a detail found also in the *Utrecht Psalter*, a manuscript executed at Rheims... The insignia in the picture of Satan's rebellion resemble in detail those of Charles the Bald and, to a lesser extent, those of his father and grandfather, Louis the Pious and Charlemagne... From all this a Carolingian ancestor for the third, main group of illustrations in the Junius manuscript [Frontispiece, and pages 2-3, 9-51, 60-1 and 65-88] can safely be inferred.

3   [lines 49-69; Artist A] There are four horizontal registers containing depictions of episodes from the Fall of the Rebel Angels. In the top register Lucifer, holding a flowered sceptre in his left hand, stands on a dias facing the observer in the central area, surrounded by three groups of adoring angels, some of whom wear wreathes. The four angels at the lower right offer crowns to Lucifer, perhaps referring to regions of the world or his new kingdom. Lucifer addresses the group of angels on the upper right, while pointing with his right hand to a two-storied palace, which has a vacant cushioned throne in the opening of its upper level. The roof of the palace has fish-scale or scalloped tiles, and some of its windows have shutters. Considerable effort has been made to draw the building using perspective. There is a less substantial architectural frame behind the group of angels on the upper right. Most of the

---

- Artist B of MS Junius 11 also drew the Virtues and Vices illustrations in the 'Corpus Prudentius' (Cambridge, CCC MS 23), a known Malmesbury book.

- there was an abbot of Malmesbury from *c.*1043-6 named *Ælfwine*, the name in the medallion on p. 2 of MS Junius 11.

He also notes that there is evidence of smoke damage to the folded edge of the gatherings, which occurred before the manuscript was bound; he suggests that this may have been caused by a fire at Malmesbury during the reign of Edward the Confessor (recorded by William of Malmesbury), in which the monastery suffered considerable damage.

figures and artefacts on this folio are either outlined or drawn with red ink. A partially cropped caption in the top margin reads, *Hu s<e> engyl ongon ofermod wesan* ('How the angel began to be proud'); see Section 10.

Raw 1976 (pp. 145-6) has analysed the paraphernalia associated with the crowning of Lucifer here and has shown that it is depicted in terms of imperial insignia and ceremonies of the 9th century. While the lily staff has an ancient history, the lily sceptre is first known from an illustration depicting the investiture of Charles the Bald in 869. So too the crowns worn by Satan and the second and fourth angels below him on the right are not English, but Continental in style. Figures bearing palm branches or fronds (see below) are also associated with the investiture ceremony, and the four angels bearing gifts can be associated with depictions of 'the homage of the provinces'.[3] The inclusion of these details here are compelling evidence of the Continental origin of the illustrations in Junius 11.

In the next register Lucifer stands in the centre with three worshipping angels standing to each side of him holding palm branches in their hands. He wears a wreath (perhaps ironically here, the palm of victory) on his head. Alternatively, the scene may depict one of the victorious angels handing out fronds or palms of victory to the faithful angels, as suggested by Jane Rosenthal 1974 (pp. 190-1) but this seems less likely in light of Raw's compelling analysis).

In the next register God (cross-nimbed and bearded), with three angels (wearing wreathes) on his right and two on his left, casts the rebellious angels into Hell, which he has prepared for them; he holds three spears or javelins in his raised right hand and a scroll in his left. A caption at the top right of this register reads, *Her se hælend gesco<p> helle heom to wite* ('Here the Healer/Saviour created hell as a torment for them'), but this is clearly out of place and should be beside the lower illustration.

In the lower register Lucifer, now Satan, lies chained in the 'Mouth of Hell', with the loops of the chain hooked over the canine teeth of 'Hell' (personified). Ohlgren 1972 (p. 204) notes that the chaining of Lucifer motif derives from Apoc. 20:1-3; it was interpolated from the Apocalypse by the early Church Fathers into their commentaries on Genesis. Isaiah 14:11-15 provides the Bible's most extensive description of Satan, the cause of his Fall and his plight:

> Thy pride is brought down to hell: thy carcass is fallen. Under thee shall the moth be strewed and worms shall be thy covering. [12] How art thou fallen from heaven, O Lucifer, who didst rise in the morning? How art thou fallen to the earth, that didst wound the nations? [13] And thou saidst in thy heart: I will ascend into heaven. I will exalt my throne above the stars of God. I will sit in the mountain of the covenant, in the sides of the north. [14] I will ascend above the height of the clouds, I will be like the most High. [15] But yet thou shalt be brought down to hell, into the depth of the pit.

The Old Saxon/Anglo-Saxon poet has included a number of these details in his development of the story of the rebellion and Fall of Lucifer; he says, for example, 'Then there fell upon them grievously, the envy, presumption, and pride of the Angel who first began to carry out the evil plot, to weave it and promote it, when he boasted by word... as he thirsted for

---

[3] See, for example, *The Gospel Book of Otto III*, Munich Bayerische staatsbibl., Clm. 4453, f. 23ᵛ-24ʳ.

conflict... that he wished to own the home and high throne of the heavenly kingdom to the north' (28^b-34^a; trans. Mason 1990 (pp. 7-8).

The inclusion of the chaining of Lucifer is further evidence that the artist is creatively adapting the iconographic tradition (as is the inclusion of the tempter in angelic form in the temptation scenes on pages 20, 24, 28, 31 and 36). Gollancz 1927 (p. xxxix) notes that the teeth of Hell have theological significance; he quotes a passage describing Jonah being swallowed by the whale in the Middle English poem *Patience*, which reveals an awareness of this: *wythouten towche of any tothe... tult in his þrote* (l. 252, 'Without ever touching a tooth, he tumbled in the throat').

The rebel angels tumble into the abyss, together with fragments of Satan's destroyed palace; he and his followers lose their robes as they fall and are subsequently naked in their banishment, symbolic of their humiliation (later in the manuscript (e.g. on p. 16) the devil and a rebel angel are depicted as wingless, further indication of their fallen status). An incomplete caption of the upper left between registers 3c and 3d reads, *her se* ('Here the...), and the word *inferne* ('below, underneath') is written (probably later) next to one of the fallen angels on the top left.

There are three ways of illustrating 'hell' in the manuscript: as the personified 'Mouth of Hell' (here and on p. 16), as a walled enclosure (as on pages 16, 17 and 20), and as a 'fiery pit' (an oval shape with flames surging from its interior wall as on p. 36); there is a similar depiction of the 'pit of hell' with red surging flames, in the *Eadwine Psalter* (fols. 1^v and 5^v; see Gibson 1992, Figs. 20a, 21a [*Utrecht Psalter* source]). Raw 1976 (p. 144) notes that the 'architectural' type of hell is probably derived from an ancestor of the illustrations in Junius 11, but that the depiction of the 'mouth' image was probably added in England to an earlier Continental model; she notes a similar image in BL Cotton MS Titus D.xxvii (f. 75^v), the main part of which is derived from three images illustrating Ps. 103 in the *Utrecht Psalter*.[4]

Isaiah 5:14 refers to 'Hell' personified: 'Therefore hath hell enlarged her soul and opened her mouth without any bounds: and their strong ones and their people and their high and glorious ones shall go down into it'. The War of the Angels, with Michael battling against Satan's minions, is mentioned in Apoc. 20:1-3. See also the discussion of the creation of the angels in the Commentary on the next image (p. 6). Jude 9 refers to Michael contending with the Devil over the body of Moses, and Daniel 10:13, 21 and 12:1 contain references to Michael as humankind's defender. Other Biblical passages which may have been influential in the evolution of the iconography of Hell and the fall of Satan include Osee 3:14, Ps. 57:7, Ps. 123:4-7, Luke 10:17-20 and 2 Peter 2:4. Several passages in the Gospel of Matthew describe the 'outer darkness', a 'furnace of fire' and 'wailing and the gnashing of teeth' – see 8:12, 13:37-43, 22:13, 24:51 and 25:30. For further critical discussion, see Bernstein 1993 and Schmidt 1995.

6 [lines 103-34; Artist A] The first and second days of Creation are depicted here: the creation of light and the separation of light from darkness. God, cross-nimbed but here

---

[4] There are also depictions of the gaping 'Mouth of Hell' in the *Paris Psalter*, in the images accompanying Psalms 1, 5 and 33 (fols. 5^v, 10 and 56^v); see similar depictions in the *Utrecht Psalter* (fols. 8, a 'Harrowing of Hell' scene, and 90, a *Credo* illustration), *Tiberius Psalter* (BL Cotton MS Tiberius C.vi, f. 14 [the bound Satan beside the gaping Mouth has an animal head and claws on both feet and hands; Christ stands on Satan while bending forward to rescue the Old Testament Just]) and the Winchester *Liber Vitae* (BL MS Stowe 944, f. 7). For a recent study of the 'Mouth of Hell' see Schmidt 1995.

beardless, sits on the rim of the firmament with a footstool beneath his feet. Above him an angel holds an inverted dome, out of which stream light rays, which have just been created. With his right hand, God seems to be directing the rays towards the darkness below, towards which he points with his left hand. Raw 1976 (p. 137) notes that this bowl of light is similar to an object 'shown in the hands of a standing angel in an eleventh-century drawing on the flyleaf of Oxford, St. John's College 28.' Gollancz 1927 (p. xxxix) thinks that this may be a depiction of 'the brightness of the everlasting light' which is equated with divine wisdom in Wisdom 7:26; verses 29-30 read, 'For she is more beautiful than the sun, and above all the order of the stars: being compared with the light, she is found before it. [30] For after this cometh night: but no evil can overcome wisdom.'

Above the agitated waters at the bottom of the illustration there is an angel covering his eyes/face with drapery, representing darkness – the Biblical account says, *et tenebrae erant super faciem abyssi* ('…and darkness was upon the face [surface] of the deep', Gen. 1:2). Some critics believe that this figure represents the 'spirit of God' moving over the waters, but this seems less likely, in that it doesn't account for why the winged figure would be covering its eyes with a cloth. Henderson 1985 (p. 167) cites analogues in various Italian mosaics for the personification of light and darkness, and notes further that, 'The Greek Octateuchs show the division of light from darkness in very similar form to the Junius MS, though only God's hand is shown. Light (Day) is a dancing figure with a torch, darkness (Night) a dark robed figure covering its face with a scarf.'

At the top left there is a cropped caption which reads, *<Her he> gesyndrode wæter and eorðan* ('[Here he] separated water and earth'), which is clearly out of place – it goes with the illustration in the upper register of p. 7.

The Fathers of the Church and subsequent medieval theologians have sometimes reflected on the question of at what point angels were created – they are not specifically mentioned in the Biblical Creation narrative, but tradition, as reflected in the illustration cycle here, places the War in Heaven and the Fall of the Angels before the Creation event, even though the only reference to it in the Bible is with respect to the end of time (in Apoc. 20:1-3). St Augustine, for example, noting that the creation of the angels is not specifically mentioned, points out that in the Book of Job God is recorded as saying, 'When the stars were made, all my angels praised me with a loud voice' (38:7). The stars were fashioned on the fourth day of Creation, so Augustine places the creation of the angels before that. Since they are not mentioned in the accounts of God's creative acts on either the second or the third day, he concludes that they must have been created on the first day:

> The obvious conclusion is that if the angels are among the works of God on those days, they are that light which received the name of 'day'. And the unity of that day is underlined by its not being called 'the first day', but 'one day' (*City of God*, XI.10; Bettensen 1972, p. 439).

Gen. 1:2-8.

7   [lines 154-68; Artist A] The third to sixth days of Creation are depicted here in four areas enclosed in intersecting circles: the separation of water and land (the Earth and the Seas), the creation of plant life, of day and night, of the stars and the sun and the moon, of birds, animals and fish (but not humans, at this point). Temple 1976 (p. 76) notes that the Creation sequence is out of order in the illustration; this is because there is a bird and a stag

in the upper scene, and they were not created until the fifth and sixth days respectively, after the stars in the firmament had been created (on the fourth day).

The upper two circles and lower two should be read as narrative unities. In the topmost circle a cross-nimbed and bearded God stands within a mandorla, cradling a book in his left arm and holding up his right hand in a blessing gesture; the ends of his robe appear to flap in the wind. Between the double lines of the mandorla frame on the left-hand side is the word *salvator* ('Saviour'). Here, as in the Old Testament poetic narratives, there is no theological impropriety in Anglo-Saxon scribes and poets referring to the God of Creation as the 'Saviour', even though humanity has not even been created at this point, or to the Trinity, even though the doctrine of the Trinity was only formulated by the Church much later in the Christian era, because the triune God is eternal – He always was, is and will be Saviour and a Trinity.

The circle below this illustrates the creation birds, animals and vegetative life; below the earth's surface the artist has depicted the waters beneath the earth. It has been suggested that the bird may be the pelican mentioned in Ps. 101:7 (Ohlgren1992, p. 89) and that it may be symbolic, but other birds are also mentioned in the same passage and there is no compelling reason for making that association here. The same author suggest that the stag may be intended to allude to Ps. 41:2 and also be symbolic, but again the suggestion is not compelling. There is a small cross at the centre of the acanthus tree, which suggests that it is the 'Tree of Life'; Swanton 2002 observes:

> The same Trinitarian sensibility is at work in the illumination of the unique, if late, manuscript of the poem, which depicts a small cross, the symbol of atonement, concealed in the uppermost branches of the tree of life in the Garden of Eden – the salvation of fallen man prefigured from the very moment of creation – and which shows the figure of Jesus blessing those who enter the Ark' (p. 86).

Gollancz 1927 (p. xl) observes that the cross in the tree 'is evidently a reference to the legend of the Holy Rood Tree as created from the beginning.'[5]

A caption in the right hand margin beside this scene reads, *her he* (added above) *todælde dæg wið nihte* ('Here he separated day from night'), which properly goes with the illustration below this one. Henderson 1985 (p. 167), however, entertains the possibility that it may not be positioned incorrectly:

> It seems to me possible that in the drawing on p. 7 we are shown a naive and literal illustration of day and night, day being represented by the open sky, full flowering

---

[5] The Cross is sometimes treated as a mystic ladder by medieval theologians; it is a towering link between heaven and earth:

> *Vere crux Christi scala est a terra in coelum attingens quia per fidem crucis, per imitationem passionis, redit homo de exilio ad patriam, de morte ad vitam, de terra ad coelum, de deserto huius mundi ad paradisum.*
>
> ['Indeed, the Cross of Christ is a ladder reaching from earth to heaven, because through the faith of the Cross, through the imitation of the passion, man returns from exile to his homeland, from death to life, from earth to heaven, from the desert of this life to paradise.' Alanus de Insulis, *PL* 210.224].

plants and animals sunning themselves, while night is represented by the stars filling the sky, and the dark stiff plants. If so, then curiously enough the inscription on p. 7 correctly interpreted the subject.

In the two circles in the lower half of the illustration the iconography resembles that found on the previous folio (p. 6). Again, God is cross-nimbed and beardless, but here he *stands* on the rim of the firmament and holds a book in his left hand; his right hand is extended in a blessing gesture. The end of his robe flaps in the breeze. Above him an angel holds an inverted dome, out of which stream light rays; in the circle below the newly-created stars dot the heavens, lighting up the plants and vegetation below. It is interesting to note that the artist does not depict the sun and the moon, since their importance is singled out in the Biblical account (Gen. 1:16-18).

Since the artist has clearly depicted the Creator as both bearded and beardless on the same folio, it may well be concluded that he intended to depict both the 'Father' and the 'Son' as 'Creator'; this would be consistent with his understanding of their co-eternal nature. There is also a bearded and a beardless Creator in the 'Creation of Eve' sequence on p. 9. [In the *Lambeth Bible* (Maidstone Museum and Art Gallery), vol. 2, the illustration for Psalm 109 on f. 32^v shows God the Father and the Son seated together on a bench (they are virtually identical); the Son, on the left (but the *right-hand* side of the Father) has his feet upon his enemies, that is, they are depicted following the Psalm as his footstool (*scabellum*).]

The book which the Creator is holding here (and in the topmost register) is the 'Book of Life' (see Apoc. 3:5, 13:8, 17:8, 20:12 *et passim*), which was written 'from the foundation of the world'; in it are recorded the deeds by which everyone will be judged at the end of time.

At the very top of the folio, in the space to the right of God as Creator, there is a figure added much later, who is positioned looking over God's shoulder as he is in the act of creating. Finnegan 1988 argues that this figure was added later by the Artist B and that it is in his style; the face does, in fact, resemble that of God in the lower register on p. 84. He argues that Artist B's figure 'secretly scrutinizes... and perhaps judges the work of his predecessor' (p. 31); he concludes:

> The second artist has complicated the character of page 7 by bringing us, the viewers, into the artistic frame. A merging of perspective results when we discover this figure doing exactly what we are doing: studying and judging the first artist's execution of the original creation. The observing figure is our, the viewers', double, literally marginalized, but definitely there. (p. 32)

Gen. 1:9-25

9 [lines 169-85; Artist A] The narrative structure of this illustration is neither vertical nor horizontal; it depicts the *second* account of the creation of the human race (the Yawist's) in which Adam is created before Eve, the first being the Priestly formulation in Gen. 1:27 (which states that God created humans, both 'male and female' at the same time). The scenes are contained within a crudely drawn architectural frame, which is not even perpendicular. Much of the outlining is done in red ink and a green wash has been used to fill in some areas at the top of the illustration. Note that here, as on p. 7, one Creator is bearded and the other beardless, suggesting that the artist intends to depict both the 'Father' and the 'Son'. The cross-nimbus of the bearded Creator is coloured in with a red wash.

Haines 1997 (p. 152) discusses the patristic and homiletic tradition concerning the 'doctrine of replacement' [i.e. of how humans will fill the vacant places left in Heaven after the Fall of the Rebel Angels], which is treated in both *Genesis A* (86-102) and *Genesis B* (364-8); Augustine comments in the *City of God* (XXII.1):

> For out of this mortal progeny, so rightly and justly condemned, God by his grace is gathering a people so great that from them he may fill the place of the fallen angels and restore their number. And thus that Heavenly City will not be deprived of its full number of citizens; it may perhaps rejoice in a still more abundant population. (Bettensen 1972, p. 1023).

He also treats this doctrine in the *Enchiridion ad Laurentium* 62 (*CCSL* 46.82]. Haines shows that Gregory I was aware of a slightly different version of the doctrine, which held that the number of humans who would ascend into Heaven would equal the number of angels remaining there (p. 152). The doctrine is also treated in the English vernacular homiletic tradition in *Blickling Homily XI* and elsewhere by Ælfric and Wulfstan; other than the account here in *Genesis A*, Ælfric was the first writer to discuss the 'Doctrine of Replacement' in a creation narrative (Haines 1997, pp. 152-3). Ælfric, in addition to speaking of the replacement of numbers of citizens, also mentions the filling of dwellings [*wununga*] elsewhere in his exegesis (p. 153). The *Blickling* treatment is closest lexically to the account in *Genesis A*, in its use of the words *eþel* and *setl*, corresponding to *setl* and *eþelstaðolas* in lines 86 and 94 of the poem respectively.

> And their joy and bliss was moreover increased when they became aware that their home [*eþel*] in heaven should thereafter be inhabited and peopled by holy souls; and that the holy seat [*setl*], from which the devil had previously been cast out for his pride, should be occupied by mankind (Kelly 2003, pp. 84-7).

Having examined the vernacular homiletic evidence for this doctrine, Haines 1997 concludes:

> Certainly, the poet's rendering of the doctrine reveals not patristic, but distinctly Anglo-Saxon origins. The kinship of the *Genesis A* account to those in the vernacular homilies, particularly Ælfric's and *Blickling XI*, is most clearly discernible in its creation narrative setting and in its portrayal of the vacancies as fair dwellings or thrones in the celestial homeland which await their new inhabitants.

In the lower right Adam sleeps while the cross-nimbed, bearded Creator removes a rib from him with his right hand, while holding Adam's shoulder with his left; note that his neck is not aligned properly with the curve of his arched back. Although Adam and Eve are naked, their genitals have not been drawn; some care has been taken to distinguish between male and female breasts (this is important for later discussion). A caption above the scene reads, *Her drihten gewearp sclep on adam and genam him an rib of þa sidan and gescop his wif of þam ribbe* ('Here the Lord cast sleep upon Adam and took a rib from his side and he created his wife from the rib'). On the left hand side of the illustration a cross-nimbed, beardless Creator holds newly created Eve's left hand in his while blessing her with his right. She looks up at him, her hair flowing down over her breasts (perhaps to suggest innocence or modesty: Gen. 2:25 says, 'And they were both naked, to wit, Adam and his wife: and were not ashamed'). A caption identifies her as *Eva* ('Eve'); another above the Creator's head reads, *Her drihten gescop adames wif euam* ('Here the Lord created the wife of Adam, Eve'). Henderson 1985

(p. 169, n. 23) notes, 'The creation of Eve on p. 9 on MS. Junius xi strikingly parallels the version in the S. Paolo Bible' [i.e. Rome, S. Paolo fuori le Mura].

The Creation of Eve from one of Adam's ribs is associated typologically with the piercing of Christ's side at the Crucifixion and Moses striking the rock in the desert to produce a spring of water for the Hebrews in the *The Bible of the Poor* (*Biblia Pauperum*, London, BL Blockbook C.9.d.2, printed in the Netherlands *c*.1470, edited by A.C. Labriola and J.W. Smeltz (Pittsburgh, 1990), pages 40 (facsimile), 82 (Latin transcription) and 125 (English translation); it is image '.f.'. The Biblical texts associated there with these three images are Gen. 2:21, Ps. 68:27, Lamen. 1:12, Exod.17:1-7, Zach. 13:6 and Amos 8:9. Though this book is dated much later than MS Junius 11, its typological treatment of the Enoch story reflects the medieval interpretative tradition. See also the Commentary for p. 60.

The scene at the top of the panel is complex. At the top Michael (he is identified by a caption above his head), wearing a wreathe, stands in the doorway to heaven; the door, which has two elaborate hinges, is held open by another angel standing to Michael's right side who holds a double-warded key in his right hand. If this is intended to be St Peter, then he is in angelic form with wings now that he is in heaven (see Matt. 16:19, where Peter is given the keys to the Kingdom of Heaven). Raw 1976 (pp. 140-1, n. 1) says that the depiction of Saints Peter and Michael in this configuration is typical of Last Judgment scenes, and cites parallels in BL Cotton MS Claudius B.iv (f. 43^v) and Stowe MS 944 (fols. 6^v and 7).

Several angels stand watching from either side, holding various items – a palm frond, a book and a musical instrument. An angel ascends/descends a ladder (*astigan* [in the caption] can mean either 'ascend' or 'descend'), which extends from below up to the doorway where Michael is standing. The source for this ladder is Jacob's vision as recounted in Gen. 28:12-14, though in his dream he saw angels both ascending and descending; it is probably significant for the scenes depicted here that the passage describing Jacob's vision concludes with God's promise that Jacob's 'seed' will be as ubiquitous (i.e. numerous) as the dust of the earth and that they shall have a homeland (the promised land). In Apoc. 4:1 a door opens up in heaven and the narrator is summoned up into Heaven, but there is no mention of a ladder. Gollancz 1927 (p. xxxv), Raw 1976 (p. 140), and others describe the angel on the ladder as 'descending', but often when angels are depicted descending 'Jacob's ladder' they are upside down, facing downwards (as, for example, on the ladders on the West Front of Bath Abbey). The Anglo-Saxon caption reads, *Her godes englas astigan of heouenan into paradisum* ('Here the angels of God ascend/descend *from Heaven into Paradise*'); if the angel is 'going from Heaven into Paradise', then he must be descending, even though he is shown as upright and facing upwards.

Gen. 2:21-2.

10   [lines 192-205; Artist A] Prior to the Fall there is no account in Genesis 2 of God addressing Adam and Eve together, as depicted here. In Gen. 2:16-7, just before God creates Eve as Adam's companion, he instructs Adam not to eat of the fruit of the Tree of Knowledge of good and evil. The inclusion of this scene may be explained by the fact that there are two accounts of the creation of Adam and Eve (as noted in the comments to the illustrations on p. 9), which the artist has failed to take into account. Alternatively, the scene may merely depict a 'generic' blessing scene, either added by the artist on his own initiative or suggested by an earlier Genesis cycle.

If this scene *is* out of sequence and intended to depict God cursing Adam and Eve after the Fall (as described in Gen. 3:9-24), then they should be wearing the aprons they sewed together for themselves from fig leaves (Gen. 3:7), and clearly they are not. In any event, God's cursing of Adam and Eve is treated in the illustration on p. 41, in which they conceal their genitals with fig leaves. Adam and Eve are also depicted covering themselves with fig leaves in several other illustrations treating events after the Fall, namely 34, 36, 39 and 41.

The figures of God, Adam and Eve stand within an architectural frame, which is more elaborate and better executed than that on p. 9. God, who is cross-nimbed and bearded, stands upon a small mound on the right hand side, holding the 'Book of Life' (see Apoc. 3:5, 13:8, 17:8, 20:12 *et passim*) in his left hand and extending his right in a blessing gesture. His nimbus is coloured with a yellow wash and part of his robe is outlined in red ink. Adam and Eve stand in an 'orans' pose and look up towards God; as on p. 9, Eve's hair flows down over her breasts, suggesting her innocence or modesty.

There is an animal at the pediment of each of the columns of the architectural frame, a lion on the left and a dragon (or basilisk, perhaps) on the right; both animals are depicted on a reduced scale. The source for this grouping of animals must be Ps. 90:13, 'Thou shalt walk upon the asp and the basilisk: and thou shalt trample under foot the lion and the dragon.' Traditionally, this passage was associated with Gen. 3:15, 'I will put enmities between thee and the woman, and thy seed and her seed: she shall crush thy head, and thou shalt lie in wait for her heel.'[6] Eve's foot extends out of the frame and steps on the hind leg of the lion. This crushing of the lion and dragon is associated typologically with the Last Judgement and the Harrowing of Hell; see Karkov 2001 (pp. 60-1) for further discussion. It is worth considering, however, that the placing of Eve's foot may be not deliberate, but rather due to spacial constraints upon the artist, since in the illustration on the facing page (11) Adam's foot is firmly planted upon a ram's neck, for no apparent reason. In his monograph study of English drawings from this period, Wormald 1952 (p. 28) comments on how artists treated frames:

> When, however, there is a frame, the figures, though vaguely attached to it, are not really restrained by it; they climb in and out just as they wish.

Karkov 2001 (p. 61) argues that Eve's intrusion into the margin is not accidental or casual, but rather that the artist has done this deliberately and that the positioning has great significance:

> Eve, pushed to the border of the architectural frame, stands with one foot on a lion who slinks off into the margins of the page with its tail between its legs – both it and Eve are simultaneously within and outside paradise. The transgression of space is further enhanced by the way in which the lion looks out at us rather than at God, a detail that helps to link the viewer with the fallibility of the first couple.

There is clearly a great distance between these two understandings of the Anglo-Saxon artist's use of the frame.

Gen. 2:16-17, 3:15.

---

[6] See Kartsonis 1986 (p. 72), who discusses the development of the theme of Christ trampling the asp and the basilisk in her study of the *anastasis;* she notes that Christian art borrowed the theme of the trampling of an enemy from imperial art at an early date.

11   [lines 206-10; Artist A] God, cross-nimbed and beardless, and with a fillet around his head, stands on a dias within a pentangular walled city or fortress (presumably meant to be the heavenly kingdom); he cradles the 'Book of Life' in his left arm [see the Commentary for the illustration on p. 7] and holds up his right hand in a blessing gesture. The ends of his robe (which is painted in green and brown) appear to flap in the wind; his hair is also painted brown. Adam and Eve, both naked, stand below in the space between three acanthus trees, with Adam on the left and Eve on the right; they each clasp an acanthus branch in one hand and raise the other in an 'orans' position while looking up towards God. They are surrounded by various animals strolling and grazing in the Garden (2 birds and a peacock, 2 lions, a stag, a dog and 3 goats or rams). Adam's right foot is placed upon the neck of one of the ram's, apparently without significance. Again, this illustration does not have a direct textual source in Genesis, but is probably intended to depict God resting on the seventh day and blessing his creations.

Gen. 2:2-3.

12   [no textual source; a 12th century (?) artist] There is an unfinished drypoint sketch in the 'blank' area at the lower half of this folio, which has been identified as St Michael fighting the dragon – see Ohlgren 1972 for a discussion of this image. The style of this etching is unrelated to the original Anglo-Saxon illustrations – it seems to be from a later period, perhaps the twelfth century. The warrior figure holds up a shield bearing a cruciform pattern in one hand and perhaps a lance in the other; Ohlgren associates this person with Apoc. 20:1-3, but the Biblical passage makes no mention of a shield:

> And I saw an angel coming down from heaven, having the key of the bottomless pit and a great chain in his hand. [2] And he laid hold on the dragon, the old serpent, which is the devil and satan, and bound him for a thousand years. [3] And he cast him into the bottomless pit and shut him up and set a seal upon him, that he should no more seduce the nations till the thousand years be finished. And after that, he must be loosed a little time.

13   [lines 237-45; Artist A] Adam and Eve stand between two trees in the Garden, which is enclosed by an architectural frame. The top of the frame comprises two arches which, however, have no central supporting column. Above the juncture of these two arches a beardless figure sits in profile within a mandorla, looking inwards, which is most unusual, since when God is depicted in a mandorla he usually faces directly outwards. The 'mandorla', from which light beams are radiating downwards upon Adam and Eve, looks more like the light-emitting dome of the illustrations on pages 6 and 7, turned on its side, than a mandorla. Adam and Eve are looking at each other and seem to be pointing to the trees beside which they are standing, presumably meant to be the 'Tree of Life' (*lifes beam*, l. 468^b) and the 'Tree of Death' (*deaðes beam*, l. 478^b). There is a small plant between Adam and Eve, but it seems to lack specific meaning. At the bottom of the illustration several birds and animals are depicted, and beneath them there are several fish swimming in water identified as *q<u>oddam mare* ('a certain sea'). The two animals in the centre are fantastic looking, perhaps intended to be a basilisk and a winged horse. Some of the illustration is outlined in red, and some leaves are also coloured in red.

16   [lines 292-320; Artist A] The Fall of the Rebel Angels. This the second illustration of the rebel angels being cast out of Heaven and into Hell; the other is in the lower register on p.

3 (see that note for further bibliographical and Biblical references). The illustration of this incident properly belongs here at the beginning of the *Genesis B* poem (lines 235-871), where it is described. The illustration on p. 3 was probably moved from its proper place in the existing illustration cycle by the scribe and/or artist and reallocated to the preliminary materials at the beginning of *Genesis A* when they were planning the layout of the present poem, which is a conflation of *Genesis A* and *Genesis B*.

The defeated, rebellious angels fall headlong into the gaping Mouth of Hell, which is personified as a beast (Isaiah 5:14; see the Commentary for p. 3); all of the fallen angels are naked and one has male genitals (the artist draws genitals on the fallen angels to emphasise their loss of perfection – the good angels in heaven are not sexualized).[7] Note too that two of the angels, and Satan himself, have no wings. The poet describes the expulsion of Lucifer and his followers from Heaven in these words:

> The good God was grown hostile to him in his heart, for which cause he would have to go to the abyss of hell's harsh punishment, because he fought against heaven's ruler. He banished him then from his favour and threw him down into hell, into those deep pits where he turned into a devil, the fiend with all his companions. Then they fell from on high, from out of the heavens, for as long as three nights and days, those angels, from out of the heavens into hell, and the Lord transformed them all into devils. Because they were not willing to esteem his deed and word the almighty God therefore deposited them, thwarted of their triumph, in a worse existence underneath the earth in black hell. There during nights inordinately long they endure, each and every one of those fiends, ever-replenished fire; then with the dawn comes an east wind and frost intensely cold. Fire or piercing cold, they constantly had to endure some harsh wringing torment; it had been created in the first instance for their punishment – their world was changed – and hell was filled with those conflicting elements. (302-20^a, Bradley 1982, pp. 20-1)

Satan lies shackled to stakes in the abyss of Hell; he has devilish features now – a tail, clawed feet and flaming hair. This is 'Personified Hell' – Satan and his minions reside within an architectural hell, which has crenelated walls and a tower. Flames surge through the window of the tower and a devil swings a flail at one of his companion inmates. Above this in heaven, which is delimited by a downward sweeping double arc embellished with six stars, God, cross-nimbed and beardless and cradling the 'Book of Life' (see Apoc. 3:5, 13:8, 17:8, 20:12 *et passim*) in his left arm, stands in the centre, with three (faithful) angels behind him to the right. He is confronting Lucifer and two of his followers, who have declared their rebellion against him openly (278-291, especially 291, *Ne wille ic leng his geongra wurþan*, 'I will no longer remain his subordinate'). Red, green and brown inks/paints have been used to outline and colour in elements of the decoration.

Apoc. 20:3.

17 [lines 320^b-37; 371-88; Artist A] God in Majesty and Satan bound in Hell. In the top register God, beardless, sits on a cushioned throne with his feet on a footstool within a decorated mandorla; he holds the open 'Book of Life' (see Apoc. 3:5, 13:8, 17:8, 20:12 *et*

---

[7] In the illustration for Psalm 2 in the *Utrecht Psalter*, three of the angels with weapons in the upper left corner are naked; in the equivalent illustration in the *Harley Psalter*, these 'angels' are clearly understood to be 'bad' and are thus depicted as both naked and wingless, and some have genitals. In the related *Eadwine Psalter* and *Paris Psalter* illustrations the figures, now interpreted as being 'good', are fully robed.

passim) in his left hand and extends his right in a gesture of blessing. His hair is reddish. He is flanked by two six-winged angels wearing wreathes, who are standing on clouds; these are drawn in red ink and have eyes on their wings [see the Commentary for the Frontispiece (p. ii) for a discussion of the Biblical sources for this iconography].

In the lower register the fallen angels torment each other with flails; they are all naked, and the one in the upper centre has male genitals. Satan, bearded, is seated on a bed of flames in the abyss with his hands and feet shackled; he is also secured by a chain encircling his neck (the devil nearest him on the left is also chained by the neck). Satan is *not* wearing a crown, as Ohlgren 1992 (p. 91) observes; rather curly strands of hair protrude from his head. The upper and lower registers have an architectural frame. Hell has fortified walls and a roof enclosing it; surging flames project downwards from the roof of hell. As the following lines from the poem show, the artist has paid great attention to detail in depicting Satan's situation in hell:

> But bonds of iron encircle me; a halter of chain yokes me. I am powerless, such hard hell fetters have fast laid hold of me. There is a great fire here, above and below. Never have I seen a landscape more hostile. The flame, hot throughout hell, will not die down. Fetters of links, a cruel chain, have impeded my movement, deprived me of my motion. My feet are shackled, my hands tethered. The ways are blocked through these hell-gates so that I cannot escape at all from these trammels. Great bars of tough iron forged in fire surround me and with them God has tethered me by the neck: thus I know that he was aware of my purpose, and this he has also realized, Lord of the multitudes, that it needs must turn out evilly between Adam and me over that realm in heaven if I had the use of my hands (371-88, Bradley 1982, p. 22).

Apoc. 20:3.

20   [lines 356-546; Artist A] Adam and Eve in the Garden being tempted by the serpent. This illustration was apparently intended to set the scene for the ensuing narrative in that it shows the serpent talking to Eve prematurely. In this illustration the narrative sequence is from bottom to top, and at the top from right to left: the devilish emissary is seen making a pact with Satan and then exiting from hell in the lower register and has been transformed into a serpent in the upper. In the lower register four devils fly about, two of whom carry flails with which to torment each other. Satan, naked and with wings and flaming hair, lies shackled in a prostrate position with flames surging up from below towards his belly; he touches the hands of his emissary to confirm their pact.[8] The devilish messenger is the depicted immediately above exiting from hell through a hatch. Given the attention to details in the preceding illustration, it is interesting that the artist did not try to represent the 'helmet of invisibility' (*hæleðhelm*, 444[a]) here, since the poet gives very specific details: 'He set on his head a concealing helm and fastened it very tightly and secured it with straps' (Bradley 1982, p. 25). Hell has the same fortified walls as in the previous illustration (on p. 17).

In the upper register on the right side Adam and Eve are in the Garden looking at one of its trees – perhaps the Tree of Life since it is described as being beautiful by the poet (467-76). On the left the tempter has transformed himself into a serpent: 'He turned himself into the

---

[8] Ohlgren 1986 (p. 204) notes that the emissary, who is a non-Biblical addition, is a necessity since Satan is shackled in Hell. It is perhaps of interest that in the final poem in the anthology, *Christ and Satan,* Satan is not bound captive in Hell, but is doomed to visit earth periodically (see Gollancz 1927, p. ciii).

form of a snake and then wound himself about the tree of death with the cunning of a devil' (491-2, Bradley 1982, p. 26). There is an apparent inconsistency here in that the poet says that the snake took the fruit of the tree and then went off to try to tempt Adam, and the artist has depicted the snake talking to Eve. But the artist seems to have chosen to follow the Biblical narrative to introduce this dramatic sequence: it begins:

> Now the serpent was more subtle than any of the beasts of the earth which the Lord had made. And he said to the woman: Why hath God commanded you, that you should not eat of every tree of paradise?

It is noteworthy that Eve seems to be restraining her left hand as it reaches towards the tree with her right hand, denoting a degree of disinclination to be disobedient in the first instance. In the Bible, the tempter never speaks directly to Adam; it is Eve who offers Adam the fruit to eat, after she has eaten of it herself.

The top scene is drawn in reddish ink and the lower in browns, perhaps a device used by the artist to emphasise their difference.

Gen. 3:1.

24   [lines 547-625; Artist A] This illustration, if it is of the tempter handing *Eve* the fruit, properly goes with the narrative which begins at line 22 of page 26; this suggests that the scribe has left the space for an illustration too early to match the sequence of illustrations already selected (and perhaps planned or sketched) for inclusion by the artist. Alternatively, Karkov 2001 (pp. 13-14), while admitting that the person depicted here does look female, argues that it is meant to be an androgynous Adam, commenting that 'the androgyny of the first couple prior to the fall is one of the characteristic features of this Genesis cycle'. She notes that the text following this illustration describes the temptation of Adam and his successful resistance, and that the angel looks less than angelic; this is something that Adam himself points out and which raises his suspicion: 'You are not like any of his angels whom I saw before…' (538^a-9, Bradley 1982, p. 27). The artist has given the reader a visual clue to the true identity of the messenger: the tempter's tail, which is clearly visible on p. 31, is concealed beneath the flap of his garment which arches out behind him! It seems likely that the artist should have depicted Adam here, but has mistakenly drawn Eve, for the figure here is definitely Eve and not Adam – the treatment of the nipples here is consistent with the artist's depiction of Eve elsewhere in the cycle (for example, on p. 28). Ohlgren 1992 identifies the figure as Eve and accepts that the illustration is merely misplaced (p. 91). As noted in the Commentary for p. 20, in the Biblical account the tempter never speaks directly to Adam; note too that the tempter is described as a serpent when it addresses Adam in the poem (491-6).

Doane 1991 (pp.140-53), following Burchmore 1985, offers a plausible explanation for the artist's introduction of an alternative 'angelic' form for the tempter, who is usually depicted exclusively as a serpent, following the Biblical account. He examines the psychology of sin in the patristic tradition and concludes that Eve is not deceived by the serpent, but rather is self-deceived; that is, the 'angelic' form of the tempter is a depiction of Eve's deluded perception of his appearance – after Eve eats the fruit, the poet refers explicitly to the tempter as a serpent (589^b-90^a).

The main scene of the illustration, which has a double-lined plain frame around it, is supported by a series of arches and columns in the lower register.

Eve and the tempter stand in the centre of the upper register between two large acanthus-leaved trees, probably the Tree of Life and the Tree of Death; the exuberant leaves of the trees protrude over the frame. Eve is positioned on a mound so that she stands above the tempter – perhaps significantly, since after the Fall, Adam and Eve and the tempter are all depicted as standing at the same level (p. 31). The tempter is disguised as a winged angel of God: he is robed and wears a red fillet or crown on his head; his hair is coloured black. His robe is in red ink.

Gen. 3:1-5.

28   [lines 533-625; Artist A] This illustration does not have a Biblical source: Gen. 3:1-5 describes the temptation of Eve (illustrated on p. 20) and Gen. 3:6 tells of her giving the fruit to Adam. There are two main narrative stages here in this drawing, moving from right to left, and with the tempter in the middle participating in both: on the right the devil first offers the fruit to Adam, whose gestures suggest that he is countering the arguments forwarded by the tempter (522-46). In the *Paris Psalter* the scribe uses blank scrolls (known as 'phylacteries', and usually inscribed with words) to indicate that a person is either speaking to someone or talking about something; the scroll begins with the speaker and ends at either the addressee or thing spoken about. Noel 1996 (p. 159) notes that such scrolls are a common feature in English art of the second half of the twelfth century, and 'is, in part, a pictorial concession to the nature of reading performance'. [An example of a quite complex use of scrolls can be seen in the illustration for Psalm 2 in the *Paris Psalter* (f. 6^v).] He says, furthermore, that '[t]he *Utrecht*, *Harley*, and *Eadwine* artists indicate speech by gesture and by glance'; this is also the case in Junius 11.

On the left the scene has two 'frames' or narrative stages: with her left hand Eve accepts the fruit from the tempter and with her right she is shown eating it afterwards (547-622). The devil has a fillet around his head and his hair is light brown. Both Adam and Eve are naked. The illustration has a simple double-arched architectural frame, which is decorated with acanthus leaves along the top. For further discussion of the frame and attitudes towards it see Broderick 1982 (pp. 31-42).

The artist's use of colour in drawing the robes of the tempter may be significant: the garment is for the most part executed in red ink, but the bit closest to Adam is drawn in brown, perhaps reflecting the fact that Adam does not believe the messenger to have been sent by God and has dismissed him.[9]

31   [lines 626-839; Artist A] The scribe left room for a full page illustration of this dramatic moment in human history, the Fall from Grace; it is unclear why the original artist did not use the lower part of the folio. At a later date someone has incised the image of an elaborately drawn lion or dog in the space originally left blank. Both scenes have a simple line frame.

---

[9] Ohlgren 1986 (206) observes that this systematic use of colour is an original contribution by the artist and concludes that the illustrations elaborate upon the text and thus are essential to a proper understanding of it.

The upper register depicts Gen. 3:6, but there is no Biblical source for the scene in the lower register, where the initial remorse of Adam and Eve is shown as the tempter exits to the right. At the top Eve, on the left, offers the forbidden fruit to Adam with her left hand, and he takes it with his right. Both are naked. They gesture towards each other with their free hands, which seems to be the artist's way of depicting dialogue in progress. The tree behind him is presumably the tree which was 'in the midst of Paradise', from which the fruit had been picked. Behind Eve stands the tempter, with his left hand extending upwards in a gesture of encouragement or approval. The artist has outlined an increased proportion of his robe in brown, perhaps suggesting that his true nature is becoming increasingly clear as the scene unfolds (if, as suggested elsewhere (see the Commentary for p. 28), he is using colour purposefully). Both Adam and the tempter have brown hair.

The illustration in the lower register corresponds to a long passage of text (723-839), which describes the tempter's delight in his success as he skips off the stage ('then the cruel-minded messenger laughed and skipped'), the initial remorse of Adam and Eve, their praying together to God for forgiveness, and the dialogue between them as they reflect upon the repercussions of their deed. The tempter's flowing robes have shrunk to an animal-skin loincloth, which will eventually disappear – on p. 36 he stands naked before Satan as he reports on his mission's success. His tail is now clearly visible and the artist has drawn lines emanating from his mouth, suggesting either spitting or some other gesture of scorn. The treatment of his hair is similar to that of Satan on p. 17. In the centre, Eve prostrates herself beside the tree 'in the midst of Paradise', with her face in her hands. Adam kneels at the left with his face and hands directed upwards; it may be significant that he looks away from Eve, since the first words he utters to her afterwards are reproachful: 'See, Eve; you, by your wickedness, have sealed the destiny of our two selves' (791-2[a], Bradley 1982, p. 34).

Gen. 3:6.

34   [lines 839[b]-51; Artist A] This illustration, together with the next two (on pages 36 and 39), shows Adam and Eve in their fallen state; they have become aware of their nakedness and cover their genitals with one hand and their faces with their free hand out of shame (much as the fallen condition of the rebellious angels is indicated by their being sexualized – see p. 16): 'They saw their bodies were naked' (783[b]-4[a], Bradley 1982, p. 33). It seems to be without significance that Eve is positioned on a mound, and looks downwards at Adam. Both scenes on this folio are contained within simple lined frames.

The lower scene illustrates lines 840[b]-4, 'They turned away, the two of them, and walked sorrowing into the green forest...' (Bradley 1982, p. 35). Adam stands to the left of three acanthus-leaved trees and Eve to the right. They again cover their faces and genitals out of shame.

Gen. 3:7-8.

36   [lines 760-76; Artist A] The tempter has successfully completed his mission; the poem reads, 'I will go back now towards the fire and there I will seek out Satan – he is shackled in black hell with a yoke of chains.' The most cruel of messengers one more departed downwards. He meant to make his way to the broad flames, those canopies of hell, where his master lay bound in chains' (760[b]-5[a], Bradley 1982, p. 33). Adam and Eve are again pictured standing disconsolately in the Garden – aware of their nakedness, they cover their genitals with acanthus leaves and their faces with their free hand out of shame. Here for

the first time Adam is depicted with a short beard (as he is also on pages 39 and 44). The top register is enclosed by a three-sided simple lined frame.

Wearing only an animal-skin loincloth the devilish emissary leans forward to dive back into the surging flames of the abyss through the hatch by which he had earlier exited from hell. In the lower register hell is depicted as an oval enclosure with surging flames (i.e as the pit of hell) leaping from its internal walls, which are very dark brown. Satan, who has flaming hair, lies tethered and shackled as before while his emissary, now once again naked reports his success to him. Four other winged devils stand or tumble into hell.

39   [lines 838-46; Artist A] The upper register again shows Adam and Eve standing among the trees of the Garden, covering their genitals with acanthus leaves out of shame, and speaking to one another (note the use of gesture to indicate conversation). Adam is depicted with a short beard (as he is also on pages 36 and 44). A narrow decorated strip separates the upper register from the lower. A simple lined frame encloses the whole illustration, and at several points acanthus leaves overlap the frame and extend into the margins. In the lower register Adam and Eve sit apart, but facing each other, among the trees of the Garden; aware of their nakedness, they cover their genitals with acanthus leaves and their faces with their free hand out of shame or remorse.

Gen. 3:8.

41   [lines 852-917; Artist A] The narrative sequence in this illustration is from lower to upper register, and then from right to left in the upper. In the lower image God, cross-nimbed and beardless and holding a ringed scroll in his left hand, comes walking in the Garden and calling out to Adam, the 'guardian of the world's creatures' (*weard woruldgesceafta*, 863[b]). Adam and Eve, kneeling among the trees of the Garden and covering themselves with acanthus leaves out of shame, both look up towards God; Adam and God gesture towards on another to indicate that they are conversing – Adam, aware now of his nakedness, explains that he is in need of clothes. A column forming the right side of the frame extends to the top of the illustration; it has both a pediment and a capital. Acanthus leaves from the tree on the left cross over in front of the column.

The top of the frame is formed by a double arch, and God, beardless and cross-nimbed stands beneath its center, as if in place of the central (missing) column. He holds the closed 'Book of Life' (see Apoc. 3:5, 13:8, 17:8, 20:12 *et passim*) and looks and points downwards to the left, the gesture indicating that he is addressing the serpent. The edge of the Book is coloured red and his hair is light brown. There are two 'frames' or narrative stages dealing with the snake: in the first, before God has cursed it, it stands upright on its tail; in the second, it slithers off to the left on its belly (Gen. 3:14, 'Because thou has done this thing, thou art cursed among all cattle, and beasts of the earth. Upon thy breast thou shalt go, and earth shalt thou eat all the days of thy life'). The body of the snake is decorated with ringed patterns highlighted with red ink and its tongue is forked. The serpent is twice referred to as *fahum* and *fah* (in lines 904[b] and 913[a]), which can mean both 'decorated' or 'stained (with guilt)'. There is a pedimented column on the left which begins at the top of the tree in the lower register and supports one of the arches at the top of the illustration. In place of a capital it has an animal's head, out of whose mouth an acanthus leaf vine descends to entwine the column. Red ink has also been used to highlight features of the animal face. The animal resembles the face of 'Hell personified' on pages 3 and 16, and it seems that the artist wishes to depict the snake as about to slither up the vine foliage and back into the mouth of Hell; Karkov 2001 (p. 76) does not make this connection, observing rather that 'the serpent crawls off into the foliate scroll of a marginal column, symbolic of the marginal wilds it is henceforth doomed to inhabit'. The body of the serpent is clearly turning upwards, however, indicating that it is about to slither up the column, which favours the interpretation proposed here. The left frame element here should be compared with that on p. 61; see also the Commentary there.

For further discussion of the frame and attitudes towards it see Broderick 1982 (p. 38).

Gen. 3:8-15.

44 [lines 918-38; Artist A] This illustration, depicting God's curses upon Adam and Eve, has two narrative sequences, proceeding from left to right. God, cross-nimbed and bearded, is pictured twice in the centre of the scene, standing on a rocky mound above Adam and Eve. On the left he holds the closed 'Book of Life' (see Apoc. 3:5, 13:8, 17:8, 20:12 *et passim*) in his left hand and points downwards at Eve, who covers her body with acanthus leaves held in both hands while looking up at him. Part of God's robe is outlined in red ink. On the right God holds the closed 'Book of Life' in his right hand and points downwards at Adam, who covers his genitals with an acanthus leaf held in his left hand. He looks up and gestures towards God; he is depicted here with a short beard (as he is also on pages 36 and 39). The illustration has a simple double-lined frame, over which Adam's left elbow extends. A large tree with acanthus leaves extends from the base of the frame up to just below the feet of God.

Gen. 3:16-19.

45 [lines 918-44; Artist A] The artist has struggled with perspective in attempting to provide a view of the Paradise enclosed within walls with columns, which have pediments and capitals, and a gate in the foreground – the uppermost section of the frame for this illustration, which has three windows in it, is clearly meant to be the interior view of the far bounding wall of Paradise; note how the side walls slant inwards in an attempt to create a perspective of depth.

In the top register God, bearded and cross-nimbed, banishes Adam and Eve from the Garden; he stands on a mound, indicating his spiritually superior position. He cradles the 'Book of Life' (see Apoc. 3:5, 13:8, 17:8, 20:12 *et passim*) in his left arm. Adam and Eve wear the clothes God has fashioned for them to cover their nakedness, but they are of cloth, following the poem (*wædum gyrede*) rather than the account in Genesis, where he clothes them in skins (*tunicas pelliceas*). Adam, beardless, and Eve, with a head covering, look up towards God as he addresses them; the artist again uses gesture to indicate conversation. Eve's right hand extends over the column of the frame. Although not mentioned in either the Biblical account or the poem, Adam and Eve have also been provided with shoes.

In the lower register Adam and Eve exit Paradise through a columned entrance; note that a gate is not depicted here, though it features in the following illustration (on p. 46), where the poetic narrative says, 'Behind them at the Lord's behest a holy angel with a fiery sword closed the hope-filled home of joys and pleasures' (945-7, Bradley 1982, p. 38). The lintel of the doorway is decorated with a vine pattern and other shapes. Eve carries a whorl/spindle in her right hand and hold's Adam's upper right arm, suggesting her dependence on him henceforth for safety (the poem says, 'you are to be in the power of the male, strictly constrained by your awe of the man', 919^b-21^a); see the Commentary for p. 88 for discussion of the typological association of Eve with Sarai (Sarah). Adam carries a metal-tipped spade over his right shoulder and a bag of seeds (it seems) on a string in his left hand.

Gen. 3:21-4.

46 [lines 945-64; Artist A] This illustration properly goes with the narrative which ends on the preceding folio (p. 45), and so it would have been better if the scribe had left the top of this folio blank for the illustration.

On the left side the 'holy angel', who is fully-robed (as the loyal angels always are), takes up guard of the entrance to Paradise; he wears a fillet around his head and holds a sword in his right hand. The sword is *not* flaming, however, as it is in both the poetic (*fyrene sweorde*, 947[b]) and Biblical accounts (*flameum gladium*). The doorway has pedimented columns from which its arched top springs. The archway has five windows and decorative motifs at is corners. The door is not the same shape as the opening, so when it is closed there will be a semi-circular gap at the top. The artist has tried, unsuccessfully, to use perspective to indicate the door's thickness and to show the advance of the four steps upon which the angel stands towards the foreground. The door is hung on two large, elaborate hinges.

On the right, Adam and Eve enter into a land 'fraught with cares'; this scene illustrates details from the poetic text which are not in the Biblical narrative:

> However, from the beginning the almighty Father did not at all wish to strip Adam and Eve of favours, though they had cheated him, but for their comfort he nevertheless let the sky continue, decorated with the holy stars, and gave them the broad bountiful land… (952-7; Anlezark 2002, p. 71).

The artist depicts the sky above and some vegetation below the figures of Adam and Eve. Adam looks back towards the gate of Paradise as he stands on a hill or mound. He now holds the metal-tipped spade in his left hand and the bag of seed in his right. Eve does not look back, but stands facing the right, with her hands extended outwards; she no longer holds her spindle – compare this with the previous image (p. 45).

Gen. 3:24.

47 [lines 965-9[a]; Artist A] The birth of Abel. The architectural background consists of an arcade with three arches supported on four columns with capitals. The column on the right side has a pediment, but the bases of the other three columns are hidden behind the bed in the foreground. There are seven windows and openings along the top of the arcade (a clerestory). There is a curtain between the first and second columns on the left; it hangs from a rod on five rings and is drawn aside to the right. There are problems with perspective in treating Eve's bed, so the artist may have intended to show that Eve had given birth to Abel in privacy, but now that he has been born the curtain can be pulled aside so that he may be seen. A reclining Eve, whose veil is outlined in red, holds up Abel; he is wrapped in swaddling clothes and looks back towards her. A second child, also wrapped in a garment and 'floating' in the central archway, must be Cain (he is 'unfinished' in that he lacks a mouth). Adam, bearded, sits on a cushioned throne and looks and gestures towards Eve and Abel.

Gen. 4:2.

49	[lines 969ᵇ-1013ᵃ; Artist A] This illustration treats five related scenes in the story of Cain and Abel. The narrative begins with the two scenes on the upper left, which show Adam and Cain working the earth with metal-tipped spades and Abel attending his flock of goats. Adam, who has a beard, uses his right foot to force the spade into the ground. The figure beside him is not Eve, but Cain, as dictated by sense and the fact that he wears a short skirt or tunic like Adam; the artist denotes Eve by showing her wearing a full-length dress or robe (on pages 45 [twice], 46 and 47). Adam wears stockings with garters, and shoes with pointed toes, but Cain just wears shoes. Cain holds his spade in his right hand, but is not yet using it. Below them, Abel holds a roughly hewn staff in his left hand as he watches over his flock. On the upper right, Cain and Abel offer the fruits of their labour to God, traditionally represented by a robed hand (the *manus Dei*) extending down through clouds from heaven. They wear short tunics, stockings with garters, and shoes with pointed toes. Abel places a live goat upon the altar and Cain, standing behind him, holds up a bowl with four ribboned items projecting upwards out of it (they could be anything, but perhaps are flames intended to show that the offering is already alight).

In the scene on the lower right Cain bludgeons Abel to death, perhaps with his own staff; neither the poem nor the Biblical account mentions the instrument used. Blood, drawn in red, streams from Abel's head. With his right hand he is pointing towards Cain and with his left he is gesturing towards his own face; the artist may be trying to represent Abel's disbelief as his brother strikes him, as if he were asking, 'What is going on? Do you not recognise me?' The scene on the lower left depicts 'the blood' of Cain crying out to God from the earth; the artist, confronted with the problem of how to depict 'blood crying out from the earth', has drawn Abel as half buried and half above the earth, with hands and face turned upwards toward God. God, bearded and cross-nimbed, gestures with both hands towards Abel's torso.

Typologically, Cain is associated with the Jews and Abel with Christ; these associations are a commonplace in medieval exegesis – see, for example, St Augustine's discussion of these typological relationships in the *City of God*, XV.7 and 18:

> [Cain] also symbolizes the Jews by whom Christ was slain, the shepherd of the flock of men, who was prefigured in Abel, the shepherd of the flock of sheep... For Abel's name means 'lamentation', and the name of Seth, his brother, means 'resurrection'. And so in those two men the death of Christ and his life from among the dead, are prefigured.' (Bettensen 1972, pp. 606, 628).

Gen. 4:3-10.

51	[lines 1013ᵇ-68; Artist A] In the upper register Cain stands before God, who is pronouncing his decree of banishment upon him. God, bearded and cross-nimbed, cradles the closed 'Book of Life' (see Apoc. 3:5, 13:8, 17:8, 20:12 *et passim*) in his left hand and gestures towards Cain with his right, to indicate that he is speaking to him (likewise, Cain gestures towards God). The jagged like between them is meant to illustrate that henceforth Cain will be hidden from God's face (Gen. 4:14 and lines 1034ᵇ-5, 'Accursed, O Lord, I must turn from thy sight').

In the middle register Cain is depicted as a fugitive in the land 'east of Eden' (Gen. 4:16); the poem refers to him as a *wineleas wrecca* ('a friendless exile', l. 1051ᵃ). He carries a barbed spear in his right hand and gestures upwards towards the city, Enoch, which stands before him. It is perhaps premature to depict him approaching the city, since in the Biblical narrative (and the poem) he builds it after Enoch is born, and the poet mentions specifically that, 'this was the first beneath the skies of all the walled strongholds that sword-bearing princes have ordered to be founded' (1058-60, Bradley 1982, p. 41). The city is represented by a tall, narrow, three-tiered edifice, whose right side forms part of the frame. The lowest section of the building is an arcade enclosed by two columns with pediments and capitals. The second and third levels become incrementally narrower, and each has scalloped or fish-scale shaped roof tiles. There are several windows in the building.

The family of three in the lower register is presumably Enoch and his wife with Irad/Jared, if it is assumed that the artist is attempting in each scene, beginning here and continuing in the next illustration (on p. 53), to depict successive generations. The figures stand in a walled fortress with a domed roof; it has four towers, one at each corner. The artist has again had difficulty with perspective. Enoch is bearded. He and his wife appear to be looking at the 'star-like' items in the space between them, but their significance is not clear. There are two half arches springing from the sides of the city's walls to the outer frame; the artist seems to be familiar with architectural principles in that the thrust of the two external vaults will help to stabilize the internal walls taking the thrust of the main dome.

The full-page illustration is enclosed within an elaborate frame – piecemeal might be a more appropriate term, since it is comprised of a number of disparate elements. On the left the vertical element of the frame extends from top to bottom, although two-thirds of the way up it has a capital (unmatched on the right). At the top corner of each of the columns there is a beast's head; the left column emanates downwards out of the beast's mouth, while the chin of the beast on the right rests on the top of the column (or else the head is merely superimposed on the corner of the frame). The column on the right extends upwards from the city wall depicted half way down the page; below the building the frame becomes a single line. The base of the city wall in the lowest register provides the bottom of the frame. For further discussion of the frame and attitudes towards it, see Broderick 1982 (pp. 39-40).

Gen. 4:11-18.

53   [lines 1066^b-77^a; Artist A] Three generations of the descendants of Cain are depicted here; they are described on the facing, preceding folio (p. 52). Each register has its own frame, though on the left side the outer element of the frame runs from top to bottom. The four columns in the lowest register have pediments and capitals; the three in the central image have capitals, but their bases are not visible. In the top register the left side has both capitals and simple pediments, and the image on the right side has one capital and no visible pediments.

The series of illustrations depicting the descendants of Cain beginning here and continuing on pages 54, 56, 57, 58, 59, 62, and 63, has no specific analogue; their design and arrangement may be an original contribution by the Anglo-Saxon artist; Raw 1976 (p. 137) speculates that there may have been a number of models available to the artist, but if so, none of them survives:

> These pictures cannot be linked to any specific source, and the wide variety of arches, arcades and buildings which serve to frame them, and the haphazard nature of their composition, suggest that several models may have been used.

In the top register Irad, bearded, sits beneath a pointed arch on a cushioned chair or throne with his feet on a footstool (*scabellum*). The 'roof' of the archway has scalloped or 'fish-scale' tiles. The background looks architectural, so the artist may have intended him to be seated outdoors looking into the room on the right. Ohlgren 1992 (p. 94) identifies the scene in the right panel as Irad's wife in bed, attended by a midwife, but it is more correctly probably Irad's wife tending her child Maviael in his cradle, as Karkov 2001 (p. 86) also observes. [The Bible does not list wives' names in its genealogical lists, so unless they feature in the narrative they remain anonymous.] The mother is veiled and wears a full-length robe and the child is wrapped in swaddling clothes.

In the central register on the left, the wife of Maviael ('Malalehel' in the poem) is seated on a cushioned chair holding her son, Mathusael ('Mathusal' in the poem), on her lap and looking towards her husband, who stands in an 'orans' position in the panel on the right-hand side. Maviael is bearded and wears a short tunic, stockings and pointed shoes; his wife and son also wear pointed shoes.

In the lower register Lamech (the slayer of Cain), who is bearded, stands in the central archway; he is flanked by his two wives, Adah and Zillah (though it is unclear which is which, since they are not identified). The women are fully robed and veiled and Lamech wears a short tunic, stockings and pointed shoes. Both women look and gesture towards Lamech; he stands in an 'orans' position, with one hand gesturing towards each wife, but is looking at the one on his left. All three figures stand on small earthen mounds.

See Doane 1978 (pp. 249-52) for a detailed discussion of the names of the descendants for Cain and Seth.

Gen. 4:18-19.

54 [lines 1077[b]-1127; Artist A] The three illustrations on this folio depict further descendants of Cain [Jabel, the father of herdsmen and those who dwell in tents (Gen. 4:20) is, however, *not* depicted in this sequence.[10]] The upper and lower registers have architectural frames, whereas the central panel contains an outdoor scene.

Two figures are shown in the top register. On the left Jubal, who is bearded, plays a twelve-stringed harp; his body is drawn as if in a seated position, but the artist has not drawn a chair for him. Unlike the other male figures thus far depicted, he is clothed in a full-length robe; he also has pointed shoes. His fingers are very long and spindly (a great asset for players of any stringed instrument). The capitals of the two columns framing him do not match. On the right Tubal-Cain, also bearded, works at his trade as a blacksmith: with his left hand he holds a piece of hot metal with tongs while he prepares to strike it with the hammer held in his right. He wears the characteristic short tunic of males in the illustrative sequence. The capital of the columns of his frame match each other.

The central register also shows a bearded Tubal-Cain; it depicts a detail mentioned in the poetic narrative that is not found in the Biblical narrative, namely, that he was the inventor of agricultural implements. He controls a plow drawn by two oxen with his left hand and holds up an axe (it seems) with his right.

---

[10] Henderson 1985 (p. 162) identifies the harp player as 'Jabal'.

The lower register shows Adam, bearded and in an 'orans' position, standing facing Eve, who is seated on a cushioned chair and is holding Seth on her lap. The poetic narrative relates that Seth was born to Adam and Eve to replace Abel, who had been murdered:

> he was happy and contributed greatly to the comfort of his elders (or parents), Adam and Eve, his father and mother, and was Abel's substitute in worldly affairs' (1107-10^a).

With her right hand she gestures towards Adam; with her left she holds Seth safely on her lap. He wears a short tunic, stockings and pointed shoes. Eve wears a full-length dress and is veiled; her pointed shoes are coloured in. Seth, who gestures towards his father with his left hand, is bare-footed. The two columns framing this scene, which have pediments and capitals, are carelessly drawn. There is a diamond-shaped decoration or keystone at the centre of the archway. Though Adam, Eve and Seth are indoors, the artist has drawn a jagged line to indicate that they are standing on uneven ground.

Gen. 4:21-5.

55   [artist uncertain] Ohlgren 1972a (Fig. 2) attempts to reproduce the faintly incised image in the 'blank' lower half of this folio. The person who made this etching seems to have been trying to make a copy of the harp held by Jubal on the facing page (p. 54). The etching is so poor that I am disinclined to attribute it to an artist. Ohlgren (p. 230) himself is tentative: 'If the drawing on page 55 is by the early eleventh-century artist, it was probably a trial sketch…' Nothing more need be said about this.

56   [lines 1128-42; Artist A] The architectural frame of this image (and some of the other which follow) is so much more sophisticated than those on pages 53 and 54 that it is hard to believe that they were drawn by the same artist; it must be concluded that for the most part the frames were not a central concern of the Artist A. Artist B shows even less concern for frames: a number of his illustrations lack them completely (73, 74, 87, and 88), while in others he uses simple single- or double-line frames (also occasionally used by Artist A).

The columns here have elaborate pediments and capitals, with many compositional elements. The 'arch' between the two columns is more like a canopy or tent than a stone archway; at its centre is a decorative element in the Ringerike style.[11] The artist seems to be depicting a room within a fortress, since he has drawn towers inside the columns on the left and right, and also in the decorated wall in the foreground; a central door in the fortress wall has elaborately decorated hinges. Once again the use of perspective has caused problems for the artist.

Seth, who is bearded and wears a short tunic, stands on the left, facing his wife and gesturing towards her; he holds a long lance over his shoulder with his right hand. His wife, who is veiled and wears a full-length robe, faces him, cradling her son Enos in her left arm and gesturing towards Seth with her right hand. Enos, who is bare-footed, also points towards his

---

[11] Kendrick 1941 (pp. 125-41) and Wormald 1952 (pp. 38-9) are the early major discussions of the Ringerike style in Anglo-Saxon art; however, the three later studies by Fuglesang (in 1980, 1981, and 1986) have largely superseded them and led to a re-evaluation of the relationship between Anglo-Saxon and Viking art. Lockett 2002 (pp. 145-8) summarizes the evidence for dating the decorated initials in Junius 11 to the tenth rather than the eleventh century.

father. The caption above Seth's head, *Seth wæs sæli* ('Seth was happy') is derived from the poem (l. 1138ᵃ, but with the reading *gesælig*).

Gen. 4:26 and 5:6-11.

57   [lines 1149-50ᵃ, 1155-66; Artist A] The scene in the foreground is framed by two columns with capitals decorated in the Ringerike style; the decorative motif projects beyond the capital as if it were made from living acanthus plants. The interlace on the left column is made from a single strand of vine, which if followed eventually becomes the outline of the capital itself; the interlace on the right column is made of three separate vine strands, which wrap around the frame of the capital as if it were standing free of the stone itself. The artist has failed to close the frame on the right hand side completely. The external wall of the fortress springs (confusingly) from these two columns in place of an arch – another example of the Artist A's problem in handling perspective (note too the treatment of the top levels of the towers on the left and right). There are three towers along the wall in the background. There is a slender central column in the middle of the scene in the foreground, around which a curtain extending from the capital on the right is wrapped; the column has a stepped pediment and a simple capital.

Cainan, the son of Enos, who has a forked beard and wears a crown, is seated on a faldstool (a folding stool) – note how the crossed supporting elements interlock. Two cords or ropes, which are affixed to the column behind him, seem to be attached to the back of his chair and then extend back out to the lower left; their ends are frayed so that they have the appearance of clawed bird's feet. [The exact significance of these securing cords is not clear.] He holds a sword upright in his right hand and gestures with his left hand towards the seven warriors assembled before him (some of whom are bearded), two of whom in the foreground hold swords that are pointing downwards. All the male figures here wear short tunics and pointed shoes; Cainan's shoes are coloured in and he also has ankle stockings. There is a riveted shield, with pointed boss, at the front of the group of warriors. The tunic of the soldier at the font of the troop is held fast at the neck by a disk brooch or fastener; Cainan's robe is secured with a similar brooch on his right shoulder. Cainan's wife, veiled and with a full-length robe, sits on a chair with her feet on a footstool, holding her son Malaleel ('Malalehel' in the poem) on her lap; they both look towards Cainan.

Gen. 5:12-14.

58   [lines 1167-80ᵃ; Artist A] Malaleel, who has a beard, stands in an 'orans' position between two columns with rounded capitals. The column on the right has a simple pediment, but the artist has used a zoomorphic initial *h* either in place of or as the pediment on the left side. The initial *h* is formed from the bodies of two interlaced winged creatures, both of whom have acanthus leaves sprouting from their mouths. The creature forming the second element of the *h* is a fierce-looking bird, whereas the winged beast forming the ascender has the body of a bird, but an animal's head. The arch has been drawn over the Fitt number *.viiii*.

Malaleel wears a short tunic fastened at the right shoulder with a disk brooch, stockings with garters, and pointed shoes. He stands on a mound of earth before an altar draped with a cloth, which is on a stepped platform (as if in a church); the artist has had trouble with perspective in drawing the top of the altar. There is nothing in either the Biblical account or the poem to explain why Malaleel is depicted standing before an altar; the artist may have chosen to portray him as giving thanks for his long and prosperous life (as detailed in the poem).

Gen. 5:15-17.

59 [lines 1175-80ª; Artist A] The Biblical account states that Malaleel lived 895 years and had many sons and daughters. This scene depicts the death of Malaleel. Bearded and wrapped in a burial cloth from the waist down he lies in a coffin or sarcophagus with his hands placed together. One son, perhaps Jared, his eldest (born when he was 65 years old), cradles his head in his right hand. Six other men, some of whom have beards, stand looking on from the right side; these may be his other sons. The one closest to Malaleel's body leans over him, holding a censer by a ring looped over his right index finger. Three women, two of whom cover their faces with napkins or veils, stand to the left. The frame element on the right side is a column, with a pediment and capital; the outer wall of a building or fortress forms the left side of the frame. The building has a tower, whose apex extends slightly above the top line of the frame; it has two arched windows and a roof with scalloped tiles. There is a smaller tower in the foreground, which also has two arched windows. Once again, the artist has had considerable difficulty in dealing with perspective in drawing the roof lines and the sarcophagus.

Gen. 5:15-17.

60 [lines 1197-1217ª; Artist A] This scene and the next, facing it on p. 61, depict the story of Enoch, who was specially favoured by God; as the poem relates, he was taken up bodily into heaven without having to suffer death:

> From this world the hero sought in the body the joy and bliss of the Lord; in no wise did he die the death of this earth, as men ordinarily do here, young and old, when God takes away from them their possessions and substance, all earth's treasures, and their life as well: but while living he set forth with the King of Angels out of this transitory life into bliss, clad in the robes which his spirit received before his mother brought him forth to men.

The Biblical narrative says that Enoch 'walked with God', indicating his just and perfect state; later it is also said that Noah 'walked with God' and that he was 'just and perfect' (Gen 5:9), which is why God chooses to save Noah, just as he 'saved' Enoch earlier (Noah, however, is never drawn with a halo, as Enoch is here). Enoch is said to have lived 365 years; in assigning him an age equal to the number of days in the year, the writer of the Old Testament may have intended to indicate the moral perfection of Enoch, which led to God's selecting him for special treatment. The only other Old Testament figure to be assumed bodily into heaven was Elijah, as recounted in 4 Kings 2:11-12, where,

> …a fiery chariot, and fiery horses parted them both asunder [Elijah and Elisha]: and Elias went up by a whirlwind into heaven. [12] And Eliseus saw him, and cried: My father, my father, the chariot of Israel and the driver thereof. And he saw him no more.

In Ecclus. 44:16 in the Vulgate (Eccesiasticus is not in the Septuagint) it is reported that, 'Henoch pleased God, and was translated into paradise, that he may give repentance to the nations'. This story is also found in various apocryphal traditions.

Temple 1976 (p. 77) notes that this Translation of Enoch is an unusual subject and that it 'may have inspired the Anglo-Saxon iconography of the Ascension with 'the disappearing Christ' whose legs alone are shown'. The typological association of the images of Christ's Ascension, and the taking up into heaven by God of Enoch and Elijah is found in the *The Bible of the Poor – Biblia Pauperum*, London, BL Blockbook C.9.d.2, printed in the Netherlands *c*.1470, edited by A.C. Labriola and J.W. Smeltz (Pittsburgh, 1990), pp. 48 (facsimile), 90 (Latin transcription) and 133 (English translation); it is image '.o.'. The Biblical texts associated there with these three images are Gen. 5:22-4, Ps. 46:6, 4 Kings 2:9-14, Is. 63:1 and Mich. 2:13. Though this book is dated much later than MS Junius 11, its typological treatment of the Enoch story reflects the medieval interpretative tradition. See also the Commentary for p. 9. For St Augustine's discussion of his typological understanding of Enoch, see the *City of God*, XV.19.

In this scene Enoch, bearded, wearing his full-length robe and nimbed to indicate his blessed status, looks up towards an angel who addresses him from clouds in the upper right corner of the frame; the gesturing of their hands indicates that they are conversing with each other. He holds up a book with in his left hand; text can be seen written on its open pages, an allusion to the Hebrew legend that he was the inventor of writing. Enoch is a type of Christ, and thus the artist singles him out for special attention by depicting his life in more than one image; the treatment of his assumption into heaven on p. 61 is strikingly similar to traditional depictions of Christ's (bodily) Ascension forty days after his Resurrection. The angel, as God's messenger, is intended to indicate Enoch's special calling by God. He stands upon the dragon, presumably meant to represent to the red dragon with 'seven heads and ten horns and on his heads seven crowns' of Apoc. 12:3 (though it only has two horns here). The Apocalyptic dragon is identified as Satan, 'the old serpent' (v. 9), and the Biblical account then describes briefly the war in heaven between Satan and Michael and their followers (vv. 7-9). Thus this episode pulls together the beginning and the end, Creation and the Last Day, through its typological associations. Moreover, as a type of Christ, Enoch's standing on the vanquished dragon also alludes to Christ's harrowing of hell. The typology is further strengthened by the reference to Enoch's mother having 'brought him forth to men', for Apoc. 12:1-4 describes the 'woman clothed with the sun' who brings forth a son 'who was to rule all nations with an iron rod.' For further discussion of this image see C. Farr, *The Book of Kells: Its Function and Audience* (London, 1997), pp. 114-15 and Karkov 2001 (pp. 87-8).

The artist has drawn a double-lined frame around the scene; despite the simplicity of its design, he has still erred in trying to create proper perspective in the lower left corner.

Gen. 5:21-4.

61   [lines 1197-1217[a]; Artist A] Here the artist depicts the Assumption of Enoch into heaven (he is clearly 'taken up', and is not ascending on his own); the narrative sequence is from the lower to upper register. In the lower scene Enoch, bearded, bare-footed, and wearing a full-length robe with sash and a phrygian cap, stands in an 'orans' position on a mound and looks towards heaven. He is flanked by two fully-robed angels who support him at the elbow and waist, preparing to lift him upwards. Twelve beardless and bare-footed youths in full-length robes and with arms uplifted (five on the left and seven on the right) watch on; they are probably intended to represent the sons of Enoch, but in depicting *twelve* individuals the artist is clearly strengthening the typological association of this event with Christ's Ascension, described in Acts 1:9-13, for neither the Old Testament narrative nor the poem is a source for the iconographic details here; in the passage describing events just after the

Ascension, Acts (v. 13) lists the twelve apostles individually by name. Schapiro 1943 argues that this image reflects a new type of Ascension iconography, which was developed by Anglo-Saxon artists around the year 1000.

In the upper register Enoch disappears into a bank of clouds – he is visible from the waist down. He is flanked by two fully-robed angels who have their hands on his waist as they lift him skywards.

Only blank space separates the lower scene from upper, and the earth upon which the figures in the lower panel stand completes the frame at the bottom of the page. The right and left elements of the frame are each made from four vertical parallel lines forming a central wide panel enclosed by two narrower panels. The simple top element of the frame is made by two parallel lines.

Gen. 5:21-4.

62 [lines 1224^b-34^a; Artist A] Here the artist depicts the birth of Lamech, the father of Noah. The illustration is comprised of a single scene divided into two sections by a central column. It has the same basic structure as the scene on p. 53, which depicts Jared watching his wife attend to their son Maviael. Mathusael (*Malalehel* in the poem), who is bearded, sits to the left on a backless, cushioned chair or throne with his feet resting on a footstool, and looks towards his wife and child on the right; he wears a full-length robe and pointed shoes. Behind him stand a group of four men, one of whom is bearded, who represent either his followers or his kinsmen. On the right side his wife reclines on a bed; she is supported from behind by a midwife or female attendant, who has assisted in the birth. A second female attendant holds the infant Noah, who is wrapped in swaddling clothes, in her arms.

The central column has both a pediment and a capital. The column on the right hand side has a capital, but its base is hidden behind a mound in the foreground, upon which the bed seems to rest. A more slender column provides the left side of the frame. Two animals are affixed to or entwined about the column, one of which is merely a head situated at the angle where the vertical and horizontal frame elements meet. The second is a hybrid bird whose neck and head enter the beast's head and exit from its top, and whose tail feathers consist of a spray of acanthus leaves which are entwined around the column. Ohlgren associates the bird body with the beast head, and describes the neck and head of the bird above the beast-mask as a (discrete) serpent (1992, p. 95), but this seems not to be so. The treatment of the frame here should be compared with that on p. 41, where, it is suggested, the accursed serpent is about to slither up the acanthus entwined column and back into the mouth of hell, mimicking the action in the image on p. 36 (though, of course, the bird here has no agenda in passing through the mouth of the beast – the configuration is merely decorative). For purposes of comparison, on p. 73 the loop of the initial 'thorn' is made up the bodies of two beasts, the upper of which seems to seems to protrude from the mouth of the lower (this may, however, be an illusion – the tail of the upper animal may only pass behind the head of the lower beast and then wrap around its neck).

Gen. 5:25.

63 [lines 1234^b-45^a; Artist A] The narrative of the birth and life of Noah begins. The illustration here is in three scenes positioned in archways and separated by columns; the narrative flows from left to right. In the left panel the birth of Noah is depicted. A midwife

supports Noah's mother, who has just given birth, with her right arm and against her left arm holds a checkered cushion for her to rest her back on. An unfinished figure in the blank area above may have been intended to be either the infant Noah or an attendant holding him (compare the treatment of the birth of Lamech on the facing page (p. 62). The bed is embellished with a variety of decorative patterns. In the central panel, Noah – now fully grown, bearded and crowned – stands in front of a cushioned throne/chair and gestures in salutation to a group of men standing before him (perhaps his followers). He wears a short tunic, stockings with garters and pointed shoes. Details of the heads of seven men in the group have not been finished by the artist; the men in the foreground also wear short tunics and pointed shoes. They stand on a mound (though apparently indoors). In the right panel, Noah – bearded, crowned, holding a slender staff and dressed as in the centre – sits on a cushioned throne/chair and addresses his three children, Sem, Cham and Japheth (named in Gen. 6:10); they wear short tunics and pointed shoes. Karkov 2001 (p. 89) observes that '[s]he and her husband are the only couple not depicted facing each other, perhaps reflecting the primacy of Noah as father and creator, and the rebirth of the earth that his story initiates.'

The architectural frame is comprised of four columns and three arches; the pediments of the two arches on the left are visible. The columns are topped with small, multi-leveled towers or turrets, which have double openings. The top of the frame is made of a stone fortress wall. The area above the central arch is decorated with scalloped or fish-scale shaped tiles to indicate that it is supposed to represent a roofed area.

Gen. 5:28-9; 6:10.

65   [lines 1285-1326; Artist A] This illustration has an upper and lower register, with only blank space separating them (as on p. 61); the narrative flow is from top to bottom. In the upper register God, in a full-length robe, bearded and wearing a crown rather than having a nimbus, addresses Noah (as indicated by his raised right hand, which is pointing towards Noah and blessing him); in his right hand he appears to hold the rolled-up plans for the ark – note that it is *not* a book that he is holding (as Ohlgren 1992, p. 95 asserts), since it is clearly encircled by his hand. Noah leans forward, indicating that he is listening attentively to what God is saying; his raised right hand also denotes that he is conversing with God. He is bearded, and wears a short tunic, stockings with garters, and pointed shoes. A jagged line running across the scene beneath the feet of God and Noah indicates the earth's surface.

In the lower register, Noah (dressed as above) begins to build the double-prowed ark; he wields an axe or adze with both hands. The prow on the left is outlined with a punched banding motif similar to that commonly found in Anglo-Saxon metalwork. The side of the ark is made from planks; it has an arched doorway the width of three planks in height. The complete illustration is enclosed in a double-line frame, which is plain, three-sided, and carelessly drawn.

Typologically, the Ark is associated with Christ; this association is a commonplace in medieval exegesis – for example, the following is from St Augustine's discussion of this typological relationship in the *City of God*, XV.26:

> The actual measurements of the ark, its length, height and breadth, symbolize the human body, in the reality of which Christ was to come, and did come, to mankind. For the length of the human body from the top of the head to the sole of the foot is six times its breadth from side to side, and ten times its depth, measured on the side from

> back to belly... That is why the ark was made 300 cubits in length, fifty cubits in breadth, and thirty in height. And the door which it was given in its side surely represents the wound made when the side of the crucified was pierced with the spear. This, as we know, is the way of entrance for those who come to him, because from that wound flowed the sacraments with which believers are initiated. And the squared beams in the ark's construction refers symbolically to the life of the saints which is stable on every side; for in whatever direction you turn a squared object it will remain stable. [Bettensen 1972, pp. 643-4]

For further typological associations, see also the discussion of the next image (p. 66).

Gen. 6:13-16, 22.

66   [lines 1327-62; Artist A] God instructs Noah to take representatives of every created species into the ark, and also his family. The two multi-winged angels flank the upper decks of the ark. They recall the angels attending God before the Creation of the world (see the Frontispiece and p. 2 and the Commentaries there), and may be intended to signal the impending flood as the end of the era of disobedience in the world and the beginning of a new life and covenant on earth, and thus function typologically. St Augustine believes that the purpose of the Flood was to bring about the extinction of the whole of Cain's posterity (see the *City of God*, XV.21).

The ship has three stories above the main deck. It looks like a sweeping, curve-prowed viking ship, with a fish-tail stern and dragon-head prow. The dragon-head has a florid horn projecting from above its eye (this is clearer in the two images on p. 68, where there are two horns on the dragon's head), recalling the multi-horned dragon of Apoc. 12:3, and typologically associating the destruction of life by the flood here with the destruction that will come on the Last Day. The apocalyptic dragon is also typologically associated with Enoch on p. 60.

There are six red rivets or bosses decorating the gunwale; there are six similar motifs on the fish-tail stern. God – cross-nimbed, bearded and in a full-length robe – holds the door to the ark open as members of Noah's family ascend a ladder to enter. Noah, bearded and with a disk brooch holding his tunic together at the right shoulder, steers the ark. Typologically, Noah stands for Christ and the ark for the Church, of which Christ is the helmsman; this association is a commonplace in medieval exegesis – see, for example, St Augustine's explication of the significance of the ark in the *City of God*, XV.26:

> It was to Noah that God gave instructions to make an ark in which he was to be rescued from the devastation of the Flood, together with his family, that is, his wife, his sons and daughters-in-law, and also the animals that went into the ark in accordance with God's directions. Without doubt this is a symbol of the City of God on pilgrimage in this world, of the Church which is saved through the wood on which was suspended 'the mediator between God and men, the man Jesus Christ' (1 Tim. 2:5) [Bettensen 1972, p. 643]

For further typological associations, see also the discussion of the preceding image (p. 65).

There seem to be two stages of narrative run together here in that waters lap the stern of the ark and Noah is steering it, while at the front end people are still embarking. The upper stories of the ark are drawn as if they are a fortress flanked by two multi-level towers, each of which has a cock sitting atop it (suggesting that they are weathercocks, as often depicted in Anglo-Saxon manuscripts). Various small roofs on the towers have scalloped tiles.

There are two arched doorways on the first level of the ark. In the left archway two sons of Noah are visible, one of whom is bearded and talks to Noah (note the gesturing). The doorways are flanked with columns, which have both pediments and capitals. The door, which God is holding open, has two ornate hinges; two women are visible through the doorway. Animals can be seen through the planks of the ark, as if they were transparent (i.e. windows). The second level of the ark has a central pointed archway, through which various birds and animals can be seen. There is a columned archway at either end of this deck. The columns have pediments and capitals, and through their openings vines can be seen within the ark. The openings in the wall above these arches do not match.

The upper deck is made up entirely of three arched openings formed by four columns, which have both pediments and capitals. The central archway is taller than the two that flank it. Once again, through the openings in the two outer archways vines can be seen within the ark. In the central opening a man can be seen lifting up or releasing a bird, and at the top of the right hand archway a bird is about to pluck off the top of the vine; this may anticipate the story of the dove returning with a bough in its mouth after the waters had subsided (Gen. 8:10-11), a scene which seems to have been intended for the 'blank' space on p. 70. There is a decorated pointed roof at the top of the ark. The two upper decks are secured at either end by knobbed cables. Red ink is used to colour in and outline various elements of the drawing. The artist has again had trouble using perspective when drawing a building.

Gen. 6:18-21, 7:1-9.

68 [lines 1372[b]-1406; Artist A] The narrative flow of the two scenes in this illustration is from bottom to top, perhaps mimicking the raising of the ark on the rising waters. At the bottom God, cross-nimbed and bearded, locks the door of the ark now that everyone is safely inside (Gen. 7:16 and mentioned twice in the poem at ll. 1363-4 and 1391[b]). Ohlgren 1992 (p. 96) says that God is 'about to open the closed and locked door of the Ark' but this is *not* the case – the poet is about to describe God locking the door in the first words on the next (ll. 1363-4) page. Karkov 2001 (pp. 89-90) also misreads the narrative here.

The structure of the ark has been simplified on this page, so that it now has only two upper decks instead of the three in the previous illustration (p. 66); each level is also less detailed than before. In the lower register both doors of the ark have been closed and locked; in the upper image only one of the doors has an external locking bolt. God is cross-nimbed and beardless and is shown locking the lower door. In both illustrations here the dragon head on the prow has *two* horns projecting from above its eyes, whereas in the previous image (p. 66) there was one.

Gen. 7:16 (lower), 7:17 (upper).

70 [artist uncertain] There is a two-tiered image outlined in drypoint here in the space which appears to be blank; it has been discussed in detail in Ohlgren 1972a. Ultra-violet photography reveals some details of what scenes were planned for this space, which is the hand-over point between Artist A and Artist B. In the upper register there is a lemon-shaped outline of the ark, similar to that in the next completed illustration on p. 73 (which suggests

that if the etching was made by one of the main artists, it was probably 'B' – but see below and the Commentary for p. 73). In the online digital image a central door can be made out in the centre of the folio, 3-6 lines below where the text finishes. There is a bird below this to the right, but it is only visible in ultra-violet enhanced images (see Ohlgren 1972a, Fig. 4 for a reproduction of this etching). This suggests that the image intended here was of the dove being sent forth from the ark as the waters were subsiding. Broderick 1978 (pp. 424-5) discusses this composition further.

In the lower register there is a sketch of a large ark running from the outer margin to the gutter. The faint outline of its stern can be seen on the left in the outer margin, and its prow can be seen near the gutter. Since the next illustration (p. 73) is a disembarkation scene, it is not likely that another was intended here. Since the ship seems to be floating, the narrative flow here may be from the bottom upwards, as on p. 68, in which case this scene would perhaps have shown either the raven being sent forth (Ohlgren 1972a, Fig. 5 shows a flying bird superimposed upon the side of the ark) or merely the ark continuing on its voyage while the waters began to abate. Gatch, writing before Ohlgren 1975 had published his observations of the incised images on this folio, thought that it was reasonable to assume 'that had a drawing been completed on this page, it would have depicted the raven and the dove' (p. 10).

As with the etching on p. 55, the two incised images here are so poorly drawn that the present editor is disinclined to attribute them to an artist; it seems more likely that a later reader has made an attempt to reproduce the two differently shaped arks found in the images immediately preceding (p. 68) and following this (p. 73) originally unused space.

Gen. 6:8-11.

73   [lines 1483-96; Artist B] As pointed out in the analysis of the images on p. 70, the ark depicted here has the shape of a 'lemon', and is described thus by a number of critics. Gollancz 1927 is less descriptive, observing that the Artist B 'merely suggests the design of a vessel. He evidently emphasises the *nægled bord* of l. 1418' (p. xlv). Another possibility presents itself to the present editor, though it has not been advanced before. The shape suggests that the artist was trying to provide an *aerial* view of the ark at the same time as he was trying to show it from the side; that is, he was attempting to draw a three dimensional object. The artist of the *Vienna Genesis* tried to do this very thing in his depiction of the ark upon the waters (f. II, 3), where bodies are shown drowned in the flood from the side at the same time as the ark, shaped like a ziggurat/zikkurat, is viewed from above.[12] Wellesz 1960 (p. 6) describes this experimental use of perspctive:

> There is hardly any scaling of the figures: they are too large in comparison with the ark, which itself is faulty in its perspective; in contrast to the figures and the ark, the waters are seen from a bird's-eye view. Yet a third dimension is most convincingly evoked by the varied and often daring foreshortening and occasional overlapping of the figures, and by the suggestion of the atmosphere…

Gatch 1975 (p. 8) discusses the shape of the ark here, noting the existence of two traditions, one of which depicts it as a tiered architectural structure and the other as having a tub or sarcophagus shape. The shape of the ark here, however, clearly does not resemble a sarcophagus. The depiction of the ark as a sarcophagus is properly associated with early-

---

[12] The Vienna image is reproduced in colour as Plate I of Wellesz 1960 (p. 23).

Christian catacomb drawings; to describe the image here as a sarcophagus flies in the face of reality and ignores a new development in the iconographic tradition. There is a depiction of 'The Storm at Sea' in the *Gospel Book of Otto III* (*c.* 998-1001; Munich, Bayerische Staatsbibl., Clm. 4453, f. 103ᵛ) in which the ship is viewed at an angle from above; it is interesting for the present discussion to note how the artist realistically captures the 'lemon' shape of a ship when it is viewed from above. Another similar depiction of a ship from this perspective is found in the *Hilda Codex* (Cologne, *c.*1000-20; Damstadt Landesbibl., MS 1640, f. 117).

[For purposes of comparison, it might be noted that when the Scandinavians enclosed a burial site they often arranged the monumental stones in the shape of a ship which, when viewed from above, has a 'lemon-shape'; a group of these monuments is found at Lindholm Hoje in Denmark.]

The artist provides an aerial view of the ark, while at the same time showing the disembarkation of Noah and his family through a portal on its side. Noah, beardless and with his hands extended in front of him, stands beside the ark with his three sons, who are beardless; the all wear short tunics and are bare-footed. Their wives are seen in the doorway of the ark; they are represented as 'busts' rather than full-length figures; their heads are veiled. The wives names are given by the poet as Percoba, Olla, Olliva and Ollivani (ll. 1546-8)[13]. One of the sons, with red hair, looks back towards the women and signals with his hand for them to come out. God, beardless and with a double-rimmed nimbus, holds the door of the ark open with his left hand and blesses Noah and his family with his right; he wears a long, flowing robe. The door of the ark has two intricately designed hinges and a bolt *on the inside*. The artist has drawn the image using red, green and brown inks. Note that Artist B does not feel the need to frame every image. See Henderson 1962 for further discussion of Late-Antique influences on this and other images in the manuscript.

Gen. 8:13-15.

74   [lines 1497-1510ᵃ; Artist B] God blesses Noah and his sons, and Noah offers sacrificial animals to him. God, beardless and in a full-length robe, stands facing Noah and his sons; he holds a ringed scroll in his left hand and raises his right in a blessing gesture. Noah, who is bearded, leans toward God, holding a bird in his hands on a cloth or towel. In front of him stand a goat and a bird. The bird is partially hidden, which confuses Ohlgren, who merges the two animals and describes the animal in the foreground as having 'cloven hooves and wings' 1992 (p. 97). Noah's sons, Sem, Cham and Japheth, stand in a row behind him with their hands extended in front of them. Noah and his sons wear short tunics and pointed shoes. The artist again uses red and green inks extensively. The ringed scroll here is similar in design to that on pages 2 and 3, suggesting that the artist may intend to associate this new beginning for mankind with the *first* beginning depicted there.

Gen. 8:20-1.

---

[13] For a detailed analysis of these names, and especially the possible etymology of *Percoba,* see Gollancz 1927 (pp. lxiii-lxvii). Gollancz notes that the metrical irregularities in the poem at this point (ll. 1543-9) suggest that the names may originally have been given in a marginal gloss, which was subsequently incorporated into the body of the text during re-copying. Other than in Junius 11, the names are found only in the Irish tradition and the Old English *Solomon and Saturn.*

76   [lines 1510ᵇ-54; Artist B] The blessing of Noah by God here, as he re-establishes humanity and a new line descending from Noah, is perhaps meant to recall the similar blessing of Adam and Eve earlier on p. 10; both sets of parents must go forth and multiply (Gen. 9:7). God, who is beardless and in a full-length robe, again holds his ringed scroll in his left hand, strengthening the association of this event with the earlier images of him as Creator. His right hand is extended towards Noah. Noah, bearded and clothed in a short tunic and pointed shoes, kneels before God. Noah appears to hold God's hand in his, perhaps a way of indicating the establishment of the Covenant between them, symbolized by the rainbow The artist again uses red and green inks extensively; for the first time he employs a simple double line to frame the scene. The frame was drawn after the image had been drawn. Because God's head extends up into the blank space at the end of the last line of text, the artist had to draw the frame over the text and break its inner line to accommodate God's head and the top of his ringed scroll. He also miscalculated the position of God's left foot and had to interrupt the inner line at the bottom as well.

Gen. 9:1-17.

77   [lines 1555-61; Artist B] The scribe left space for an illustration at both the top and the bottom of this folio, but Artist B has chosen to override this plan. He illustrates Noah, being assisted by one of his sons, as a husbandman in the lower panel, and extends the building on the left side upwards through the text and into the otherwise blank space in the upper register. That he was uncomfortable in doing this is revealed by the way he tried to 'background' the building so that it would not obscure the text. The scribe clearly thought (or knew) that the exemplar for the illustrations had an extra image which could be used at the top here, but, for whatever reason, the artist did not include it. Henderson 1985 (p. 169, n. 25) observes, 'The upwards extension of buildings is a familiar device of medieval illustrators when they wish to eke out too little pictorial material in too large a picture-space....'

The building has two arches of unequal height, formed by three columns having both pediments and capitals. The building has two tiered towers of unequal height. Two of Noah's sons, one of whom is bearded, stand in the left archway and his wife, in a full-length robe, stands in the other one, partially obscured by a column. The third son, beardless and holding a long stick or lance in his hands works in the field with Noah, and looks back towards him.[14] The men all wear short tunics and, where their feet are visible, are wearing pointed shoes (the artist has given them 'agitated' looking lower legs as if to indicate that they are wearing stockings). Noah, who is bearded, guides a plough drawn by two oxen with his left hand and holds a goad in his upraised right hand.

The artist again uses red and green inks extensively; he has drawn the outline of the back and head of the ox in the background, but has not bothered to try to sketch his legs and hooves. He has the same problem with the use of perspective as Artist A, as can be seen here in the treatment of the roof of the taller tower.

Gen. 9:20.

---

[14] Raw 1976 (p.136) notes that the tradition of Noah and his sons plowing after the Flood is evidenced only here and in the Old English *Solomon and Saturn*: *Saga me, hwylc man aþohte ærest mid sul to erianne? Ic ðe secge, ðæt wæs Cham, Noes sunu.*

78   [lines 1562-1601; Artist B] This illustration depicts three narrative stages flowing from top to bottom. In the top section Cham looks upon the nakedness of Noah as he lies drunk. Cham, who is beardless and wearing a short tunic, stockings and pointed shoes, raises his hands as if to indicate surprise at, or shock of, the impropriety of what he is seeing. Noah, who is bearded, lies on an ornate bed with his head on a patterned pillow; he holds up the edge of his sheet with his right hand so that his genitals are revealed. The bed is supported by two columns with pediments; extravagant growths of acanthus leaves sprout from their capitals, and other plants wrap around the lower parts of the columns.

In the foreground and below the bed, Cham excitedly tells his brothers, Sem and Japheth, what he has seen; they gesture towards each other, indicating that they are conversing. One of the brothers is bearded, and all wear short tunics and pointed shoes (and perhaps stockings). In the lower section of the illustration Noah lies on his side asleep in his bed. Sem and Japheth cover their faces with cloths as they cover Noah's nakedness with the sheet. The bed is framed by columns similar to those in the top scene. The artist again uses red and green inks extensively. Mason 1990 (p. 69) identifies this illustration incorrectly as 'Noah's Death and Burial'. [Biblical scholars see the residue of an ancient myth here, in which a son castrates his father in a struggle for power; the story of Uranus and Cronus represents this myth in Greek and Roman literature.]

Gen. 9:21-7.

81   [lines 1644-50[a]; 1661-78[a]; Artist B] There is some disagreement about the subject of the lower register here. If this image is intended to depict lines 1649-50[a] ('Then they set out, taking their possessions, cattle and treasure, from the east'), then the narrative flow here is from lower to upper register. This would mean that it is Heber/Eber, from whom the Hebrews take their name (1644-8), who is depicted here with his followers. [See the *City of God* XVI.11 for St Augustine's discussion of how Hebrew, named after Heber, was the original language.] This is how Broderick (1978, 348) identifies the lower scene.[15] Heber, bearded and wearing a fillet or head band, is shown leading a band of his followers, driving their herds before them. The artist intends to depict them all holding spears in one of their hands, and a number of them have sword sheathes. They wear short tunics and pointed shoes. The points of their spears project onto and above the simple double-line frame.

In the upper scene Heber supervises his followers, who are busy building a fortified city; they wield axes in their upraised arms. The city has crenelated walls, towers and a gate locked *on the outside*. Heber and his men are dressed as below. The artist again uses red and green inks extensively, and has had a problem with the use of perspective in drawing the fortress.

Ohlgren 1992 (pp. 97-8) identifies the upper register as a depiction of Nimrod planning to build the Tower of Babel, which makes for a confused narrative sequence, for Nimrod is descended from Chus, and the story of the Tower of Babel is associated with Heber and the descendants of Sem in the Biblical narrative.

Gen. 11:2, 11:4.

---

[15] Henderson 1985 (p. 162) says that this image depicts Nimrod 'discussing the proposed Tower', apparently following Temple 1976 (p. 77).

82   [lines 1678^b-1701, 1730-8; Artist B] There are three stages in this illustration; the narrative flow is from top to bottom. In the upper scene God – in a full-length robe, cross-nimbed and beardless – has come down from Heaven to inspect work on the Tower of Babel; he holds a ringed scroll in his right hand and gestures towards a group of four workmen, two of whom are bearded, to indicate that he is speaking to them. The two workers nearest God turn towards him. The workers wear short tunics and pointed shoes; one has stockings. Three of them hold axes in their hands. Two of the group look towards the Tower at the right, which has three upper levels supported on a double-arched arcade; the three columns have pediments and capitals. There are three rectangular green windows in the next level up, and there is a single arched window (painted red) in the level above this, whose opening forms a cross pattern. Two men, one with a beard, wield axes/picks while working on the upper stories of the Tower; they too wear short tunics. A trumpet of acanthus leaves sprouts down from the upper right corner of the frame.

The scene below this depicts the dispersal of the Babylonians. Two groups of men and women, facing in opposite directions, are depicted leaving Babylon. Some of the men have beards, and three hold spears or javelins; they are wearing short tunics and pointed shoes. The women are veiled and wear full-length robes. The artist has not bothered to draw the lower parts of the women on the left who are in the background.

The lower scene depicts Abram's family leaving 'Ur of the Chaldees' and entering the land of Chanaan; they advance to Haran and settle there. [Abram's name is not changed to Abraham by God until he renews his covenant with him in Gen. 17:5; Sarai is renamed Sara(h) in the same passage, at Gen. 17:15.] St Augustine discusses the significance of their names being changed in the *City of God* XVI.28. Typologically, Sara(h) prefigures the heavenly Jerusalem, the City of God, according to Augustine (XVI.31), who is following Galatians 4:22-6. The bearded figure at the front of the group is probably intended to be Abram's father, Thare. The veiled woman behind him is Sarai, the wife of Abram; the Biblical account also names Lot, Thare's grandson, as being among the group. Thare and one of the other male figures hold spears. The men wear short tunics, pointed shoes and stockings. The multi-leveled building before them represents the city Haran. The artist again uses red and green inks extensively and has had a problem with the use of perspective in drawing the rooflines of the city.

The simple double-line frame enclosing the illustration is similar to those on pages 76, 81 and 84 where the frames also extend upwards in order to accommodate a figure from the scene, and sometimes also enclose the last line of text. Here the topmost workman projects up above the frame. The bottom right corner of the frame is interrupted by the image of the buildings of Haran. Jagged lines representing the surface of the earth separate the scenes from each other.

Gen. 11:5-9, 31.

84   [lines 1744-90^a; Artist B] There are three scenes from the life of Abram here; the narrative flow is from top to bottom. On the left in the top register God – beardless, cross-nimbed and holding a ringed scepter in his left hand – raises his right hand in a blessing gesture as he makes his promise to Abram; he orders him to leave Haran (*Carran* in the poem, 1772^a). God wears a full-length robe and Abram, who is bearded, wears a short tunic, stockings and pointed shoes; he gestures towards God with both hands, indicating that he is conversing with him. On the right Sarai stands with Lot in an arched doorway; the columns

of the archway have pediments and columns. The building here is the most sophisticated architectural image yet found in the manuscript. The walls and towers in the background are angled so as to suggest that they are enclosing a space; thus the edifice may be intended to represent either a house with an enclosed courtyard or a walled city. The artist again uses red and green inks extensively, and has had a problem with the use of perspective in drawing the rooflines of the city. The tympanum above the doorway is pointed.

In the middle scene Abram – bearded and wearing a short tunic, stockings and pointed shoes – leads Sarai, Lot and his family away from Haran and into the land of Canaan. He has a sword sheath attached to his belt. The building on the right represents a city in Canaan; the Biblical account relates that, 'Abram passed through the country into the place of Sichem'. Abram holds a spear in his left hand, as does one of his followers in the foreground (but in his right hand).

In the bottom scene God – bearded and cross-nimbed – promises Abram that he will give that land to him and his seed. God and Abram gesture towards each other to indicate that they are conversing; they are dressed as in the topmost scene.

The simple double-line frame enclosing the illustration is similar to those on pages 76, 81 and 82 where the frames also extend upwards in order accommodate a figure from the scene, and sometimes also enclose the last line of text. Here the building on the right projects up above the frame. Jagged lines representing the surface of the earth separate the scenes from each other.

Gen. 12:1-3, 5-6, 7.

87 [lines 1790^b-1810; Artist B] This illustrations has three scenes, with the narrative flow from top to bottom. In the top scene Abram stands between two buildings, intended to represent Hai and Bethel (*Bethlem* in the poem; Gen. 12:8); he holds an axe or adze in his two hands. This seems intended to depict his building of an altar, which is mentioned in both the Biblical and poetic narratives; the Anglo-Saxon poet, however, seems to have conflated the two visits to Bethlem mentioned in the Biblical account, as Karkov 2001 (p. 99) also observes. Ohlgren 1992 (p. 98) identifies the subject of this page as the *second* visit to Bethel, described in Gen. 13:4, but such an interpretation means that the artist has reversed the chronological order of the illustrations on this page and the next (p. 88) since the latter depicts Gen. 12:10. This seems to complicate matters unnecessarily.

The poetic narrative adds a detail to the Biblical story, that Abram 'offered sacrifice to his Lord of life' (1807^b-8^a, *tiber onsægde / his liffrean*); this is the scene depicted in the middle, where Abram holds up what appears to be a pot of incense in front of a building – probably a temple, since it must house the altar (note the cruciform window openings in the two buildings at the top; perhaps too much should not be read into this since there is a similarly shaped window in the Tower of Babel on p. 82). In the bottom scene God – with full-length robe, beardless and cross-nimbed – blesses Abram; the poem reads:

> Not at all sparingly did God, through his own hand, give him reward for this, rich bounty, in that place of sacrifice' (1808^b-10).

This detail is not mentioned in the Biblical account. In each of these scenes Abram is bearded and wears a short tunic, stockings and pointed shoes.

The artist has not framed the illustration. Jagged lines representing the surface of the earth separate the scenes from each other. The artist has again had trouble using perspective in drawing the buildings. There are steps leading up to each of the three buildings here, which is particularly relevant, if they are intended to represent temples. The buildings are all multi-tiered and have arched doorways. The artist again uses red and green inks extensively, and has had a problem with the use of perspective in drawing the rooflines of the city.

Gen. 12:7-9.

88   [lines 1811-23; Artist B] In this, the final medieval drawing in the Genesis sequence, the artist depicts Abram, Sarai and their family and followers approaching a fortress with towers and battlements intended to represent Egypt. Abram holds a spear in his right hand and Sarai a whorl/spindle in hers. Eve was depicted earlier holding a whorl/spindle in her right hand as she exited from the Garden (see p. 45); in this subtle manner the artist associates Sarai typologically with Eve, both of whom give birth to sons who are typologically associated with Christ – Abel (see the Commentary for p. 49) and Isaac. Gollancz 1927 (p. xxxiii) draws attention to the fact that Eve and Sarai both hold the same object in their hands, but does not make a typological association; rather he suggests that this will be of 'archaeological interest'. Karkov 2001 (p. 99) also notes the typological significance of linking Eve and Sarai in this way.

St Augustine offers an explication of Abraham's typological relationship to God the Father and of Isaac's to Christ in the *City of God* XVI.32:

> Then he [St Paul] went on, 'Hence he brought him also to serve as a type' [Hebr. 11:17ff.]. A type of whom? It can only be of him of whom the Apostle says, 'He did not spare his own son, but handed him over for us all' [Rom. 8:32]. This is why, as the Lord carried his cross, so Isaac himself carried to the place of sacrifice the wood on which he too was to be placed. Moreover, after the father had been prevented from striking his son, since it was not right that Isaac should be slain, who was the ram whose immolation completed the sacrifice by blood of symbolic significance? Bear in mind that when Abraham saw the ram it was caught by the horns in a thicket. Who, then, was symbolized by that ram but Jesus, crowned with Jewish thorns before he was offered in sacrifice? [Bettensen 1972, p. 694].

[It was, in fact, the Roman soldiers who fashioned the crown of thorns (Mark 15:16 and John 19:1).]

Abram and the other men wear short tunics, stockings and pointed shoes; Sarai has a full-length robe and veil (another female figure behind her also wears a veil). A group of five figures, 3 men and 2 women, who are standing within the walls represent the Egyptians [Ohlgren 1992 (p. 99) inadvertently observes there are 'four']. The buildings are all multi-tiered and have arched doorways. The artist again uses red and green inks extensively, and has had a problem with the use of perspective in drawing the rooflines of the city.

Gen. 12:10.

96   [lines 1811-19] The illustration here is of uncertain date, but is much later and not by an Anglo-Saxon artist. Ohlgren 1992 (p. 99) believes that the scene depicts 'Abraham and the

messenger' from lines 1811-19 of the poem. This is possible, but that incident is recorded two pages earlier (on p. 94), which makes the identification less than certain. In any event, the image is not relevant for a discussion of Anglo-Saxon illustration.

99   [lines 2136-61] Ohlgren 1972a reproduces an incised sketch in this 'blank' area as Fig. 6, identifying it as a bird's head and relating it to lines 2157^b-61 of the poem (which appear on the preceding page (p. 98):

> You need not fear for a while the attack of the hostile warriors, the battle of the northmen, for the birds of prey sit all smeared with blood beneath the mountain cliffs, fully gorged with the slaughter of the armies.

A less likely association would be with Gen. 15:9-11, where Abraham slings stones at birds, but this is not mentioned by the Anglo-Saxon poet.

Milton Keynes UK
Ingram Content Group UK Ltd.
UKHW052029150823
426832UK00007B/17